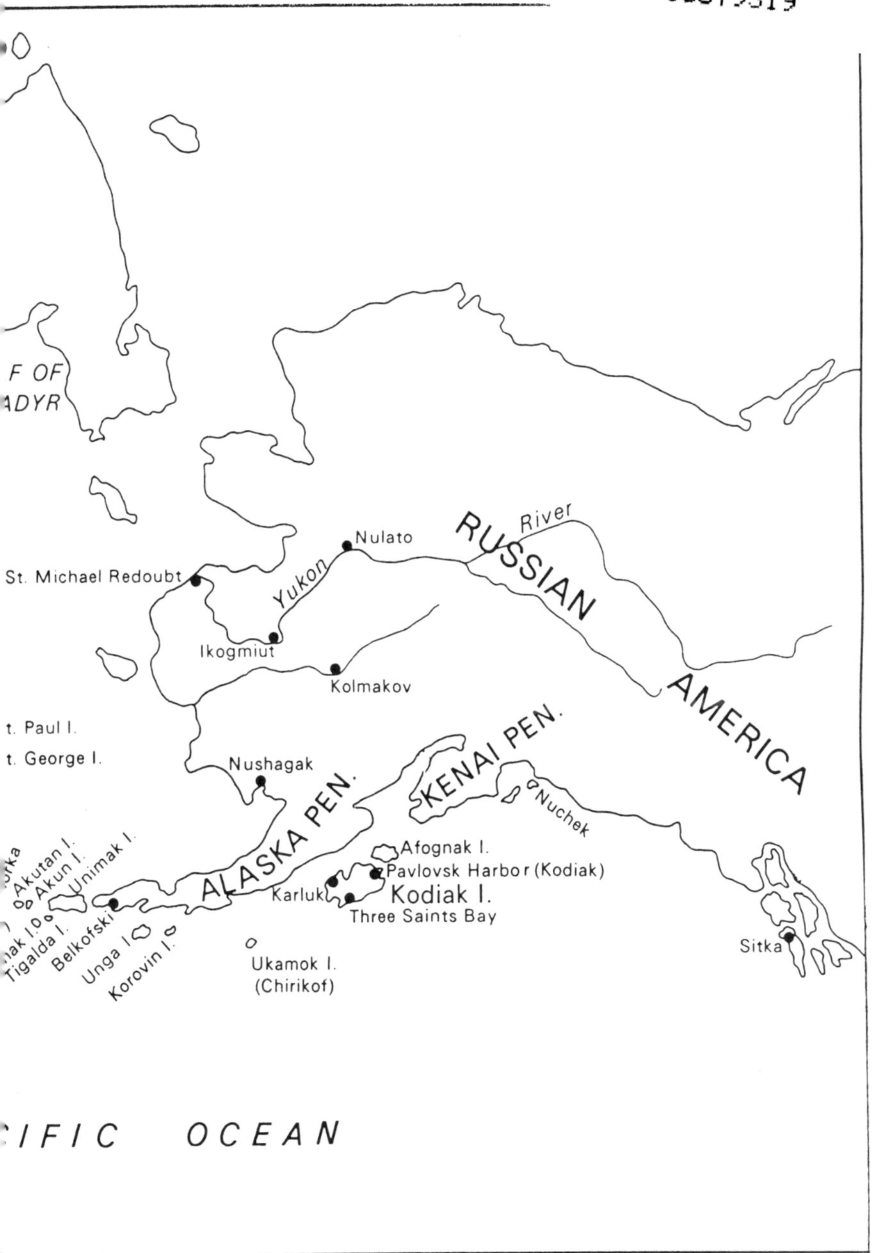

RUSSIAN AMERICA
Yukon River
Nulato
St. Michael Redoubt
Ikogmiut
Kolmakov
Nushagak
ALASKA PEN.
KENAI PEN.
Nuchek
Afognak I.
Pavlovsk Harbor (Kodiak)
Kodiak I.
Karluk
Three Saints Bay
Ukamok I.
(Chirikof)
Sitka
Akutan I.
Akun I.
Unimak I.
Tigalda I.
Belkofski
Unga I.
Korovin I.
OCEAN

KIRIL TIMOFEEVICH KHLEBNIKOV

NOTES ON RUSSIAN AMERICA

PART I: NOVO-ARKHANGEL'SK

We . . . stood watching the shores of France. My God! — I thought. — To think of where I was then and where I am now! Here lies England, there lies France and the rest of Europe — all things great and glorious! However, Mt. Edgecumbe, Sitkha, Kamen', the Kolosh, Mamais, Yamans, etc. — it all has become so deeply impressed upon my memory that it has crowded out all my thoughts about Europeans. Sighing, I said: there spreads a realm of nature, here all is vanitas vanitatum.

— K. T. Khlebnikov

Alaska History No. 43

NOTES ON RUSSIAN AMERICA

PART I: NOVO-ARKHANGEL'SK

by
KIRIL TIMOFEEVICH KHLEBNIKOV

Compiled, with an Introduction
and Commentaries
by
SVETLANA G. FEDOROVA

Translated
by
SERGE LeCOMTE
and
RICHARD PIERCE

Edited
by
RICHARD PIERCE

THE LIMESTONE PRESS
Kingston, Ontario : Fairbanks, Alaska
1994

Box 1604
Kingston, Ontario
Canada K7L 3N6

U.S. Office:
The Limestone Press
℅ History Department
University of Alaska Fairbanks
Fairbanks, Alaska 99775-0860

International Standard Book Number 1-895901-04-9

Publication was funded in part by the Alaska Humanities Forum, Anchorage, and the National Endowment for the Humanities.

Production: J. Ketz

CONTENTS

CONTENTS

CONTENTS

PREFACE

This volume, No. 43 in the Alaska History Series, comprises Part I of K. T. Khlebnikov's "Notes on [Russian] America" [*Zapiski ob Amerike*] concerned with Novo-Arkhangel'sk (Sitka), the administrative center of Russian America, known after sale of the region to the USA in 1867, as Alaska. The work is a translation of *Russkaia Amerika v "zapiskakh" Kirila Khlebnikova. Novo-Arkhangel'sk*, compiled by Svetlana G. Fedorova from several versions, with introduction and commentaries, and published by Nauka, Moscow, 1985. Parts II-V of Khlebnikov's work, No. 42 in the Limestone Press Alaska History Series concerning Kad'iak (Kodiak) Island and other subordinate districts, compiled by Svetlana Fedorova and the late Roza G. Liapunova, was published as *Russkaia Amerika v nepublikovannykh zapiskakh K. T. Khlebnikova* by Nauka, Leningrad, in 1979.

Because of Khlebnikov's long service with the Russian-American Company (from 1801) and his many years in Russian America (1818-1832), his collection of historical, ethnographical, and commercial information will join the works of Veniaminov, Wrangell, Zagoskin, Litke and other indispensable sources on this distinctive period in the history of European colonization in North America. Part VI, on Fort Ross, will appear under other auspices.

Footnotes in the Russian edition which supplement the main text have been renumbered consecutively and placed in one section. However, cost factors have required omission of notes on minor differences between versions (unlikely to be of use to the foreign reader), glossaries of ethnic and geographic terms and personal names (most of which are either explained in the text or generally known), and the color illustrations in the Russian edition.

— Richard A. Pierce

ABOUT RUSSIAN AMERICA AND THE AUTHOR OF THE *NOTES*, KIRIL TIMOFEEVICH KHLEBNIKOV

Novo-Arkhangel'sk, Novoarkhangel'sk, Sitkha, and Sitka — all of these designate the present-day town of Sitka on Baranof Island[1] in the Alexander Archipelago on the southeastern coast of Alaska. For nearly six decades Novo-Arkhangel'sk was the capital and residence of the chief manager of the Russian possessions in America. And even after their sale by Russia to the United States of America in 1867, Sitka (the Americans kept the Indian name) remained the chief town of Alaska until 1906, when the capital was moved to Juneau where it is today.

In 1732 the Russian vessel *Sv. Gavriil* (Saint Gabriel) approached the shores of the "Great Land" (America), and for the next 135 years the Russians continued to discover and master the Aleutian Islands and Alaska, making them a component part of the Russian Empire.

As soon as the survivors of the Second Kamchatka Expedition of V. Bering and A. I. Chirikov (1741-1743) returned to Kamchatka with news of the newly discovered Aleutian Islands, which abounded with valuable furs, a stream of promyshlenniks and navigators rushed to the islands of the Aleutian chain of Northwestern America. Subsidized by merchants from Vologda, Tot'ma, Velikii Ustiug and other north Russian towns, small merchant fur hunting companies built vessels and sent them east from Okhotsk and Kamchatka toward unknown lands in the Pacific Ocean. In 1759 the islands of Umnak and Unalashka, in the Fox [Lis'ei] chain, were discovered. In 1761 the Russians spent the winter on Unimak and the Alaska Peninsula. In 1763 they reached Kad'iak Island.[2] Larger companies replaced the smaller ones because only they could equip expeditions for such long and more distant stays.

As a result it became necessary to create permanent settlements on these faraway islands.

Thus, the village of Illiuliuk (later known as Dobrogo Soglasiia) became the first Russian colony in Northwest America on Unalashka between 1772-1775.[3] In July 1784, almost a decade later, G. I. Shelikhov's vessels, from the port of Okhotsk, arrived for repairs and provisions in order to sail farther east to Kad'iak. The trading factory on Unalashka served as an intermediate base for G. I. Shelikhov to create new permanent settlements in August at the Gavan' Trekh Sviatitelei [Three Saints Harbor, or more accurately, Three Hierarchs Harbor] on Kad'iak Island and then others on Afognak and on the shores of Kenai and Chugach bays. Thus, G. I. Shelikhov continued the Russian tradition of fur hunting from permanent settlements.

The Shelikhov settlements, however, were more than just trading posts. They attempted for the first time to create a complex economic system in these newly developed regions, which included, besides the fur-based economy, such related industries as shipbuilding, forging of iron tools, copper smithing from imported copper, tanning and brick making. A beginning was made in the search for copper, clay, slate and other useful minerals, and experiments were made in the fields of agriculture, gardening, and raising cattle and poultry.

A. A. Baranov, who arrived on Kad'iak in 1791, played an important role in bringing these plans to fruition and subsequently became the chief manager of the Russian colonies in America. Baranov decided to move the main Russian settlement from Three Saints Bay on the southwestern corner of Kad'iak Island and built a new settlement — Pavlovskaia Harbor — which for 16 years (1792-1808) was the capital of the Russian colonies in America and the residence of the chief manager.

The beginning of this new stage in Russian mastery of the Pacific coast of Northwest America coincided with the definitive formation on 8 July 1799 of the Russian-American Company and presentation of exclusive privileges on all continental and island territories of the northern part of the Pacific

Ocean. Writing about that era, N. N. Bolkhovitinov states: "With good cause we can say that, as a result of Russian expeditions in the eighteenth century, Russia became not only a European and Asiatic power but to a certain extent an American power. The term 'Russian American' made its appearance and earned its civic rights."[4] The Russian-American Company succeeded the small Russian mercantile companies of the late eighteenth century and inherited everything that had been built and developed in Northwest America. This company had trading and governing functions. The Russian government was interested in transforming the scattered trading posts in the Aleutians and in Northwest America into bases.

Having secured the government's support, the Russian-American Company took a new step southward in 1799 toward the fertile Columbia River basin and California. The main object of this trip was the island of Sitka in the Alexander Archipelago.

Let us remember that the islands of the archipelago were discovered by Russians during the Second Kamchatka Expedition in June 1741. During the last decade of the eighteenth century, English and American merchants traded with the Tlingits at will, supplying them with firearms, powder and lead. In July 1799, A. A. Baranov sailed from Kad'iak to Sitka on the vessel *Ol'ga* in order to found another Russian settlement — Fort St. Michael the Archangel. From then on the small inlets of the Alexander Archipelago became the main area for sea otter hunting. "However," K. T. Khlebnikov remarked, "Mr. Baranov also had political reasons in mind: to extend Russia's possessions as far as Nootka and to take possession of the entire coast before other nations did. These reasons were sanctioned by our government." [5]

The acute competition among European powers for spheres of influence on the Northwest American mainland complicated the Russian position in Sitka. Originally, the Russian-American Company was unable to obtain goods from European Russia, which were in demand by the natives, and categorically forbade the sale of firearms, powder and alcoholic beverages. In the summer of 1802 Tlingits attacked the fort of St. Michael the Archangel and burned it down, killing many of its inhabitants.[6] In 1805 another Russian settlement, Yakutat in Bering [Yakutat] Bay, suffered the same fate. These unfortunate incidents delayed but did not stop the Russians from moving south.

In order to solve the problems of supplying the Russian colonies in America with goods, the Russian-American Company decided to undertake round-the-world expeditions. The first Russian round-the-world voyage (1803-1806) gave decisive support to the Russians who were establishing the second Sitka settlement. With the help of the sloop *Neva*, captained by Iu. F. Lisianskii, A. A. Baranov raised the Russian flag on 29 September 1804 [7] above the Sitka settlement, which had been abandoned by the Tlingits. From August 1808 Novo-Arkhangel'sk became the main residence of the chief manager and the capital of Russian America.

* * * *

Kiril Timofeevich Khlebnikov (1784-1838),[8] a native of the Ural town of Kungur in the Perm guberniia, arrived in Novo-Arkhangel'sk on 20 November 1817 as an agent [commissioner] for the Russian-American Company on the ship *Kutuzov*, which was under the command of Captain-Lieutenant L. A. Hagemeister. He relieved the 72-year-old A. A. Baranov [9] of all his duties and on 27 November 1818 took him along on his voyage home. It was to be A. A. Baranov's last voyage. He died on 16 April 1819 not far from Batavia, and by maritime custom his body was consigned to the waters of Sunda Strait. He was the last chief manager from the merchant class. In his place came naval officers experienced in round-the-world and polar voyages, educated and inclined toward diplomatic and business activity, which reflected the aim of the Russian government to establish control over the Russian-American Company.[10-11] During K. T. Khlebnikov's 15 years in the colonies (20 November 1817 to 17 September 1832), there were five chief managers: L. A. Hagemeister, S. I. Ianovskii, M. I. Murav'ev, P. E. Chistiakov, and F. P. Wrangell. K. T. Khlebnikov developed good relations with all of them, and with some he was a close friend. "He knew how to make his superiors love him, his subordinates respect him and foreigners with whom he had relations to be his friends," wrote Khlebnikov's first biographer, the writer and journalist N. A. Polevoi.[12] During these years, Khlebnikov served as assistant chief manger and managed the main office at Novo-Arkhangel'sk, subordinate to which were managers of the various colonial "districts" [*otdel*]: Atkha, Unalashka, Kad'iak, the Northern region, and Ross.[13] In a manner of speaking, K. T. Khlebnikov "kept his finger on the pulse" of life in Russian America throughout his 15-year stay. Upon his return to St. Petersburg (13 September 1833), he continued to push for improvements in Russian America, from 6 March 1834 as acting office manager of the Main Office and from 7 March 1835 as one of the directors of the Russian-American Company.

It is interesting to follow K. T. Khlebnikov's growth as business organizer, scholar, traveler and writer as an unusual personality. Khlebnikov's so-called "diary" [14] allows us a glimpse of that process. For almost 38 years (28 December 1800 to 1 November 1837), he set down short notes concerning his trips, memorable meetings with people, ships and the progress of his work. In a family tree drawn up by Khlebnikov, found on the last page of the diary, we can count five generations of "Kunguriaks," the first of whom was his great-great-great-grandfather Koz'ma Khlebnikov, resettled in Kungur during the Novgorod uprising. His father, Timofei Ivanovich Khlebnikov who was town mayor, died young when Kiril was only six years old. His mother, Mar'ia Ivanovna née Chekin, lived to be 84 and saw her son return from America. There were seven children in the family (three sons and four daughters). Kiril was the fifth child and the youngest of the brothers. He began the diary on 28 December 1800 when he was sixteen. At this time he ran away from home and went to Siberia with Mr. Gornovskii, an agent of the Russian-American Company.

The very idea of starting a diary and the regular entries in it, shows the seriousness and business ability of this novice traveler. The road we travel allows us to learn about the world and, in this case, knowledge of a bigger world, because it led Khlebnikov from Kungur to the Pacific Ocean and Okhotsk, Gizhiginsk, and Kamchatka.

The Demidov factory at Nizhnii Tagil, the Irbit and Yakutsk fairs, where Russian-American Company goods came, served as "universities" for Khlebnikov. On 30 March 1801 he signed a contract in Irkutsk with the Russian-American Company to serve the company for one year in Okhotsk. There, he made the significant acquaintance of Sidor Andreevich Shelikhov, a veteran of the company who sailed with G. I. Shelikhov on the ship *Three Saints* to Kad'iak Island in order to organize a permanent settlement (1783-1786).[15]

The beginnings of Khlebnikov's life were hard but interesting: On 21 July 1801 he agreed to serve as store manager in Gizhiginsk for a year. "During the winter, I rode on sleds pulled by dogs and reindeer and lived in Koriak and Tungus yurts." In July 1802, upon arrival in Okhotsk by ship, he was met by the manager of the Okhotsk office, A. E. Polevoi, also an associate of G. I. Shelikhov. Khlebnikov renewed his contract for another year in Gizhiginsk. In August 1803 Polevoi "promoted" him to company accountant for another year in Kamchatka. He did not get to witness the arrival of the first Russian round-the-world ship under the command of I. F. Kruzenshtern in the port of Petropavlovsk in July 1804, but a year later, in August 1805, Khlebnikov came to the port from Nizhnekamchatsk and helped prepare the *Nadezhda* for its homeward voyage via Canton.

In March 1807 he traveled throughout Kamchatka with the naturalist G. I. Langsdorff, who had just returned from Alaska and California where he had accompanied N. P. Rezanov. N. A. Polevoi wrote that "acquaintance with this famous scientist, with whom Khlebnikov traveled around Kamchatka and sailed to Okhotsk, developed his inclination toward nature."[16] That same year he met the naval officers N. A. Khvostov and G. I. Davydov on the eve of their departure for Sakhalin and the Kuril Islands.

However, the most important moment in K. T. Khlebnikov's life occurred when he met L. A. Hagemeister, who had sailed into Petropavlovsk on the *Neva* (June 1800), and V. M. Golovnin on the *Diana* (September 1809 to May 1810). While traveling in Kamchatka and across the Sea of Okhotsk, Khlebnikov underwent privations, and his life was in danger more than once: he was in several shipwrecks, he froze, he fell through the ice, he almost drowned, he spent the night under a sled in a snowstorm, and he starved . . . . From July 1808 he began his services as Kamchatka agent, and from that day on his life was tied to Russian America. Russian-American Company vessels sailing to and from Novo-Arkhangel'sk passed through Petropavlovsk. These ships had to be supplied with fresh water and food, cargos loaded and unloaded, and a close account of things had to be made. This was no easy job, and often ships with these cargos became prey to the ocean. Meanwhile, in spite of his endeavors and his loyal work, K. T. Khlebnikov's indebtedness to the Russian-American Company grew.

In July 1813 Khlebnikov left Petropavlovsk forever. He traveled through Okhotsk and then Yakutsk and in December arrived in Irkutsk, where he stayed through the year of 1814. While still on Kamchatka, he received the news on 1 July 1813 that Napoleon had taken Moscow and had later been defeated outside the Russian borders.[17] That is how long it took to find out about the events of 1812. It was in Kamchatka that Khlebnikov the writer was born. His letters about Kamchatka, his first steps in literature, were of a detailed, compiled nature.[18] Not until much later, in 1836, did he publish an account of his adventures in Kamchatka — "Looking at Fifty Years of My Life" ["*Vzgliad na polveka moei zhizni*"].[19]

On 17 January 1815 Khlebnikov left Irkutsk by the Siberian road, recalling the places he had seen 15 years before: Krasnoiarsk, Tomsk, Tiumen, Ekaterinburg, and finally Kungur (7-10 February 1815), where he met his relatives, and a day in Perm (11 February). He then took to the road again, in a winter carriage drawn by two horses, for Kazan, Nizhnii Novgorod, Murom, and Vladimir, and after a short stay in Moscow (21-25 February), continued on to Tver, Vyshnii Volochek, and Krestsy to his final destination, St. Petersburg (2 March). Although it was his first time in the capital, Khlebnikov did not feel alone. And after September 1815, when his old friend L. A. Hagemeister arrived in Kronshtadt and preparations began for the round-the-world voyage on the ship *Kutuzov*, a year went by like a day because of the work.

On 7 September 1816 Khlebnikov sailed out of Kronshtadt as an agent for the company on the *Kutuzov*, under the command of Hagemeister, bound for Novo-Arkhangel'sk. Sailing by way of Copenhagen, Norway, and the Cape Verde Islands, they arrived in Rio de Janeiro, Brazil (11 December 1816-7 January 1817). Rounding Cape Horn (13 February 1817), they entered the port of Callao, Peru (17 March-7 May), and from there went to Lima. Their next stops were in Guayaquil Bay opposite the islands of Santa Clara (20 May-17 June) and at the mouth of the River Tumbes (9-16 July).

We shall spend more time on the *Notes* that deal with the southernmost Russian colony, known as Fort Ross, located on the Pacific coast of North America. The *Kutuzov* arrived at Port Rumiantsev (in Little Bodega Bay) on 15 September 1817. After five days, on 20 September, "we went to Fort Ross in three-hatch baidarkas." On 27 September "we returned in a large baidara." On 30 September they left Bodega and sailed to San Francisco Bay. This was K. T. Khlebnikov's first visit to Fort Ross, which he would visit many times in the future. They spent a month at San Francisco (1-30 October 1817). From there, on 30 October, "Mr. Kuskov sailed to Ross in baidarkas."[20] This is all we know about K. T. Khlebnikov's first meeting with A. A. Baranov's assistant Ivan Aleksandrovich Kuskov, who had founded Fort Ross.

On 20 November 1817 the *Kutuzov* sailed into Sitkha Bay. A new stage in Khlebnikov's life was beginning. On 11 January 1818 L. A. Hagemeister told A. A. Baranov that he personally was taking command of the colonies as the new manager. On the following day, 12 January, Khlebnikov was appointed manager of the Novo-Arkhangel'sk office and assistant to the chief manager. His time was taken up with business dealings; keeping accounts; sending cargos to Okhotsk; repairing the chief manager's house; finishing construction of a new pier; meeting his old friend V. M. Golovnin, who had come to Novo-Arkhangel'sk on the *Kamchatka* (28 July-20 August 1818); carrying on business dealings with Bostonians who had come there; and other duties. However, we cannot find a single entry in his "diary" concerning the above-mentioned: there is a gap of one year and five months (13 January 1818-4 June 1820). This gap, however, is compensated for by another source of information, "The Journal of the Novo-Arkhangel'sk Office Manager Khlebnikov" (19 July 1818-15 July 1821),[21] which includes the texts of reports to the Main Office, reports to the chief manager, and counter orders. This "Journal" gives us a precise account of Khlebnikov's varied duties and his complications with new relations. Thus, on 15 August 1818 Khlebnikov notified the Main Office: "Although the stores [warehouses] were all completed and the lists for incoming goods checked, I have yet to receive the account with prices from the former chief manager Mr. A. A. Baranov. When asked about this, he stated that no one can do it but he but because of constant attacks on his health, he doesn't have time."[22]

Khlebnikov did not expect that he would have to stay in America for as long as fifteen years. In a letter dated September 1818, Khlebnikov addressed L. A. Hagemeister: "I do not wish to serve more than three years from the day I signed my contract. I ask not to be held here [in America] past that time."[23] However, his plans did not coincide with those of the directors of the Main Office of the Russian-American Company. On 6 February 1819 the company in St. Petersburg wrote:

> We agree not to recover the debt that you brought upon yourself in Kamchatka due to various circumstances. Take courage now, forget the past, ask for God's help and be ready to face the future. The continuation of your duties, which have gained the respect of others, such as Mr. L. A. Hagemeister, and your attention to the needs and advantages of the Russian-American Company will give you the right to be respected ever more greatly.[24]

After expressing his gratitude for having had his debt written off, Khlebnikov answered 25 March 1820:

> The warrant which I received from my superiors gave me the opportunity to find out how things work in the Russian-American Company, as far as my knowledge could take me. However, I cannot say anything about many various enterprises, because I don't know any area other than Novo-Arkhangel'sk . . . . It seems to me that in order to know what goes on in such a vast area, one needs to be everywhere to gain the knowledge and to conform to the surroundings.

Further on, after declining the offer of the directors to make him the chief manager, Khlebnikov with characteristic directness and humility wrote:

> Allow me to say openly that I have no proper abilities and am not worthy of accepting such an important position. Strength of mind, foresight, decisiveness and even daring are qualities needed to run things here; I, however, do not have these qualities. I would gladly wish for such a burst of energy and zeal . . . . I don't think I ever dreamt of having qualities other than those with which I have been endowed.[25]

K. T. Khlebnikov's active nature gave him no rest, and his thirst for knowledge had no boundaries. During his 15-year stay in Russian America, he left Novo-Arkhangel'sk on 15 voyages:[26] he sailed around the Aleutian chain three times and visited the islands of Unalashka (1825 and 1829), Atkha (1825 and 1827), Attu, and Amchitka (1827); he also visited Kad'iak (1825), Bering Island (1827), and the Pribylov Islands (1825 and 1829). And, to provide still more statistics, Khlebnikov visited California thirteen times(!) (this includes his visit there on the *Kutuzov* and the transport *Amerika* on his way back to Russia). During these voyages, he visited Fort Ross nine times and was in Port Rumiantsev (Little Bodega) eleven times. He visited Guatemala, Peru, and Chile once. He also visited Brazil and Pitcairn Island, which belonged to England. However, only once, with F. P. Wrangell, did he manage to travel to Ozerskii Redoubt which is near Novo-Arkhangel'sk. During his service in the colonies, Khlebnikov spent a total of five years traveling through Russian America![27]

Khlebnikov's personal observations; his conversations with round-the-world voyagers, company employees, Boston and English merchants and sea captains, Spanish missionaries and diplomats, Aleuts, Eskimos, Indians and simple Russian workers; his studies of the Novo-Arkhangel'sk office and the documents of other offices; and, finally, his passionate love of historical literature, geography and natural sciences; his thirst for knowledge and his unswerving determination to become self-taught, which allowed him to study Spanish and English on his own, and to collect geological and ethnographic specimens — all of these things formed the basis of his monumental work which Khlebnikov entitled *Notes on the Colonies in America*, the first part of which we have published in this volume. Writing about Khlebnikov's St. Petersburg period, N. A. Polevoi wrote the following:

> Every time a conversation led to the topic of America, people would come for his advice, and he would willingly relate to each and every one what he had learned. His readings, observations, and taste made K. T. an intelligent and pleasant writer, although as a young man he had received no academic or literary training of any sort. K. T. was so humble that he gave way to others' requests, but he himself never wanted to print anything . . . .[28]

K. T. Khlebnikov's *Notes on the Colonies in America* is a unique work. These are not the notes of a traveling tourist, but of an observant and intelligent researcher making notes on historical economic situations and geographical, statistical and ethnographic conditions of this area. This is not just a remarkable monograph because of its completeness and circumstances, but a wise, theoretical work based on applied practice. His sober, realistic approach to the material is an honest attempt to understand the psychology and customs of the native peoples of Russian America whom he treated with kindness, without falling into idealization. Let us keep in mind that this was the first work of its kind and that its aim had a practical application for the further development of the Russian possessions in America.

I. E. Veniaminov, F. P. Litke and F. P. Wrangell — these are three names which are inseparable from the history as written by K. T. Khlebnikov in his *Notes on the Colonies in America* — therefore, we should mention a few words concerning the role of these three men.

Khlebnikov's first meeting with I. E. Veniaminov might have taken place directly when Veniaminov arrived in Novo-Arkhangel'sk, but at that time Khlebnikov was on the ship *Riurik* in Monterey. "The priest for Unalashka arrived on the *Konstantin*; he seems in all appearances better than our Aleksei [Sokolov]," Grigorii Sungurov wrote to California on 25 October 1823 after Veniaminov's arrival.[29] Khlebnikov returned from California to Novo-Arkhangel'sk on 6 February 1824, and only then did they meet personally (Veniaminov left Novo-Arkhangel'sk for Unalashka on 29 July 1824). They met again when Khlebnikov visited the Aleutian Islands on the brig *Baikal*.[30]

After his arrival, Veniaminov was constantly on the road, going beyond his boundaries to study customs and mores of the natives, including their superstitions and legends. Thus began his first literary sketches of what would become his internationally recognized work on the islands of the Unalashka department (office). On 9 August 1829 Veniaminov wrote from Unalashka to Khlebnikov in Novo-Arkhangel'sk: "In your appraisal of my notes you say that they are full of lively descriptions and for that reason you wish that I put my name on them [and publish them]. I beg you not to do that: first of all, I do not want to become any kind of writer or scribbler,[31] and, second, the style is not good; that's the way I feel about it; and besides, as you yourself state, by following its thread does one reach the ball [of yarn]; consequently, it takes work and strain to do so; thus, if my notes can be considered the thread, it will take you a lot of work to get to the ball. Thus, I humbly beg you to do me the favor of correcting them and to publish them in your name."[32]

Khlebnikov continued to gather materials for his *Notes* and Veniaminov helped him in this. On 6 August (not earlier than 1831 — S. F.), I. E. Veniaminov wrote from Unalashka to K. T. Khlebnikov in Novo-Arkhangel'sk:

> You ask me to get you information about Solov'ev[33] and others. I must tell you that never having thought of becoming a writer, I did not gather any information. But if it pleases you, I will send you whatever I can find out, gather, notice, or say about local events. Last year, I promised to send you my topographical observations about the western section of Unalashka and Umnak islands. However, I will not be able to send them to you at present, because I consider my observations about the western section inconsequential and incomplete, and they quite resemble those made by Mr. Sarychev.[34]

Thus, it was none other than Khlebnikov who awakened in Veniaminov an interest in scientific and literary activities, and their mutual help can serve as a great example of unselfish creativity. Let us quote from yet another letter written by

Veniaminov on 1 September 1831 from Unalashka to Khlebnikov in Novo-Arkhangel'sk:

> Along with this I am including a map of the Unalashka Department with the names of villages and the numbers of inhabitants and river .... Only forgive me that the map isn't well drawn because I do not know how to perform such things; and besides, it is incorrect because it has not been checked out. However, the names of the villages, the bays in Alaska and the islands (including the Shumagin Islands, which I did not have the opportunity to see) are all correct.[35]

In turn, as director of the Main Office for the Russian-American Company in St. Petersburg, Khlebnikov continued to help I. E. Veniaminov to complete his "Notes on Unalashka." On 27 April 1835 Veniaminov wrote from Novo-Arkhangel'sk to F. P. Litke in St. Petersburg:

> Kiril Timofeevich wrote to me that he gave you a compilation of my "Notes" describing the Aleutian Islands. I must inform you that these are notes or rough drafts that I gave K. T. and call them *Notes of the Aleutian Islands* from the second section. The first section consists of a general description of the islands, such as their location, a description of the islands, the climate, water, etc.; the third section deals with the life of the inhabitants. I am very sorry that I cannot send you the entire manuscript at this time. However, if I finish it, I assure you that you and Ferdinand Petrovich [Wrangell] will be the first to know about it. The first two sections are finished; the third is half complete.[36]

Understanding how anxious Veniaminov and Wrangell were, waiting in Novo-Arkhangel'sk for news of publication of Veniaminov's work and knowing how much of a role F. P. Litke had played in Veniaminov's writing of an Aleut grammar and dictionary, K. T. Khlebnikov wrote to Wrangell on 13 April 1835: "Today, they bought me a copy of Father Ioann's *Catechism*; I have sent a copy to F. P. Litke."[37]

Litke and Wrangell first met with Khlebnikov when they were all in their early twenties. While midshipmen on the sloop *Kamchatka* under the command of V. M. Golovnin, they arrived in the Sitka roads on July 1818. The unifying link between them and Khlebnikov was none other than

Golovnin, who remembered Khlebnikov's good will and help given to his expedition in Petropavlovsk, Kamchatka, where the *Diana* entered port in September 1809 — after a 13-month imprisonment at the Cape of Good Hope among the English.

Litke came back to Novo-Arkhangel'sk as a famous polar researcher and commander of the sloop *Seniavin* (12 June-19 July 1827). However, contrary to the supposition that Litke again met Khlebnikov in Novo-Arkhangel'sk and that he became familiar with his *Notes*,[38] we can now definitely confirm that that meeting never took place, and the Khlebnikov *Notes* (judging from the above-mentioned letters between Khlebnikov and Veniaminov) were not yet finished. A month before the arrival of the sloop *Seniavin* in Novo-Arkhangel'sk, K. T. Khlebnikov had left on 9 May 1827 on the brig *Kiakhta* for Atkha, Attu, Amchitka, and Bering Island and only returned on 6 September of the same year.

Actually, Litke did read Khlebnikov's *Notes*, but this occurred much later in St. Petersburg, when Litke was getting his notes on his voyage on the naval sloop *Seniavin* ready for publication. The three volumes came out in 1834-1836.[39] "It pleases me," wrote Litke, "to acknowledge my gratitude to the present manager of the colonies, my long-time friend Baron Wrangell, who obtained many interesting materials for me. I equally want to express my gratitude to the former manager of the Novo-Arkhangel'sk office, Khlebnikov, who allowed me to use detailed notes which he compiled during his 15-year stay there." Litke borrowed from Khlebnikov (with first-source footnotes) information on the discovery of the Pribylov Islands, their climate, population, and fur trade; a description of the climate on Kad'iak, and information on the Tlingit Indians. Litke did not fail to mention "how interesting" K. T. Khlebnikov's recently published article "The First Russian Colony in America" had been. It was published in the magazine *Raduga* in Revel in 1833.[40] We have already written about F. P. Litke's fruitless attempt to publish K. T. Khlebnikov's "Notes about the Colonies in America." [41]

At the time that F. P. Wrangell was made the chief manager of the Russian possessions in America (June 1830-

October 1835), he was already a famous polar researcher. In Novo-Arkhangel'sk K. T. Khlebnikov was under his direct subordination, but they were also united because of their great and sincere friendship. It is well known what a great role Wrangell played in preparations for the publication of Khlebnikov's *Notes.* But almost nothing is known about Wrangell's own attempts to continue the study of Russian America. The Russian ethnographer S. A. Tokarev justly remarked that "the results of F. P. Wrangell's work on the history and ethnography of Russian America have not come to light or been greatly appreciated."[42] Meanwhile, the manuscript of Wrangell's "information concerning Russian Possessions in America" was scattered through various archives[43] and only a small part has ever been published. The other manuscript, entitled "F. P. Wrangell's Notes on Russian Colonies in America" (1831-1835),[44] begins with a mention of Khlebnikov's work *Notes on the Colonies in America*, which undoubtedly served as a springboard for Wrangell.

On 13 September 1832, after saying goodbye to Wrangell, Khlebnikov left Novo-Arkhangel'sk forever on the naval transport *Amerika* under the command of V. S. Khromchenko. On his way to Russia he visited California one last time, and after going around Cape Horn, a year later the ship sailed into the Kronshtadt roads on 13 September 1833.

After arrival, work at the Main Office of the Russian-American Company occupied a lot of his time, but Khlebnikov continued his literary endeavors. On 28 August 1837 Aleksandr Shenin, one of the editors for the *Entsiklopedicheskii Leksikon* (Encyclopedic Lexicon) published by A. A. Pliuchar, wrote to Khlebnikov:

> The biography of Admiral Golovnin has not yet reached the editor's desk. F. P. Wrangell states that Rear Admiral Rikord wants to write this biography since he served with him and was a close friend of his. I know absolutely nothing about N. I. Grech's intentions to write his biography. I am sending back your articles: Hagemeister, Kad'iak, the people of Kad'iak, the Gvozdev Islands, Golovnin Bay, and Hagemeister Island so that you may make any change you deem necessary.

> Should you need your other articles, we can also send them to you. I respectfully ask you to send me your new article "Aliaska." I will soon be able to correct and complete the first volume of the *Encyclopedic Lexicon*.[45]

Khlebnikov's principal work, his *Notes on the Colonies in America* was not published during the author's lifetime, in spite of the diligent efforts of his friends F. P. Litke and F. P. Wrangell. The reason for that, one can suppose, was not only the departmental barriers of the Russian-American Company, not wanting to publicize a critical survey of its activities in America. We recall that for a while Khlebnikov's name figured in the "Decembrists' alphabet" after the committee of inquiry discovered among D. I. Zavalishin's papers a copy of a letter to K. T. Khlebnikov, written 14 July 1824 from Okhotsk to Sitkha.[46]

While in America, Khlebnikov had met and corresponded, not only with D. I. Zavalishin, but also with the future Decembrist Vladimir Romanov. K. T. Ryleev was the head of the Main Office from the beginning of 1824. G. S. Baten'kov and O. M. Somov were also in the service of the company. Here, for example, is a letter from V. P. Romanov from Kronshtadt to K. T. Khlebnikov in Novo-Arkhangel'sk, dated 24 July 1824:

> I am sending you a copy of the *Poliarnaia Zvezda* [Polar Star] and the "Prisoner of Chillon," a translation of the famous author Lord Byron. Unfortunately, he has been sent to the Elysian Fields . . . . I do hope that you will send me some information on the Koliuzh [Tlingits] so that I might complete my dictionary with their words and small conversations. I would also appreciate something about the Aleuts.[47]

The almanac *Polar Star*, published by A. A. Bestuzhev and K. F. Ryleev, was a pocketbook for lovers of the Russian language. It only came out three times (1823, 1824, and 1825); a fourth book had been ready for publication for 1826, but the events on 14 December 1825 prevented it from being published. The almanac was a great success. Some of the most popular writers of the day contributed their works to the *Polar Star*: Zhukovskii, Pushkin, Krylov, Del'vig, Gnedich, Pletnev, V. Panaev and others. "For me, 1823 was a turning point in my life, especially when the almanac *Polar Star* came out in print," the Decembrist V. I.

Shteingel wrote. "Ryleev's translation of Juvenal's satirical work 'For My Favorite' appeared in the first almanac. It is apparent that this article was aimed at Count Arakcheev, and for that reason the prank seemed very daring and put the poet-translator in the public eye."[48]

Judging from the date of V. P. Romanov's letter (24 July 1824), he could only have seen the first almanac. The mention of Lord Byron, who had died in 1824 in Missolonghi in a battle for Greece's independence (the idea being camouflaged in the phrase "he was sent, unfortunately, to the 'Elysian Fields'" showed that Zavalishin and Romanov and their ideas could be understood and find support in K. T. Khlebnikov.

Khlebnikov's friendly relations with the Moscow merchant I. V. Prokof'ev continued to the last days of his life. I. V. Prokof'ev was the principal director of the Russian-American Company and a man of very liberal views. The future Decembrists would gather at I. V. Prokof'ev's flat in the company headquarters at 72 Moika Street near the Blue Bridge (*Sinii most*)[49] and discuss future plans. K. F. Ryleev and his family occupied a modest apartment on the lower floor. O. M. Somov also lived in this house, along with his roommate A. A. Bestuzhev; V. I. Shteingel would sometimes spend the night there.

> Writers and many close friends would often gather at the Ryleev's. Besides the above-mentioned (A. O. Kornilovich), there were: Wilhelm Karlovich Kiukhel'beker, a comrade of Pushkin at the Lyceum; Faddei Venediktovich Bulgarin; Nikita Mikhailovich Murav'ev; Prince Sergei Petrovich Trubetskoi, Prince Aleksandr Odoevskii . . . . The conversations were usually lively but did not always deal with literary subjects; they often led to lively contemporary social questions with which all those present agreed.[50]

The Russian colonies in America apparently were often discussed by the members of the Northern Society. Russian America, and in part Fort Ross, occupied a special place in the Decembrists' plans.[51] According to V. I. Shteingel's recollections, when the dispatch concerning Aleksandr I's failing health arrived on 27 November 1824, "the apartment of the never-to-be-forgotten author of 'Dum' and 'Voinarovskii,' K. F. Ryleev, located in the house of the Russian-American Company where he was office manager, became the center of dealings, information and meetings."[52] "Ryleev's and Obolensky's apartments were the central points from which the revolutionary impulses originated. The conspirators met constantly at Ryleev's apartments . . . "[53]

Here, in September 1833, we have K. T. Khlebnikov at 50 returning to St. Petersburg. What was he thinking when he went up the steps of the famous St. Petersburg house of the Russian-American Company? "On the following day after unloading the cargo from the transport *Amerika* in Kronshtadt on 17 September 1833, I sailed into the capital and took two rooms in the company house, where once thoughts had been expressed by the council of the impious," he wrote to Novo-Arkhangel'sk to F. P. Wrangell in a letter completed in December 1833, almost on the eighth anniversary of the revolt in Senate Square.[54] In these lines we can clearly feel his compassion toward those Decembrists who had perished for their ideas.

But here he was in St. Petersburg in 1833. Where were those hotheads and those passionate hearts? Where were his former friends? K. F. Ryleev, "the Knight of the *Polar Star*," had been sent to the gallows, along with four of his friends; V. P. Romanov was sent under close watch to serve in the Black Sea naval forces; D. I. Zavalishin sentenced to hard labor for life and sent to Siberia . . . .

We must remember while reading *Notes on the Colonies of America* that they were written before K. T. Khlebnikov's return to St. Petersburg. We assume that it is not by accident that the official historian for the Russian-American Company, P. A. Tikhmenev, concealed K. T. Khlebnikov's name under the initial "Kh." in his work *A Historical Survey of the Russian-American Company* and mentions him far less than he deserves.

* * * *

In all, the *Notes* include six parts and a "Supplement" to Part Six. Each part corresponds to those administrative departments of the Russian possessions in America before 1830:

(1) Novo-Arkhangel'sk on Baranof Island (Sitka); (2) Kad'iak and surrounding areas; (3) Unalashka, the Fox Islands, and part of the Alaska Peninsula; (4) Atkha, the Andreianov, Rat, Near and Bering islands; (5) the Pribylov Islands, St. Matthew Island and part of North America; (6) Fort Ross on the coast of New Albion and the supplement "Notes on California." Only the "Notes on California" were published in Khlebnikov's lifetime (in 1829).

If we are to give credence to authoritative literary research, then Khlebnikov's *Notes on the Colonies in America* should have opened with a large "Introduction." This "Introduction" attracted the special attention of Pushkin experts, because Khlebnikov's story is tied to the name of the great poet. On 7 January 1837 Khlebnikov wrote A. S. Pushkin in a letter in which, on the advice of "one of the local writers" (probably the poet A. G. Rotchev, the future manager of Fort Ross in California),[55] he asked Pushkin to read the "Introduction to a Historical Overview of the Russian Possessions in America" for publication in the journal *Sovremennik*, which was published by A. S. Pushkin. The letter was written three weeks before the poet's tragic death. L. B. Modzalevskii, who discovered this letter in the archives of the Institute of Russian Literature (Pushkin House) in Leningrad and published it twice (in 1937 and 1938),[56] suggested that the "Introduction" is truly Khlebnikov's fundamental work *Notes on the Colonies in America*, parts of which (One and Six) were published in *Materials for the History of the Russian Settlements on the Shores of the Eastern Ocean* (St. Petersburg, 1861, No. 3).

On the subject of the letter sent by K. T. Khlebnikov to A. S. Pushkin, B. V. Lukin (in 1956) saw the "Introduction" in a different light. He considered it a small article which was to serve as a foreword to a multi-volume work on Russian America. In B. V. Lukin's opinion the *Notes on the Colonies in America* was that work.[57] In searching for the manuscript that Khlebnikov sent to A. S. Pushkin, B. V. Lukin studied the contents of one of the folios stored in the Leningrad Archives AN SSSR, on the back of which the gilded letters read "A Historical and Statistical Overview of the Russian Possessions in Northwest America and the Aleutian Islands by K. T.

Khlebnikov." Among the letters gathered in one portfolio, he found one entitled "Introduction" on five full (recto and verso) pages with the author's dedication to F. P. Wrangell.[58] The second page had the title: "A Historical and Statistical Overview of the Russian Possessions in Northwest America and the Aleutian Islands" and in the hand of the author the following note: "By K. Khlebnikov. Remark: worth remembering." Thus, there was a binding with a title, a title page, and an introduction. The only thing missing was the article itself, for which the introduction was prepared. Then it was suggested that this was the "Introduction" to *Notes on the Colonies in America.* This suggestion, however, is doubtful. S. B. Okun even remarked that the *Notes on the Colonies in America* is a work half memoirs and half research in nature. The "Introduction" was written in the form of a historical-philosophical essay and dedicated to a comparative analysis of the Russian and Spanish colonization of America. B. V. Lukin suggests this is in all probability the "Introduction" that Khlebnikov sent to A. S. Pushkin to be published in *Sovremennik.* After the poet's death, the "Introduction" was sent back to its author by A. A. Kraevskii.[59] However, we still need to find out to which work the "Introduction" was assigned.[60]

In 1861 "Historical Materials concerning the Russian Colonies along the Shores of the Pacific Ocean" was published in St. Petersburg as a supplement to *Morskoi Sbornik* [Naval Anthology] (ed. 1-4) by the Ministry of the Navy; combined in these historical sources, "Materials . . . " was supposed to strengthen the position of those groups in Russia that insisted on the elimination of the Russian-American Company's monopoly in Northwest America. That same year a new charter for the Russian-American Company was supposed to be instituted; however, it was discussed from 1860 to 1867, basically until the very moment Russia sold its American possessions to the United States. Issue No. 3 of the "Materials," entitled "K. T. Khlebnikov's Notes on America," [61] includes Part One and Part Six of his six-part *Notes on the Colonies in America.* The first page of the published work had the following note on it: "The manuscript was found at a second-hand book dealer's, to whom it was sent by the heirs of Mr. Prokof'ev, the former director of the American Company" (note by A. Sokolov).

The naval historian A. P. Sokolov (1816-1858), who prepared Khlebnikov's manuscript for publication, did not live to see "Materials for the History of the Russian Colonies. . . " in print. He died three years before it was published. The evidence that Khlebnikov's manuscript *Notes on the Colonies in America* was at A. P. Sokolov's disposal is corroborated by the fact that A. P. Sokolov's article "The Russian Library in America,"[62] published in *Morskoi Sbornik* in 1850, included an extract from Khlebnikov's manuscript, with a description of the Sitka library and a list of donors. Thus, there is only a five-year gap between I. V. Prokof'ev's death (1845) and the first partial publication of Khlebnikov's manuscript by A. P. Sokolov (1850).

Khlebnikov's original manuscript published in "Materials for the History of the Russian Colonies . . . " has yet to be found in the archives. Therefore, it is impossible to establish whether it contained a manuscript which the publishers believed to consist of only two parts, "Novo-Arkhangel'sk" and "Fort Ross," or whether it also included other parts of Khlebnikov's work; were these two parts abridged? We can say one thing for certain: this manuscript contained data which went up to 1829 exclusively, and consequently it was the earliest copy of *Notes on the Colonies in America* which has survived to our day.

* * * *

K. T. Khlebnikov's *Notes on the Colonies in America*, the clerks' copies of which are now preserved in several Soviet archives, have long attracted the attention of researchers. Even the Perm historian D. Smyshliaev, while studying his fellow countryman K. T. Khlebnikov's materials, published a list of his works in 1876, in which he mentioned the "Notes on the Colonies of the North American Company," whose manuscript is preserved in the archives of the Imperial Russian Geographic Society . . . . This enormous work attests to K. T. Khlebnikov's unusual conscientiousness and inquiring mind on the subject at hand; it consists of six notebooks, written with a fine handwriting on old, large format postal paper. The seventh part, which is the appendix to the main work, includes half the history and description of the former Russian California."[63]

In 1939 S. B. Okun used these *Notes* in his monograph on the Russian-American Company. Other historians who followed used it in their studies of the history and ethnography of Russian America.[64] In the 1950s A. I. Andreev proposed to the Geographic Society of the Soviet Union that they possibly publish the full text of K. T. Khlebnikov's *Notes*. In the 1960s co-workers D. D. Tumarkin and R. G. Liapunova, under the leadership of A. V. Efimov, all with the Institute of Ethnography AN SSSR, made this idea reality. They gathered (in the form of photocopies) the entire text of K. T. Khlebnikov's *Notes* (from the archives of the Leningrad department of the Institute of History AN SSSR and the Leningrad department of Archives AN SSSR) after noticing the existence of yet another copy in the Archives of the Geographical Society of the USSR.[65]

The copy which is the basis of our publication is located in the Archives of the Geographical Society of the USSR (Leningrad) in the collection of materials of the Russian-American Company, gathered by the Russian naval historian F. F. Veselyi (1817-1895), and supplemented by other members of the Geographical Society (AGO-112).[66] We have included in our publication only Part One, "Novo-Arkhangel'sk Fort on Baranof Island (Sitka)." We published Part Two through Part Six in 1979.[67] Part Six, "Fort Ross on the Shores of New Albion" and the supplement "Notes on California" will come out in our publication *Russian America in the Notes of Kiril Khlebnikov: California and Fort Ross as Seen through the Eyes of Russian Travelers.*

The version AGO-112 is the fullest account (it consists of all six parts and the supplement to Part Six), and that is the main reason why it forms the basis of our publication. The other versions, spread throughout two archives (LOII-447, LOAAN-275, LOII-275),[68] only have Part One through Part Five. The version AGO-111 has only Part One, "Novo-Arkhangel'sk fortress . . . " This version, however, is more important because it not only contains the author's notes but also has a considerable amount of data for 1830-1832.

Our publication does not limit itself to version AGO-112 or the third issue of the text *Materialy dlia istorii russkikh zaselenii po beregam vostochnogo okeana* [Materials for the History of the Eastern Ocean] (St. Petersburg, 1861). We combined into one the three existing manuscripts of Part One (AGO-112, LOII-447, and AGO-111)[69] and the 1861 publication, after noting down in each instance the proper place of each text according to the appropriate manuscript. Therefore, the present publication will not be a mechanical reproduction of the 1861 publication for our reader. It is considerably more complete and offers new archive materials for scientific research. A recalculation of all the tables revealed that inaccuracies in certain cases were due to a clerk's slip of the pen; corrections are indicated to the footnotes.

Yet another of Khlebnikov's articles, published here, gives us a picture of the administrative divisions of the Russian colonies in America in 1821. The manuscript is located in the Central Government Archives of the Navy, USSR.[70]

"A Questionnaire for the gathering of information about the American tribe, the Kolosh," by V. P. Romanov, is published here as a supplement. It is preserved in the K. T. Khlebnikov collection of the State Archive of Perm Oblast.[71] In addition, the present volume includes "a song composed by Mr. Baranov on the Northwest Coast of America" (in K. T. Khlebnikov's notes).[72]

The texts in this volume are written using the modern alphabet along with certain linguistic peculiarities of the first third of the nineteenth century. The dates have been left in the Old Style. Personal names and geographical terms have been retained as the author recorded them; their contemporary names appear in brackets in the cases where they have been changed. Words, sentences, names, dates and so forth, belonging to the author, have also been included in brackets. Deletions from the original have been marked by ellipses (. . .).

The notes of the compiler are designated by asterisks. Notes and supplements belonging to K. T. Khlebnikov are set apart by capital letters (sometimes by letters with hyphens to the left and right of them, which designate the beginning and end of a text) along with the archive number; notes by other authors are marked by small letters.

I would like sincerely to offer thanks to all who helped complete this volume: namely, staff members of the Archives of the Geographical Society of the USSR; the Archives of the Leningrad Department of the Institute of History AN USSR; the Central State Archives of the Navy, USSR; the Central Naval Museum; the State Russian Museum; the Museum of the Academy of Arts, USSR (Leningrad); the Central State Historical Archive of the Estonian SSR (at Tartu); the State Archive of Oblast (at Perm); the State Historical Museum (Moscow); to the Soviet historian, the late Ia. M. Svet; and to American colleagues Antoinette Shalkop and Richard Pierce.

NOTES

1. All of these names are found in the nineteenth century Russian sources. On the origin of the term *Sitkha*, I. E. Veniaminov states: "The island of Sitkha is called by the Kolosh *shig*, which properly means 'a tree branch,' and Novo-Arkhangel'sk, where the Sitkha Kolosh live, is called *shit'ka* or *shitiika*; *t'ka* or *-tiika* comes from the word *at'ika* — 'on the sea side.' Thus, *Shitka* or *Sitkha* signifies 'place on the sea side of the island' called *Shig* by the Kolosh." (I. E. Veniaminov, *Zapiski ob ostrovahk Unalashkinskogo otdela* [Notes on the islands of the Unalashka district], St. Petersburg, 1840, *ch.* 3, p. 29.)

2. R. V. Makarova, *Russkie na Tikhom okeane vo vtoroi polovine XVIII v* [Russians on the Pacific Ocean . . .], Moscow, Nauka, 1968, pp. 182-188.

3. S. G. Fedorova, *"Pervoe postoiannoe poselenie russkikh v Amerike i Dzhems Kuk," Novoe v izuchenii Avstralii i Okeanii*, Moscow, Nauka, 1972, pp. 228-236.

4. N. N. Bolkhovitinov, *Stanovlenie russko-amerikanskikh otnoshenii, 1775-1815* [The establishment of Russian-American relations, 1775-1815], Moscow, Nauka, 1966, p. 272.

5. K. T. Khlebnikov, "*Zapiski K. Khlebnikova o Amerike,*" *Materialy dlia istorii russkikh zaselenii po beregam vostochnogo okeana* [Materials for the history of Russian settlements on the shores of the Eastern Ocean], *vyp.* 3, supplement to *Morskoi Sbornik*, 1861, p. 3.

6. K. T. Khlebnikov describes these events in *"Pervonachal'noe poselenie russkikh v Amerike"* ["The first Russian settlement in America"], *Raduga*, Revel, 1833, books II, III, V, and then reprinted in *Materialy dlia istorii russkikh zaselenii . . .*, *vyp.* 4, St. Petersburg, 1861, pp. 40-56. See also *K istorii Rossiisko-Amerikanskoi Kompanii* (*Sbornik dokumental'nykh Materialov*), Krasnoiarsk, Krasnoiarskii kraevoi gos. arkhiv; Krasnoiarskii Gos. Ped. In-t, 1957, p. 120. The site of the former fort of St. Archangel Mikhail on the coast of Baranov [Baranof] Island now bears the name "Old Sitka." There are no buildings whatever, and there has been preserved only a fence surrounding the supposed site of the graves of the Russians who perished in 1804.

7. All dates here and in the source are given in Old Style.

8. The basic dates of the life and activities of K. T. Khlebnikov are given on pp. xlv-lvii.

9. S. B. Okun', *Rossiiskogo-Amerikanskaia Kompaniia* [The Russian-American Company], Moscow and Leningrad, 1939, p. 96.

10-11. That Khlebnikov had a distant acquaintance with A. A. Baranov while Khlebnikov was in the service of the Russian-American Company in Kamchatka is indicated by a letter from A. A. Baranov from Novo-Arkhangel'sk to Khlebnikov dated 22 September 1809 (GAPO, *f.* 445, *op.* 1, *d.* 143, *l.* 1-1 *ob.*):

> My dear sir, Kirilo Timofeevich!
>
> Although I have not had the honor of knowing you, your politeness and greetings have placed me in your debt. I thank you sincerely for your letter sent with Toropogritskii and for the newspapers and magazines. Let us continue such good relations in the future, if it suits providence to keep me here and the Main Administration does not see fit to honor my many requests for a successor and to release me after so many

years and so much trouble. [Note in the hand of K. T. Khlebnikov: "received 24 May (1810)."]

12. N. A. Polevoi, "*Kirilo Timofeevich Khlebnikov, Nekrolog*," *Syn Otechestva*, 1838, v. IV, *otd.* VI, p. 3.

13. The Kuril Islands received the status of a colonial section under the manager of the Novo-Arkhangel'sk office only in 1830 (AVPR, *f.* RAK, *op.* 888, *d.* 343).

14. TsGIA ESSR, *f.* 2057, *op.* 1, *d.* 381, *l.* 1-13 *ob.* There is no doubt that N. A. Polevoi used this source in the obituary of K. T. Khlebnikov he wrote in 1838.

15. "The first book on the vessel of accounts of workers of the Northeast American Company of the companion Grigorii Shelikhov, sailing on the vessel *Sankt Trekh Sviatitelei* from 1783 to 1790," containing 70 accounts, is in AVPR (*f.* RAK, *op.* 888, *d.* 881, *l.* 1-93 *ob.*). An analogous book (but not a copy of this one) is in the Library of Congress in the Yudin Collection (RO, Iudin Coll., box 1, folder 3) and was used by Professor R. Pierce in making a list of the participants of the voyage of G. I. Shelikhov to the coasts of America on the vessel *Sv. Tri Sviatitelia* in 1783-1786. In this list, under No. 66, is Sidor Andreevich Shelikhov (G. I. Shelikhov, *A Voyage to America, 1783-1786*, translated by Marina Ramsay and edited by R. A. Pierce, Kingston, the Limestone Press, pp. 114-117).

16. N. A. Polevoi, "*Kirilo Timofeevich Khlebnikov. . .* ," p. 3.

17. TsGIA ESSR, *f.* 2057, *op.* 1, *d.* 381, *l.* 10.

18. RO GPB, F. IV. (f. Oleninskaia sistema), *l.* 1-43 *ob.*: [K. T. Khlebnikov], "*Pis'ma o Kamchatke.*"

19. K. T. Khlebnikov, "*Vzgliad na polveka moei zhizni*" ["A look at a half century of my life"], *Syn Otechestva*, 1836, *ch.* 175.

20. TsGIA ESSR, *f.* 2957, *op.* 1, *d.* 381, *l.* 13.

21. AGO, R-99, *op.* 1, *d.* 14, *l.* 1-72 *ob.*

22. *Ibid.*, *l.* 11-11 *ob.*

23. *Ibid.*, *l.* 20.

24. *Ibid.*, *l.* 50-50 *ob.*

25. *Ibid.*, *l.* 51 *ob.*-52.

26. For a complete list of K. T. Khlebnikov's journeys, supplemented by references to journals of his voyages preserved in manuscripts, see pp. li-lvii.

27. AGO, R-99, *op.* 1, *d.* 112, *l.* 2.

28. N. A. Polevoi, "*Kirilo Timofeevich Khlebnikov. . . ,*" p. 5.

29. GAPO, *f.* 445, *op.* 1, *d.* 343, *l.* 2 *ob.*

30. *Ibid.*, *d.* 15, *l.* 3.

31. K. T. Khlebnikov also sometimes called himself a "scribbler," critically evaluating his own literary work. Thus, during the voyage on the military transport *Amerika* from Novo-Arkhangel'sk to Kronshtadt (1832-1833) he wrote the *Life of A. A. Baranov* in a very short time — before the ship reached Brazil.

> The voyage of 85 days, could not be without monotony; but we as passengers having nothing else to do, scribbled on paper; Pavel Fedorovich [Kuzmishchev] wrote his proposal for improvement of Kamchatka or transfer of it from the government to management by Russian-American Company; and I, by your [F. P. Wrangell's] kind counsel somehow scribbled the *Life of Baranov* . . . I had the honor to mention that, while en route across the sea, I wrote the *Life of A. A. Baranov.* It turned out to be long, but I did not want to exclude curious details of the events. Most honored Pavel Fedorovich helped me in setting down my thoughts and corrected grammatical errors. On arrival [in Kronshtadt], I copied it and gave it to Ivan Vasil'evich [Prokof'ev]. He says that he has not had time to read it yet, but that they will print it. I do not know whether this will occur, but if it does, I will have the satisfaction of sending you a copy on the transport [TsGIA ESSR, *f.* 2057, *op.* 1, *d.* 489, *l.* 8, 28 *ob.*; K. T. Khlebnikov, St. Petersburg, to F. P. Wrangell, Novo-Arkhangel'sk, 20 December 1833].

32. *Ibid.*, *d.* 161, *l.* 14 *ob.*-15. It is worth noting that the historiography of Russian America includes many examples worthy of imitation today where the researcher-historian, using numerous historical sources and extracts from the work of predecessors, places his name on the title page only as the

compiler and not as the author. We recall only the names of fundamental works: *Zapiski ob ostrovakh Unalashkinskogo otdela, sostavlennye I. Veniaminovym* (ch. I-III, St. Petersburg, 1840); *Statistische und ethnographische Nachrichten über die Russischen Besitzungen an der Nordwestkuste von Amerika, Gesammelt von dem ehemaligen Oberverwalter dieser Besitzungen, Contre-Admiral von Wrangell . . .* , St. Petersburg, 1839; *Istoricheskoe obozrenie obrazovaniia Rossiisko-Amerikanskoi kompaniia i deistvii ee do nastoiashchego vremeni, sostavlennoe P. Tikhmenevym* (ch. I-II, St. Petersburg, 1861, 1863). K. T. Khlebnikov himself signed his publications only with the initials "*K. Kh.*" or "*Iz zapisok K. T. Kh.*" His article "*Statisticheskie svedeniia o koloniiakh Rossiisko-Amerikanskoi kompanii,*" the original of which is found in LOAAN (R-II, *op.* 1, *d.* 275, *l.* 2-15 *s ob.*), appeared in 1834 in *Kommercheskaia Gazeta* (Nos. 80, 81, 87, 90, 93, 96, 98, 99) generally unsigned. Khlebnikov wrote to F. P. Wrangell in Novo-Arkhangel'sk 9 January 1835:

> The departure from here of Mr. Physician Blashke and Lieutenant Voronkovskii presented an opportunity to send for your information the balance of the Russian-American Company and newspapers about the state of affairs. This information was provided by the Minister of Finance and printed in *Kommercheskaia Gazette* and, from them, in *Invalid* and in the German *Vedomosti* published at the Academy [Nauk]. Mr. Keppen, publisher of the *Gazette*, on the proposal of His Excellency I. F. Kruzenshtern has asked me to provide notes. I quickly did so, and in thanks for that Mr. Keppen sent ten copies of specially printed information [TsGIA ESSR, *f.* 2057, *op.* 1, *d.* 489, *l.* 56].

One can determine the majority of K. T. Khlebnikov's unpublished works only by handwriting or by content, as for example the "Letters about Kamchatka" (43 *l.*), the authorship of which B. N. Vishnevskii established in 1953 (RO GPB, F. IV, 815 [Oleninskaia sistema], supplement: copy of letter of 27 July 1953 from B. N. Vishnevskii, Kungur, to the GPB).

33. Ivan Maksimovich Solov'ev was a Tobol'sk merchant, foreman on the vessel *Iulian* (1758-1762) and seaman on the vessel *Petr i Pavel* (1764-1766). He was on Unalashka twice and left a bad memory about his visit (I. E. Veniaminov, *Zapiski ob ostrovakh . . . , ch.* 2, pp. 186-194).

34. GAPO, *f.* 445, *op.* 1, *d.* 161, *l.* 29.

35. *Ibid.*, *d.* 161, *l.* 23 *ob.* In this file, as in descriptions of the entire *fond* 445, geographical maps are not counted. However, in TsGAVMF we found a map of the islands of the Unalashka district (*f.* 1331, *op.* 7, *d.* 777), which according to the description given in this letter, is like the map of 1831 by I. E. Veniaminov.

36. *Pis'ma Innokentiia, mitropolita moskovskogo i kolomenskogo, 1828-1835, sobrany Ivanom Barsukovym*, St. Petersburg, 1897, *kn.* 1, p. 23.

37. TsGIA ESSR, *f.* 2057, *op.* 1, *d.* 489, *l.* 44 *ob.* (K. T. Khlebnikov, St. Petersburg, to F. P. Wrangell, Novo-Arkhangel'sk, 13 April 1834).

38. B. N. Vishnevskii, *Puteshestvennik Kiril Khlebnikov* ["The traveler Kiril Khlebnikov"], Perm, Permskoe knizhnoe isd izd-vo, 1957, pp. 42, 45; B. N. Lukin, "*Neopublikovannaia stat'ia 'letopistsa Russkoi Ameriki' K. T. Khlebnikova* ["On unpublished articles by the 'chronicler of Russian America' K. T. Khlebnikov"] in *Ot Aliaski do Ognennoi zemli* [From Alaska to Tierra del Fuego], Moscow, Nauka, 1967, p. 131; L. M. Paseniuk, *Zhorzh Blon, Gavriil Pribylov i drugie, Kamchatka Lit-Khud. sb.*, Petropavlovsk-Kamchatskii, Dal'nevostochnoe knizh. izd-vo, 1981, p. 160.

39. F. P. Litke, *Puteshestvie vokrug sveta, sovershennoe po poveleniiu imp.* Nikolaia I *na voennom shliupe* Seniavin *v 1826-1829 godakh* [Voyage Around the World on the Naval Sloop *Seniavin*, 1826-1829], St. Petersburg, 1834-1836, in three volumes with atlas.

40. *Ibid.*, v. 1, pp. 84-85.

41. R. G. Liapunova and S. G. Fedorova, *Russkaia Amerika v neopublikhovannykh zapiskakh K. T. Khlebnikova*, Leningrad, Nauka, 1979, p. 13.

42. S. A. Tokarev, "*Vklad russkikh uchenykh v mirovuiu etnografischeskuiu nauka,*" *Ocherki russkoi etnografii, fol'kloristiki i anthropologii*, Moscow, AN SSSR, 1956, *vyp.* 1, p. 10.

43-44. TsGIA ESSR, *f.* 2057, *op.* 1, *d.* 347, *l.* 1-23 *ob.*

45. GAPO, *f.* 445, *op.* 1, *d.* 395, *l.* 11.

46. D. I. Zavalishin's letters to K. T. Khlebnikov are preserved in several archives: in the Archive of AN SSSR (*fond* N. F. Dubrovina), see list in collection of materials: *Pamiati dekabristov*, Leningrad: AN SSSR, 1926, v. 3, p. 230; in TsGVIA see list in *Dvizhenie dekabristov Imannoi ukazetel' k dokumentam fondov i kollektsii TsGVIA SSSR. Otv. sost.* L. P. Petrovskii, Moscow, GAU in Sovet Ministrov SSSR, 1975, *vyp.* 3, p. 687; there is a letter of 21 December 1824 in GAPO, *f.* 445, *op.* 1, *d.* 195, 3 *l.* For commentaries on letter of D. I. Zavalishin to K. T. Khlebnikov from 14 July 1824, which fell into the hands of the investigatory commission in the case of the Decembrists, see L. B. Modzalevskii, "*Pushkin i Khlebnikov,*" in *A. S. Pushkin i Sibir'*, Moscow and Irkutsk, Vostsiboblgiz, 1937, p. 158; B. N. Vishnevskii, "*Puteshestvennik . . . ,*" p. 46; L. S. Kashikhin, "*Pis'ma dekabristov,*" [v GAPO] *Zvezda* (Perm') 26 December 1975.

47. The manuscript text "*Zapiski o Kalifornii*" (clerk's copy) has in only one of the lists the work of K. T. Khlebnikov (AGO, R-99, *op.* 1, *d.* 112, *l.* 408-550 *s ob.*) published in *Syn Otechestva*, 1829, v. 174, *ch.* II, III.

48. "*Zapiski barona V. I. Shteingelia,*" *Obshchestvennye dvizheniia v Rossii v pervuiu polovinu XIX v*, St. Petersburg, 1905, v. 1, p. 410.

49. Today, the Leningrad lombard is in this building.

50. [V. I. Semesvskii], "*Vospominaniia kniazia Evgeniia Petrovicha Obolenskogo,*" in *Obshchestvennye dvizheniia v Rossii . . .*, v. 1, p. 235.

51. The theme "the Decembrists and Russian America" still awaits a major study. It was touched upon in A. G. Mazour, "Dimitry Zavalishin: Dreamer of a Russian-American Empire," *Pacific Historical Review*, March, 1936; S. B. Okun', *Rossiisko-Amerikanskaia kompaniia*, Moscow and Leningrad, Gos. sots.-ek. izd-vo, 1939, pp. 90-114; N. N. Bolkhovitinov, *Russko-amerikanskie otnosheniia, 1815-1832 gg.*, Moscow, Nauka, 1975, pp. 492-521; V. M. Pasetskii, "*Dekabristy o russkom Severe,*" *Puteshestviia i geograficheskie otkrytiia v XV-XIX vv.*, Moscow and Leningrad, Nauka, 1965, pp. 76-92; V. M.

Pasetskii, *Vperedi neizvestnost' puti*, Moscow, *Sov. Rossiia*, 1969, pp. 43-52 (about V. P. Romanov); V. M. Pasetskii, "*Arkticheskie puteshestviia rossiian*," Moscow, *Mysl'*, 1974, pp. 108-117; V. M. Pasetskii, *Geograficheskie issledovaniia dekabristov*, Moscow, Nauka, 1977.

52. "*Zapiski barona V. I. Shteingelia*," p. 435.

53. [V. I. Semesvskii], "*Kniaz' Evgenii Petrovich Obolenskii*," *Obshchestvennye dvizheniia v Rossii . . .* , v. 1, p. 214.

54. TsGIA ESSR, *f.* 2057, *op.* 1, *d.* 489, *l.* 19.

55. B. N. Vishnevskii devoted a chapter in his book to the theme "*Dekabristy i A. S. Pushkin v zhizni K. Khlebnikova*," in which he gives the text of the notes of A. G. Rotchev to K. T. Khlebnikov, on the necessity of publishing certain manuscripts. B. N. Vishnevskii rightly assumes that this concerns the manuscripts of the same "*Vvedeniia* [Introduction]," which K. T. Khlebnikov sent with an accompanying letter to the poet (B. N Vishnevskii, *Puteshestvennik . . .* , p. 47 fn). On the friendly meetings of K. T. Khlebnikov with A. G. Rotchev, see also V. I. Bez"iazychnyi, "*On byl chelovek . . .* " (*Postranitsam odnoi neobyknovennoi biografii*)," Volga (Saratov), 1970, No. 12.

56. L. B. Modzalevskii, "Pushkin and K. T. Khlebnikov," pp. 155-164; L. B. Modzalevskii, "*Iz arkhiva Pushkina*," in *Literaturnyi arkhiv: Materialy po istorii literatury i obshchestvennogo dvizheniia*, Moscow and Leningrad, Izd-vo AN SSSR, 1938, pp. 28-30. This same position is repeated by A. N. Nikoliukin in his book *Literaturnye sviazi Rossii i SShA: Stanovlenie literaturnykh kontaktov*, Moscow, Nauka, 1981, p. 246.

57. B. N. Lukin, "*Zagadka ischeznuvshei rukopisi*," *Ural'skii sledopyt*, 1966, No. 9.

58. LOAAN, R-II, *op.* 1, *d.* 275, *l.* 23-27 *ob.* See B. N. Lukin, "*Neopublikovannaia stat'ia . . .* ," pp. 130-135.

59. For A. A. Kraevskii's reply, see "*Russkaia Amerika v neopublikovannykh zapiskakh . . .* ," pp. 14, 15.

January 20 is a date set in A. S. Pushkin's hand on the cover of one part of a synopsis of S. P. Krasheninnikov's work *Opisanie zemli Kamchatki*, first printed in 1755. "Why did Pushkin make a large extract? Probably for his journal *Sovremennik* . . . Seven days until the last duel, nine days before death . . . the fire of work on the fifth volume of *Sovremennik* . . . , the firm intention to write new chapters for '*Istorii Pugacheva* . . . ' However, Pushkin sits and stubbornly makes extracts from two volumes," writes the Soviet historian N. Ia. Eidel'man in his newest study of Pushkin. Eidel'man searches for the answer to this question in his *Pushkin: Istoriia i sovremennost' v khudozhestvennom soznanii poeta* [Pushkin: History and current affairs in the poet's artistic consciousness], Moscow, 1984, in chapter IX — Kamchatka affairs dela). In these same days, it appears, Pushkin read also the introduction sent to him by K. T. Khlebnikov which was returned to the author without publication after the poet's death. We, too, together with N. Ia. Eidel'man, ask: why, on the eve of his death did "Pushkin send his thought and imagination such a vast distance?"

60. Upon close examination of the stated archive folio in LOAAN (R-II, *op.* 1, *d.* 275), it can be seen that the paper upon which the introduction is written is in format, color and structure like the paper on which was written yet another section, headed "Supplement" (*l.* 16-22), beginning with the words: "I add to this some information about the peoples of the Russian-American Company colonies at the time of Baranov's replacement . . . " The scribe's copy is similar. The "Supplement" is devoted to anthropology and linguistics and includes a dictionary of the Kolosh and the Kad'iak languages, and also words "of Greenland origin" (collected by K. T. Khlebnikov, G. I. Davydov, V. S. Khromchenko and Iu. F. Lisianskii). Can the "Introduction" and "Supplement" be component parts of a one, still not discovered or unknown work by K. T. Khlebnikov?

At the same time we note that there still exists a dictionary begun by I. I. Banner (d. 1816) and continued by K. T. Khlebnikov, including the languages of the Kolosh, the Fox Island Aleuts, the Kad'iak "Aleuts," and inhabitants of the Kuskokwim River, Norton Sound, Bering Strait, and the Sandwich Islands (GAPO, *f.* 445, *op.* 1, *d.* 47, 17 *l. s ob.*).

61. Issue No. 3 of *Materialy dlia istorii russkikh zaselenii po beregam Vostochnogo okeana*, containing "*Zapiski K. Khlebnikova o Amerike*" was published by the Oregon Historical Society in English translation under the title *Colonial Russian America: Kyrill T. Khlebnikov's Reports, 1817-1832*,

translated by B. Dmytryshyn and E. A. P. Crownhart-Vaughan, Portland, Oregon Historical Society, 1976.

62. A. P. Sokolov, "*Russkaia biblioteka v Amerike*," *Morskoi Sbornik*, 1850, v. 4, no. 7, pp. 34-39.

63. D. D. Smyshliaev, *Istochniki i posobiia dlia izucheniia Permskogo kraia: Prilozhenie k Sborniku permskogo zemstva*, Perm, 1876, pp. 92-93.

64. S. B. Okun', *Russiisko-Amerikanskaia kompaniia*; S. G. Fedorova, *Russkoe naselenie Aliaski i Kalifornii, Konets XVIII v. - 1867 g.*, Moscow, Nauka, 1971; N. N. Bolkhovitinov, *Russko-amerikanskie otnosheniia*; R. G. Liapunova, *Ocherki po etnografii Aleutov*, Leningrad, Nauka, 1975; G. I. Dzeniskevich, *Vklad russkikh puteshestvennikov v etnografiiu atapaskov Aliaska (XVIII-XIX vv)* in the book *Ocherki istorii russkoi etnografii, fol'kloristiki i antropologii*, Leningrad, Nauka, 1977, *vyp.* VII and others; J. R. Gibson, "Bostonians and Muscovites on the Northwest Coast, 1788-1841," in *The Western Shore: Oregon Country Essays Honoring the American Revolution*, Portland, Oregon Historical Society, 1975; J. R. Gibson, *Imperial Russia in Frontier America: The Changing Geography of Supply of Russian America, 1784-1867*, New York, Oxford University Press, 1976; J. R. Gibson, "Russian Sources for the Ethnohistory of the Pacific Coast of North America in the Eighteenth and Nineteenth Centuries," *Western Canadian Journal of Anthropology*, 1976, VI(1); J. R. Gibson, "Old Russia in the New World: Adversaries and Adversities in Russian America," in J. R. Gibson ed., *European Settlement and Development in North America: Essays on Geographical Change in Honor and Memory of Andrew Hill Clark*, Toronto and Buffalo: University of Toronto Press, 1978; J. R. Gibson, "European Dependence upon American Natives: The Case of Russian America," *Ethnohistory*, 1978, 25(4):359-385; G. Barratt, *Russia in Pacific Waters, 1715-1825: A Survey of the Origins of Russia's Naval Presence in the North and South Pacific*, Vancouver and London, University of British Columbia Press, 1981.

65. R. G. Liapunova, "*Rukopis' K. T. Khlebnikova Zapiski o koloniiakh v Amerike kak istochnik po etnografii i istorii Aliaski i Aleutskikh ostrovov*," *Ot Aliaski do Ognennoi Zemli*, Moscow, Nauka, pp. 136-141.

66. AGO, R-99, *op.* 1, *d.* 112, *ch.* I-VI.

67. *Russkaia Amerika v neopublikovannykh zapiskakh K. T. Khlebnikova*, compiled by, with introduction and commentary by R. G. Liapunova and S. G. Fedorova, Leningrad, Nauka, 1979.

68. LOII, 447 (*ch.* I); LOAAN, R-II, *op.* 1, *d.* 275 (*ch.* II); LOII, *koll.* 115, *d.* 344 (*ch.* III-V).

69. AGO, R through R-99, *op.* 1, *d.* 112, *ch.* I-VI.

70. TsGAVMF, *f.* 213, *op.* 1, *d.* 144. An English translation: James R. Gibson, "Russian America in 1821: The Colonies of the Russian-American Company by K. T. Khlebnikov," *Oregon Historical Quarterly*, LXXVII(2):174-188, 1976.

71. GAPO, *f.* 445, *op.* 1, *d.* 120, *l.* 1 *s ob.* The document is not dated, but it is known that V. P. Romanov published an article "*O koliuzhakh i koloshakh voobshche*," *Severnyi Arkhiv*, St. Petersburg, 1825, ch XVII).

72. TsGIA ESSR, *f.* 2057, *op.* 1, *d.* 354, *l.* 18-19.

Approaching Novo-Arkhangel'sk (Khlebnikov ms., artist unknown).

MAIN DATES IN K. T. KHLEBNIKOV'S LIFE AND ACTIVITIES[1]

1756-1790. Khlebnikov's father, Timofei Ivanovich Khlebnikov, mayor of the town of Kungur, Perm guberniia, died 9 October 1790.

1751-1835. Khlebnikov's mother, Mar'ia Ivanovna Khlebnikov, née Chekina, died 19 August 1835.

1773-1835. Khlebnikov's brother, Aleksei Timofeevich Khlebnikov, the eldest of the children, died 15 October 1835. After him were born: Anna (married N. S. Prokof'ev), Ivan, Olimpiada, Kiril, Aleksandra, and Ol'ga.

1784 18 March(?). Kiril Timofeevich Khlebnikov was born.[2]

1800 28 December. Khlebnikov, Stolbov and Krotov, accompanying Russian-American Company agent Gornovskii, left Kungur for Siberia via Irbit, Tiumen, Tobol'sk, Tomsk, Krasnoiarsk, Nizhneudinsk.

1801 30 March-8 May. Irkutsk. "Here in the office of the American company, obligated myself for a year trip to Okhotsk and back."

7 July. Arrived at Okhotsk via Yakutsk.

21 July. Agreed for a year to set out for Gizhiginsk and signed a contract with the Russian-American Company.

21 September. Arrived in Gizhiginsk by sea and appeared before Russian-American Company agent Vorob'ev as prikazchik.

1802 "During the winter traveled by dogs and reindeer to Koriak and Tungus iurts."

1802 July. Arrived in Okhotsk by sea with the chief manager of the Okhotsk office, A. E. Polevoi. "Signed on for another year at Izhiga."

30 August. From Okhotsk on the galiot *Konstantin*, under command of Kirilov, left for Gizhiginsk, but "for more than twenty days suffered contrary winds and for three days didn't have a drop of water, so turned back and on 6 October arrived in Iamsk."

1803 21 May. "Went on skis across the bay to the lighthouse and because of a strong thaw almost drowned, weakened and barely reached the shore and fell."

22 June. Left by sea from Iamsk and arrived at Gizhiginsk. In July left Gizhiginsk by sea.

2-30 August. In Okhotsk manager A. E. Polevoi and agents Mesnikov and Vykhodtsev "signed me on for one year in Kamchatka," as Russian-American Company prikazchik.

27 September. Arrived for service in Nizhnekamchatsk, where served in Russian-American Company store as prikazchik.

1804 Spent the year in Gizhiginsk in Kamchatka "occupied in the store and traveled no farther than Kliuchevsk settlement."

3 July. From reports of Vykhodtsev, learned that the ship *Nadezhda*, under command of I. F. Kruzenshtern, arrived in Petropavlovsk Harbor and on 26 August left for Japan with the ambassador N. P. Rezanov.

1805 12 August. Arrived from Nizhnekamchatsk at Petropavlovsk port. "Here, I found the ship *Nadezhda* and prepared for the voyage to Canton and Russia. Mr. Shemelin was agent."

27 September. The ship *Nadezhda* went to sea.

5 October. "Mr. Mesnikov arrived from St. Petersburg and took over [as agent] in place of Vykhodtsev . . . . I signed on with him in the

1805 former occupation," that is, as prikazchik in Nizhnekamchatsk.

1806 Spent the year in Nizhnekamchatsk.

1807 February. Left Nizhnekamchatsk for Tigil'. "Here, I purchased deer and meat sent to Petropavlovsk port for the expedition [of Khvostov and Davydov?].

March. "Left Tigil' with Mr. Langsdorff, naturalist and traveler."

30 March. Arrived in Petropavlovsk Harbor. "Here, I found the Japan expedition of Mr. Khvostov. In 1806 he took Mr. Rezanov from America to Okhotsk, and after approaching the shores of Japan, wintered in Kamchatka on the ship *Iunona*. Mr. Davydov on the tender *Avos*.

April. The expedition put to sea.

9 May. "Put to sea on the cutter *Rostislav*. Commander: the Bostonian Wolf; passenger: Mr. Langsdorff.

14 May. We struck a sleeping whale.

14 June. Entered the mouth of the Okhota River."

July. The expedition of Khvostov and Davydov arrived in Okhotsk from the voyage to Japan.

30 August. Left Okhotsk for Petropavlovsk port on the brig *Mariia*, under command of Ia. E. Potapov, and arrived there 21 September. "Found there the other company vessel *Sitkha*, arriving from America, on which the hieromonk Gedeon and the Englishman Barber arrived. Mr. Mesnikov loaded it with goods and sent me to Kamchatka."

3 October. "At entrance to the mouth of the Kamchatka River our vessel turned over. We saved ourselves on the small boat, but lost the vessel, cargo and all its property."

1808 1 July. From Nizhnekamchatsk arrived at Petropavlovsk Harbor and remained for the summer.

MAIN DATES IN KHLEBNIKOV'S LIFE

1808 1 October. "Orders of the Main Office, replaced Mr. Mesnikov as Kamchatka agent."

10 October-16 December. Went from Petropavlovsk Harbor via Verkhnekamchatsk to Nizhnekamchatsk and on the return trip at night on 6 December. "There was heavy rain and almost drowned in the River Kamchatka at Kozyrevsk settlement."

1809 1 February. Left Petropavlovsk with Mesnikov and naval officers V. N. Berkh and Kozlianinov via Verkhnekamchatsk to Nizhnekamchatsk. On 17 March V. N. Berkh left in Petropavlovsk Harbor, and the three remaining via the Tigil' set out for Bol'sheretsk, thence 24 April arrived in Petropavlovsk.

1 June. Put to sea on brig *Sv. Pavel* under command of Narmanskii. On it left 22 officers, Mesnikov and Zakaharov.

8 June. The sloop *Neva* under command of L. A. Hagemeister arrived with a cargo of salt from the Hawaiian Islands. On 21 July the *Neva* put to sea, holding course for Novo-Arkhangel'sk.

2 August-25 September. Trip with prikazchik Titov to Nizhnekamchatsk and Verkhnekamchatsk. At Nizhnekamchatsk Titov replaced prikazchik Guznishchevskii.

25 September. Arrived in Petropavlovsk. "Soon after that the sloop *Diana* entered port, which under command of Mr. Golovnin was held thirteen months at Cape of Good Hope by the English, and from there escaped . . . "

1810 3-15 January. Left from Petropavlovsk Harbor with the inspectors Pasko and Panaev for Verkhnekamchatsk to replace prikazchik Sorokin with Anisimov.

20 January. Arrived in Nizhnekamchatsk.

15 March-5 April. By way of Tigil' arrived in Bol'sheretsk.

9 April. Returned to Petropavlovsk.

MAIN DATES IN KHLEBNIKOV'S LIFE

1810 26 May. Sloop *Diana* went to sea, going to Novo-Arkhangel'sk.

28 May. The sloop *Neva*, coming from Novo-Arkhangel'sk arrived in the roadstead under command of L. A. Hagemeister, "who left the ship here and proceeded to St. Petersburg with the crew. June. Went to sea with the brig *Pavel*, on it Mr. Hagemeister and merchantry."

17 August-2 October. Trip to Nizhnekamchatsk and Verkhnekamchatsk, return to Petropavlovsk.

1810 25 October. Coming from Okhotsk with Mr. Kokh and family, the brig *Mariia* entered the roadstead under navigator Kuritsyn.

1811 14 January-12 February. Trip from Petropavlovsk to Verkhnekamchatsk (on 5 February received a letter that Kokh had died suddenly on 24 January). Verkhnekamchatsk to Petropavlovsk.

13 May. Sloop *Diana* under V. M. Golovnin set sail for the coasts of Japan.

23 June. Brig *Finliandiia* under command of Sukin arrived from Kad'iak and 14 August set out for Okhotsk. On 6 October the *Finliandiia* under command of I. F. Vasil'ev returned, and 12 October Vasil'ev sailed on the *Finliandiia* to Atkha.

7-20 October. Ia. E. Podushkin took command of the sloop *Neva*.

5 November. Received word of "wreck of ship *Iunona* on the shore of Viliui on 3 November."

1812 22 February-26 May. Traveled with the agent Iudin from Petropavlovsk to Verkhnekamchatsk, then to Nizhnekamchatsk; with Guznishchevskii went to Tigil' range "and for two days in big storm took shelter in the snow under a sledge without food. Returned back because of impossibility [of continuing]." Via Kliuchi and Verkhnekamchatsk to Petropavlovsk.

1812 19 August-1 October. Trip from Petropavlovsk to Nizhne Kamchatsk, Verkhne Kamchatsk and back with the Bostonian Dobell from Manila and Lieutenant Colonel Sibiriakov.

1813 16-26 February. Trip from Petropavlovsk to Malininskii ostrozhek and return to port with General Petrovskii.

11 March-11 July. Trip with company agent Iudin to Bol'sheretsk "for cash" by way of Icha, Tigil', Tigil' range, and Kliuchi to Nizhnekamchatsk; from Nizhnekamchatsk en route to sea on 1 July "received the Russian post, where we learned of the taking of Moscow by the enemy and of his defeat outside Russia." Put to sea with Iakushkin, Petrovskii and officers to Petropavlovsk.

18 July. K. T. Khlebnikov quit [left] Petropavlovsk forever on the vessel (commander Iakushkin); 16 August-1 September to Okhotsk; 30 September-1 October to Yakutsk.

3 December. Arrived in Irkutsk.

1814 "Spent the whole year in Irkutsk, not going anywhere." Wrote "Letters about Kamchatka" [1814?].

1815 17 January. Paired up with A. A. Berezin and left together for Krasnoiarsk, Tomsk, Kainsk, Tiumen, Ekaterinburg, Kungur (7-10 February), Perm (11 February), Kazan, Nizhnii Novgorod, Murom, Vladimir, Moscow (21-25 February), Tver, Vyshnii Volochek, Krestsy, St. Petersburg (2 March).

1 September. "Mr. Hagemeister arrived in Kronshtadt from operations on the *Hannibal*."

1815-1816 5 September 1815-29 August 1816. Trips with directors of the Russian-American Company and independently: Kronshtadt, St. Petersburg, Petergof. Preparations for voyage around the world on the ship *Kutuzov*.

1816 7 September. On the ship *Kutuzov*, under command of L. A. Hagemeister, as Russian-American Company agent left on voyage from Kronshtadt to Novo-Arkhangel'sk: Copenhagen, Norway, Cape Verde Islands, Rio de Janeiro (Brazil, 11 December 1816-7 January 1817).

1817 Cape Horn (17 February): Port Callao with trips to Lima (Peru, 17 March-7 May); stop at mouth of River Tumbes (9-16 July); stop at Port Rumiantsev (Little Bodega Bay, 15-30 September); 20 September "went to Fort Ross in three-hatch baidarkas. On 27 September returned in a large baidara." San Francisco (1 October-30 October): "On 30 October Mr. Kuskov set out for Ross in baidarkas."

20 November. Arrived in Sitkha Bay.

1818 11 January. L. A. Hagemeister proclaimed himself chief manager of the Russian possessions in America in place of A. A. Baranov.

12 January. K. T. Khlebnikov was appointed assistant to the chief manager and manager of the Novo-Arkhangel'sk office.

SEA VOYAGES OF K. T. KHLEBNIKOV FROM NOVO-ARKHANGEL'SK

4 June-20 November 1820. On the brig *Il'mena* (*Il'men'*) under the command of the Englishman Stevens (command transferred to K. I. Shmidt). At Cape Barro de Arena the brig was wrecked. Khlebnikov in a baidara went to Fort Ross (3 July). From Bodega Bay 29 July continued voyage on the brig *Buldakov*: Monterey, Santa Cruz, return to Bodega (11-22 September without visiting Fort Ross), Santa Barbara, Novo-Arkhangel'sk.[3]

6 October 1821. Given "as prize" 5,000 rubles. "The Main Administration hopes that you, after this, will not hasten to leave the colonies and continue your service at least until your honored commandant [chief manager of the colonies M. I. Murav'ev] will leave the colonies."[4]

13 September 1822-10 January 1823. On the brig *Buldakov* from Novo-Arkhangel'sk to Bodega Bay (2-7 October) and trip to Fort Ross (4-6 October); Monterey (Mexico) (12 October-20 November); San Francisco (23 November), where I transferred to the brig *Volga*. Put to sea (10 December); Bodega without visiting Fort Ross (11-13 December); Novo-Arkhangel'sk.[5]

15 September 1823-6 February 1824. On ship *Rurik* [*Riurik*] under command of V. S. Khromchenko from Novo-Arkhangel'sk; Bodega Bay (14-31 October) and trip to Fort Ross (18-20 October); Monterey (3-13 November); Santa Cruz (Upper California) (14-19 November); San Francisco (21 November 1823-12 January 1824); Novo-Arkhangel'sk.[6]

1824. On 1 January in place of 2,000 [r.] began to receive salary of 3,000 rubles.[7]

24 May-20 December 1824. On brig *Baikal* from Novo-Arkhangel'sk; Bodega (3-27 June) and trip to Fort Ross (4-12 June); Monterey (28 June-12 July); Santa Cruz (12-19 July); Monterey (19 July): "Mr. Etolin on the *Baikal* went to Sitkha and I remained on the coast. On 22 August the newly built brig *Kiakhta* arrived from Bodega." On this brig went from Monterey (15 September) to Santa Cruz (16-25 September); Bodega (25 October-20 November) and trip to Fort Ross (2-5 November); Novo-Arkhangel'sk.[8]

2 June-3 August 1825. On the brig *Baikal* from Novo-Arkhangel'sk to Kad'iak (8-20 June); Unalashka (26 June-5 July); St. George Island (9 June); St. Paul Island (10 June); Atkha (19-23 June); Novo-Arkhangel'sk.

23 September 1825-25 January 1826. On brig *Baikal* under command of Kh. Benzeman from Novo-Arkhangel'sk to Bodega Bay (9-17 October) and trip to Fort Ross (11-14 October); to Monterey (21 October): here transferred to the brig *Kiakhta*. Put to sea (9 December); San Francisco (7 December 1825-3 January 1826); Novo-Arkhangel'sk.

MAIN DATES IN KHLEBNIKOV'S LIFE

23 June 1825. Awarded gold medal "for diligent service" on Vladimir ribbon to be worn around the neck. Message from the Minister of Finance to the Main Administration of the Russian-American Company states: "We intend to take it up with the Kungur burgher community about his transfer from the [burgher] estate to the merchant estate, freeing him [Khlebnikov] from it and elevating him to merchant status.[9]

26 November 1825. He received an expression of appreciation "for excellent service" on behalf of the shareholders of the Russian-American Company.[10]

31 August 1826-22 March 1827. On brig *Baikal* under command of Kh. Benzeman left Novo-Arkhangel'sk for Bodega Bay (18-22 September) without visiting Fort Ross; Monterey (24-29 September); San Pedro (3-29 October); Catalina Island (30 October-3 November); San Diego (6-22 November); Monterey (2-19 December) and trip to Mission San Juan (5-6 December); Santa Cruz (21-23 December); and Monterey (23 December), where he transferred to brig *Okhotsk*. Put to sea (11 January 1827); San Francisco (16 January-24 February) and trips to missions San Jose and Santa Clara (23-27 January); to New mission (6-9 February); and Novo-Arkhangel'sk.[11]

9 May-6 September 1827. On brig *Kiakhta* from Novo-Arkhangel'sk to Atkha (8-22 June); Bering Island (10-12 July); Attu Island (26 July-4 August); Amchitka (16 August); and Novo-Arkhangel'sk.[12]

20 September-24 December 1827. On brig *Golovnin* from Novo-Arkhangel'sk to Bodega Bay (15-17 October) without visiting Fort Ross; Monterey (18 October-1 November); Santa Cruz (1-20 November); Monterey (20 November-3 December); and Novo-Arkhangel'sk.

31 August 1828-17 February 1829. On the brig *Kiakhta* from Novo-Arkhangel'sk to Bodega Bay (18-25 September) and trip to Fort Ross (19-22 September); San Francisco (26 September-23 November); thence trips to mission Santa Clara (4-7 September), Rancho San[ta] Paula (11-12 September), Mission San Jose (14-17 September), to mission Santa Clara (20-25 November); Monterey (25 September); here transferred to brig *Okhotsk*. Put to sea (27 December); San Diego (2-21 January 1829); Novo-Arkhangel'sk.

1 June-18 July 1829. On brig *Golovnin* from Novo-Arkhangel'sk to Unalashka (14-26 June); island of St. Paul (2 July) and island of St. George (5-6 July); Novo-Arkhangel'sk.

Published "Notes on California" in journal *Syn Otechestva*, 1829, v. 174, ch. II, III.

18 October 1829-15 May 1830. On brig *Okhotsk* under command of D. Zarembo from Novo-Arkhangel'sk went to Fort Ross (2 November); Monterey (6 November); here transferred to sloop *Baikal* under command of midshipman A. K. Etolin. Went to sea (2 February 1829); Concepcion Bay (Chile, 9 February-9 March); went to town of Concepcion (11 February-1 March); Novo-Arkhangel'sk.

18 March 1830. Awarded gold medal "For Zeal" on Aleksandr ribbon to be worn around the neck.[13]

23 October 1830-28 March 1831. On sloop *Baikal* under command of podporuchik M. Prokof'ev went from Novo-Arkhangel'sk went to Fort Ross (13 November); San Francisco (15-20 November); Monterey (23 November-3 December); San Francisco (6 December 1830-9 February 1831); thence trips to the New Mission (7-8 December), to missions San Jose and Santa Clara (13-18, 29 December; 1, 8, 12-18, 27-29 January), to Mission San Pedro (1-2 February); Monterey (12-27 February); Novo-Arkhangel'sk.[14]

29 September 1831-21 January 1832. On sloop *Urup* went from Novo-Arkhangel'sk to Fort Ross (10 October 1831): "went to fort in baidarka." Left Bodega Bay (11 October); Monterey (14 October-10 November), thence trip to Mission San Carlos (27 October); Santa Cruz (10-12 November), "went in row boats to Santa Cruz;" Monterey (12-19 November); San Francisco (24 November-19 December); thence trips to missions San Francisco (26, 28 November), Santa Clara, San Jose, San Antonio, and again San Francisco; Novo-Arkhangel'sk.

MAIN DATES IN KHLEBNIKOV'S LIFE

26 March 1832. K. T. Khlebnikov and F. P. Wrangell went by sea from Novo-Arkhangel'sk to Ozerskii redoubt (on Baranof Island).

20 November 1832-13 September 1833. On the sea transport *Amerika* under command of V. S. Khromchenko went from Novo-Arkhangel'sk to San Francisco (12 December 1832-13 January 1833), thence to the missions San Francisco (14 December 1832), San Jose (21-25 December), the New mission (26-28 December), San Francisco (9 January 1833), and Rancho San Antonio (10 January); Pitcairn Island (12 February); Cape Horn (18 March); Rio de Janeiro (7 April-18 May); England (19 November); Copenhagen (5 August-September); Kronshtadt.

29 September 1833. To St. Petersburg. "Went to the botanical garden and Mr. Fisher showed me around." On 6 November "went to Egor Vasil'evich Wrangell." On 23 December with I. V. Prokof'ev went from St. Petersburg by diligence to Novgorod, Tver, Moscow (27 December 1833-3 January 1834); Vladimir, Nizhnii Novgorod, Kazan, Perm (14 January); Kungur (15 January-7 February); Perm (8-10 February), Kazan, Nizhnii Novgorod, Moscow (21-23 February); St. Petersburg (27 February).

Published article "Pervonachal'noe poselenie russkikh v Amerike" in the journal *Raduga* (Revel'), 1833, *kn.* II, III, V.

1834. St. Petersburg. Visits to F. P. Litke in Winter Palace (February) and to P. F. Anzhu in the house on Elagin Island (1 July), to N. S. Mordvinov in Cabinet (August).

Published article "Statistical Information about the Russian-American Company Colonies," *Kommercheskaia Gazeta*, 1834, Nos. 80, 81, 87, 90, 93, 96, 98, 99.

6 March 1834. "Because of Mr. Bokovikov's illness, occupied the duty of office director of Main Administration of Russian-American Company."

1835. Trips to Kronshtadt: accompanied ship *Elena* under command of I. I. Schants to Russian America (1 August).[15] Visits to F. P. Litke, N. S. Mordvinov, A. P. Gel'mersen. Meeting with English polar researcher John Ross.

Published book *Life of A. A. Baranov*, St. Petersburg, 1835.

7 March 1835. "Elected as director in general meeting of shareholders."

1836. St. Petersburg. Visits to M. I. Murav'ev in Pavlovsk (17 May); thence in company of N. I. Grech (and his son), Pavel Murav'ev (and his brother) and N. I. Prokof'ev (31 May); thence also (21 June, 5 July, 2 and 9 August, 13 September); to Tsarskoe Selo and Pavlovsk with F. P. Wrangell (23 August). Met transport *Amerika* from Novo-Arkhangel'sk (20 July).

Published memoirs "A Glimpse of a Half Century of My Life" (*Syn Otechestva*, 1836, v. 175).

1837. St. Petersburg. Trips to Vyborg, Helsingfors, Abo and back (14-27 January); to Moscow and back (3 April-10 May); to Kronshtadt with N. I. Kusov (7 July) and to accompany ship *Nikolai* (10 August), to M. I. Murav'ev in Pavlovsk (10 August); to Tsarskoe Selo with P. I. Rikord (18 August); there again with A. S. Golovnin (30 August); there again with E. V. Wrangell (3 September); "there by railroad" (1 November).

2 July 1837. Awarded Order of St. Anna, third degree.[16]

25 November 1837. Elected, with F. P. Wrangell, by a general meeting of Russian-American Company shareholders to committee of five for compilation of "new roles and privileges of company employees."[17]

22 December 1837. Elected by St. Petersburg Academy of Sciences as member-correspondent of divisions of political science, departments of historical, philological and political science; informed of same by letter of 15 January 1838.[18]

1838. Published article "Life of G. I. Shelikhov" (*Syn Otechestva*, 1838, part II).

Published memoirs "Extract from Notes of a Russian Traveler (K. Kh.) in Brazil in 1833," *Severnaia Pchela*, 1838, Nos. 56, 57).

14 April 1838. "On Easter Sunday he was in good spirits, he appeared healthy, and did not even feel his constant rheumatic pains. On 14 April he came on foot, bold and gay, from the Russian-American Company house, at the Blue Bridge, to the house occupied by the Department of ship timbers, in Griaznaia Street, to the honored commandant of the department Baron F. P. Wrangell . . . Mr. [I. Ia.] Vasil'ev, appointed for a journey to Siberia, Kamchatka and America, was also there. Dinner and time until evening flew by in conversation, and K. T. had never been so nice and talkative, particularly in recalling the years he had spent in America. He started home on foot with Mr. Vasil'ev, but had hardly taken several steps when he lost consciousness. They hastened to carry him again into Mr. Wrangell's, where several minutes before he had so gaily said goodbye, but nothing science could do nor any friendly efforts could save his life. K. T. never regained consciousness and died in the night on 15 April. Numerous friends and people of all callings accompanied his casket on the way to Volkov Cemetery, with sincere grief. Without family and alone in St. Petersburg, he had awakened the love and friendship of so many, who, loving him as their kin saw his casket lowered into the earth with sincere regret."[19]

NOTES

1. Based upon: Diary of the employee of the Russian-American Company Kiril Khlebnikov (28 December 1800 — 1 November 1837), TsGIA ESSR, *f.* 2057, *op.* 1, *d.* 381, 20 *l. s ob.*; and Letters, K. T. Khlebnikov to F. P. Wrangell (11 October 1832 — 31 March 1838), *ibid.*, *d.* 489, 66 *l. s ob.*

2. For an exact rendering of K. T. Khlebnikov's date of birth, see introduction to the book *Russkaia Amerika v neopub-*

likovannykh zapiskakh K. T. Khlebnikova, Leningrad, Nauka, 1979, p. 6.

3. See K. T. Khlebnikov, "*Dnevnye zapiski o pokhode v Kaliforniiu na brige Il'mena i obratno no brige Buldakov, 1820 g.*" ["Diary of a voyage to California on the brig *Il'mena* and back on the brig *Buldakov*, 1820"], AGO, R-99, *op.* 1, *d.* 18, *l.* 1-15.

4. GAPO, *f.* 445, *op.* 1, *d.* 6.

5. K. T. Khlebnikov "Second trip notes about voyage on the *Buldakov*, 1822," AGO, R-99, *op.* 1, *d.* 18, *l.* 16-74.

6. K. T. Khlebnikov, "Report of the manager of the Novo-Arkhangel'sk office to Chief Manager M. I. Murav'ev about inspection of affairs in the fort and settlement of Ross, 19 January 1823" and "Report to Chief Manager M. I. Murav'ev about demands of the Mexican government to remove the settlement of Ross at Bodega, 1823," AGO, R-99, *op.* 1, *d.* 26, 5 *l.*

7. GAPO, *f.* 445, *op.* 1, *d.* 14.

8. K. T. Khlebnikov, "*Zapiski putevye v Kalifornii i kreposti Ross na brigakh Baikal i Kiakhta, 1824*" ["Travel notes of journey in California to Fort Ross on the brigs *Baikal* and *Kiakhta*, 1824"], AGO, R-99, *op.* 1, *d.* 28, *l.* 1-77; K. T. Khlebnikov, "[Notes about Ross Colony], 3 November — 20 December 1824," *ibid.*, *d.* 143, *l.* 1-22.

9. GAPO, *f.* 445, *op.* 1, *d.* 16, *l.* 1 *ob.*

10. *Ibid.*, *d.* 18.

11. K. T. Khlebnikov, "Report to the Main Office of the Russian-American Company about the state of affairs in the Ross office" [*l.* 1-2] and "Travel diary of the manager of the Novo-Arkhangel'sk office: Bodega — Monterey Bay, 18 September 1826 — 10 January 1827," AVPR, *f.* RAK (341), *op.* 888, *d.* 323, 31 *l.* (that is, lacks notes about beginning and end of expedition).

12. K. T. Khlebnikov, "Travel notes on the brig *Kiakhta* to the islands of Andreianov, Bering, Near, and Rat sections, 4 May — August 1827 [incomplete]," AGO, R-99, *op.* 1, *d.* 34, 29 *l.*

13. GAPO, *f.* 445, *op.* 1, *d.* 23, *l.* 1 *ob.*

14. K. T. Khlebnikov, "Travel notes of the manager of the Novo-Arkhangel'sk office on the sloop *Baikal*, 1830 — 1831," AGO, R-99, *op.* 1, *d.* 46, 43 *l.*; K. T. Khlebnikov, ["Daily journal of visit of the Spanish missions, 19 January — 27 February 1831"], *ibid.*, *d.* 143, *l.* 23-41.

15. K. T. Khlebnikov wrote F. P. Wrangell 26 April 1834: "Ivan Ivanovich [Shants] is getting ready on his coming voyage to go past the Cape of Good Hope and New Holland [Australia] and visit both of these places. I would like to go along as supercargo, although I do not know whether the directors will approve. However, I am dying to go, and [if I go] it will probably be the death of me" (TsGIA ESSR, *f.* 2057, *op.* 1, *d.* 489, *l.* 48).

16. GAPO, *f.* 445, *op.* 1, *d.* 31.

17. *Ibid.*, *d.* 32, *l.* 1.

18. *Ibid.*, *d.* 33, *l.* 1.

19. N. A. Polevoi, "*Kirilo Timofeevich Khlebnikov (nekrolog)*," *Syn Otechestva*, 1838, v. IV, *otd.* VI, p. 6.

Pavlovsk settlement on Kad'iak I. By Voznesenskii, 1842-1843.

PART ONE: *NOVO-ARKHANGEL'SK FORT ON BARANOV ISLAND [SITKHA]*

I
REASONS FOR FOUNDING OF SAME [NOVO-ARKHANGEL'SK FORT ON BARANOV ISLAND, SITKHA]

It is common knowledge that during several years after occupation of Kad'iak Island by Mr. Shelikhov's company (1783) and in the years following that when the company artels belonging to Mr. Lebedev-Lastochkin (a companion of Mr. Shelikhov) occupied Kenai and Chugach bays and nearby areas, the number of sea otters gradually declined. The main reason for establishing these settlements was to hunt sea otters. It was for this reason that Mr. Baranov, the chief manager of the colony, suggested sending parties of Aleuts in baidarkas farther along the American coast in a southeasterly direction.

The first such expedition, headed by Purtov, reached Yakutat (Bering) Bay in 1794 and took up to 2,000 pelts.[1] In 1795 a ship was dispatched to Yakutat to establish a settlement, but because of the commander's miscalculations, resulting in a shortage of water, the ship returned to Kad'iak. In the following year, 1796, a fort was founded and in accordance with an Imperial order settlers were established in the neighboring areas to cultivate the land and to raise livestock. In an order of 11 May 1794, the Governor-General of Siberia, Mr. Pil', directed Mr. Shelikhov to accomplish the following:

> In accordance with an Imperial Decree, you have been assigned twenty families in order to build shipyards at Cape St. Elias and ten families to settle and cultivate the land there or in more suitable areas on the mainland of the American continent. These settlers have been assigned 36 rubles a year, which are to be paid to them as soon as possible.

The area of Yakutat Bay, surveyed by Purtov and later by Mr. Baranov himself, was found to be more suitable than Cape St. Elias because of its pleasant harbor, forest and the contact already established with the savages known as the Koliuzh [Kolosh].

Yakutat Bay abounds in deciduous and coniferous trees. The land is generally hilly, but there are also flat areas covered with tall grasses. The ocean air is probably the main reason why no grain of any type will ripen, although there have been several attempts to grow it.[2] The bay is located at 59½° latitude; off to the WNW, at a distance of 60 miles, you can see in all its beauty Mount St. Elias, the highest mountain in North America. According to La Pérouse's observations, Mount St. Elias is located at latitude 60°23′ and longitude 140°45′ west of Greenwich. He estimated Mount St. Elias to be 12,672 English feet high. The Spanish navigator Malaspina estimated the height to be at 2,793 toises or 18,829 feet. If his calculations are correct, then the mountain is as high as those in South America[3] and higher than Mauna Kea in the Sandwich Islands. I have dwelled on these details simply because they contradict the opinion of naturalists who contend that mountains have a tendency to be lower at the poles than in equatorial areas.[4]

From 1796 parties of Aleuts were sent out continuously from Kad'iak to areas farther than the Yakutat settlement, which was already used as a warehouse depot for pelts which were left by the baidarkas and then transferred to sailing vessels. In 1798 they reached the so-called Khutsnovsk Strait. In 1799 they discovered new sea otter grounds in various smaller bays. Sometimes, their catch consisted of 3,000 to 5,000 pelts. A party of Aleuts usually consisted of 250 to 300 baidarkas under the leadership of two or three Russians. The Yakutat settlement served as a resting place, but its distance from the hunting parties made it necessary to have a place to store the pelts gathered during the hunt. The parties were nearly always sent out without the support of sailing vessels. The great distances they had to cover took them into late fall during which time the detachments were exposed to the dangers of storms. From Ledianoi Strait (Cross Sound) to Yakutat all the way to Chugach Bay, the entire coast is rocky or full of shoals. There are few good harbors even for baidarkas. Consequently, if the baidarka parties had a successful hunt and decided to hunt farther, they would be late in returning and in danger of perishing at sea because of autumn storms, or they might have to spend the winter out and suffer food shortages and possible attacks by the Kolosh.

Mr. Baranov had also political reasons in mind for enlarging Russia's possessions as far as Nootka. He wanted to prevent other nations from taking possession of this coast. The government approved his reasoning. Mr. Baranov referred to the settlement of Sitkha in a letter to Mr. Larionov, dated 24 June 1800, in the following manner:

> (1) Only now have we begun to enjoy the advantages of the fur trade in these areas which have become known to us. (2) We cannot allow the English or Americans to develop any trade with the savages, to whom they have been supplying firearms; we cannot allow them to settle these areas which have been explored by Russian navigators.

In July 1799, Mr. Baranov arrived in Sitkha on the galley *Ol'ga* which he commanded; meanwhile, a party which had come there with 1,500 pelts had not waited for his arrival and returned to Kad'iak with the pelts.[5] Medvednikov, the appointed manager of the settlement, arrived there with his people on the vessel *Orel*.

After finding a suitable location, Mr. Baranov gave the natives presents and asked their permission to build a fort there, offering them protection against their neighbors. Fifty Aleuts were left behind to perform this work along with the crew of the ship *Ekaterina*, which had been out at sea to survey Bucareli Bay. Mr. Baranov wrote:

> We first built a large *balagan* [storehouse] where we stored foodstuffs which we unloaded from the ship. Then we built a small ordinary bathhouse, which I moved into in October. Earlier, I had lived in a torn tent in rainy weather, and I suffered all winter long because of the smoke and the rain which came through the leaky roof until the end of February. Then we built a two-storied barracks with two watchtowers which were eight sazhens long and four sazhens wide. Then we built a *kazhim* for the Aleuts.

The newly established fort was named for the St. Archangel Mikhail. During the winter the Russians and Aleuts killed 40 sea lions and 150 seals, which were used for food. In the spring they began to catch halibut, and in March they caught large quantities of herring. In the winter the Aleuts caught nearly 300 sea otters near the settlement. During his stay, Mr. Baranov became acquainted with foreigners who had come there on five ships. He found out about their dealings and became aware of the profits we were losing because of their trade.

At first the Kolosh were indifferent to us, but when they became aware that we were establishing a settlement, which they had not expected, they took up their spears and attempted to take the fort from us. Because of Mr. Baranov's good judgement and prudence, their attempts were unsuccessful. On 20 April 1800, he left for Kad'iak on a galley, leaving Medvednikov in charge with 20 Russians. In 1802, because of the garrison's carelessness, the Kolosh attacked and destroyed the settlement.

With the help of the ship *Neva*, which had just arrived from Russia, Mr. Baranov seized the Kolosh strongholds on 8 October 1804 and founded a fort nearby, which was named Novo-Arkhangel'sk, which thanks to God's help is still standing today.

Novo-Arkhangel'sk in the 1830s. From Belcher, artist unknown.

II
BENEFITS FORMERLY DERIVED FROM THE SAME AND CIRCUMSTANCES ATTENDING [MR. BARANOV'S ADMINISTRATION]

Mr. Baranov decided to found the main office here. Even before informing the Main Office [of the company] he concluded that:

> the advantages of this location would insure millions in profits to the Empire. Consider that six to ten English and American ships have been trading here each year for the last ten years, taking with them 2,000 to 3,000 pelts in various places. An average of 2,000 pelts can be transported by each ship. One must suppose that every year an average of 12,000 pelts are taken out. And even if the figure were reduced to 10,000, this would mean that 100,000 pelts were exported in a period of ten years. Supposing they were sold in Canton at 30 piasters (or 45 rubles) apiece, the revenue would amount to 4,500,000 rubles. If the cost of getting these pelts were 1,500,000 rubles, there would still be a profit of 3,000,000 rubles in ten years.

Mr. Baranov goes on to say that "these very circumstances which benefit our fatherland are the same incentives which compelled me to occupy Sitkha at an opportune time. I decided that in spite of our small number of men and the circumstances of the company, we would establish a settlement, acquaint ourselves with the local conditions and wait for results with time."

This very view must have been quite important because (1) we had given up the idea of rebuilding the settlement and thus concealed our weakness. Having established our presence here, Mr. Baranov could put the Aleuts to work and not have to send for new people from Kad'iak every year. Thus, he could settle them here as the focal point of the fur industry; (2) because of the deep water and abundant forests it was possible to build a shipyard. And finally, (3) it became advantageous to trade with the Americans who after trading along the Northwest Coast on their homeward trips would sell their goods at a moderate price. This situation, of course, cannot be considered profitable, because if the Americans knew that the company would purchase their goods, they would have come to Kad'iak and even more remote places.

The first contact with Americans took place on Kad'iak in May 1801 because there had been a shortage of supplies due to the unfortunate accident suffered by the ship *Phoenix*. We bought 12,000 rubles' worth of goods and paid for them in fox pelts. In 1802 the Englishman Barber and the American Ebbets ransomed several prisoners from the Kolosh and brought them to Kad'iak. We bought more than 70,000 rubles' worth of goods from them. In 1803 the American O'Cain sold goods to us, and he concluded an agreement dealing with the hunting of sea otters in California.

After the second occupation of Sitkha in 1804 and before Mr. Baranov was replaced, a period of 14 years went by. It is now apparent that he changed his mind many times due to various circumstances which occurred. The fur trade took a different direction; shipbuilding was not always successful, but trade with Americans increased greatly, and through them we found a new trade route with Canton. We shall now examine in detail the course of these significant developments.

A. SEA OTTER PROCUREMENT IN THE SITKHA VICINITY

The year following the second occupation of Sitkha, in June 1805, a party of Aleuts in 300 baidarkas was sent out into the straits to hunt otters under the leadership of Bykadorov. Two sailing vessels, the *Ermak* and the *Rostislav*, sailed out to escort them. They hunted in Khutsnovsk [Chatham] Strait and Kek Bay [Prince Frederick Sound] until 21 August; in all they gathered 1,645 pelts under the constant harassment of the Kolosh. When the party returned to Sitkha, 200 baidarkas were sent to Kad'iak under the leadership of Demianenkov. On the way this party learned from Kolosh loyal to us that the Kolosh had destroyed the Yakutat settlement. The leader of the party took careful measures as he proceeded forward. Having reached the settlement at night, they confirmed the unfortunate incident. After spending several days in their baidarkas without setting foot on land, they grew tired, but there was no place for them to rest. Unable to hope for safe passage along the shore, the leader of the party and many of the Aleuts set out for Nuchek. Some 31 baidarkas with exhausted Aleuts left everything up to God and rowed towards the shore. Suddenly, a violent storm rose from the southeast and the entire party perished at sea without any exception. Those who had made it to the shore were fortunately not captured by the Kolosh. They continued, on their way finding baidarkas and the bodies of their companions who had drowned at sea.

This unfortunate incident put a stop to successful hunts, and in 1806 not a single party set out from Sitkha. In 1807 a party of 75 baidarkas under the leadership of Eremin was sent through Chatham Strait by way of Cape Ommaney with the intention of going to Kaigani Strait. However, they were met by a strong Kolosh force and had to return with little gain. Mr. Kuskov, who had stayed in Sitkha, took the party into the Chastye Islets [Bay of Islands], where after hunting on both sides, they took some 300 pelts and then returned on 10 September.

In March 1808 a party of 100 baidarkas sent into the Chastye Islets [Bay of Islands] returned 22 April with 130 pelts. Ninety-five baidarkas were added to this party and sent around Cape Ommaney to Kek Bay [Prince Frederick Sound]. They were escorted by the vessel *Nikolai*, commanded by Benzeman. The vessel *Kad'iak* was sent there to trade with the Kolosh. The party hunted 1,700 pelts, but did not trade because the Kolosh were unwilling to sell their sea otter pelts. Upon their return on 21 July, a new party of 110 baidarkas was sent out to Cape Edgecumbe and returned on 30 August with 170 pelts.

On 16 June 1809 a party was sent out to the straits under the command of Kuglinov and escorted by the schooner *Chirikov*. They returned in September after the Kolosh opposed them throughout the hunt.

On 10 March 1810 a party led by Shvetsov was sent out to the Chastye Islets [Bay of Islands]. After ten days there, they gathered 150 pelts. According to Shvetsov's report, the Aleuts came down with diarrhea due to the water they got from melted snow. As a result the 52 Kad'iak baidarkas and 10 from the Fox Islands could not take part in the hunt. Only two men died, however.

In May of that year another party was sent out into the straits. The *Juno*, under the command of Benzeman, and another, under the American Winship, escorted the party with the intention of trading with the Kolosh. The commander of the expedition was Mr. Kuskov. After reaching Dundas Island, near the Queen Charlotte Islands, they began their hunt under constant danger of Kolosh attack. At the time there were American ships trading there. A certain Mr. Hill expressed his dissatisfaction and threatened Mr. Kuskov that, should the occasion arise, he would unite with the Kolosh and use every possible means to hinder [our hunt]. And eventually a large number of armed men with canoes surrounded both of our ships, while Hill tacked his vessel at a distance ready to help the Kolosh. To avoid any conflict with them, Mr. Kuskov decided to sail from there, because eight Aleuts had already perished in various incidents. Even on his return trip he encountered armed Kolosh ready to attack our party at the least carelessness. On 2 August Kuskov returned with both ships and 1,400 pelts. After his return no more parties were sent into the straits. Meanwhile, a new area for hunting sea otters opened along the coast of California.

In 1815 the ship *Otkrytie* was dispatched to trade in the straits under the command of Mr. Podushkin. Prikazchik Toropogritskii traded 340 large sea otters, 107 yearlings and 39 pups. They sailed for 46 days. The party hunted down 276 sea otters and 73 yearlings.

In 1816 the hunting parties gathered 63 beaver pelts. Between 1815 and 1818 we purchased from the Kolosh in the surrounding Sitkha area 108 sea otter pelts, 37 yearlings and 18 pups.

B. SEA OTTERS PROCUREMENT IN CALIFORNIA IN COLLABORATION WITH FOREIGNERS

After arriving on board the vessel *Eclipse* in Kad'iak in 1803, the American O'Cain sold Mr. Baranov part of his goods and told him that he had discovered a new island off the California coast which abounded in sea otters. He was the first to suggest that Mr. Baranov give him several baidarkas for the purpose of hunting sea otters and then divide the catch. Mr. Baranov immediately agreed to it and concluded an agreement with him. As security O'Cain left goods worth 12,000 rubles with Mr. Baranov. Shvetsov and Tarakanov were assigned to the expedition along with 20 baidarkas. They left Kad'iak on 26 October 1803, stopping in San Diego on the way to San Quentin where they gathered 1,100 pelts. O'Cain bought up to 700 pelts from the Spanish missionaries and officials in various places, for which he paid no more than three piasters apiece. Shvetsov found out from one of the American sailors that O'Cain had never really discovered any island, but since he had been here in 1801 he had seen a great number of sea otters. Since he had no means of taking them, he decided to entice Mr. Baranov in this manner. In June 1804 O'Cain safely returned to Kad'iak. Because of this first successful venture, Mr. Baranov turned his attention to California.

In 1804 and 1805 the occupation of Sitkha and the arrival of Mr. Rezanov put an end to these ties. But in May 1806 an agreement was concluded with Winship which would give him 70 baidarkas under the leadership of Slobodchikov. He was to sail to the mouth of the Columbia River. From there he was to begin the hunt and proceed to Cape Barro de Arena.[6] In California Winship and Slobodchikov quarreled. While on the island of Seros, Slobodchikov bought the schooner *Nikolai* in exchange for 100 sea otter pelts and 50 yearlings. He persuaded an American to sail the schooner to the Sandwich Islands, and from there returned to Sitkha on 22 August 1807. Winship returned with his party 8 September. The catch consisted of 3,006 otter pelts, 1,264 yearlings and 549 pups, all of which were divided in Sitkha.

After Winship's departure Mr. Baranov went to Kad'iak and there he met an American named Campbell, and on 25 October 1806 they concluded an agreement that he would take twelve baidarkas under Tarakanov's leadership and sail along the coast of California. He would begin hunting at Trinidad Bay, but was to avoid the Spanish settlements. On 3 August Campbell returned safely to Novo-Arkhangel'sk with a catch of 753 otter pelts, 228 yearlings and 250 pups.

In May 1808, Mr. Ayres, commander of the *Mercury*, agreed to take 25 baidarkas under Mr. Shvetsov's leadership. On 26 June they left Kad'iak, sailed to the [Queen] Charlotte Islands and the Columbia River to trade. They began hunting at Trinidad, then they went to Bodega and San Francisco bays. Mr. Ayres returned to Sitkha and gave the company its share, which consisted of 844 pelts, 128 yearlings and 68 pups. Shvetsov had also bought 37 pelts of various sea mammals and 190 river otter pelts in various places.

Various other hunting contracts were concluded: in December 1809 with Jonathan Winship, captain of the *O'Cain*; in October 1810 with Nathan Winship, captain of the *Albatross*; in November 1811 with Thomas and William Blanchard of the *Amethyst* and *Katherine*; with William Davis, captain of the *Isabella*; in 1813 with Whittemore, captain of the *Charon*. They all took baidarkas and all successfully fulfilled their agreements. The table below shows the extraordinary profits made with the cooperation of Americans.

The Company's Share

	Ship	Sea otter and mature females	Yearlings	Pups	Total
Jonathan Winship	*O'Cain*	2,251	267	208	2,726
Nathan Winship	*Albatross*	389	70	101	560
William Davis	*Isabella*	989	216	283	2,488*
Thomas Meek	*Amethyst*	655	49	17	721
William Blanchard	*Katherine*	626	93	39	758
Whittemore	*Charon*	798	68	30	896
		5,708	763	678	7,149

*[Sic; should be 1,488.]

C. SEA OTTER PROCUREMENT IN CALIFORNIA BY OUR OWN DETACHMENTS

Knowing nothing about California, Mr. Baranov depended on men who had taken part in expeditions there. From them he learned about the climate and natural resources of that region. He waited for the right moment for his own hunting parties to hunt sea otters along the California coast. After returning to Kad'iak in August 1808, Mr. Baranov sent out the schooner *Nikolai* under the command of Bulygin to trade and hunt sea otters; part of the hunting party was assigned to prikazchik Tarakanov. They were supposed to go to the Columbia River, then up to Grays Harbor and meet up with the ship *Kad'iak*. The unfortunate wreck of the *Nikolai* and the immediate imprisonment of the crew were described by Mr. Tarakanov and published in the *History of Shipwrecks*. The *Kad'iak* was sent out on 20 October under the command of navigator Petrov who was accompanied by Mr. Kuskov, the active associate of Mr. Baranov. They were sent out to personally become acquainted with these yet unknown areas. Due to strong head winds, they were unable to reach Grays Harbor and instead went to Trinidad and from there sailed on to Bodega Bay on 15 December. There they began hunting and took 1,453 otter pelts, 406 yearlings and 491 pups. Five Russians and Americans [Aleuts] jumped ship in Bodega Bay. The *Kad'iak* then left California for Sitkha, but because of strong head winds they sailed for 49 days.

On 22 January 1811 Mr. Kuskov again set off for California on the schooner *Chirikov* under the command of Mr. Benzeman. They reached Bodega Bay on 21 February. Because of the poor hunt, they sent 22 baidarkas into San Francisco Bay where they found Mr. Tarakanov and his party of 48 baidarkas, which had been left there by Mr. Davis of the *Isabella*, and another party of 60 baidarkas sent by Mr. Winship. In three months' time Mr. Kuskov's party had gathered 1,160 otter pelts and 78 yearlings. At first the Spanish did not object to the hunt, but later they decided to prevent them from taking on fresh water supply by placing guards near the sources. They had orders to capture any Aleuts. Therefore, the hunting party was forced to leave. The brig left Bodega Bay on 20 July and sailed for the Farallon Islands to stock up on sea lions. They arrived in Sitkha on 28 July.

In November of that same year [1811] Mr. Baranov again sent Kuskov out on the schooner *Chirikov* along with 40 baidarkas and Aleuts with the intention of founding a settlement on the shores of New Albion, which abounded with sea otters and fruit-bearing trees. The Ross settlement was established in June 1812 by this hunting party and the crew of the *Chirikov*. Meanwhile, hunting parties were sent out when the weather was favorable. From March 1812 to 1815 they took 714 otter pelts, 143 yearlings; in 1815, 114 otter pelts, 39 yearlings; in 1816, 84 otter pelts and 13 yearlings; in 1817, 44 otter pelts, 11 yearlings. Based on the above-given figures, it is obvious that the number of pelts decreased. The reason for such a decrease was as much the fault of the Spanish, who prevented the Russians from hunting, as well as, if not more so, the fault of the Aleuts, who caused the sea otters to disperse.

In 1815 Mr. Baranov sent out the brig *Il'mena* with a party of Aleuts under the command of Tarakanov with trading goods with prikazchik Nikiforov. The captain of the vessel was an American named Vozdwit [Wadsworth?], but the chief agent was an American, a certain Dr. Eliot. The hunting party brought back to Sitkha 322 otter pelts, 50 yearlings, and 20 pups. Eliot received 10,000 piasters. He continued to pursue his smuggling activities along the shores and was eventually caught by the Spanish who also took a few Russians and many Aleuts. Due to a major leak, the *Il'mena* was unable to sail directly to Sitkha. Instead, it sailed for the Sandwich Islands. It reached those shores on 2 May 1816. The ship came under the jurisdiction of Dr. Schaeffer, whom Mr. Baranov had put in charge there.

D. IMPORT OF WHEAT FROM CALIFORNIA

After an attempt at establishing trade with California, which had been carried out by the order of Mr. Actual Chancellor N. P. Rezanov in 1806, no other opportunity arose to renew this aim. But through Americans who had hunted along the shores with parties [of Aleuts], the Russians received wheat, barley, beans, bacon, salt and salted beef. Mr. Kuskov, who had settled on the shores of [New] Albion, became acquainted with the missionaries and several Spanish officials. He visited the port of San Francisco and traded for wheat:

in 1813 — 2,886 puds
in 1815 — 1,695 puds

Through the commissioner Eliot, Fort Ross obtained 4,838 [puds], from which Kuskov sent a certain quantity to Sitkha:

in 1814 on a Boston vessel	419
in 1815 on the *Chirikov*	1,510
in 1815 on the *Chirikov*	4,369½
in 1816 on the *Il'mena*	1,723¼
Total	8,022½*

*Error in original; should be 8,021¾

Governor de Sola, who arrived in California in 1816, was indignant because the former [Spanish government in California] had allowed the Ross settlement to be established there. As a result, he terminated all relations and trade [with Ross]. He also ordered [his troops] to keep an eye on the hunting [by Russians] along the California coast.

E. SHIPBUILDING IN SITKHA

N. P. Rezanov arrived in Sitkha in 1805. Noticing the lack of sailing ships which were necessary for an expedition planned to Japan, he ordered the building of a tender. Two shipwrights began building it in September, and in June 1806 it was launched and named the *Avos'*. The tender was put under the command of Mr. Davydov, who sailed it to Japan and wintered in Kamchatka. It was later wrecked near Cross Sound by Mr. Karpinskii.

Mr. Baranov could not cope with the shipwrights and was forced to send them both back to Russia. Since he lacked vessels, he bought some from the Americans, but he thought it would also be more advantageous to build some himself. As a result, he concluded an agreement in 1806 with the American Lincoln, who completed the building of the brig *Sitkha* the following year and was paid 2,000 rubles for his labor. The old vessel *Aleksandr* was re-timbered; in June 1807 the keel for the *Otkrytie* was laid, and the vessel was launched on 16 July 1808. Lincoln received 2,500 rubles for building it. That same year he built the *Chirikov*, and repairs were made on the *Juno* for 2,500 rubles. After Lincoln's departure from the company's service in 1809, no more ships were built. The promyshlennik Mukhin repaired the old ships without much success. The ships built by Mr. Lincoln deserved mention. The *Sitkha*, a fine vessel, was wrecked on the shores of Kamchatka, while the *Chirikov* was used until 1825. From 1820 the *Otkrytie* was used for five years as a storage place for wheat.

Meanwhile, the promyshlennik Grudinin, who was stationed at Fort Ross and had helped Lincoln, volunteered to build a ship. He selected oak timber unfamiliar to him, and in 1816 he laid the keel of the vessel *Rumiantsev.*

F. TRADE WITH FOREIGNERS IN SITKHA

Above, we mentioned the trade which was carried on by the Americans and English in Kad'iak. After the occupation of Sitkha [by the Russians in 1804] foreign ships frequently sailed here after May 1805. Due to a shortage of goods and foodstuffs, Mr.

[Table 1. Monetary Value of Trade with Foreigners and Quantity of Furs Transferred to Them, 1805-1817.]

Names of Captains and Ships and Total Cargos Purchased	[r.]	[k.]	Number of Fur Bearing Animals Bartered and Their Prices		[r.]	[k.]
1805. May Captain D'Wolf and the ship *Juno* goods worth	12,320		112 84	sea otters and mature females at yearlings at	80 40	
1805. August Captain Treskott [with vessel *Mary*] goods worth	9,040	50	113	sea otters at	80	
1805. September Captain D'Wolf ship *Juno* with entire cargo worth	136,000		300 472 101	piasters at sea otters at yearlings at Bills of exchange on St. Petersburg, 54,637½ piasters at	2 100 50 2	
1806. May Captain Winship with ship *O'Cain* goods worth	9,767	60		Credit	9,697	25
1806. June Captain Brown (ship *Vancouver*) goods worth	3,529	60	1,520 6	fur seals at sea otters at	2 80	
1806. July Captain Campbell (vessel *Peacock*) goods worth	345		5	sea otters at	63	
1806. September and October Captain O'Cain (vessel *Eclipse*) goods worth	8,689	80		[. . .]	[. . .]	

[Table 1.] — continued

Names of Captains and Ships and Total Cargos Purchased		[r.]	[k.]	Number of Fur Bearing Animals Bartered and Their Prices		[r.]	[k.]
1807. February Captain Barber [vessel *Myrtle*]							
	furs worth	20,557	80				
	various foreign goods at	38,729	30	40,050	Piasters transferred to Main Office at	2	
	artillery shells at	4,388	77				
	vessel with tackle and sails at	20,324	13	950	Piasters at	2	
		84,000					
1807. August From Captain Campbell	goods worth	7,921	28	2,296	fur seals at	3	
1807. October Captain Jonathan Winship per account 1806 in:				1,315	river beavers at	3	
				170	Aliaska red fox at	5	
				65	Kad'iak fox at	3	
				9	sea otters at	80	
				1	sea otter at	75	
	Credit	9,697	25	20	tails at	4	50
	Plus goods	4,048	83	1,391	fur seals at	2	
	[Total]	13,746	08				
Captain Swift (ship *Derby*):					*1807*		
1807:	goods worth	18,036		258	sea otters, various, at	18,036	11
					1808		
1808:	goods worth	34,516		2,485	river beavers, 1st sort, at	6	
				1,200	river beavers, 2nd sort, at	5	
				732	river beavers, 4th sort, at	4	
				100	river beavers, 2nd sort, at	2	
				47	unborn fetuses at	7	

[Table 1.] — continued

Names of Captains and Ships and Total Cargos Purchased		[r.]	[k.]	Number of Fur Bearing Animals Bartered and Their Prices		[r.]	[k.]
Captain Swift — *continued*				1,407	beaver tails at	6	
				377	female sea otter tails at	5	
				1	sea otter	80	
						34,516*	
Captain Ayres, ship *Mercury*:					*1807*		
1807:	Goods worth	4,709	80		Payment made from general fur catch		
1809:	Goods worth	1,209	67		*1809*		
1810:	Goods worth	[. . .]		190	rivers beavers at	1,140	
1811:	Goods worth	25,400	17		*1811*		
				5,000	fur seals at	2	
1812:	Goods worth	12,425	36	3,000	fur seals at	1	50
					5 puds, 18 funts bone	18	
Captain Winship, ship *O'Cain*					*1813*		
1809:	Goods worth	40,427		3,000	fur seals	1	50
				72	sables	2	
1811:	Goods worth	10,889	34	1,619	river beavers at	6	
	346 barrels of tar			823	otters at	7	
	14 fur seals			908	sea otter tails at	3	60
				7,470	fur seals at	1	20
				4,844	fur seals for tar at		
Captain Blanchard, ship *Katherine*				3,000	fur seals at	2	
1811:	Goods worth	22,050	45	7,458	fur seals at	1	50
				136	beaver tails at	3	60
Captain Whittemore, ship *Charon*							
1812:	Goods worth	22,617		12,565	fur seals at	1	80

[Table 1.] — continued

Names of Captains and Ships and Total Cargos Purchased		[r.]	[k.]	Number of Fur Bearing Animals Bartered and Their Prices		[r.]	[k.]
Captain Whittemore, ship *Charon* (cont.)					Calculated per sea otter hunting in payment of Aleuts		
1813:	Goods worth	6,065					
Captain Suter				3,160	fur seals at	3	
1813:	Goods worth	27,753	30		*Transferred to [St. Paul] Island*		
				2,175	bachelors at	2	80
				6,768½	small at	1	80
					Transferred to receive on St. Paul Island		
Captain Bennett							
1813:	Goods worth	55,512	40	28,000	fur seals at	2	
	brig *Ledi* [*Lydia*] with armament	20,000		13,000	fur seals at	1	50
	brig *Atahualpa* with armament	20,000		10,000	fur seals at	2	
					Transferred to St. Paul [Island]		
Hunt, agent of Astor, with vessel *Beaver*				20,000	bachelor fur seals at	2	
1812:	Goods worth	124,056	74	53,045	small fur seals	1	50
					Transferred to St. Paul [Island]		
Captain Clark				3,996	fur seals at	2	80
1813:	Goods worth	22,377	62	6,216	small fur seals at	1	80
Captain Ebbets, ship *Enterprise*					*1810*		
1810:	Goods worth	53,731		3,722	sea otters and yearlings worth	36,988	
				10,852	fur seals worth	16,873	50
					1811		
1811:	Goods worth	94,843	12	1,477	river beavers at	6	
				41	otters	2	
				16,646	bachelor fur seals	2	
				34,764	small fur seals at	1	50

[Table 1.] — continued

Names of Captains and Ships and Total Cargos Purchased				Number of Fur Bearing Animals Bartered and Their Prices			
		[r.]	[k.]			[r.]	[k.]
Captain Davis, ship *Isabella*					*1810*		
1810:	Goods worth	24,750	10	2,363	fur seals at	2	
				10,440	small fur seals at	1	50
1811:	Goods worth	19,693	08		*1811*		
				529	river beavers at	6	
				297	beaver tails	3	60
				70	sables	2	
				7,470	fur seals at	1	20
					1813		
				535	fur seals at	2	
1813:	Goods worth	2,432		713	small fur seals	1	50
Captain Thomas Meek, ship *Amethyst*					*1812*		
	goods worth	25,477	32	2,000	bachelor fur seals at	3	
	Amethyst	10,000		2,219	fur seals, medium, at	2	
				5,128	fur seals, small, at	1	50
				700	beaver tails	3	60
1815. Vessel *Brutus*	Goods worth	43,287	84	5,749	fur seals at	1	50
					Payment for this sum soon after Mr. Baranov's replacement		
Captain Gyzelaar from schooner *Ledi* [*Lydia*], goods belonging to Wilcox and Liugsten [Ljungstedt]. 1817:	Goods worth	33,204			Payment made after replacement of Mr. Baranov		
Captain Pigot, *Peddler*							
1814:	Goods worth	75,981	81	15,000	fur seals, medium, at	1	75
	Transferred at	24,000		50,768	fur seals, small, at	1	50

*[Sic.]

Rezanov purchased the vessel *Juno* from Mr. D'Wolf with its entire cargo.

In order to have a clearer picture of the amount of money spent on goods and the number of pelts given to foreigners in exchange for goods, I propose [Table 1, pp. 14-18].

Based on the figures given above, 1,170,000 rubles in trade took place with the Americans, which included the purchase of five vessels: the *Juno*, *Myrtle* (renamed *Kad'iak*), *Lady* (*Il'mena*), *Atahualpa* (renamed *Bering*) and *Amethyst*.

The Americans were paid in otter pelts:

various sea otters:	4,884 pelts	fur seals:	362,730 pelts
sea otter tails:	3,845 pelts	otters:	864 pelts
river beavers:	9,694 pelts	foxes:	235 pelts

[The sum of] 94,587½ piasters was transferred to the Main Office.

Mr. Baranov calculated the piaster at the exchange rate of two rubles, but when the rate fell in Russia, the company took great losses on the exchange.

Out of these accounts, the fur goods went for:

sea otters — from 40 to 50 piasters, that is, 80 to 100 r.
yearlings — from 20 to 25 piasters, or 40 and 50 r.
fur seals as the main goods — from ¾ to 1½ piasters, or 1 r. 50 k. to 3 r.

[Table 2.] When and at What Prices Principal Goods Were Purchased from Foreigners, [1805-1811]. *

[Name of Goods and Supplies]	[Measure]	1805 from Treskott and D'Wolf		1806 from Winship		1808 from Ayres		1810 from Davis		1811 from Ebbets and Vitirs	
		In piasters and cents									
		p.	c.	p.	c.	p.	c.	p.	c.	p.	c.
Barley flour	barrel	10						16			
Corned beef	barrel	25				13		10			
Rum and brandy	gallon	3	50	4		3 & 3	50	3 & 4		1	50
Molasses	gallon	1	50	1	75	1	25	1		1	

[Table 2.] — continued

[Name of Goods and Supplies]	[Measure]	1805 from Treskott and D'Wolf		1806 from Winship		1808 from Ayres		1810 from Davis		1811 from Ebbets and Vitirs	
		In piasters and cents									
		p.	c.	p.	c.	p.	c.	p.	c.	p.	c.
Virginia tobacco	per 100 [funts?]	25		25		50		15		9	
Tar	barrel	10									
Soap	per 100 [piculs?]	25		25				20			
Rifles w/ bayonets	[. . .]	6									
Frieze	150-[. . .] yards	2	14			4		20		2	
Plates	dozen			3							
Pompenoi coffee	funt				75						
White wine	gallon			3				2			
Vinegar	gallon				75	1					30
Tar and pik	barrel			11	25					9	
Wheat	barrel					7	50	7		2 puds†	
Blue nankeen	100 funts					1	50				
Large blanket	piece					3	50			2	
Salt	100 funts							4			
Sugar candy	picul							16	80	5 puds†	
English flour	100 funts							8	72		
Granulated sugar	100 funts									15	

*For continuation of the table of prices for 1818-1830, see Chapter 6, below. †Thus in the original.

G. TRADING IN CANTON THROUGH AMERICANS

Captain O'Cain of the ship *Eclipse*, who had already done business with Mr. Baranov in Kad'iak in 1803 and had first suggested the mutual hunting of sea otters along the California coast, arrived in Novo-Arkhangel'sk in August 1806. He suggested that the company attempt trading in Nagasaki, Canton and other ports in East India [sic]. Mr. Baranov sent a considerable number of otter pelts with him, along with Mr. Bykadorov and Toropogritskii as his agents. O'Cain exchanged the pelts in Canton with very little profit. On the return trip he stopped in Kamchatka where he gave the agent Miasnikov 200,000 rubles' worth of cotton and other goods. He sailed on to Kad'iak with the remaining goods, wrecked his vessel near Sannakh Island, and he lost most of the cargo.

I have appended [Table 1, pp. 22-23].

When Mr. Baranov received information concerning this trade transaction, he realized that his agents could not have done anything and that O'Cain had cheated him. But when O'Cain died in a shipwreck at the same island, the matter was closed.

Mr. Ebbets, an agent of the rich and powerful merchant Mr. Astor, was a man whom Mr. Baranov had known for some time and trusted in trading matters. Mr. Ebbets arrived in Sitkha in July 1810 where he concluded an agreement to trade company fur goods in Canton. In exchange for his services Mr. Ebbets was to receive five percent of the transaction as his share. Mr. Baranov was obliged to pay 18,000 piasters for the freight on goods to Canton and on goods coming from Canton. [Table 2, p. 24] lists the goods sent by Mr. Baranov and the prices they sold for in Canton. The main goods traded by Mr. Ebbets in Canton were as follows:

123 piculs 55 catties of sugar candy — at 10 taels[7] 7 mes per picul
24 piculs 65 catties of sugar candy — at 11 taels 7 mes per picul
273 piculs 95 catties of sugar candy — at 7 taels 9 mes per picul
1,000 piculs of wheat — at 3 taels 4 mes per picul

Total: 8,637 taels, 7 mes

[In conversion to piasters], counting a piaster as 72 kondorins — 11,996.80 piasters

4,000 pieces of nankeen — at 90 centimes
2,000 pieces of blue nankeen — at 1 piaster 20 cents
800 pieces of flesh-colored nankeen — at 90 cents
300 pieces of black nankeen — at 2 piasters 75 cents
200 pieces of fustian — at 2 piasters 75 cents
600 pieces of cotton from 3½ to [. . .] — at 6 piasters 50 cents
10 piculs of velvet — at 28 piasters
250 pieces of demi-cotton — at 1 piaster 50 cents
10 piculs of thread — at 100 piasters
6,520 English pounds 48 piculs 90 catties of Hyson tea at 45 taels per picul;

13,515 English pounds 101 piculs 36 catties of pekoe tea at 54½ taels per picul;
13,400 English pounds 100 piculs 50 catties of Sushon tea at 35 taels per picul;
5,085 English pounds, 38 piculs, 14 catties of gunpowder tea at 62 taels per picul

Total: 13,606.8 taels

Counting in piasters at 72 kondorins — 18,896.33 piasters

100 boxes of tea services — at 2 piasters 40 cents
22 boxes of table plates — at 23 piasters
2 boxes of plates — at 50 piasters
55 pieces of seersucker — at 4 piasters
595 silk waistcoats for 840 piasters
500 pieces of silk material — at 9.20 piasters

Table 1. Goods Issued in Sitkha to Mr. O'Cain and Exchange of Same in Canton, 1806.

Sent from the Colonies			
		Each [r.]	Total [r.]
1,180	sea otters	60	70,800
615	yearlings	[. . .]	7,680
22	pups	4	88
105	new-born fur seals	8	840
592	otter tails	6	3,552
109	yearlings	2	218
104,813	fur seals	2	209,626
2,472	river beavers	6	14,832
189*	otters	8	1,496
56	sables	1½	84
50	red foxes	6	300
	26 puds 37 funts walrus tusks	15	403.87
	21 puds 15 funts baleen	8	211
		Total	309,290.87*

Sold in Canton					
		[r.	k.]	[r.	k.]
1,915	sea otters of all sorts	27		51,705	
690*	sea otter tails	3	60	2,512	80
104,241	fur seals		80	83,392	80
229	fur seals	[. . .]		160	

Table 1. — continued

Sold in Canton					
		r.	k.	r.	k.
2,474	river beavers	6		14,844	
186*	otters	8		14,888	
56	sables	[. . .]		90	
50	red foxes	3	20	160	
5*	piculs tusks	50		275	
	7 piculs 20 catties baleen	20		144	
		Total		54,777	57†

NB. Sale is counted in piasters, at 2 r., that is, the sea otters sold for 13½ piasters, etc. *[Sic.] †Error in original.

		Unit Cost [piasters/cents]	
500	pieces of silk material	6	85
200	pieces of silk material	5	
147	pieces of satin	20	25
50	packets of handkerchiefs	9	75
70	pieces of satin	from 18 to 19	
150	pieces of satin	16	50
30	pieces of taffeta	12	75
28	catties of silk	6	50
5	pieces of camelot	26	
	Total for all goods:	64,388	34

Mr. Baranov received these goods along with accurate accounts and documents from Mr. Ebbets. Mr. Baranov remained satisfied with Mr. Ebbets' trade transactions. As mentioned above, Mr. Baranov continued to figure the piaster at the exchange rate of two rubles throughout his administration. Based on that rate, he marked up his prices by 60 percent and imposed a tax on the sale of these goods in the colonies.

[Table 2. Goods Supplied to Mr. Ebbets at Sitkha and Their Sale in Canton, 1810]

Sent from the Colonies						Applied in Canton					
				[Sum in:]						Total	
		r.	k.	r.	k.			[p.	c.]	[p.	c.]
2,391	beavers and mature females	50		119,550		2,503	sea otters and yearlings	21	50	53,814	50
112	yearlings	20		2,240		518	pups	4		2,072	
165	pups	6*		495		3,555	tails	2	15	7,643	25
356	pups	3		1,068		822	land otters	4		3,288	
67	unborn	1		67		23*	river beavers	6	50	182	
3,055	sea otter tails	3		9,165		3	small sea otters	2		6	
13	yearling tails	1		13		30	foxes }				
326	large otters	8		2,608		30	cross foxes }				
285	medium otters	6		1,710		10	silver foxes }	1	50	255	
183	small otters	3		459*		100	red foxes }				
21	small otters	1	50	31	50	6,405	fur seals	1		6,405	
31	various river beavers	[. . .]		167		200	fur seal rejects			100	
30	white foxes	[. . .]		30		11	sable cloaks			132	
122	sables	[. . .]		89	60	75	mink mantles		25	18	75
61	mink	[. . .]		30	50		101 puds, 36 funts			63	
100	Kad'iak foxes	[. . .]		200			whiskers			42	
30	Unalashka foxes	[. . .]		150			17 puds, 33 funts				
10	silver foxes	15		150			tusks				
6,220	fur seals	[. . .]		6,220							
	17 puds, 33 funts tusks	10		178	25						
	101 puds, 36 funts whiskers	5		509	50						
				145,611	35†					74,021	50
										or 148,043 rubles	

*[Sic.] †Error in original: should be 145,131 r. 35 k.

[Table 3. Prices Set by A. A. Baranov on Foreign Goods Sold in the Russian Colonies in America (after 1810).]

Name of Goods	Measure	Length	Width	Price in Sitkha		Price in Districts	
		arshins	vershoks	[r.]	[k.]	[r.]	[k.]
Sugar candy	pud			16		18	20
Wheat	pud			5	50	6	
Fine white nankeen	piece	8 14/16	9	3		3	50
[Dull] cherry nankeen	piece	14	7½	4		4	20
Black nankeen	piece	13 5/16	12½	8	80	9	
Half cotton	piece	14¼	8	5		5	50
White fustian	piece	14¼	8½	6	50	7	
Bengal linen:							
1st sort	piece	47	10	21		25	
3rd sort	piece	47	10	18		22	
4th sort	piece	48½	8½	14		18	
Velvet	piece			89	60	18	
Thread	funt			3		4	20
Seersucker	piece			7		9	
Velvet waistcoat	piece			7		9	
Table services	piece			80		100	
Pearl (gunpowder) tea	[funt]			2	25	2	50
Green (Hyson) tea	[funt]			1	70	2	
Black flower (Pekoe) tea	[funt]			2		2	50
Sushon tea	[funt]			1	30	1	60
Taffeta	piece	22½		29	30	35	
Smooth foulard	piece	20½	11½	22		28	
Semi-dimity	piece	16¾		17		20	
Colored dimity	piece	23 6/16		65		70	
Black dimity	piece	23	16	62		68	
Blue dimity	piece	16		65		70	
Trimming	piece	37	1	60		65	
Silk [second-rate]	piece	23½	1	42		50	
Serge kerchief	[piece]			1	75	2	
Silk	catty	1 38/96 Russian		16		18	

III
MR. BARANOV'S REPLACEMENT AND THE STATE OF THE COLONIES AT THAT TIME

In November 1817 the ship *Kutuzov* sailed into Sitkha under the command of Captain-Lieutenant and Cavalier L. A. Hagemeister. The cargo brought by the *Kutuzov* was turned over to Mr. Baranov, but the advanced age of this honorable man had weakened his health and mental faculties. Since there was no competent man to help, Mr. Hagemeister was compelled to take over his duties in order to prevent any further mismanagement. He declared his intentions in the following instructions:

> *The Council which was established by Imperial decree on behalf of the Main Administration [Office] of the Russian-American Company, under the protection of His Imperial Majesty, has directed the following to the office in Novo-Arkhangel'sk:*
>
> Due to the advanced age of the chief manager of the American territories, the Collegiate Councillor and Cavalier, Mr. Baranov, the state of his health and his 25-year stay there, under constant work and anxiety, have given him the right to ask to be dismissed from his obligations. Two men were sent to replace him (Koch and Bornovolokov) but both of them died before reaching their destination. After that the company was unable to find a suitable third man. Now, it has found a qualified person in Captain-Lieutenant L. A. Hagemeister, commander of the *Kutuzov* and the *Suvorov*. After deliberating on the matter, the Russian-American Company asked Mr. Hagemeister to write to Mr. Baranov, so that the latter would relinquish his power, capital and business affairs. With this change of events, the Novo-Arkhangel'sk office, naval officers, and employees of the company will be informed of this change and all shall obey Mr. Hagemeister, the newly appointed manager of these regions. If anyone should disobey this order, he shall be subject to severe punishment according to the law.
>
> Dictated in St. Petersburg, 25 August 1816 and signed by: Gavril Sarychev, Ivan Veidemeier, Iakov Druzhinin, Mikhailo Buldakov, Venedikt Kramer, Andrei Severin, Legal Councillor Ivan Zelenskii.

A. GENERAL MAKEUP OF THE POPULATION, PARTICULARLY IN SITKHA, AND THE CONDITION OF RUSSIAN, CREOLE AND ALEUT EMPLOYEES

On 11 January 1818 Mr. Hagemeister summoned the captain of the ship *Suvorov*, Mr. Z. I. Ponafidin, and then both went to Mr. Baranov to present the instructions of the Council. Without belittling the important contributions which Mr. Baranov made to the fatherland and to the company, it must be mentioned that lately he had been dealing with matters in a rather superficial manner. And because he did not have any competent assistant to rely on, he eventually realized that all of his business affairs had become unprofitable.[8] In spite of his lack of successes in business because of his advanced age, he reassured himself that he was not neglecting his duties, a neglect which had already deeply become rooted. Mr. Hagemeister was compelled to replace him. After announcing this to Mr. Baranov, he appointed the agent on his ship, [K. T. Khlebnikov], as manager of the office. Mr. Hagemeister then forwarded the Council's directives to all officials and employees of the company informing them of Mr. Baranov's replacement. The following day they began assessing the capital belonging to the company. As they did so, they collected information concerning the various ethnic groups which, according to census reports between 1815 and 1817, consisted of the following:

Table 1. Population According to Censuses of 1815 and 1817

	Males	Females
On Kad'iak, islanders	1,483	1,769
Kad'iaks at Novo-Arkhangel'sk	142	35
Fox Islanders at Novo-Arkhangel'sk	42	26
On Aliaska [Alaska Peninsula]	402	467
On Kenai Bay	723	747
On Chugach Bay	172	188
At various places in Kad'iak district	345	425
On Unalashka and other Fox Islands	465	559
In Northern [Pribylov] Islands district	188	191
	3,960*	4,407

*[Sic.]

At Novo-Arkhangel'sk:

Russian males including children	190
Creole males including children	72

Aleut males including children	173	
	435	
Russian and Creole women including children	110	
Aleut women including children	75	
	185	
Total	620	[persons]

In addition to these, there were 24 Russians and Creoles, 37 Aleut males, and three Aleut females, a total of 64 persons, left on the Sandwich Islands from Dr. Shaeffer's expedition.

[2. Wages in the Russian Colonies in America.]

Except for the chief manager, 190 of the company employees hunted for one and a half shares, and 101 received salaries. The Aleuts were paid for their otter pelts at a rate set by the chief manager; this was determined at about one-tenth of the catch after taxes, and sometimes it was more. The Aleuts were given laftaks for their baidarkas and kamlei for the pelts.

Between 1,000 to 1,200 rubles were paid out at half shares in the last four years. The yearly average sum spent was the following:

To the chief manager for 13 shares[9] at 600 [r.] — 7,800 [r.]
To prikazchiks: 3 dry shares, half shares — 6
To promyshlenniks and other participants in half shares — 183
Creoles — 3
Aleuts — 1

[Total:] 193 at 300 [r.] — 57,900 [r.]

Beyond half-shares, three men's salaries:

On Salary:

Creoles and Aleuts			Creole Students		
45	men at 60 r.	2,700 r.			
19	men at 80 r.	1,520 r.			
5	men at 100 r.	500 r.	1	man at [180] r.	180 r.
9	men at 120 r.	1,080 r.	2	men at 400 r.	800 r.
8	men at 150 r.	1,200 r.	1	man at [450] r.	450 r.
	[Total:]	7,000 r.		[Total:]	1,450 r.*

Carpenter Burtsov	1,000 r.	Prikazchik Nosov	3,000 r.
Seafarer Benzeman	2,000 r.	The two Sukhanovs	4,000 r.
Seafarers Jones and Young at 1½ [thousand r.]	3,000 r.	Accountant	600 r.
		Priest [Aleksei Sokolov]	600 r.
Seafarer Domashnev	2,450 r.		
[Total:]	8,450 r.	[Total:]	8,200 r.
		Bonuses made per year	6,850 r.
Lt. Podushkin's salary	5,000 r.	[Total]:	120,000 r.†
600 piasters	3,000 r.		
	8,000 r.		

*[Sic.] †Error in original.

In addition to the workers listed above, 20 Aleuts were hired to perform various types of work. They received no wages, but they were given clothing and footwear suitable for the seasons on company account. These workers were known as kaiurs.

B. CAPITAL IN NOVO-ARKHANGEL'SK. SHIPS; PRINCIPAL GOODS AND THEIR PRICES

Capital[10] received from Mr. Baranov during 1818 consisted of the following:

Russian and foreign goods, materials, and supplies in warehouses, store, and other magazines	at	1,066,904 r.	43 k.
Sea furs and land animals	at	202,750 r.	70 k.
Economic things, i.e., laftaks, gut, and kamleis	at	21,784 r.	62 k.
Debts of officials, promyshlenniks, and Aleuts	at	338,903 r.	96 k.
Debts on Aleuts for 2,534 sea otter pelts	at	21,698 r.	96 k.
Sailing and row boats	at	125,363 r.	12 k.
	Total	1,777,404 r.	61 k.*

*Error in original; should be 1,777,404 r. 83 k. [sic].

At the beginning building properties were not counted as having a monetary value. Subsequently, so that the accounts could be put in some sort of order, the buildings were appraised.

At the time that Mr. Baranov was replaced the only building worth anything was the large warehouse. The rest of the buildings generally had to be replaced. The barracks had no stoves; and it was so dilapidated that it was on the verge of collapse. It was for this reason that there were no quarters for the employees. Several of the promyshlenniks had built five small houses outside the fort.

Sail boats and rowboats were included in the following list:

Otkrytie	45,550 r.	*Amethyst*, used for storehouse	3,000 r.
Il'mena	35,440 r.	And two row boats or barkazas	650 r.
Chirikov	28,030 r.	Total:	125,360 r.*
Konstantin	6,400 r.		
Zlatoust	4,300 r.		
Platov	2,000 r.		

*Error in original; should be 125,370 r.

At that time the brig *Finliandiia* was harbored here, but it belonged to the Atkha district and was not part of the company's capital, but it remained here for over two years due to the shortage of vessels.

Principal goods traded with foreigners were the following:

1,550	pieces blue Canton nankeen	200	puds powder
48	pieces black Canton nankeen	115	English sole leather
165	pieces telemby [a fabric — ed.]	19	boxes gin
360	black serge kerchiefs	540	buckets rum
1,664	Bengal cotton kerchiefs	40	puds Virginia tobacco
1,180	second grade kerchiefs	220	kegs tar and pik
1,467	arshins frieze	2,500	puds Sandwich [Is.] and California salt
712	arshins lesser type cloth at 8 r.		
822	arshins baize	568	puds molasses
556	arshins flannel	654	puds wheat
1,596	arshins bombazine	9	puds Boston hardtack
400	baize blankets	2,717	puds Boston flour
45	pieces Canton silk	596	puds California wheat
187	puds sugar candy	596	puds barley
323	puds hard sugar	43	puds coffee
6,060	funts various grade Canton tea	290	pieces Bengal and California calico
920	puds lead and cartridges		

The new chief manager [L. A. Hagemeister] noticed that because the piaster was falling in value, the prices of foreign goods were being set without proper consideration; therefore he ordered his office to set actual prices of goods as closely as possible based on the

List of Newly Set and Old [until 1818] Prices on Principle Goods

	Measure	New Prices		Former Prices	
		[r.]	[k.]	[r.]	[k.]
Boston flour	pud	10		8	
Tallow	pud	9			
Millet	pud	8		6	
Molasses	pud	10		8	
White sugar candy	pud	36		18	
Yellow sugar candy	pud	32		16	
White granulated sugar	pud	24		14	
Yellow granulated sugar	pud	20		12	
Flowered tea	funt	5		2	50
Sushon tea	funt	3		1	60
Coffee	funt	1			
Provence butter	bucket	2			
Vinegar	vedro	6		4	
Virginia tobacco	funt		50		40
English soap	funt		60		50
Bombazine	arshin	2			
Ordinary English cloth	arshin	8			
Flannel	arshin	1	25		
Frieze, 1st grade	arshin	6		5	
Frieze, 2nd grade	arshin	5		4	50
Frieze, 3rd grade	arshin	4			
Blue nankeen	piece	6		4	
Bengal calico	piece	24		18	
Silk scarves	piece	30		22	
Atlas [silk material]	piece	120		65	70
Taffeta	piece	50		29	
Black serge kerchiefs	piece	4		2	
Canton cloth kerchiefs	piece	1	50	1	20
English cloth kerchiefs	piece	2	50	2	
English sole leather	piece	18		12	
Baize blankets in 3½ marki	piece	12		10	
Baize blankets in 3 marki	piece	10		8	
English plates	dozen	7	20	6	
Rum and gin	bucket	40		16, after 40 [sic]	24
Large, black nankeen	[piece]	10		8	80

present value of the piaster, without taking into account expenditures, or including the usual commercial interest. All of this was done so as not to cause dissatisfaction among the employees, since they were not aware of the economic situation. The tax he proposed was approved and posted in the store [see *List*, above].

However, the prices set earlier were not constant and fluctuated depending on the prices paid for the goods. We must note the unjust setting of prices: for example, in Novo-Arkhangel'sk the price for hard sugar was set at 16 rubles a pud, but in other offices the price was set at 18 to 20 rubles a pud even though the price of purchase was taken into consideration. In general a 10 to 25 percent increase was imposed on goods for sale, in spite of the fact that all employees had the same rights everywhere.

According to a new regulation, it became impossible to lower the rate of the piaster, and subsequently there were constant increases on the prices of newly purchased goods and provisions. For example, 100 funts of millet went for 8 piasters; and considering 1 piaster to be equal to 5 rubles, the cost was 40 rubles or 14 rubles a pud. Considering the loss caused by rats, it could not be sold for less than 16 rubles a pud. But if the rate of the piaster suddenly rose to 6 rubles, the price would be three times as high. But this equalization was not as obvious due to the gradual transition of things.

However, the Main Office issued the following regulation No. 523, Paragraph 11:

> Ordinary cloth, work cloth, tick and treacle must be sold at the lowest possible prices. A 30 percent increase must be imposed on goods bought in St. Petersburg for expenses incurred. A 10 to 15 percent increase must be imposed on goods bought elsewhere to pay for transportation without making a profit. In general, it has been decided that the company should only make a profit from imported goods, various fragile objects and goods traded from foreigners. [Paragraph 10]: Married personnel with families should receive bread depending on the size of their families at a price which will not profit the company.

The store issued the workers goods according to authorization of the chief manager and were put on their accounts once a month or sometimes every three months. They received several funts of flour and other provisions.

But this reevaluation of prices was difficult for the people and those in charge. The workers could not always get their supplies when they needed them, while the authorities accumulated so many petty bills that they could never prepare a correct account. It was impossible for them to get their business account in order, not only while they were here, but also when changes in management took place in the stores.

IV
REORGANIZATION OF THE COLONIES BY MR. HAGEMEISTER

Mr. Hagemeister set into motion many of the Main Office's regulations which had not been previously in effect in all areas. He forwarded the regulations governing the duties of the chief manager and the various offices, according to a directive written in May 1811. These articles, which deal with the relations to the islanders (natives), were explained by the various offices. As we shall see from the following review of things, Mr. Hagemeister put into action almost all the suggestions made by the Main Office, which had been sent to him through the Novo-Arkhangel'sk office 23 June 1817, directive No. 523.

A. EMPLOYEES' AGREEMENT TO PAYMENT BY WAGES [INSTEAD OF IN SHARES]

On 20 February 1818 in No. 61, paragraph 14, Mr. Hagemeister ordered the office to announce to the promyshlenniks that instead of receiving half shares they would now be receiving 300 rubles in wages and one pud of flour per month. The office announced this suggestion, and all promyshlenniks in Sitkha expressed their opinion in the following statement:

> In fulfilling the proposal sent to this office by Your Excellency on 20 February with the suggestions of the Main Office, all of which has been explained to us, you are asking each one of us to be paid in wages instead of shares normally paid for pelts. We are also to receive foodstuffs from the company along with flour whenever possible if shipments from California ever become regular; we are also to receive 300 rubles in monies a year and one pud of flour a month free of charge. We accept this proposal with the following conditions:
>
> 1. The proposed wages of 300 rubles per person per year should be retroactive to the last sharing, in May 1815.

> Since the Main Office also suggests a ration of one pud of flour per month, we hope they will be humane in their dealings with us in our needs; after realizing that we owe the company considerable sums of money we hope the Main Office will deduct our debts from our wages, but based on the prices of goods when the debts were owed.
>
> 2. If there should be no regular shipment of flour and the suggested amount of flour is not issued, then we should receive payment for the flour.
>
> 3. In the future for as long as we work for the company, we ask that the prices of necessary goods (clothing and footwear) not be raised, especially on foodstuffs, above the established tax which is presently at the stores.
>
> 4. Those who excel in the service of the company should expect remunerations above the 300 rubles and rations per year, at the discretion of Your Excellency, at the expense of the company.
>
> 5. Should we get sick or injured while in the service of the company we would hope that no deduction would be made from our wages.
>
> 6. Finally, we humbly beg Your Excellency that you take into our account our needs and that you decrease prices on necessary goods and foodstuffs needed by our livelihood based on previous prices and that you fix a stable tax. The company, as we are aware, will not suffer any losses from this.

Subsequent to this agreement, Mr. Hagemeister ordered that the promyshlenniks be issued one pud of flour per month, subject to the management's approval.

A plan for substituting sharing with wages had been drawn up by N. P. Rezanov (already deceased). In a report to Mr. Baranov written on 9 September 1805, Mr. Rezanov clearly stated (in paragraph 4):

> Hunting is being carried out by the Americans, while those who enter the service of the company in order to hunt animals are being employed only to build and reinforce the settlement's defense, navigation and security. In a word, it is unfortunate to have to say that our forces in America consist of less than 400 men on shares. These men are being used to keep the natives under control; they help in construction and at the same time they defend the vast American shores even though they form a small force. For their work they receive

> half shares of the animals taken, while the masters get one whole share. Considering the extent of the colonies, the number of men at the present in service is extremely insufficient. This fact has stifled our successes, but it would be disadvantageous for the company and to them to increase the number of men based on the present situation; the profits of the hunt would become so diluted that both the company and the workers would be in dire straits. Moreover, the promyshlenniks are uncertain of their situations after a four-year period when the sharing occurs. And instead of the expected bonus they could very well lose their work. While expanding its activities the company should seek to make a profit in trade carried on by agents for the company and not by the promyshlenniks. The latter, it goes without saying, cannot continue to exist and work based on the present system much longer. I think that eventually the sharing system should gradually decrease and all benefits go to the company and its employees should be paid wages.

This reorganization enhanced the welfare of the people, and luckily it was carried out without much opposition. Naturally, the older promyshlenniks, who prior to 1803 had had the opportunity to receive shares (in pelts), had found this advantageous. But in the following three periods, when the animals were taxed, they received no more than 1,531 rubles in a four-year period. It is true that sometimes the number of furs was great and sometimes larger than at other times. But the number of people had also increased, and there were officials in the company who received a large salary from the general sum, which decreased as a result of this. However, the promyshlenniks and many others would rather feed on hopes of an uncertain future instead of being satisfied and counting on a definite and permanent situation. With the establishment of wages, each person knows what he is going to make.

The truth is incontestable. It is a fact that under the terms of previous companies and regulations the promyshlenniks were able to exist only on shares, on the basis of which they received animal skins in kind, selling them at free prices, thus obtaining some profit. When a set price was substituted, the profits disappeared completely. Those with common sense subsequently noticed that the present situation was more helpful and advantageous than the former arrangements.

B. REGULATIONS FOR ALEUTS ENGAGED IN SEA OTTER AND OTHER ANIMAL PROCUREMENT: CONDITION OF THE KAIURS

In order to carry out the orders of the Main Office (mentioned in No. 523, paragraphs 7 and 8), Mr. Hagemeister issued No. 14: Aleuts are to be issued, at company expense, lavtaks for their baidarkas, a gut kamlei and a bird skin parka per man; they are to be paid in goods which are to be taxed at one-fifth of the fixed price for the hunted furs, as agreed in a general contract with all the promyshlenniks.

The kaiurs were given enough to pay for their clothes and footwear.

C. USEFUL CHANGES INTRODUCED BY MR. HAGEMEISTER AND HIS SUCCESSOR [MR. IANOVSKII]

1. Because of the inadequate pay of the Creoles, Mr. Hagemeister ordered the office to issue them, in addition to their wages, a pair of seaman's outfits, two pairs of shoes, and one kamlei, all of which was worth nearly 35 rubles.

2. From this time [20 February 1818] paper tokens came into general use and the practice of using notes for goods issued from the store on credit was stopped; instead, even salaried employees received tokens from the cashiers office every month and used them to buy the items needed. In dispatch No. 177 Mr. Hagemeister ordered the following: any employee of the company owing money would have one-third of his pay withheld and be allowed to keep two-thirds to live on. The cashier of the store observed this regulation.

3. Several responsible promyshlenniks were now used as prikazchiks. They had formerly been on the sharing system, but this had been insufficient to earn a living; therefore 25 rubles per month was given to them in form of foodstuffs during the time they went out hunting.

4. In order to clarify the sources of the various pelts (from the various offices) article 63 stated that each pelt should be stamped with the letters PAK (Rossiiskaia Amerikanskaia Kompaniia) which signified that the pelt was of good quality. The symbols for the various offices were the following:[11]

Novo-Arkhangel'sk	+
Kad'iak	X
Unalashka	O
Ross office	∞

Types of goods are distinguished by the following letters:

Maritime		*Mainland Foxes*	
1st grade of sea otter	Н	1st grade of prime	М
2nd grade of sea otter	М	2nd grade of immature fox	К
3rd grade of sea otter	Л	3rd grade of summer	И
1st grade of mature females	К		
2nd grade of mature females	И		
3rd grade of mature females	Ж	*Island Foxes*	
1st grade of yearlings	Д		
2nd grade of yearlings	Г	1st grade	И
1st grade of pups	В	2nd grade immature fox	
2nd grade of pups	Б	3rd grade of summer	

River Beaver and Otter

1st grade of prime	М
2nd grade of yearlings	К
3rd grade of pups	
4th grade of small	

5. Under Mr. Hagemeister's management the various offices took on an orderly nature. The prikazchiks who ran the various stores and warehouses gave him their accounts three times a year; agents and prikazchiks also turned in their accounts upon returning from voyages. The office administrators in charge of cash turned in his accounts every month, and the offices turned in their information every four months to the chief manager.

6. On 23 October 1818 Mr. Hagemeister turned over his duties to Mr. Ianovskii and left for Russia on the *Kutuzov*. His successor made two useful decrees (No. 293 and 296): he ordered the ships' commanders who received no monies according to the agreement to issue sailors' foodstuffs during the duration of sea voyages:

To the Commander [per month]		*To the Crew [per month]*	
Flour	1 pud	Hardtack per day	1 funt
Corned beef	30 funts	Meat (sea lion or beef)	½ funt

To the Commander [per month]		*To the Crew [per month]*	
Butter	10 funts	Groats per month	6 64/96 funts
Tea	1 funt	Peas per month	8 funts
Sugar, brown	12 funts	Tallow per month	8 funts
Peas	10 funts	Rum per month	5 cups
Rum	1½ mugs		

Which at prices then in effect came to 36 r. 45 k. per month.

The fort at Novo-Arkhangel'sk from SSW. By Assistant Navigator 14th Class I. F. Vasil'ev, 1808.

V
THE NOVO-ARKHANGEL'SK LOCATION [LOCALITY]

A. CLIMATE AND NATURAL RESOURCES

Having mentioned Sitkha, I did not say anything about its climate and the natural resources of the area, which were and still are the reasons for settling this area. Therefore, it is necessary to examine these details.

Cape Edgecumbe on Baranof Island (Sitkha) lies at latitude 57°03′ N and longitude 135° W from Greenwich.[12] This cape is distinguished by a beautiful mountain, which the first Spanish navigators called Engaño and later Hyacinth. Captain Cook called this mountain Edgecumbe after a lieutenant who had served on his ship; Russian sailors called it St. Lazarus and Cape Trubitsin; the promyshlenniks added *Krasnaia sopka* to it.[13] Mt. Edgecumbe is an extinct volcano; our sailors who visited this region in 1798 under the command of Shields saw it smoking. Its height was barometrically measured by Mr. Gofman at 2,500 feet, but it can be seen at sea from a distance of 70 miles, according to this by the table: "For finding the distance of terrestrial objects at sea [by defining the height of terrestrial objects from sea level], the height must be 3,800 feet. Mt. Edgecumbe, however, seems of average height in comparison to other mountains along the entire coast; the rest are almost all higher. L'tuiskaia sopka (Mt. Fairweather) can be seen at a distance of 130 miles on a clear day. Most of the other mountains remain covered with snow all summer long, but Mt. Edgecumbe is free of snow for two to three months every other year.[14]

All the hills are covered with coniferous forests, but only the upper rocky elevations are covered permanently with snow. Sitkha is an island separated from the mainland by Khutsnovskii Strait (Chatham Street) and separated by shallower straits to the north. The entire island is almost two degrees, stretching from Cape Ommaney to Ledianoi Strait. There is probably not even a square mile of level space. The area is covered with mountain ridges. For the most part it consists of granite and various types of gneiss and mica shale. The small valleys, plains and mountain slopes are covered with wet tundra and moss. Old forests have been knocked down by winds and undermined by the flow of melted snow water. They are piled on one another and overgrown with moss; the trees have rotted because of this process and make the area impassable. This wilderness is a reason for the bad weather and fierce winds. According to many observations, it can be said truly that in general in a good year it rains two-thirds of the time and that it is moderately clear for one-third of the year. But there are times when only one-fifth of the year is clear.[15]

The incessant gloom, light drizzle and humidity in the air are common atmospheric phenomena. But here as elsewhere, there are no rules without exceptions. Good weather does occur. In general the winters are warm; sometimes it snows, but it melts quickly when it rains. The winter does not last long and is mild; sometimes the temperature reaches 10 or even 14 degrees Reaumur (1820). Sometimes, spring begins early, with raspberries blooming in February (1825) and berries ripening in May. It is a beautiful sight to see roses blooming on still leafless bushes. But sometimes in March the temperature might be 8 degrees in the morning and 4 in April. And in May (1826) there may be hardly any greenery showing. Sometimes, the snow remains on the ground from November to February (1824). The usual weather picture is to have clouds and rain the entire fall. Gusts of wind are sometimes so strong that they rip out the trees by their roots. Mr. Baranov noticed that light earthquakes occurred when strong east winds blew.[16] The main winds are from the east and southeast and are usually accompanied by rain and overcast skies; with winds from the south the weather is sometimes clear; with southwestern winds there are gusts of wind; in the winter it is accompanied with hail, rain and snow. Almost all mariners coming upon Edgecumbe with the intention of resting after a long voyage at sea encounter terrible squalls; sometimes they have to bear these squalls for ten days. With winds from the west, northwest and north, one can expect clear weather. In the winter one can often observe the Aurora Borealis, and on a moonlit and starry night one can take delight in this wonderful natural phenomenon in the darkest corner of the world.

[Table 1.] Extract from Journal on Atmospheric Conditions at Sitkha, 1828.

Mo	Condition of Atmosphere			Barometer [English]		Thermometer		Winds		
	Clear Days	Variable with Rain	Overcast with Constant Rain	Max [Inches]	Min [Inches]	Max	Min	Gen	Mod	Str
Jan	10	16	5	29.80	29.20	+5	-7	28	2	1
Feb	5	13	11	29.8 ¾	29.23	+6	-1	17	8	4
Mar	6	12	13	30.44	29.6	+8	-2	20	5	7
Apr	4	14	12	30.27	29.38	+13.5	-4	14	10	6
May	1	13	17	30.12	29.57	+12	-5.5	15	6	
Jun	5	17	8	30.20	29.45	+16	-7	6	24	
Jul	7	14	10	30.20	29.75	+18	-9	9	22	
Aug	10	13	8	30.17	29.34	+15	-5	8	23	
Sep	3	19	8	30.20	29.20	+12	-2	14	10	6
Oct	2	18	11	30.1	28.78	+10	-1	3	20	8
		rain and snow								
Nov	2	21	7	30.10	28.66	+6	-2	9	15	6
		rain and snow								
Dec	11	10	10	30.57	28.72	+6.5	-10	16	10	5
		rain and snow								
Total	66	180	120	30.57	28.66	+18	-10	158*	165*	43

NB. The first snow fell on 11 November, but soon melted; during December snow fell several times and with clear weather remained for ten days and then melted because of rain; the thermometer dropped below zero on 18 January, 2 February, 2 March, 2 October, 6 November, and 22 days in December — a total of 52 days. *[Sic.]

[Table 2.] Extract from Journal on Atmospheric Conditions at Sitkha, 1829.

Mo	Condition of Atmosphere			Barometer [English]		Thermometer		Winds		
	Clear Days	Variable with Rain	Overcast with Constant Rain	Max [Inches]	Min [Inches]	Max	Min	Gen	Mod	Str
Jan	4	17	10	30.25	29.10	+7	-6.5	11	10	10
		rain and snow								
Feb*	2	19	7	30.40	28.82	+8.5	-1	13	9	6
		rain and snow								

[Table 2.] — continued

Mo	Condition of Atmosphere			Barometer [English]		Thermometer		Winds		
	Clear Days	Variable with Rain	Overcast with Constant Rain	Max [Inches]	Min [Inches]	Max	Min	Gen	Mod	Str
Mar	4	14	13	30.33	29.22	+8	-1.5	12	10	9
		rain and snow								
Apr	1	11	18	30.30	29.33	+10	-1	8	18	4
May	8	14	9	30.16	29.10	+16	+4.5	8	17	6
Jun	10	19	1	30.36	29.28	+19.5	+4.5	7	17	6
Jul[*]	14	13	4	30.32	29.90	+20	+7	26	2	3
Aug	14	10	7	30.8	29.50	+17	+9	22	3	6
Sep	15	8	7	30.5	29.45	+15	+7	18	6	6
Oct[*]	7	11	13	30.35	29.5	+11	+4	16	7	8
Nov	4	14	12	30.9	29.30	+6	-3	16	8	6
Dec	—	10	13	30.39	29	+2	-11	25	2	4
Total	85[†]	168[‡]	114	30.40	28.82	+20	-11	182	109	74

The first snow fell on 6 November and remained several days. The thermometer fell to 0° on 9 October and was under 0° for the first time on 19 October: the thermometer showed 4° below zero. The thermometer fell below freezing in October, November, December [1829], 10 January, February and March [1830], in all [. . .] days; at the same time the barometer changed from [. . .] to [. . .].

[*]The number of days of each month is shown in accordance with the source. [†]Error in the original; should be 83. [‡][Sic.]

[Table 3.] Extract from Journal on Atmospheric Conditions at Sitkha, 1830.

Mo	Condition of Atmosphere			Barometer [English]		Thermometer		Winds		
	Clear Days	Variable with Rain	Overcast with Constant Rain	Max [Inches]	Min [Inches]	Max	Min	Gen	Mod	Str
Jan	6	8	17	30.42	29.00	+4.5	11.5	19	12	
		rain and snow								
Feb	16	9	3	30.33	28.80	+4	12	10	13	5
		rain and snow								
Mar	15	17	9	30.20	28.90	+5.5	-4	11	16	5
		rain and snow								
Apr	10	17	3	30.22	29.40	+15	0	25	3	2

[Table 3.] — continued

Mo	Condition of Atmosphere			Barometer [English]		Thermometer		Winds		
	Clear Days	Variable with Rain	Overcast with Constant Rain	Max [Inches]	Min [Inches]	Max	Min	Gen	Mod	Str
May	8	18	5	30.38	29.34	+13	+4	19	9	3
Jun	6	11	13	30.17	29.70	+14	+7	16	7	7
Jul	7	13	11	30.18	28.10	+16	+9	15	10	6
Aug	17	11	3	30.15	29.75	+17.5	+6	8	23	
Sep	6	9	15	29.94	29.10	+17	+1.5	8	16	6
Oct	1	13	17	30.10	28.50	+11	-1.5	7	16	8
		rain, snow and								
Nov	6	20	4	30.30	28.84	+5	-6.5	20	8	2
		rain and snow								
Dec	5	19	7	30.48	29.30	+5	11.5	24	4	3
Total	92*	165	108*	30.48	28.50	+17.5	11.5	182	137	46*

Strong winds were from southwest squalls with hail and snow; east and southeast with rain. At a great height of the barometer was clear weather and overcast — at the very least, from 28.50 [height of barometer]; rain, hail, and strong wind for more at change of winds from southeast to southwest. *[Sic.]

[Table 4.] Extract from Journal on Atmospheric Conditions at Sitkha, 1831.

Mo	Condition of Atmosphere			Barometer [English]		Thermometer		Winds		
	Clear Days	Variable with Rain	Overcast with Constant Rain	Max [Inches]	Min [Inches]	Max	Min	Gen	Mod	Str
Jan	3	21	7	30.32	29.4	+8	[illeg.]	21	5	5
		rain and snow								
Feb	3	14	16	30.26	28.64	+6.5	-1	20	6	2
		rain and snow								
Mar	3	19	9	30.47	28.90	+7.5	0	18	7	6†
		rain and snow								
Apr	2	17	11	30.46	28.98	+8.5	+.5	10	13	7†
		rain and snow								

[Table 4.] — continued

Mo	Condition of Atmosphere			Barometer [English]		Thermometer		Winds		
	Clear Days	Variable with Rain	Overcast with Constant Rain	Max [Inches]	Min [Inches]	Max	Min	Gen	Mod	Str
May	7	17	7	30.25	29.23	+14.5	+2.5	17	8	6
Jun	7	20	3	30.26	29.60	+16	+4	15	11	4
Jul	5	15	10	30.14	29.42	+15	+7.5	19	9	3
Aug	1	15	15	30.38	29.41	+14	+7.5	25	5	1
Sep	4	18	8	30.29	29.23	+13.5	+2.5	18	7	5
Oct*	1	19	16	30.43	29.13	+8.5	+2	9	15	7
		rain and snow								
Nov	3	18	9	30.43	29.11	+6	-4	13	7	10
		rain and snow								
Dec	—	14	17	30.24	28.80	+5	-1.5	9	12	10
		rain and snow								
Total	39	208‡	118‡	30.47	28.64	+16	-4	194	105	66

In the mountains the first snow fell on 26 September, and then followed by rain; then the mountains were covered with snow 31 October with the maximum of the barometer at 30.47. On 2 March the thermometer showed +2½°, gentle northwest wind, sky cloudy; with the very least fall [of the barometer] +4½°, wind east fresh, cloudy and small constant rain; 6 November at 29.30 on the barometer, 3½° on the thermometer, with gloomy condition of the atmosphere, wind southeast and south — squalls, with rain and lightening.

*Number of days in October correspond with the source. †Squalls. ‡[Sic.]

[Table 5.] Extract from Journal on Atmospheric Conditions at Sitkha, 1832.

Mo	Condition of Atmosphere			Barometer [English]		Thermometer		Winds		
	Clear Days	Variable with Rain	Overcast with Constant Rain	Max [Inches]	Min [Inches]	Max	Min	Gen	Mod	Str
Jan	11	11	9	30.40	28.40	+3	-9	14	10	7
		rain and snow								
Feb	12	10	7	30.49	29.20	+4.5	-6	6	20	3
		rain and snow								
Mar	5	11	15	30.41	29.16	+9	-4	14	10	7

[Table 5.] — continued

Mo	Condition of Atmosphere			Barometer [English]		Thermometer		Winds		
	Clear Days	Variable with Rain	Overcast with Constant Rain	Max [Inches]	Min [Inches]	Max	Min	Gen	Mod	Str
		rain and snow								
Apr	12	10	8	30.44	29.16	+13.5	-1.75	16	9	6
May	11	13	7	30.30	29.30	+18	+5	17	9	5
Jun	4	14	12	30.13	29.60	+15	+7.5	19	8	3
Jul	4	20	7	30.20	29.79	+17	+8	18	6	7
Aug	7	10	14	30.27	29.54	+16	+8	20	9	2
Sep	1	8	21	30.25	29.12	+12.5	+2	13	8	10
Oct	—	9	24	30.30	29	+8.5	+1	8	16	7
Nov										
Dec										

On 8 January with the barometer between 28.76 and 29.00, the thermometer from 0° to +1°, a strong southeast wind blew, the condition of the atmosphere: dense overcast and rain and snow, 9 January barometer at 29.33, thermometer from +2° to 2°, in the afternoon at three o'clock a noticeable earthquake lasting for more than one minute. With the fall of the thermometer [barometer?] to 28.40. On 4 January the thermometer showed +3°. Wind south, strong, gusty, sky cloudy, with black clouds, wind and wet snow.

With the maximum height of the barometer at 30.49, on 10 February the thermometer stood from +3° to -2°, quiet, sky clear. March: height of the barometer reached 20, thermometer at +5°, sky dark, cloudy, wind northeast, moderate changing from east to southeast: until the 25th the barometer dropped to 29.21, thermometer was at +3½°, wind east, strong, with rain, sky cloudy.

April: At the maximum height of the barometer 30.44, temperature 19°, wind southwest calm weather. Clear, lasting with quiet from northwest winds to the 28th. Meanwhile, the barometer dropped gradually to 29.48. Then in the evening, the wind changed to southwest, and after that rain began. The lowest height [of the barometer] on the 11th — 29.16, the thermometer at 7°, winds gentle from southwest, cloudy and pouring rain.

May 5th: the maximum height of the barometer 30.38, the thermometer +9°, sky brightening, with sunny periods, wind northwest changing force. After that, clear weather continued for ten days, the barometer [dropped] to 29.77. The lowest height on the 18th was 29.30, the thermometer [had plus] 6½°, wind fresh, cloudy and rain. Snow fell on the mountains.

June: the maximum height of the barometer 30.3 on the 21st, thermometer at +10°, cloudy, wind southwest.

July: maximum height of barometer 30.20 began the 21st and continued four days; weather cloudy, wind northwest changing force; thermometer showed from 10° to 14°.

August: maximum height of barometer 30.27 on 17 August, wind southwest gentle, wind cloudy, light rain.

[Table 5.] — continued

September: maximum height of the barometer 30.25 on 30 September, wind northeast gentle; bright, cloudy. Minimum height of barometer 29.12 on 21st; gentle, weather cloudy and rain, thermometer +9°.

On 2 September snow fell on the mountains, during the night thunder and lightning; barometer 29.30, thermometer 8°, wind east and southeast, 3rd and 4th barometer 29.50 and 29.0 thermometer from 7° to 10°, winds east and southeast, weather cloudy and gloomy, rain. Thunder, lightning and pouring rain.

October: barometer maximum 21st was 30.30, thermometer 2½°, wind southwest, weather cloudy, snow and rain. The lowest [height of barometer] 29 [...] October 7; thermometer +4° and 5°, wind east, fresh, weather gloomy with rain.

Mr. Baranov's observation that the weather is clear on the third day after a new moon and that it may continue for the entire lunar month is right some of the time. The weather at sea is often different than along the coast. Sometimes after leaving shore, one goes through a darkness which gradually clears, and one comes out in a clear area from which you can see dark clouds in the distance near snowy peaks. The winds at sea are not constant; in the spring and summer, the winds are from the east and south and southwest and northwest in the fall. But sometimes there are northeast and northwest winds in the spring and summer, and sometimes they last for the great part of fall and winter months, but at times the complete opposite can happen.[17]

The fort of Novo-Arkhangel'sk is located within the bay 14 miles from Cape Edgecumbe, which can be seen west of here. A chain of snowy ridges stretches from north to east from Mt. Edgecumbe; from east to south the mountain ridges are not as high; they are forested, from south to west the blue ocean stretches into infinity to the poles without any obstacles. The fort is sheltered from the sea by highly elevated islands.

B. THE INHABITANTS OF SITKHA [ISLAND] AND THE ENTIRE NORTHWEST COAST OF AMERICA, THE KOLIUZHI [TLINGIT]

The Koliuzh or Kolosh inhabit the Northwest Coast from 40° to 60° latitude. The natives of Trinidad Bay are as different as those of the Columbia River as much as the latter are distinctive from those of the Juan de Fuca Bay and so on. According to the Russians and Aleuts who had visited these regions, the natives of Trinidad Bay look more like the Kolosh than like the Indians living south of Cape Mendocino. Therefore, I am probably correct in grouping them with the Kolosh (this resemblance can be seen in their rituals and way of life).

The Indians of New Albion cannot understand one another at a distance of ten miles. Consequently, it is very possible that peoples scattered across a distance of 20 degrees will naturally develop a distinct difference in their way of life and language simply because of intermixing with the inhabitants of interior America, such as the Kolosh of Bering [Yakutat] and Trinidad bays.

How can one understand a people without a permanent way of life, without any true traditions and without any living monuments? Only the shamans have the people's trust, and everything told by them serves as religion. The shamans drew their knowledge from those shamans before them who imparted it to their followers with new significance. The wisest of them established rituals based on circumstances using extraordinary happenings. Without a written language what signs could they have used to preserve the immutability of their ancestors' traditions? Who can now confirm that the tales of present-day natives are the same as those their ancestors told one hundred years ago? Who can confirm that these wise elders did not change their stories from time to time? The shamans, of course, impart ideas (concepts) even to the elders of the tribe; how many are the tribes and how varied are their ways of looking at the same concept?

In order to understand a people like the Kolosh, one ought to make a thorough investigation of them. It is possible that one tribe is more intelligent than another and, consequently, has a better understanding of concepts and knowledge. It is probable that at a distance of 20 degrees the climate and other factors can influence a people's way of life.

We became acquainted with the Kolosh in 1783, but the first navigators had no means of gathering information about their concepts without the aid of translators. After the occupation [by the Russians] of Yakutat in 1794 and Sitkha in 1799,

Mr. Baranov of course gathered important data, but they have been lost. My data consist of the following:

1. The Kolosh Concept of a Supreme Being; the Creation of the World (and of Humanity; of Evil Spirits)

The Kolosh have no understanding of a supreme being or creator of the world. But their understanding has led them to look at the origin of things in the world near them. In the mythology of the Sitkha Kolosh, animals are considered active participants in life: man is perceived as a demigod and ravens as life-givers.

> Kitkh-ugin-si,[18] the first being on earth, had a sister, and he killed her children so that the tribe of people would not multiply. Besides him, there were other inhabitants on this earth over whom he exercised his power. For their sins he would bring floods and cause them to drown, but he could not kill them all because these people saved themselves [by going] on rafts and boats to the top of mountain peaks where the flood could not reach them. There, they would tie up their boats to the rocks with ropes and remain anchored there. The rafts and ropes have been preserved on these mountain tops until this time.
>
> Kitkh-ugin-si's sister, tired of her brother's abuse, decided to run away. She went far away along the seashore, and there she built herself a cabin out of tree bark. One fine day, she came out onto the shore and saw playful whales in the sea. Not knowing what these animals were, she began to yell so that they would come closer to her hut and bring her food because she was starving. The whales disappeared without answering her. That night, however, a handsome man appeared in her cabin, asking her why she was here alone and starving. She told him that her brother had not allowed her to raise her children and that, feeling sorry for them, she had been compelled to run away and endure starvation. The man who had come sent out one of his slaves (*kalga*) to the shore and ordered him to bring a small round pebble which he placed in the fire. When it burned red hot, he gave it to her to eat. After she had done so, he told her that she would give birth to a son, whom no one would be able to kill. The man then vanished.
>
> Soon thereafter, she sensed that she was pregnant and gave birth to her son, El'kkh. She raised him, bathing in the sea every morning. When he had grown bigger, she made him an arrow and showed him how to use it to kill birds. While

walking through the forests, he killed many humming birds from which his mother sewed herself a mantle made of bird skins. Once, he saw something white in a tree. He shot his arrow and killed a large bird. He skinned it and put on the skin. Looking at the wings, he understood that the bird had been able to fly through the air with them. When he realized this, he said, "How happy I would be if I could fly like a bird." Saying this, he rose through the air but was unable to maneuver the wings. So, he faded behind the clouds. Feeling sorry for himself, he repented by saying, "I would have been better if I had stayed with my mother." After saying these words he found himself in front of his mother's cabin.

After living together a certain time, his mother told him about Kitkh-ugin-si, and how he had killed her children, and why she was in this cabin. Feeling his strength, the young man begged his mother to let him take vengeance on his uncle. Sure that he would not come back to her alive, she would not allow him to do this. Finally, however, she agreed to let him go because of his relentless requests. He then left. When he came to his uncle's cabin, he did not find him at home. The people (kalgas) told him that his uncle had left. Because his uncle was jealous, he would lock up his wife in a chest and hang it in the middle of the cabin before he left home. The young guest asked what was in the chest. When the people told him that his uncle's wife was in it, he broke the lid open and freed her in spite of the people's objections. Several days later, they saw a boat coming from the sea. It was Kitkh-ugin-si coming home. At that moment the people put his wife back in the chest and hung it back in the middle of the cabin.

Having come ashore, Kitkh-ugin-si noticed that there was a change in his house. After stepping out of his boat, he asked, "Who took down the chest?"

The people answered him in fear. They told him that his nephew had done this and that they had not had the strength to hold him back. The old man came home and gathered his people in his cabin and ordered the waters to rise and drown all of those who were not with him. His nephew was sitting on top of the cabin. He was wearing the bird skin and was not afraid of his uncle's threats and ordered the waters to recede immediately. After that, he came down from the roof and locked all the exits of the cabin so that no one could escape from it. He then commanded the waters to rise and flew into the sky using his bird wings. He flew for a long time. Finally, he grew tired and fell down to earth and hurt himself on a rock. It was for this reason that people began to feel pain after that. He lay motionless in that spot for a long time, but one morning after falling fast asleep he heard a voice saying, "Go, they are calling you." He woke up but saw no one. Thinking that this had been a dream, he fell asleep again. But the voice called out again with the same words. He woke up but saw no one. He gathered his strength and walked towards the shore. He saw beavers swimming in the water, and he thought, "Could it be possible that these sea animals called out to me?"

A beaver swam out to him and said, "Sit on me, and I shall take you to those calling you."

"You won't drown me?" El'kkh asked.

"Close your eyes and sit down. Don't be afraid of anything," the beaver said. El'kkh obeyed the voice calling him and sat down on the beaver. He sailed for a long time. Later, the beaver said, "Open your eyes and look." Looking at the shore, he noticed a multitude of people on it. The beaver told him, "Go and there you shall find your mother and your uncle." Coming ashore, he saw his mother and uncle who were glad to see him. They wanted to feed him, but he could not eat anything. His uncle gathered all the people who were there into his cabin. Among these people, there was one with two bellies, and he ate a lot. El'kkh asked him why he was like that. At first, the two-bellied man did not want to say anything, but then he acquiesced to El'kkh's request. He told him that once he saw a raven who was sick, and the raven asked him to scrape the skin off one of his feet near the joint. He did so until he drew water from it. After he recovered, the raven was able to create all living things. Then, the raven ordered the two-bellied man to eat the skin that had been scraped from the raven's leg, and thus the man became a glutton.

El'kkh became acquainted with the raven through the glutton. Through the raven, El'kkh received the right to become the forefather of the Kolosh.

Since they could not figure out how people were created or what the raven's power is, they think that things are the way they are because they are. The only truth emerging from this dark fairy tale is the flooding of the world; the rest is a figment of the imagination.

The Kolosh believe in evil spirits. They think that these inflict sickness upon people. They (the spirits) inhabit the waters, and therefore sickness is transferred through eating fish and shellfish which are possessed by evil spirits. The Kolosh beseech them through the shamans in order to avoid sickness, but they do not honor these spirits. They think that the herring asked the evil spirits to give them Kabachkov, because he did not give them any peace in the past. The spirits told this to the shamans.

2. Concept of the Soul and What Happens to It after Destruction of [the Bond to] the Body

Once a man dies, the Kolosh burn the corpse and erect monuments to the rich people in that place where they were burned. They believe that the soul is eternal, but they do not believe in reward and punishment in the other world. The souls retain the same social status that they had in this lifetime, especially the chiefs and those subject to them. If a chief dies with his servants, the latter remain the chief's eternal servants.

3. Birth Rituals

After giving birth to a child, the mother remains in bed for a month without leaving the cabin. After this period, she washes herself, the child and her clothing and puts on clean clothes. Then, they call the relatives to celebrate the event. At this time the mother gives the child the name of one of her dead relatives, and the ritual ends. The women usually have six to eight children but no more than ten.

4. Child Rearing (Love between Parents and Children)

The mother breast-feeds the child until he is able to walk. The mothers teach their children to eat fish by putting well-chewed pieces of iukola into their mouths until they grow their own teeth and are able to feed themselves. They make their children's clothing out of animal pelts. When the child begins to speak, his relatives, uncles and others are obliged to bathe him in a river or sea water every morning in spite of the freezing weather until the child gets used to the cold. The mothers and fathers avoid this ritual, because the cries and tears of the child would cause them pain. Instead, the uncle carries out the ritual by hitting the child if he cries and is being disobedient.[19] Children of all ages show respect for their parents, and moreover, it is noteworthy that the old and helpless are well taken care of. Generally, the children are related to the maternal side of the family, and inheritance rights come from the mother's lineage. The Kolosh, in general, are a sturdy people; they are of average height; their facial structure is regular; they have black hair; they do not have rough beards. Whatever little hair they have on their faces, they scrape off with sea shells. The women pierce their lower lips and insert pieces of wood in them, which gives their faces a disgusting look. Now, this custom is becoming rare.

5. Marriage and Marriage Rites

A man proposing marriage must be able to perform any type of work and be able to use a firearm. Based on his wishes and her parents' agreement, he rides to the village where he intends to marry the intended bride; upon his arrival he sends a go-between with his proposal. If the father and daughter agree to his proposal, he then goes to them and presents gifts to the parents and close relatives and obtains his bride. After this, he returns to her parents and receives gifts from them, which must be larger and more valuable than the presents he gave them. The gifts must consist of animal pelts and European things, weapons and often slaves (kalgi). There have been instances when the bride would not agree to the conditions, and the marriage did not take place. For example, one bride-to-be asked toion Nauchik[a] to send his first wife back to her relatives. The chief, who loved his first wife, refused, and the marriage proposal was broken. Shamans do not participate in marriage rituals, and no sacrifices take place.

The rich and noble Kolosh have up to five wives and sometimes more. Through these ties they attempt to obtain a large dowry and to have more relatives in order to strengthen their positions. In some tribes it is customary to marry before they even reach puberty. There are cases of jealousy and women fight to the point that they sometimes stab one another with knives. If the wife is unfaithful and is caught at the scene of the crime, the husband kills her, and her seducer without fear of reprisal from his relatives (the seducer's) whom he pays with clothing and other things of value. This punishment is meted out to the man who is not a relative of the husband. Should he be a relative, then the offended husband forces him to take her as his wife and to care for her. But hot-headed and passionate people do not always observe this moderation, and as a result relatives are often victims of the offended husband's rage. There are, however, condescending husbands who allow their older wives to have a young male helper who lives in their cabin, performs chores and sleeps with her in her husband's absence.

There are no examples of anyone marrying his mother, daughter or even niece. They always choose their brides from other tribes. It must be noted that after the death of an uncle, the nephew takes his wife in spite of the age difference. Two sisters can become the wives of one husband.

6. Female Labor

Although women have their own work such as preparing fish, sewing, basket weaving, weaving of blankets from wool and so on, they are also burdened with such chores as preparing wood, bark, etc. During wars and times of negotiation with neighboring tribes, the women do not participate in the councils; the men hide their plans from them. But during trading, holidays and other business deals, they take an active part. More often than not, the husbands carry out their wives' commands.

7. Funerary Rites

When a man dies, they make him a coffin, place his corpse in it, and the relatives and friends take him to a selected place where they burn his corpse. At this time the relatives express their grief by screaming and crying. As mentioned above, before they came in contact with Europeans, the Kolosh would kill the slaves when a chief died. Today, as the Kolosh have assured us, these killings no longer take place. The relatives of the deceased cut their hair off and paint their faces black in order to express their grief. They may mourn like this for a whole year.

8. Food Stores and Their Use

The preparation of food among the Sitkha Kolosh begins in February with the coming of herring. They do not store this fish, because it spoils quickly, becoming moldy and bitter. They usually store herring roe. When the herring begin spawning, the Kolosh cut down spruce trees and weigh them down with rocks in the water near the shore. The spawned roe sticks to the branches, which are then taken out of the water and dried in the sun or in the air. When the roe is dry it is beaten off the branches and stored for future use.

After herring, there is the constant preparation of various types of fish which come from the ocean into the rivers in the month of July. The Kolosh stock up mainly on pink salmon [*gorbusha*, humpbacks]. They separate the meat from the bones, air drying it or smoking it.

Halibut can be fished all year round. It is dried and stored. In addition to fish they store berries, raspberries which they crush with herring roe into one dish. In the spring they gather sap from trees, which is dried and stored. Seals, dolphins, sea lions and whales which have washed ashore also serve as sources of food. The fat of these animals is considered a delicacy and is served to guests in place of drinks. Of the four-legged animals they use the meat of the deer [*oleni*], mountain sheep [*barany*], but they do not eat bear meat. They also eat all sorts of birds but do not touch the raven, which they worship.

The Kolosh have never used human meat as food for any reason. But they say that a people living north in the mountains (a people called Konnan) ate human flesh during famine. They say that these people sometimes come to trade in Chil'khat. These people differ from the Kolosh in their way of life and language. These Konnans used to have bows and arrows as weapons, but now they get firearms and gunpowder from the Chil'khat Kolosh in exchange for fox and sable furs and native copper. Toion Saiginakh told us that these people have dealings with the Mednovsk and Chugach natives, and that the Chil'khat Kolosh had visited these people.

9. Diseases and Modes of Healing

It has been mentioned that the Kolosh have a strong constitution. No one has observed any indigenous diseases. There are the usual eye, head and stomach aches which are a result of their way of life. The smoke in their cabins and other factors account for their eye and head aches. Some of the stomach aches are caused by the food they eat, but none of it is fatal. Some people die from fevers because of their lack of medicine. According to Saiginakh, a smallpox epidemic broke out 50 years ago, around 1770. He was a boy at the time and hardly remembered the incident, but he remembered for sure that only one or two people remained in each family. Smallpox, according to him, had spread from Stakhin and ended in

Sitkha but did not spread farther north. At the time the Kolosh thought that this disease had been sent upon them by the raven for punishment for the constant wars which they carried on among themselves. The old women are responsible for taking care of the sick, using various herbs and roots, but the Kolosh do not depend on the old women's knowledge. While shamans do not take part in curing people, the people come to them with questions: will the sick live or die? If the answer is of a positive nature, the people reward him with gifts. There are, however, shamans who cure people. These are so rare that they are given special respect.

10. Domestic Life

The Kolosh are sybarites in their cabins. If there is food available, the Kolosh men are ready to lie around with their wives all day long. If they get bored sitting in their huts, they put on their raincoats (*plashch*), walk along the shore, sit on the rocks, or lie in the sand. They eat two or three times a day;[20] they bathe in water often and seldom warm themselves near a fire. Many are passionate players of "sticks"; they may lose all their belongings — clothing, pelts, firearms, slaves — and there have even been examples of men losing their wives. When there is a lack of food, the Kolosh go out to sea and fish for halibut. The women bring in the wood and water. They prepare the food and perform all other domestic chores. The Kolosh have a sound judgement of things that fall within their domain. They are passionate traders, but they have a childish greed as they grab rare objects for which they usually pay high prices. When they get bored with the object, they sell it for almost nothing. They have European clothing, some of them quite a bit of it, but they rarely wear it. At times you can see them change clothes three or four times a day. Others wear shirts. But the usual and main piece of clothing is a mantle made out of a flannel blanket or a piece of frieze about three arshins long. In the winter they wear clothing made of sable, fox, black bear, mink, marmot and other fur.

11. Wars and War Tactics

Wars among the Kolosh are always of an internecine nature, but they must be differentiated into internal and external wars. The former occurs when two families (Wolf and Raven) have a quarrel in the same village, and one becomes the victim of the other. Then, the relatives of the murdered demand payment for his death. If they refuse to pay, the offended party challenges them to an open fight. In this event no firearms are used by any side. Instead, they use knives and only attempt to wound, and not kill. If the offended party manages to show his superiority, the other side is obliged to pay for the death and negotiations take place. If the attacking party retreats, they have a temporary truce, and they wait for the opportunity to avenge themselves by killing any of their enemies. This vengeance may last several years among these people who live, so to speak, under one roof.

As far as it is known women are always the reasons for their quarrels and fights. Although the main reason for external fighting is women, there is also the matter of pride. If the pride of the savage is based on his strength against the helpless, it is not bridled by moderation. Instead, it is fueled by greed and vengeance. If a man from another tribe or region has been killed for whatever reason, then vengeance fills the minds of the dead man's relatives. They try not to disclose their plans until they have decided to take the offensive. It is for this reason that all discussions by the warriors are kept from the women who, being related to various villages, might warn their relatives of the oncoming danger. Having prepared themselves, they leave in boats and try to reach the enemy village by sunrise. Before attacking, they put on an armor made of wood woven with whale veins, with which they cover their chests and backs. They conceal their faces with wooden masks, which have carved images of animals and terrifying creatures. On their heads they wear wooden hats with the same type of carvings. They tie their hats down, leaving only slits for their eyes and ears. Attacking by surprise, they show no mercy for the men, killing them all, but sparing the women whom they take as prisoners (*kuukh*).

Subsequently, the defeated await the moment to take revenge by killing the same number, but if this goal is not reached in their lifetime, their heirs must avenge their ancestors. At times, however, the quarrels are settled through negotiations, and payments are made for the dead. Each side takes a peace hostage. After doing so, they perform a strange ceremony. Both sides come out on a flat area (men and women) brandishing knives. The men look aggressive as they attempt to grab the hostage (the top adversary, the most respected in lineage and age) and shake their lances and knives; they yell and rush into the adversary side and grab the hostage, who hides among his own people. With a joyous cry, they lift him up and carry him to their side, thus fulfilling their desire and ending the war. Each side performs the same ritual, keeping the hostage in good health and performing all sorts of favors for him. They do not allow him to walk, but always carry him. Peace is concluded with dances from morning to evening and lots of food. Savages almost everywhere have three things which they consider most important in life: lovemaking, lots of food (especially fatty, oily foods) and dancing. In these three things lie their need for freedom and independence. Finally, the hostages are taken to the cabins of their new friends, where they live for a year or more. Later, they return to their own villages. Again, they dance to confirm the strength of their alliance.

12. Entertainments

The remembering of dead friends and relatives, of past pleasures, new unions, new friendships, military events, new plans and other pleasures in life are expressed through dances accompanied by feasting. There are two types of dances: some occur between families and neighbors and take place yearly; others are public dances to which friends, nobles and the honored are invited. These come from far-away places.

The former occur in the fall when they begin to store fish, oil, berries and nutritious roots. Then the leader of any tribe invites his neighbors to his house and entertains them for a few days. They dance one dance after another without any interruptions; then the leader gives his guests animal pelts, blankets and other clothing. The leader of the first house goes to the next house and so on. As a matter of politeness the gifts are always returned.

Public dances are organized by the entire tribe, and invited guests remain there for more than a month. In the village where the entertainment is to take place, each yurt puts out a totem pole depicting an animal, or bird or something familiar to all. Throughout the celebration the yurt is no longer referred to by the name of the owner, but by the image on the totem pole. After they have danced in one yurt, they move on to the house of the Eagle, Raven, Sun, Moon, Bear and so forth. Special artisans carve these images with great skill. For these they receive reindeer pelts, or elk, otter or a slave woman for each carving he makes.

The guests arrive and give one another presents according to status, hoping to receive a present of the same value in the future. The dance lasts from morning to evening. It consists of standing, jumping and twisting their bodies in one place. In preparation for the dance, the Kolosh paint their faces with various images. They cover their hair with eagle down which they throw at those around them. They carry carved rattlers in their hands, while others bang on drums.

13. Shamans

Shamans are self-made people. When they want to acquire the position of shaman from a relative who was a shaman and who died, young people are assigned the following tasks: they get ready by fasting and being chaste for several years. When they feel ready, they begin their sorcery. Their main task is to foretell the future and to cure people who are afflicted by evil spirits. If someone dies from an unusual pain, this death is attributed to something evil; therefore, the people run to the shaman who calls out the name of those who have poisoned the food of the sick or dead person. The unfortunate suspect is either terribly beaten or killed.

14. Slaves or *Kalgi*

As mentioned above, prisoners were taken during wars. Today, there seldom are any internecine wars. Thus, prisoners are rare. But they can be bought from the Kolosh who live on the shores of the [Queen] Charlotte Islands. They have complete power over the prisoners' lives. From time to time slaves are killed during funeral banquets, dances and the death of an important chief. Usually, they kill the weak and disabled who cannot be sold or given as gifts. Sometimes during such rituals, slaves are given their freedom and allowed to live anywhere they please.

It is noteworthy that the Kolosh have no knowledge of suicide, and that under the most unbearable conditions, the slaves did not choose to end their lives.

15. Toions

The chiefs of each tribe are recognized as elders, but they have no power over anyone. They have no right to send anyone out to perform any kind of work. And only through good will does anyone accompany him on far-away trips or help him in his work. The status of chief is inherited.

16. Wealth and Valuables

The fortune of the Kolosh depends on how many relatives he has. But his wealth is determined by the number of slaves he has, some of whom have 20, 30, or 40 of both sexes.

Instead of using money the Kolosh pay with deer skins, zamshas (suede), which in Siberia are called *rovduga*. These are not used for clothing, but are carefully kept as a means of barter. Fifteen and twenty such skins can pay for a slave; five and six for a beaver, ten and fifteen for a good boat. In general, all items are valued according to the number of such skins.

17. Kolosh Views of [European] Peoples

The first foreigners to appear on these shores were the Spanish, English, French, and Russians, but they came ashore in various areas and were taken for gods. The Kolosh say that, when they approached a ship, they did not have the courage to go near it, but after they were beckoned, they decided to send an old man. When he returned alive and with gifts, the Kolosh became bolder; they became acquainted with the foreigners and began trading with them.

18. Handicrafts

The main skill of the Kolosh consists in making boats and canoes which are light and maneuverable and can accommodate two to six men in a small boat and from forty to sixty men in larger ones. The normal boats can accommodate ten to twenty men. These boats are used with short paddles on both sides. No rowboat can compare with these for speed.[21] The men occupy themselves by carving war masks and common masks of men's and women's faces with natural features. They also carve pipes out of wood or slate. They make rings out of copper or horns, which they wear on their hands. They make spoons out of ram's horns. They make dishes resembling wooden soup bowls which they adorn with shells and bone (ivory). Today, some of them have begun repairing guns. I saw a knife, made by a Kolosh, which looked like an English dirk, which was of equal beauty to the original. They make double-edged knives very skillfully, which they adorn with shiny shells.

The women make very beautiful blankets from soft goat's hair [*iz miagkogo koz'ego pukhu*]. They weave baskets out of grass roots, which they use to carry and keep water. The women use smaller baskets, woven from dyed roots, to keep their sewing instruments.

Today they weave hats (in the European fashion) from these roots; they are very light, durable and rather pretty.

C. WATERS AND PRODUCTS OF THE SEA AND RIVERS

There are no large rivers on the island of Sitkha, but there are small ones which flow along rocky river beds. The water is clean and abounds with fish in the summer. These small rivers all originate in the mountains. Two rather important rivers rush down in waterfalls. One of the rivers is three hours away from the fort, in Serebrennikov [Silver] Bay. These falls are more than 100 feet high. When the falls hit bottom, they turn into two rapids. The river originates at a lake one hour away from the falls. The lake is surrounded by high cliffs. The other important waterfall empties into a deep lake near Ozerski Redoubt. There are many small rivers which rush noisily everywhere, especially in the spring when the snows melt.

There are many lakes on the island. The largest, located near Ozerski Redoubt, is ten miles long. In some places the depth has been measured at 190 sazhens, and in other places they could not hit bottom. This lake lies between the mountains and seems to have been formed because of an earthquake due to the fact that massive cliffs that now stand there were torn away by some powerful force. The extreme depth of the lake also serves as an additional proof of this. The lake lies slightly above sea level. Its water and that of other lakes is fresh but has no fish.[22]

Near the Novo-Arkhangel'sk fort there is a lake with marshy and muddy soil. Bloodsuckers live in its water, but of a species which is useless for bloodletting.

Mineral springs can be found at various spots along the shore. Near the Ozerski Redoubt there are sulphurous hot springs. They have been known to the Kolosh, who used them to cure their sicknesses. Many still use them today. Wounds heal quickly, bone fractures mend and scurvy disappears because of the usefulness of these springs. As the water flows from its spring to the pool, it leaves an ash-grey color on the rocks. The water from the springs is hot but drinkable. At first the taste is disgusting, but once you get used to the taste, then the smell of it is not so bad. Most cannot sit in these springs for more than 15 minutes. After sitting in the water you feel weak, and your head begins to spin.[23]

On the Chastye Islands [Bay of Islands] there are cold waters that have a sour taste, which the Aleuts discovered by drinking it.

The Almighty distributed his various gifts in abundance everywhere. Through his industry man derives benefits from the depths of mountains and seas. No climate, no storm, nothing can prevent or impede man's endeavors and passions to become rich.

1. Sea Otters and Their Procurement

The most valuable product of the local seas has been and still is the sea beaver [*morskoi bobr*], which the English rightly call sea otter and the Spanish nutria. The Russians were the first to find out about these pelts, and soon after the Bering expedition in 1741 brought in 900 furs, the Russians began sailing out of Kamchatka to hunt the sea otters. The Spanish knew of these furs from the time they occupied California, but because they were busy with the mines of Potosi, they neglected hunting, which requires both work and time. After discovering Port Nootka, Cook observed many sea otters there and along the entire coast. He took several hundred pelts with him and acquainted the English with a new trade item. In 1784 and 1786 they sent their first ships to the Northwest Coast from Macao and the East Indies. The following year they returned to Canton and began trading there. In 1787 La Pérouse took 600 pelts aboard his ship, and from that time on there were shipments of pelts every year. The calculation made by Mr. Baranov in 1800 that during the previous ten years 100,000 pelts were shipped out is not an exaggeration. While in Canton, Mr. Shemelin gathered information that the Americans had imported 8,200 pelts in 1804 and 14,000 in 1805, while the Russian-American Company had brought in 4,628.[24]

It is true that from time to time sea otters have begun to diminish. Either because of over-hunting or because many were frightened away by the use of firearms and frequent visits by hunting parties, the sea otters have moved to areas yet undiscovered. One distinguished observer, zealous for the benefit of the fatherland, pointed out that they kill all the sea otters, just like at the town of Arkhangel'sk when they caught all the cod. "Codfish spawn roe, but sea otters give birth to only one or two young ones, and because of this inequality the sea otter could be extinguished altogether." We now see that, along the whole expanse of coast from Cape Ommaney to Kenai Bay, only two places remain where we can still hunt — namely, L'tua Bay and Yakutat; but even there, they are no longer native, but hide someplace farther along the coast to the southeast where they are more protected. Near Sitkha, almost all have disappeared, and in the innumerable straits to 46° there are ever fewer.

The Kolosh derive a great profit from hunting and leave no place where [sea otters] can find refuge.

In comparison to other sea otters, the ones from the Northwest Coast fall into three classes: (1) those from the Kuril and Kamchatka areas; (2) those from the Andreianov and Fox Islands; (3) those from the Northwest Coast; (4) those from [New] Albion and California. Those from the first three groups are large in size; the fur is longer and softer. Those which are black and have a fine gloss are considered the best pelts in Russia. In Canton they first look at the size, and then they are sorted out by quality. Pelts from the south are browner, especially when the sea otters have been hunted in the summer time. The sea otters from California are usually smaller. Some of the winter pelts are black but with short hair and no gloss. The advantage of hunting in the winter is that the pelts are darker and glossier, and there are few cubs, because the young have grown into adults by then.

The Aleuts are the only people born with a passion for hunting sea otters. They go in hunting parties of five to ten baidarkas. When they spot a sea otter, they surround it, and the person closest to the sea otter gets to shoot him with a dart and has the right to claim the kill. A sea otter cannot stay more than a quarter of an hour under water, and the more severely wounded it is the faster it surfaces. It is impossible for it to evade the skillful hand of the marksman [harpooner]. Formerly, the Kolosh used to shoot sea otters with bows and arrows, but now they own and use firearms to hunt them. The sea otters are frightened by these shots and leave their native grounds. It is a known fact that where they used to be abundant (for example in Kenai and Chugach bays and near Sitkha), they have become scarce. In other areas where they have been hunted out, they have reappeared after hunting had stopped for awhile. Such is the case along the Andreianov and Fox Islands, and in L'tua and Yakutat bays.

2. Whales, Sea Lions and Seals

At times whales appear near these shores, but neither the Aleuts nor the Kolosh hunt them. Sometimes, the whales wash ashore near the fortress, and if the Aleuts find them, they go out in their baidarkas, cut out the blubber and bring it back to the fort. More than once, they have found whales which were not far away and towed them to the village, where they cut them up. In general, these whales are small, not more than six sazhens in length.

The sea lions lie on rocks near Cape Edgecumbe and on the southern tip of the island. There are few of them in the nearby islands, and because of the difficulties, few parties are sent out to hunt them on the distant islands. The best catch occurs from December to March; and in a poor year one can get ten skins. The seals have also been hunted out, and they are rarely seen. It was mentioned above that in 1800, during Mr. Baranov's first winter here, the Aleuts killed 40 sea lions and 150 hair seals. Subsequently, because of colonization and hunting expeditions, these animals could no longer live here; they were either killed or moved to remote areas; it was observed earlier that in sea lions killed here were found arrowheads belonging to the [New] Albion [California] Indians. This is an indication that the seals migrate from north to south and back.

3. Fish and Shellfish

Fish which are found all year round are: halibut, cod, eel-pout [*kuzma*], sea perch and sea burbot. The first two kinds occur in great numbers but are not always abundant; at times there is more halibut, sometimes more codfish; however, halibut is the main source of food for the natives. Halibut tastes best from fall to spring. Periodically other fish appear: sometimes in February or March large schools of herring arrive and remain near the shores until May. Sometimes, they even appear in the fall and winter, but these runs are small and unpredictable. At the beginning of May, various types of salmon similar to those in Kamchatka begin to appear [they are known by the same names as there]. In May, June, July and August, the king salmon [*krasnaia ryba*] and pink salmon [*gorbusha*] make their run; in August the silver salmon [*kizhuch*] makes its run and stays until the end of October. In addition to these, there are various types of smaller fish, such as flounder [*kambala*] and sculpin [*byki*] all year round. White fish [*riapushka*] and loach [*gol'tsy*] come every spring.[25]

Among shellfish there are large round crayfish [crabs], shrimp and various kinds of mollusks, which are used as a food source. The best of these are *mamai* in a round white striped shell from which they make an excellent soup and are very good cooked like cutlet. These shells, known as baidarkas, are tasty when marinated in vinegar. Cuttlefish are known here under the name of button crabs. The most abundant of the shellfish are the crayfish. All of the shellfish mentioned above are used as food by the Kolosh, Aleuts and Russians. Many are suitable for preparing very fine dishes. However, they do not always have the same taste. In the summer, their flesh is more watery and tasteless; from September on they taste better and the flavor does not change until May. Sometimes, shellfish have been harmful; there have been many examples of people dying suddenly after eating them.

The esteemed Dr. B. has stated that the sea urchin is in fact a link between all three kingdoms of nature: mineral, plant and animal. The shell, which is made of lime matter, belongs to the mineral kingdom; the needles (spines) on the shell belong to the plant kingdom and smell like plants;[26] while their internal organs belong to the animal kingdom. Dr. B. believes that nature has given poor countries such creatures (shellfish) to make up for the bounties enjoyed by other countries. In his opinion, the sea urchin is highly nutritious. Besides having a great taste, they have medicinal properties. They are used to cure kidney stones, and also tuberculosis when it is in its early stage. As a matter of fact, they are a universal cure for all sorts of diseases. Without denying the views of scientists, one can conclude that nature has created nothing without a purpose; some things have been created to use as food, some as delicacies; but not everything.

4. Land Animals, Amphibians, Etc.

Sitkha is an island and therefore it is proper that it should have many animals. The important ones are: bears, which have beautiful black fur, various types of fox, and mountain sheep [*gornye barany*] which are the only meat that humans use. There are smaller animals: the marmot, which belongs to the anteater family, mink, and many rats, which were brought here on various ships from Okhotsk and Kamchatka, the Sandwich Islands, and Canton. Small mice were also brought here by these ships. There are amphibious animals, such as the river beaver and river otter, but they are few in number.

On the mainland, which is separated by a strait, you can find the same animals, in addition to moose [*losi*], deer [*oleni*], wolverine, sable and a type of mountain sheep [*nekotoryi rod gornykh baranov*] whose hair provides a soft wool, out of which the Kolosh weave blankets and the Russians knit socks and hats.

5. Birds

The birds inhabiting the cliffs and forests of Northwest America cannot be of a delicate constitution. Were it not for the birds which migrate here from the south to spend the summer and beautify the forests, waters and air, then only those belonging to this climate would be here; the average-sized white-headed eagle, which makes its nest in high mountain cliffs; the raven and the small eagle-owl. But the raven reigns everywhere. One can always hear its wild cawing. Sparrow-like birds and swallows appear in the spring but in small numbers; in the forests far from the shores there are grouse and in the tundra there are willow ptarmigan. When it cannot find food under the snow during harsh winters, the grouse comes closer to the coasts. Then one can hunt them in great numbers.

In March, but usually from the middle of April, geese, ducks, cranes, herons and swans migrate to (the) north in the spring. They fly across the mainland of North America and its islands, where they lay their eggs and raise their young. Beginning in August, they make their return flight. Sometimes, some of these birds remain on these shores to winter.

In May the humming bird (honey sucker) makes its appearance. It is three and a half inches long from its tail to its thin beak; its body and head are one and six-tenths inches, and without its head it is only one inch. The flame colored throat of this bird shines like hot coals. There are many of them when the weather is warm. They remain two but not longer than three months and then disappear. The humming bird can also be found in California. There, it is longer by almost one inch. Its throat is of a raspberry color and is not as beautiful. By comparison they appear to be of a different breed and are native to their shores and do not migrate. Like some insects, they hibernate during the winter and come back to life with the beneficent rays of the spring sun.[27]

There are various marine birds native to this climate. These taste bad because of the fish they eat. There are many other marine birds: puffins [*toporki*], cormorants [*urily*], diving birds [*ary*] and gulls [*chaiki*]. The first three make their nests in the cliffs, while the latter appears only when the herring begins its run. The grey albatross can be found along the seashore. Sandpipers of various types can be seen here in the spring and summer.

Bats appear in the summer and leave in the fall.

6. Vegetation

The sheer cliffs, deep ravines and wet tundra are all covered with a primeval forest. The granite, which has little soil, is covered with moss and enormous spruce. The old trees which have been knocked down by winds rot by themselves and allow for new growth. Together, they form a dark and impassable refuge for wild animals. The main conifers consist of spruce; then we have the larch and a type of cypress with a pungent odor. There are few pines. The deciduous trees are: the alder [*ol'kha*], willow [*iva*], and a so-called apple tree; there are various types of bushes; raspberries [*malina*], which have a watery taste; ash berry [*realina*], currants [*smorodina*], bilberries [*chernika*], the latter also taste bad; there are elderberries [*buzina*] and others. One plant, related to the blackthorn [*ternovnik*] bush, has many needles; it grows between the large forests near the shore and impedes passage. Along the shore, there are berries known as velvet berries [*barkhatnye iagodu*]. These are very tasty. Red bilberries [*brusnika*], cranberries [*shiksha*], cloudberries [*kliukva*] and crowberries [*moroshka*] all grow in the tundra area. V. N. Berkh noted that in China they prefer our native ginseng [*zhin-zhing*] to the Canadian kind. But the root which he called ginseng is really *maun* or valerian. It is common knowledge that it was brought to Canton by the Americans and was not recognized as ginseng. Therefore, they no longer import it there. Besides this root, there are other medicinal plants. They include millefolium, which is known and used by the natives. Other useful herbs are gathered in the spring: young nettle [*krapiva*], parsley [*petrushka*], sour grass [*shchavel*] and chicory [*tsikorii*].[28]

The following trees are used for shipbuilding in this order: Cypress [*kiparis*], known as *dushmiannoe derevo*, is used for the frame and planking of rowboats; it is somewhat yellowish, clean when finished and light-weight. Spruce [*el'*] is used for beams and decks; fine layered [*melkosloinoe*] trees which grow near rocks are used for making masts and spars. Those trees which grow in the wet tundra contain a lot of moisture and for that reason do not rot as quickly. Deciduous trees are used for planking and sometimes for decks, rudders and pumps, because they bend easily. The apple tree is used for making block and tackle because of its sturdiness. Spruce is used in house building. It is straight, even and up to 15 sazhens in length, without curves. The bark of cypress trees is peeled and used as roofing in the spring. In general the trees contain a lot of moisture. They are cut down in the fall and used as building material the following summer. They do not have much time to dry, and because they again quickly absorb the moisture, they rot rather quickly; they do not last more than twenty years. It must be mentioned that because of the moisture, the trees resist fires. One cannot burn down a forest in the dry summer even when the bark is full of pitch; and for this reason the houses do not catch on fire.

Several types of mushrooms and saffron milk-caps [*ryzhiki*] grow in Sitkha, but only in small numbers; in Yakutat Bay there are many milk-agaric [*gruzdei*].

7. Minerals

The mountains on the island consist of granite and other stratified rocks with layers of Shilferton slate [*aspid*] between them;[29] in L'tua and Yakutat bays, the mountains consist of gneiss [*sliudenogo slanets*], mica and granite. In many places there are quartz, horn-stone [*rogovogo kamnia*], hornblende [*rogovoi blendy*], chlorite, serpentine and talc [*dialasha*]. Large garnets [*granaty*] can be found in the mica and gneiss, many of which have one and two-tenths of an inch in diameter; few of them are clear and in general have cracks in them. Due to a lack of lead, the Kolosh use large garnets instead of bullets for hunting animals, and smaller ones, like No. 1 shot, for hunting birds. Of course, their guns are usually damaged from such use. One can also find white and grey marble, lime spar [*izvestkovyi shpat*], sometimes some carnelian [*serdoliki*] and chalcedony which occur in round pieces. The Kolosh make smoking pipes out of slate and decorate them with figures of birds with beaks and eyes. They used to make serpentine labrets [*planki*] which their women inserted into their lips. One such labret, which had been used for a long time, measured two and eight-tenths inches long, two inches wide and seven and a half inches in diameter.

Lots of pumice [*pemzy*] can be found near Mt. Edgecumbe; there are various areas sprinkled with olivine, zeolite and volcanic blends.

View of Mt. Edgecumbe and Novo-Arkhangel'sk fort, from the east. From Khlebnikov manuscript, artist unknown.

VI
COLONIAL STATUS

After Mr. Baranov's departure, Novo-Arkhangel'sk remained the main port and the seat of the chief managers. There were and still are differing opinions concerning its advantages and disadvantages as a port. The advantages of this port cannot be equalled by any other location; its disadvantages lie in rising costs and the impossibility of pacifying the natives; the two balance out. Both will long be the subject for discussions and disagreements. We should examine all of these realistically and in detail.

A. POPULATION

In January 1825 the population of the fort was as follows:

In Service		*Not in Service*		
Officials, clergy, promyshlenniks and Russians in general	309			
Creoles	58	Kad'iak Creoles	8	
Kad'iak Aleuts	17	Kad'iak Aleuts	129	
Fox Island Aleuts	13	Fox Island Aleuts	8	
Aleuts, Indians	3	Indians	2	
	400	[persons]	147	[persons]
Minors, male	66			
Women	133			
Minor children, female	67			
	200*			
Total:	813	[persons]		

*[Sic.]

The number of salaried officials and employees (400 persons) was as follows:

Chief manager	1	Priest, elder and deacon	3
His secretary	1	In arsenal, supervisor and assistants	3
Office manager and employees in office	6	Physician and employees in hospital	5
Naval officers	1	Employees at chief manager's	6
Navigation officials and seafarers	8	Teacher and superintendent	2
Their assistants	6	Vessel prikazchiks	4
Storekeepers	3		
Their assistants	5		
			54 [persons]

Crews on Voyages

On brig *Baikal*	22	On brig *Okhotsk*	10
On brig *Buldakov*	20	On schooner *Fortuna*	14
On brig *Volga*	13	On sloop *Konstantin*	16
On brig *Riurik* (crown seamen)	28	On cutter *Baranov*	8
			131 [persons]

Freed from service in Okhotsk	13
Sent to various districts	11
Transport:	209 [persons]

In Port

Draper and keeper of materials	2	Repairmen	2
Shipmasters, joiners and turners	10	Tailors	2
Smiths and assistants	6	Roofer, glazier, painter	3
Locksmiths and apprentices	6	Charcoal burner	1
Coppersmiths and apprentices	11	Fisherman	1
Coopers	4	Ship carpenters and carpenters	21
Spinners	4	Sawyers	14
Baidarshchiks	2	Caulkers	2
			93* [persons]

Watchmen	22
Cooks	4
Interpreters	2
Housekeepers	2
In Ozerskii Redoubt	24
	54 [persons]
Remainder	43
Total:	400† [persons]

*Error in original; should be 91. †Should be 397.

One can see that except for 43 men who had no real official status, who were employed as charcoal burners, and those who were sick, one could not even make up a crew of 16 men for a longboat. In 1825 when the ships were sent out on expeditions, there were usually 180 men, including apprentices, remaining in port.

Having given a detailed account of people's occupations, one can see that there was no surplus of personnel in this establishment. In reality, it was impossible to have less than 300 men trained in their jobs. If Sitkha were not the main port and if it existed because of some other circumstance, its garrison would have to consist of no less than 100 armed men. Now, after taking into account the work and sailing, the number of men mentioned above is barely sufficient at the present time.

Above we mentioned two tables of inhabitants — one of which deals with the colonies in 1818, the other with Novo-Arkhangel'sk in particular in 1825. I am adding the following detailed table for the colonies up to 1830 in order to clarify things.

[1. Table on Population in the Colonies by 1830]

	Russians		Creoles		Aleuts		Total		Both Sexes
	M	F	M	F	M	F	M	F	
At Novo-Arkhangel'sk	271	18	128	106	52	47	451	171	622
At Kad'iak proper	104	8	177	187	37	17	3,520	3,506	7,026
On Kad'iak Island in settlements					1,230	1,271			
On mainland					1,972	2,023			
In Unalashka district	23	7	51	52	569	701	643	760	1,403
In Pribylov Islands district	8		17	24	98	92	123	116	239
Fort Ross	35	2	21	32	61	51	117	85	202
In Atkha district	43	1	55	65	298	332	396	398	794
In Kuril district	11		1		59	9	71	9	80
Total	495	36	450	466	4,376	4,543	5,321	5,045	10,366

Up to January 1830, the company paid salaries to 975 of the above-mentioned people, including about a hundred female workers, as shown in the following table.

[2.] Salaries in the Colonies: Administrative Employees of Various Ranks, Promyshlenniks, Creoles, Aleuts, Male and Female, to 1 January 1830

	Number	One [r.]	All [r.]
Chief manager	1	30,000	30,000
Office manager, Novo-Arkhangel'sk	1	12,000	12,000
Naval officer	1	7,000	7,000
Naval officer	5	5,000	25,000
Naval officer	1	4,500	4,500
Employees, officials, and non-officials	4	4,000	16,000
Employees, officials, and non-officials	3	3,500	10,000*
Employees, officials, and non-officials	2	3,000	6,000
Employees, officials, and non-officials	7	2,500	17,000†
Employees, officials, and non-officials	1	2,250	2,250
Employees, officials, and non-officials	2	2,000	4,000
Employees, officials, and non-officials	1	1,800	1,800
Employees, officials, and non-officials	8	1,200	9,600
Employees, officials, and non-officials	3	1,000	3,000
Employees, officials, and non-officials	1	900	900
Employees, officials, and non-officials	2	800	1,600
Employees, officials, and non-officials	2	750	1,500
Employees, officials, and non-officials	5	700	3,500
Employees, promyshlenniks, and creoles	17	600	16,200‡
Employees, promyshlenniks, and creoles	14	500	7,000
Employees, promyshlenniks, and creoles	18	450	8,100
Promyshlenniks and creoles	29	400	11,600
Promyshlenniks and creoles	379	350	132,650
Creoles	36	300	10,800
Creoles	31	250	7,750
Creoles	9	240	2,160
Creoles	1	225	225
Creoles	9	200	1,800
Creoles	19	180	3,420
Creoles	4	175	700
Creoles	2	170	340
Creoles and Aleut workers	11	150	1,650
Creoles and Aleut workers	1	140	140
Creoles and Aleut workers	4	130	520
Creoles and Aleut workers	6	125	750
Creoles and Aleut workers	59	120	7,080
Creoles and Aleut workers	51	100	5,100
Creoles and Aleut workers	17	90	1,530
Creoles and Aleut workers	86	80	6,880
Creoles and Aleut workers	18	70	1,260

Table [2.] — continued

	Number	One [r.]	All [r.]
Creoles and Aleut Workers	32	60	1,920
Creoles and Aleut workers	14	50	700
48 workers	48	25	1,200
	975[‡]		388,125[a]

[*]Error in original; should be 10,500 r. [†]Error in original; should be 17,500 r. [‡][Sic.]
[a]Error in original.

B. RELATIONS OF OFFICIALS, OTHER EMPLOYEES AND PROMYSHLENNIKS TO THE COMPANY

All officials, from the chief manager on down, serve on salaries. They also receive free living quarters, wood, candles and fish from the company. They buy their food and other necessities, all of which is sufficient for them. They have schoolage boys as servants; they buy their foodstuffs from the company store; sometimes these goods are limited in quantity, although there is usually something there.[30] Officials are paid in colonial money every month by the company cashier. The term of service is three to five years. A year before it is time to terminate his service the official is obliged to let the company know whether he intends to continue working or to return to Russia. The return trip is guaranteed according to previous arrangements. Travel allowance and wages are determined according to rank and number of years the official has served the company. Officials cannot buy furs at all.

Formerly, promyshlenniks were hired on the basis of an overall contract [*valovoi kontrakt*]. Finally, on 14 December 1820 the Main Office made a resolution to outline the duties of the workers hired for hunting and other duties in the American colonies. The terms of this resolution are as follows:

> a) Upon entering the service of the company, the worker is to be read this resolution, and by signing it he agrees to fulfill his duties. The company will get him a passport valid for seven years. He is to be issued money so that he can buy the necessary equipment. He is to be paid 70 kopeks per diem for food while travelling. If he makes a round-the-world voy-

age at sea, he must perform his duties as a sailor as assigned. He must obey the captain; if he disobeys the captain's orders, he shall be punished according to naval regulations at sea. In Kronstadt he shall be provided with the necessary rations. Those who travel through Siberia shall receive one ruble per diem as far as the Lena River; while travelling from there to Yakutsk, they shall receive cooked meals. From Yakutsk to Okhotsk they shall walk on foot if there are not enough horses and be given their meals at company expense.

b) Upon arriving in Okhotsk they will be at the company's disposal; they shall board ship for America and begin their assignments. In Okhotsk and during their voyage at sea they shall be given rations at company expense. Upon leaving Okhotsk their accounts shall be taken aboard with them.

c) Upon arriving in the colonies they shall be under the jurisdiction of the Main Manager or office managers; and they shall carry out their duties according to their abilities; they shall pledge to obey the management at all times.

d) The promyshlennik shall not engage in fur trading with the natives or foreigners. Should he do so, everything he has gained shall be confiscated.

e) He shall avoid all vices: drunkenness, extravagance, quarrelling and other crimes and not accumulate large debts.

f) The length of service is seven years. After his service he shall return to his homeland if he has no debts and decides to do so. The company shall not stand in the way of his decision. He shall be shipped out on the first available ship by way of Okhotsk or around the world at company expense. Upon his departure he shall receive an accurate accounting: a month after leaving for Okhotsk or St. Petersburg, he shall no longer be considered a company employee. Each employee who owes debts must pay be serving the company and should not ask to be dismissed and should not complain.

g) Upon returning to Kronstadt or St. Petersburg they should not leave the ship before it has been unloaded.

For its part the company shall be obliged to perform the following duties for its employees:

Wages (Salaries)

1) It shall issue the new employee 350 rubles a year the moment he boards ship to the day he boards ship to return home.[31] If he returns home around the world he shall receive payment equal to that given to the ship's crew; if he passes by

way of Okhotsk he shall receive 15 rubles a month until the ship has been unloaded.

Payment

2) Debts shall not be deducted from the new employee's pay before arriving in the colonies; he shall be paid monthly in the colonies with up to one-third deducted to pay off his debts.

Rations

3) Upon their arrival in the colonies he shall be issued a flour ration in addition to his salary. He shall receive one pud of flour per month when available. He shall receive said ration until the day he leaves for his homeland. At sea he shall be issued rations. Should there be a shortage of flour, he shall be paid five rubles per pud.

The Payment of Taxes

4) The company shall pay government taxes on his behalf as follows: those who have money deducted from their pay for their relatives more than one-third, an annual sum of no more than 50 rubles.

Medical Treatment

5) In case of sickness he shall be treated by a doctor at company expense, and no deductions shall be made from his pay.

The Price of Goods

6) The company must have clothing and footwear in the colonies to supply its employees, but they shall pay a price set by the chief manager depending on local circumstances.

Colonial Products

7) Colonial foodstuffs shall be issued without cost by the company at a measure determined by the management. Foodstuffs for the navy shall also be issued by the company.

Bonuses

8) If anyone performs meritorious service, the company shall reward him through the chief manager, in accordance with his authority.[32]

This regulation has been made known to all entering the service of the company as part of a mutual agreement. Chief Manager Matvei Ivanovich Murav'ev decided that in addition to flour rations, the store could also sell the following on a monthly basis:

1) To unmarried promyshlenniks, 15 funts of flour, 6 funts of groats and 6 funts of peas.[33]

2) To married promyshlenniks without children, 30 funts of flour, 8 funts of groats and 10 funts of peas.

3) To married promyshlenniks with children: the same amount of flour, groats and peas as that assigned to promyshlenniks without children; with 4 funts of groats and 6 funts of peas per child.

Other products will be sold based on their availability. Each person is assigned between three-quarters and one funt of tea per month, two to three funts of sugar and one bottle of molasses and one funt of tobacco.

Goods which are abundant are sold freely.

On his name-day each promyshlennik and Creole receives a bottle of rum from the store; the best workers get two bottles. On major holidays anyone can buy half a bottle and sometimes a cup per person. When there is a surplus of rum it is sold more frequently; where there is a shortage of it, it is sold less often.

According to regulations of Chief Manager Mr. Hagemeister, a cup of rum is issued at company expense eight times a year: (1) Epiphany, (2) Easter, (3) Archangel Michael's Day on 8 November, which is a church holiday, (4) Christmas, (5) birthdays, (6) saints' (namesake) days, (7) day of ascension to the throne, and (8) day of the Emperor's coronation.

[4.] Priests' Rations Issued by the Company in Kind [per Year?]

Rye flour	30 puds	Vodka	1 vedro
Wheat flour	10 puds	Circassian tobacco	2½ puds
Rich rolls	3 puds	Sugar	2 puds
Rye hardtack	5 puds	Black tea	10 funts
Groats	5 puds	Soap	2½ puds
Butter	3 puds	Tallow candles	2½ puds

1833 [Yield of] Private Gardens

	[barrels of] potatoes		[barrels of] potatoes
From Tebenkov [Teben'kov]	28	Elisaveta Klimovskaia	27
From Razinberkh [Rozenberg]	21½	Min'ka Kalistratov	32
From Shelikhov	24	Ivan Chernov	23
From Banztinov [Benzeman?]	30	Aleksei Repin	12
From Abramov and Solodovnikov	17	Petr Kin'dlikov	16
From Ermolaev	10	Vasilii Bykov	4
Father Aleksei	20	Nikolai Chichenev	1½
Filipp Koshevarov [Kashevarov]	60	Agafei Milovidov	2
		Gedeon — interpreter	4
		Total:	337*
		Company:	190
			527*

*[Sic.] Weight of a barrel of potatoes: 4 puds, 23 funts; 530 [barrels] x 4.5 = 2,385.0 [puds] + 39 = 2,424 [puds].

C. RELATIONS OF CREOLES [TO THE COMPANY]

In a dispatch sent to the chief manager on 28 February 1827, No. 157, the Main Office (Board of Directors), stated as follows:

> The company management gives you permission to announce everywhere that should any Creole child lose his father, as well as those born out of wedlock, he shall be taken care of by the company. Up to the age of 16 he shall receive the same care which is now being given to our apprentices; from 16 to 20 he shall be assigned duties according to his abilities and be given the proper necessities according to the position they occupy; from 20 to 29 he shall be paid a salary based on his training, abilities and productivity and dedication to the company. He shall receive 100 to 350 rubles, including clothing and rations; those who show merit and outstanding work while performing as prikazchiks shall be given special privileges and awarded a rank becoming them.

Because Creoles have managed to attain Imperial privileges, which have put them in a different class status, their rights have been defined in article 41. In resolution No. 336 of the Novo-Arkhangel'sk office on December 1822, Chief Manager Matvei Ivanovich Murav'ev clarified the higher privileges in the following paragraph:

Creoles who do not have their fathers' status, that is, those born out of wedlock and are not registered anywhere in the latest census, are citizens of the colonies and Russian subjects. They enjoy all rights of this citizenship and are protected by the laws, to which they are also subject and are accountable to. The government relieves them of all responsibilities by entrusting them under the protection of the chief manager and his offices, and he is entrusted to watch over their welfare and property. In order to achieve this goal, the colonial authorities must watch over their moral behavior sternly and not allow them to regress to a wild state. Once they have become acquainted with the European way of life, the colonial authorities should make sure that the Creoles do not regress. Those who are capable of performing household chores or have an inclination towards agriculture or gardening should get the company's help in developing such industry. Married people and those with children should be given first choice; the colonial authorities should make sure that the help from the company not be wasted and that it should be allocated to those who truly are capable. Those who are not eligible for such work, that is those who are single and without children, who have been working as tradesmen and sailors for some time, may enter the service of the company freely, but this freedom to do so should be limited by the same reasons which apply to the Russian promyshlenniks. They should perform their duties well and make sure their debts to the company are paid. For the most part, the Creoles are obligated to the company because of their initial education and upbringing, and educated in such a manner, they are obliged to serve the company until the age of 29, in accordance with regulations from the Main Office.

Creoles not in the service of the company cannot by any means be used by the company for company labor without being paid or without their consent. They shall have full freedom to hunt in accordance with regulation No. 51, which states: "everything they hunt shall belong to them; it is understood, however, that they cannot and shall not obtain any privileges. That is all animal furs cannot be sold to anyone but the company, although they have the right to use furs for their own personal use. They have no right to demand wages or company goods or any contract from the company. In the event of some misfortune, however, the company shall not refuse to help them; but this hope should not allow them to get lazy; therefore, those who are incapable of feeding themselves because of their idleness vagrancy shall immediately be taken into the service of the company for one year but given less pay. He shall not, however, be taken away from his family. Should his wife and children be employed by the company they shall be paid equal wage so as to prevent any form of oppression. The office manager, before making a decision, should gather the necessary information concerning the behavior of the guilty party and write it all down in his penalty book. In case of distress and poverty resulting from illness or misfortune, then all help should be rendered by the company as means will allow it. By giving rights and privileges to the Creoles, the government charged the chief manager with the supervision of the Creoles and well-being, by establishing the following:

Censuses of the Creoles

1) The office is obliged to compile an accurate list of Creoles, showing the number of males and females, their age and status, and to determine where each person should be assigned. The office manager shall affix his own testimony concerning their behavior and abilities; no matter where they live, the Creoles shall be registered in two offices: either in Kad'iak or Unalashka; because their mothers belonged to both areas with few exceptions; but such exceptions shall not be reason for changing the rules. A person born in Unalashka can be registered as a citizen of Kad'iak and vice versa; because marriage and other family ties may put him in two areas. Before a person can move to another area, he or she must give this in writing to the office and indicate his reasons for the move. Once this has been approved he may move and register at the other office and be taken off the register of another office. It is strictly forbidden to leave without permission. Such an act shall be considered one of vagrancy.

2) All Creoles shall be gathered at the office and be read the privileges and rules granted by the Emperor, as well as the supplement to article 41.

3) They shall be asked whether they want to remain in the service of the company. Those who are willing to do so shall be paid a salary of 100 to 300 rubles, making sure that this money is sufficient for their needs and properly rewards them for their abilities. Payment shall be made according to his work and abilities to perform such work; they shall be told that while in the service of the company, they shall be subject to the same laws applicable to Russian promyshlenniks in the colonies, excluding their term of service. I believe that the Creoles' term of service should be three years. All who enter the service shall sign an agreement; those who do not wish to serve the company have the right to do so as long as they do not owe the company any debts and wish to live by themselves (and such people should be honest, mature and diligent) if they decide not to work for the company, then they should be asked

> how they propose to live and where they plan to live. They are then told that they belong to the jurisdiction of the closest artel and should they be in need of anything they should direct themselves to the local administration without whose permission they cannot move and under whose jurisdiction they shall find themselves. Should they have any complaints, they may petition the office manager and even the chief manager. The office assigns housing where they choose to live and they are registered in that area; the office allows them to move to the area of their choice as long as it does not interfere with the rights of others. The office shall give them any necessary assistance to settle seeing to it that such assistance is sufficient. If the Creole, living by himself, decided to hunt animals, with his relatives, he shall not be denied this right and he must be in the [hunting] party under the general rules.

Upon his arrival on 15 December 1820, Chief Manager Mr. Matvei Ivanovich Murav'ev issued the following regulation [No. 105] dealing with the schools:

> In an attempt to carry out the good intentions of the Russian-American Company, I have decided to establish a staff to feed and clothe the students in Novo-Arkhangel'sk. This staff, established on an economical basis, shall be provided for by the office. The office shall take notice that the list of foodstuffs may be insufficient. This was done because it was extremely hard to obtain such provisions and because the students should have fresh garden produce in addition to fresh fish, salted fish, whale and seal meat; and when possible, they should also have fats and oils. In addition to the teacher and his aid the school shall have someone to supervise minors; this person shall be responsible for all their food, linens and clothing. A woman of high morals, an Aleut, shall be assigned to wash and clean the students and she shall be paid 100 rubles a year. All expenses shall be paid from the account designated for social welfare.

Although nothing is mentioned in the regulations of the Main Office concerning rations which might be given to Creoles during shortages, from this time on they shall receive one pud or half a pud of flour per month; and if they serve at sea they will be allotted sea rations.

Due to recurring shortages of fish in Sitkha it was necessary, in addition to rations, to allow them to buy foodstuffs from the company store. Rations were set as follows: married people —

six funts of groats, six funts of peas; each child — four funts of groats and four funts of peas.

Clothing and Food Allowance of Thirty Pupils

	[No. of] Pair	For Each r.	k.	Total r.	k.
Per 1 pair warm coats of grey cloth with a lining of coarse cloth	30	@ 12	50	375	
Per 1 pair summer clothing of ticking	30	6	50	195	
Per 3 pair shoes of tanned leather	90	1	50	135	
For 3 shirts of low-quality canvas	90	2	50	202	50*
For 1 cap	30		50	15	
For 3 arshins coarse cloth for stockings	90 arshins		30	27	
		[Total:]		949	50

*[Sic.]

Provisions

	Each funts	All puds	All funts	r.	k.	r.	k.
Per month:							
flour	10	7	20				
groats	5	3	30				
peas	5	3	30				
Per year:							
flour		90		@ 5		450	
groats		45		4	80	240*	
peas		45		4	80	240*	
						930†	
Paper, ink, pencils, etc.						70	50
Washerwoman's salary						100	
Total per year:						2,050‡	

*Error in original; should be 216 r. †Should be 882 r. ‡Should be 2,002 r.

The source or richness and strength of these regions comes from the people; there is no better time than now to explain the advantages which were foreseen by the late Chancellor Rezanov while he visited these colonies. In his report No. 478, Chapter V, he wrote:

> The true strength of these regions lies in increasing the number of settlements and its population. The main subject of any well established government should be the growth of its population. It is from the people that the sources of industry flow in order to satisfy personal and social needs such as agriculture, construction, crafts, and various economic branches. With such a population we can have the men needed for a defense force, which will grow with the success and growth of popular enterprise. With this growth in industry the people will have the means to care for themselves.

In the same report, part 3, he states:

> Those who come from decent families and who have been educated by the company should have been instilled the desire to hunt and work ever since they were born. These persons should be assigned to various positions in accordance with their abilities.

In Chapter VI, on schools, he states:

> From these people you shall derive your military personnel, farmers, craftsmen, builders, prikazchiks, accountants, and in time managers themselves. With the increase of the number of schools, you will help to take care of the orphans and you will render humanity a great service.

What has education accomplished here? In 1805 Mr. Rezanov thought that in a 20-year period we would see sailors, accountants, prikazchiks, many talented craftsmen and excellent builders come from these people. It is unfortunate that because they lack basic education, they do not have maturity and firmness of character, and while understanding Russian rules for good behavior, they do fall to the temptation of vices: above all, the use of strong drink, which for many has resulted in death.[34]

For the sake of the well-being and advantages of the company, and of the fatherland we hope this generation has better success.

Earlier, it was necessary to send the Creoles to St. Petersburg so that they could be taught navigational skills. But experience has shown that they can acquire the necessary skills in the colonies without the great expenditures of sending them to the capital to be educated. There are many examples of persons who studied shipbuilding and returned without understanding either theory or the practical application of the science, and because of that they are of no use. Several of them understand navigational skills quite well, but while in the capital they developed a taste for luxurious things and acquired bad habits. Young people everywhere always follow examples: in a small society they are subject to one person along with the watchful eye of the father; in such a small society there can be no such vices as in a large city. Here crime, for example, deceit, and theft cannot be hidden for long and is quickly discovered; the guilty party is immediately punished according to his crime. But those who go into the worldly city cannot know how crimes are discovered and are punished. Therefore, there is less crime here. There were cases here of people rooted in vice; but because we did not tolerate vice, they eventually gave up their evil ways and became useful citizens.

Drunkenness is the only vice of the natives. But this is something we can understand. When drinking is done in the open, people abuse it all the time; but where can you not find people free of this passion? Here, where there are few pleasures, some take the opportunity to get drunk and have a good time. However, in the colonies it is generally impossible to find enough drink to feed this vice.

Based on examples, we have noticed that the Creoles who studied here in the local schools and ships, have worked out quite well. Some who are apprentice seafarers command small vessels; some are accountants and prikazchiks, who know their jobs; there are coppersmiths who have great skill and who are not inferior to their teachers. Soon, we hope to have students who will study medicine, surgery and navigation.

It would be desirable if Russian men were forbidden to marry Creole women and take them back to Russia so that the native population could increase. In Russia, where these women are subjected to changes in climate, they do not live very long; or, if their husbands abandon them they end up living in poverty. It would be desirable if marital life and family bonds were encouraged. Only in this manner can healthy citizens be created.

D. RELATION OF ALEUTS TO THE COMPANY

In the privileges granted to the company by the Emperor in 1821, there are rules set concerning the relationship of the islanders to the company, as stated in paragraphs 43 through 57. Chief Manager Matvei Ivanovich Murav'ev, in carrying out these rules, clarified several points in his regulations to the various offices in numbers 337, 338 and 339 for 1822 and numbers 55, 59, 98 and 211 for the year 1823 in which he states:

> Maintain the islanders in their present way of life and keep a census of the population, of both sexes, births and deaths; of the numbers of those who have been baptized and those who were newly baptized, keeping in mind the differences between the Creoles and the [native] Americans who are either present or absent, differentiating their sex and age. The other offices are obliged to send such listings to the main office in Novo-Arkhangel'sk. This particular office shall have a special file to keep this information.
>
> The islanders shall be governed by their own toions under the supervision of elders. In order to do this, two such persons shall be chosen from the best Russian employees, who shall, along with the toions, have the duties of watching over the islanders placed in their hands. They shall have to investigate fights and complaints and help them in their needs. Should any differences arise between the islanders and the toions, then the Chief Manager shall decide matters.
>
> The islanders, that is all males 18 to 50, shall be obliged to hunt for the company. Half of the islanders shall be used to perform company duties; they shall be advised of this in the month of January; zakashchiks and toions shall meet in the main settlement and get their orders from the office managers. The office should be careful that in choosing hunters they choose from families with more than one male so that a wife and children are not left helpless or without food.
>
> The colonial powers must strive to acquaint the islanders with the advantages of social (civilized) life; they should be given the necessary amount of land to develop gardening; they should receive not only advice but also tools and seeds. The office manager can render this help at company expense. In

order to encourage agriculture, those who excel shall be presented to the chief manager and rewarded for their good work.

These islanders, being Russian subjects, are protected under the law and consequently, their personal property and rights are inviolable. The office shall be obliged to prosecute with severity anyone who breaks the law. American natives not in the company service, but who hunt on their own with their own equipment, have the right to hunt land and marine animals near their dwellings and cannot go farther without the permission of the authorities. Everything they catch will belong to them. But if they want to sell the furs, they shall have to sell them to the company. Those who are engaged in hunting parties and maintained by the company, shall not have the right to keep any furs for their own use; they must turn over everything without exception to the company which shall pay the hunters in accordance with the set regulations. This particular sacrifice is the only obligation that these natives make to the Russian government, and the company takes advantage of this since it makes the initial investment in organizing these parties.

The islanders shall be paid not less than one-fifth of the amount which was paid previously to Russian promyshlenniks for their furs based on the gross catch.

This is the first real statement dealing with the relationship of the islanders to the company and it is still in effect today. It was stated above that in 1816 the company decided to issue lavtaks for each baidarka and clothing for the Aleuts. It is done in the following manner:

For a two-man baidarka:

	r.	[Sum] r.
6 bachelor fur seal lavtaks	at 3	18
2 gut kamleis	at 5	10
7 funts of seal whiskers for ties, whale sinew for sewing, portion of whale fat		at 2
	Total:	30

When Aleut hunting parties are sent out, the company supplies them with guns and a sufficient amount of bullets which they use to kill seals for food. They are also given fishhooks and line for fishing and each man receives a funt or two of tobacco. When necessary, the party is issued two to three cups of rum per person. When they travel on sailing vessels, they are issued a ration of bread; the hunting party is also issued a certain amount of flour.

When the Aleuts perform work in port or in the forest or in the company gardens, each man is paid a ruble a day, and in bad weather they are issued one cup of vodka. During the summer the Aleut women clean fish for the company at the Ozerskii Redoubt and at the [Novo-Arkhangel'sk] port, for which they receive 50 kopeks a day.

If the company needs new baidarkas or to have them repaired, it pays a particular price for them. For a three-man baidarka, 15 rubles; for repairs, 5 to 10 rubles depending on the work which needs to be done.

In general, the Aleuts and their women are always paid for their work. Should any baidarka be sent out to the Ozerskii Redoubt or to the hot springs in the winter or spring and the Aleuts are not paid, they are given lavtaks by the company so that they may repair their baidarkas in the fall and winter.

When the Aleuts are sent out in parties, they get their supplies, which cost 10 to 30 rubles, on account: then later the amount is deducted from the profit made from the hunt. But many do not do this, so that if they have return with a successful hunt they can get all the profits from it. They have various ways of making money and are allowed to buy provisions and goods from the company store. When they are in need, the company issues a ration of flour and other provisions. The Aleuts get the same amount of rum that the regular employees get during the holidays and have permission to buy a cup of rum for themselves when there is such a sale.

Payment for sea otters was set in accordance with the regulations made by the Main Office (Governing Board), at one-fifth of the sale price — that is, ten rubles for a matka [large pelt], four rubles for a koshlok [medium] and 80 kopeks for a medvedka [small one]. Considering that the prices for garden produce have gone up significantly along with the prices for Russian and foreign goods and that the prices of sea otters are also higher, the present chief manager, P. E. Chistiakov, has ordered that the payment for sea otter pelts be increased by 50 percent and has advised the Main Office of this situation.

One of the articles of rules and privileges granted by the Emperor to the company has remained unchanged till now: paragraph 56 allows the islanders to sell their pelts to the company at a sale price which the company is obliged to declare to the government for approval.[35]

So that the advantages of the company equal those of the islanders, they must be paid for their labor in accordance with government regulations but more than the prices set in the general contract. Of course, the price for pelts has increased. And in order to buy goods abroad, it is necessary to have a vessel in order to transport these goods, and there is also the cost to maintain a crew. Even today when we have a 100 percent markup, we still have a loss. In such a trade, we should have a 200 percent markup in the sale of pelts in order to make a profit at all. Or it will be impossible to continue this type of work.

If the Aleuts continue to hunt based on the aforesaid conditions, they will continue to make a profit because they will continue to hunt the sea otters in the same baidarkas, which are issued to them by the company. The land animals also have to be caught with company traps, which the Aleuts do not have and cannot make because of lack of materials, which are distributed by local authorities when needed.

Undoubtedly, there are various people working for the company who do not abide by the conditions set by contract and who can pay three times more than the company for pelts, hoping to hide their resources in some way; this should not be an example since it is an abuse which is forbidden by law.

It would be fair to say that the company, which gets goods from St. Petersburg around the world for Russians as well as the islanders, charges only 30 percent for transportation and 10 or 15 percent on goods purchased elsewhere; consequently, the company makes no profit at all; it simply sells goods at cost. If a merchant does not make a profit or earn interest on his money, then he loses all advantages.

This particular fact makes it necessary that the company and the islanders both comply with conditions of the contracts because without mutual compliance the company could lose its balance and profits.

E. MEANS OF SUPPLYING PEOPLE WITH PROVISIONS

From the time when the promyshlenniks were paid wages, that is when Mr. Baranov was replaced, the company remained obliged to supply the people with flour. For that reason ships were sent to California every year, where they traded for wheat, barley and other grain. Above, it was mentioned what amounts persons from lower ranks could receive.

In Novo-Arkhangel'sk the flour ration in the winter amounted to 300 puds or more; in the summer 200; up to 200 puds of flour, peas and groats and other grain are sold in the winter; 100 puds in the summer. The following chart [p. 89] will show expenses for 1825.

Rusks are baked in port. It is for this purpose that two bakeries were built. Two or three men work there all winter long. Five hundred to six hundred puds of rusks are baked there. Twenty-eight funts of rusks can be baked out of one pud of flour [see Table 2, p. 89].[36]

Detailed Expenditures

Rations for Promyshlenniks:

		[puds/funts]			[puds/funts]
1825:	January	337.23	1825:	April	336.04
	February	313.21		May	260.05
	March	311.36		June	177.10
1825:	July	173.10	1825:	October	269.06
	August	236.06		November	268.10
	September	248.30		December	263.10
					3.195 puds, 10 funts*

1825:	Jan. wheat	13.18	Feb. wheat	17.32
	wheat flour	129.30	flour	131.35
	hardtack	4.14	peas	1.37
	peas	4	wheat	4
	maize	6.04	barley	7.15
	barley	1.33	hardtack	1.08
		157 puds, 19 funts†		164 puds, 7 funts

*Error in original; should be 3,195 puds, 11 funts. †[Sic.]

Similar amounts were spent in later months.

1. *Table on Expenditures for Provisions in Novo-Arkhangel'sk, 1825*

Demand [in puds]	Flour	Wheat	Peas and Beans	Millet	Low Groats [by sort]	Barley	Hardtack	Total [puds, funts]
Share of employees	3,195¼							3,195.10
Ship provisions	28		33½	87¼	82		578½	809.10
Schools and hospitals	119		3	33	2		5	125.50[a]
Expenditures in port	179		8.6	2.15			105.15	294.36

[a]Error in the original; should be 162 puds.

[2. *Table of Foodstuffs Used in Novo-Arkhangel'sk and in Districts, 1825]*

Demand [in puds]	Flour	Wheat	Peas and Beans	Millet	Low Groats [by sort]	Barley	Hardtack	Total [puds, funts]
[In Novo-Arkhangel'sk]								
Sold at store	1,639½	39.35	23½	215		124¼	124.36	2,167.28 [*]
Salary of officials	90¾			20½			4.20	115.30
In Ozerskoi Redoubt								
Shares	370							370
Sale	131							131
At the jetty		424.34						424.34
	5,752½	464¾	68 [†]	358[†]	84	124¼	818¼	7,633.30 [‡]
In Districts								
Nushagak	31.20	174		40.30		82½		328.29 [a]
Unalashka		355½		72.20		132	8.27	568.30 [b]
[St.] Paul Is.		119		28.31		51.35		199.33 [c]
[St.] George Is.		60		21.14		24.30		106.4
Atkha				21.5				21.5
Nuchek		39		20.37		33		92.37
Ross office				41			9.19	51.04 [†]
Kad'iak		4,985.10		124		198	19.26	[5,328.36][†]
Total	5,784	6,197.10 [†]	68 [†]	728.32 [†]	84	646.15	856.20	14,364.20 [d]

[*]Error in original; should be 2,167 puds, 1 funt. [†][Sic.] [‡]Should be 7,670 puds, 1 funt. [a]Should be 328 puds, 30 funts. [b]Should be 568 puds, 27 funts. [c]Should be 199 puds, 26 funts. [d]Error in original.

In addition to bread, fish is the main source of food, which the company prepares in the following manner.

In February and March herring appear near the shore and are caught in nets in various areas near the Novo-Arkhangel'sk fortress. The promyshlenniks do not eat fresh herring, and for that reason they salt the fish and issue it salted. As long as the herring keeps running, they salt it and preserve in 6 to 8 vats or 20 to 30 barrels; red salmon are caught in traps built near Ozerskii Redoubt; at first few are caught, but from the middle of June more and more are caught; after that the gorbusha [pink] and khaiko [chum] salmon begins its run and then the kizhuch [silver]. They do not begin salting until the run is large; fresh fish is sent by baidarkas [to Novo-Arkhangel'sk] until then. Salting begins in June and lasts until September. One hundred twenty to 180 barrels of various fish are salted at the redoubt; five puds of salt are used per barrel. The quantity of salted fish per barrel is estimated as follows: red salmon, 200; chum and silver salmon, 100; or 150 on the average. As a result, the redoubt salts nearly 20,000 fish,[37] and in addition to that they smoke 10,000 fish into iukola for the Aleuts, which they manage to smoke with great difficulty because of the damp weather, and the already dried fish is spoiled by rats, so that only half of it is eventually used for food.

Meanwhile at the end of June and July the pink salmon makes its run near the fort; then appear the chum and silver salmon which are caught in nets. A special boat with nine men is used for such fishing. This is enough to supply those in the fort with fresh fish, and moreover 20 to 30 barrels are salted.

Based on new calculations it appears that the above-mentioned figures dealing with salted fish at the Ozerskii Redoubt are incorrect. This was brought to our attention by the commander of the redoubt, Mr. Slobodchikov; as it turned out, he was correct and therefore the fish had to be salted all over again so that the count would be correct. Salted fish for 1828 was the following:

[3. Table on Salting Fish at Ozerskii Redoubt and Consumption of Salt Fish at Novo-Arkhangel'sk, 1828]

		Amount of salt used in puds
In 1st bin salted red salmon in June	11,700 reds	195

		Amount of salt used in puds
In 2nd bin in June and beginning of July	13,530 reds	275
In 3rd bin in July and August	11,710 reds	262
	36,940 reds	732
For vessels and officials at [Novo-Arkhangel'sk] port:	11 kegs	25
12 vats of red salmon	14,500 reds	27
8 vats of herring	[. . .]	47
Total	51,440 reds	1,021*

*[Sic.]

Use [of Fish]

At fort issued daily up to 125 puds
Per week up to 900 puds
For those sent into woods for charcoal 300 to 400 puds of fish undressed

In one month used up to 5,200 puds of fish

[4.] Extracts of Figures of Fish Preparation at Various Times, for Comparison

1821	Barrels	1822	Barrels	1823	Barrels
20 July at port		*5 July at port*		*1 July at port*	
herring	8				
red salmon	20	herring	8	herring	16
chum and pink	5	red and other	30	chum and pink	28
At [Ozerskii] Redoubt		*At [Ozerskii] Redoubt*		*At [Ozerskii] Redoubt*	
red fish	37		72	red fish	58
chum and pink	40			in first store	40
	110		110		142

One and a half barrels of fish are used daily in the winter to provide food for the people. Out of this number 35 fish are issued to the artel in the barracks, and 25 are used in a common kettle from which people living in their own homes receive a portion. Those who perform outstanding service receive special rations.

From the month of November the Aleuts are equipped in two or three rowing vessels in order to fish for halibut; they are hired at ten rubles a person per month; there are usually eight rowers and two foremen in each boat. They sail to the hot springs and from there they sail into the bays where they set their lines in appropriate places. The following list will show much fish was caught:

[5. Extract, Fish Catch, 1825-1828]

		puds			puds
1825:	October	130	1827:	October	65
	November	101½		November	196
	December	107		December	146½
1826:	January	114	1828:	January	190
	February	221		February	92
	March	107		March	178
	April	79½		April	77½
	Total	860		Total	945

The first fish go to the hospital, then to the garrison and officials. The garrison is issued eight puds of fish a day.

During the holidays the garrison gets half a funt of meat per man. In all, including the meat issued to the families, the company issues six to seven puds of meat a day at its own expense.

The company also raises potatoes, of which they cultivated up to 150 puds in 1825 in local gardens. These are primarily used to feed the sick and school children daily; while six to eight kegs are issued to the garrison per month in the winter, beginning in November.

When the hunting parties return in August, the Aleuts are sent along the rivers where the fish are running and catch as much as they will need. When the weather is calm in the winter they sail out into the strait to catch codfish, halibut, turbot, and perch which they catch for their own needs. Anything above that, sometimes more than half of what they catch, they sell to the local inhabitants. There have been times when they had shortages of fish and the Aleuts were supplied food by the company.

Sea lions, which are rarely hunted, cannot be considered a part of the food used to supply the people, although this meat is eagerly eaten. If a whale happens to wash ashore, this delicacy is used by the Aleuts because they are so fond of the blubber.

Food supplies of this type can be gotten from the nearby islands — salted and smoked seal and sea lion meat, and fat. From Unalashka they get whale blubber, from Kad'iak — iukola, berries and seal oil, but nothing in great quantity.

The oil is used mainly for lighting lamps. No less than 30 barrels are used yearly for this purpose. Oil is the only source of lighting in the barracks, the Aleut kazhim, on vessels and in private homes. Oil is also issued to the Aleuts as food and is also used to grease their baidarkas, because without it they would quickly deteriorate. It is also used at the mill instead of grease. It is widely used at the tanning factory and by the caulkers. Each barracks is issued six to seven funts of oil for three lamps to be used in the wintertime. When there is not enough oil, we are obliged to buy it from the Kolosh at ten rubles a pud. If they do not have any, then they use animal fat in the lamps.

In the spring it is possible to extract oil from herring if the catch is large. In times of need it is a good substitute. It can also be used as food; it does not have a bad odor and it is pure. In one day one man can extract three buckets of herring oil using three kettles.

F. HUNTING METHODS

In the section dealing with the hunting of sea otters around Sitkha it was stated that even during Mr. Baranov's administration there had already been a gradual decline in the number of sea otters. After his replacement, Chief Manager Hagemeister concluded an agreement with Mr. Roquefeuille, the captain of the vessel *Bordelais*. This hunting agreement was similar to the one concluded by Mr. Baranov and the Americans.

On 20 April 1818 Mr. Roquefeuille sailed out of [Novo-Arkhangel'sk] port for Kad'iak for the purpose of taking on the necessary number of baidarkas and then sailing for the strait. On 15 June the *Bordelais* returned to Sitkha with the sad news that after they arrived in the strait and set up camp on one of the islands, they encountered open hostility from the Kolosh. This incident took place in an area which the [native?] Americans call by its Kolosh name *Nepada*. It is located in the Prince of Wales

[1. Table Showing Where and How Many Baidarkas Hunted and Their Catch, 1818-1832]

Year	Sailing Vessels Accompanying	Commander and Chief of Party	Where They Hunted	Number of Baidarkas	Number of Pelts
1818	*Finliandiia* *Platov*	Young and Eremin Likhachev	Frederick Sound and environs	100	416 large and medium 30 pups
1819	*Finliandiia* *Baranov*	Young, Tarakanov Tumanin	Cross Sound and Chastykh Islands	80	296 large 18 small
1820	*Baranov* *Fortuna*	Tumanin Eremin	Chastykh Islands and Chatham Strait	80	205
1821	*Chirikov* *Fortuna*	Young, Eremin Tumanin, Dorofeev	In Straits and Chastykh Islands	100	47
1822	*Rumiantsev* *Fortuna*	Pometilov, Molvistov Ingestrom	Yakutat and L'tua	60	323
1823	*Riurik* *Fortuna*	V. S. Khramchenko, Nosov Pometilov	Yakutat and L'tua	90	362
1824	*Golovnin* *Fortuna*	Young, Nosov Pometilov	Yakutat and L'tua	55	247
1825	*Rurik* [*Riurik*] *Fortuna*	V. S. Khramchenko, Nosov Ingestrom	Yakutat and L'tua	85	460
1826	*Riurik* *Fortuna*	P. D. Lipinskii, Nosov Pometilov	Yakutat and L'tua	79	268
1826, 1827	*Riurik* *Fortuna*	P. D. Lipinskii, Terent'ev Pometilov	Yakutat and L'tua		250
1828 and later	None were sent hunting.				
1832	*Polifem*	Lt. Prokof'ev, Plat[...?], Lt. Mit'kov, Pankin(?), Nosov	Yakutat and L'tua	30	145 sea otters and pups

Archipelago in a bay on the south side of Cape Pele. When the Aleuts had gathered ashore to rest, the Kolosh began to fire upon them from the forest. They killed 20 Aleuts [men] and 3 women. Twelve swam away, wounded. Captain Roquefeuille, who was walking along the shore, took off his clothes [*plat'e*] and swam towards the ship. The Kolosh also shot at him, but he got away safely. After this incident, we no longer had any more dealings with foreigners in hunting matters. In 1819, 1820 and 1821, we sent out hunting parties under the protection of well-armed ships; but the Kolosh constituted an obstacle everywhere we went.

Table 1 [p. 94] shows when, where and how many baidarkas were used by hunting parties, including the type of game taken. However, it must be noted that the party sent to Kek Strait [Prince Frederick Sound] found few sea otters. That is the area where great numbers of sea otters had been taken in previous years. In 1805, 300 baidarkas brought back 1,645 pelts. When our baidarkas began to go after the sea otters, several Kolosh boats started hunting and shooting sea otters in the same area; there were numerous fights. The Kolosh captured one of our baidarkas, but it was returned through our commander's intercession.

The number of sea otters hunted by each baidarka varies. The most experienced and successful hunters took ten to thirteen; those who were not so lucky got one or none at all. The following table shows the results of hunting along the Northwest Coast for a three-year period.

[2. Sea Otter Catch per Baidarka]

	1 to 3	3 to 5	5 to 8	8 to 11	11 to 14
1823 No. of baidarkas	36	32	10	7	3
1824 No. of baidarkas	11	18	16	6	3
1825 No. of baidarkas	13	20	32	14	5

G. TRADE METHODS

Former fur companies knew no other means of trading than the barter of fur from the islanders for goods which they brought on ships. Due to a shortage of goods and food provisions for his promyshlenniks and Aleuts, Mr. Baranov established trade with

American and British shipmasters. Mr. Baranov's successors continued these relationships even when trade was prohibited in the colonies, and it had to be carried out in adjoining areas. Mr. Rezanov established trade with California. Mr. Kuskov traded with the Spanish several times, and later he established permanent relations with that state. Mr. Baranov had intended to occupy several of the Sandwich Islands. His commissioner, Dr. Shaeffer, had begun this venture quite successfully, but it eventually ended in failure. After Mr. Baranov was replaced, there were several opportunities to have ties with these islands; salt and foreign goods were purchased there. Trade with the Kolosh also was a great source for exchange of furs for different types of goods. But the bulk of Russian and foreign goods was used to supply the people in the colonies. I propose the following detailed account of trade relations in subsequent chapters.

1. Trade Methods with Foreigners

When Mr. Baranov was replaced, trade relations with foreigners were continued by his successors. Since Mr. Baranov owed debts, they also transferred to them; while others (foreigners), who had not sold their goods, had left them here for safekeeping. All of these goods were bought from them, and it was in such a way that trade with them was established and was carried out in the following manner:

[a.] Payments Made by Novo-Arkhangel'sk Office for Provisions and Other Goods Supplied by Foreign Merchants, 1818-1832

Ships and Captains and Sum Paid for Goods	piasters	cents	Payments [by Novo-Arkhangel'sk Office]
1818			
Thomas Meek, ship *Eagle*: goods	2,346		1,211 fur seals at 1¾
Mr. Roquefeuille, French captain, ship *Bordelais*: 626 fanegas of wheat, 775 arrobas of tallow, various goods	5,514	06	Payments made with various accounts
1819			
Ship *Brutus*, Captain Nye: goods	4,917	83	2,700 fur seals at 1¾
Brig *Brutus* with armament, for 5,000 fur seals	[. . .]	[. . .]	5,000 seals

Table [a.] — continued

Ships and Captains and Sum Paid for Goods	piasters	cents	Payments [by Novo-Arkhangel'sk Office]
Thomas Meek, ship *Eagle*: goods	1,789	97	605 seals at 1¾, remainder calculated by accounts
Mr. Gyzelaar with ship *Clarion*: goods	2,288	60	1,308 fur seals at 1¾
Mr. Bennet, ship *Volunteer*: goods	380	90	Paid with Russian goods
Mr. Hill, ship *Clarion*: 239 puds of lump sugar for 5½ [. . .] for	1,863	53	671 seals at 1¾; remainder in Russian goods
Mr. Davis in Sandwich Islands, brig *Brutus*: goods bought by Schmidt	1,285	90	Credit transferred to Thomas Meek
1820			
Mr. Bennet from ship *Clarion*: goods for	302	80	Paid in Russian goods
Mr. Piggot, brig *Peddler*: goods for 2,620 seals			2,620 seals
Andrew Blanchard, brig *Thaddeus*: goods for 7,801 seals	[. . .]	[. . .]	7,801 seals
1821			
Captain Thomas Meek, with brig *Arab*: by conditions made with them in 1819, goods supplied from Boston by request:	7,528	24	Cash: Piasters — 1,500 Chervontsy — 500
Payment for credit:	1,491	96	Goods and translation — 728 [r.] 53 [k.]
Traded for money:	3,685	11	Credit — 690 [r.] 58 [k.]
For chief manager:	234		
	12,939	31	
1822			
Captain Clark, ship *Sultan*: goods	898	83	483 seals at 1¾ 54 piasters
Captain John Meek, brig *Peddler*: goods	7,775	98	4,361 seals at 1¾ 144¼ piasters
Captain Thomas Meek, brig *Arab* brought from Canton by condition of 1821: goods with levying 50 percent for	9,622	89	River beavers: 800 1st grade at 4 800 2nd grade at 4 800 3rd grade at 4

Table [a.] — continued

Ships and Captains and Sum Paid for Goods	piasters	cents	Payments [by Novo-Arkhangel'sk Office]	
Captain Thomas Meek — *continued*			4,739 seals at	1¾
			Russian goods for	3,274
Besides that, bought for	10,043	30		
On account of chief manager	821			
Credit 1821	690	58		
	21,177	77		
Captain Stevens from brig *Pearl*:[*]			373 seals at	1¾
goods for	680	75	Piasters	28

Ships and Captains and Sum Paid for Goods	piasters	cents	Payments [Goods]	[Money]
1823 in California				
Captain Newell, ship *Mentor*: goods	13,991	80	2,995 seals [for]	1.75
			Credit: 8,749 [r.] 83 [k.]	
Mr. Hartnell, Englishman trading in California.				
Goods:	1,443		3,276 seals at	1.75
Traded for wheat:	4,600		Goods for	310
	6,043			
Mr. Newell with *Mentor* at Bodega:			5,000 seals	
goods for	8,866	15	[for]	1¾ piasters
			500 seals for credit	
			1,823 r. [for]	1¾
In Monterey: goods for:	3,150		1,800 seals for	1¾
In piasters:	1,190		700 seals for	1.70
Mr. Elwill with schooner *Washington*:				
goods for	812	25	500 seals at	1.70
In Sandwich Islands from Mr. Meek:			4,428 seals at	1.75
goods [for]	34,203	17[†]	12,825 seals	1.75
			500 river beavers	4

[*]This brig [*Pearl*] was in Novo-Arkhangel'sk port at the time when the sloop *Apollon* arrived and forbade trade with foreigners in the colonies. After that shortages in goods and supplies forced [the chief managers] to have relations with them via the Sandwich Islands and California, where the following transactions were carried on.

[†]Mr. Meek brought the brig to Novo-Arkhangel'sk under the flag of the Russian-

Table [a.] — continued

Ships and Captains and Sum Paid for Goods	piasters	cents	Payments [Goods]	[Money]
Brig *Arab* 11,000 seals	[. . .]	[. . .]	11,000 seals	
1825 in Novo-Arkhangel'sk				
Mr. Blanchard with brig *Lapwing* with 1st account of goods:	11,605	89		
with 2nd account of goods:	15,657	66		
with 3rd account of goods:	1,244	50		
Brig *Lapwing*	14,000			
Account of foodstuffs	87	25	24,235 seals at	1.75
	42,655[*]			
Mr. Wells with ship *Parthian*: goods for	1,212	30	603 seals at piasters	1.75 157
1826 in Novo-Arkhangel'sk				
Mr. Hammet with ship *Sultan*: goods for	17,550	55[†]	10,[000] seal skins	1¾
Mr. Thomas Meek with *Chinchilla*: goods for	19,092	40[‡]	10,788 seal skins at Remainder in goods	1¾
Mr. MacNeil with *Tally-ho*: goods at	2,873	30[a]	1,603 seals at	1¾
1827				
Mr. MacNeil with *Tally-ho*: goods at	7,462	61	4,264 fur seals at	1¾
Brig *Tally-ho* (*Chichagov*)	14,875		8,500 yearlings at	1¾
In California				
Mr. Cunningham, ship *Kur'er* [*Courier*?]: goods for	9,400	92[b]	5,000 seals at balance	1.72½ 1,275.92
In Novo-Arkhangel'sk				
Mr. Cotting, ship *Active*: goods for	8,253	65	4,716 seals at	1¾
Mr. Briat with ship *Triton*: goods for	4,191	89	2,395 seals at	1¾
Mr. Blanchard, ship *Diana*: goods for	23,983	68		
242 doubloons at 17 piasters	4,184		13,625 seals at	1¾

merican Company, here received seal skins sent it on the brig *Riurik*, receiving obligation to load with salt, about which will be mentioned in article about trade on the Sandwich Islands. [*][Sic.] [†][Error] in original; should be 17,500 piasters, 55 cents. [‡]Should be 18,879 piasters, 40 cents. [a]Should [be] 2,805 piasters, 30 cents. [b]It is unclear where this total came from.

Table [a.] — continued

Ships and Captains and Sum Paid for Goods	piasters	cents	Payments [Goods]	[Money]
Mr. Blanchard — *continued*			1,500 bachelors for money at	2¾
piasters	11		remainder in goods	
	28,108	68		
Mr. Thomas Meek, *Chinchilla*: goods for	23,227	39	10,675 seals at Materials for	1¾ 4,545.90
1828				
Mr. Allen, ship *Sultan*: goods for	9,461	25	4,000 pelts at 895 bachelors at	1¾ 2¾
Mr. Carter, schooner *Washington*: goods for	5,650	87	1,100 skins at 400 large at 80 puds of copper at balance:	1¾ 2¾ 16 1,345.87
Mr. Meek, brig *Chinchilla*: goods for 726 kegs of salt for	12,193 3,321	10 50	7,354 seals at Goods and materials for	1¾ 3,391.35
Payment to Carter	1,345	87	row boats For work [preparing or repair] of spars and freight, wheat	400 200
1829				
Mr. Hammet with ship *Harold*, goods and supplies for	2,272	17	1,238 seal skins	
Mr. Taylor, ship *Volunteer*: 18,200 funts salt and part supplies various goods [for]	296 7,031	60 50	Materials for seal skins	4,018 296.60
Mr. Debrot with schooner *Alabama*: 517 quintals salt 154 yards of redwood	905	30	410 spruce timbers 2 row boats Part materials	

Table [a.] — continued

Ships and Captains	Sum Paid for Their Goods in piasters/cents	Payment [Sitkha Office]	[piasters]
1830			
Mr. Thompson, brig *Convoy*, rum for	27	Materials for	27 piasters
1831			
n Main Office F. P. Wrangell: Mr. Carter and schooner *Little*, California goods and supplies for	907 69	Goods and materials	
Mr. Jones and ship *Diana*, goods and supplies for	12,618	Bill of exchange on Main Office 3,800 funts of whale baleen at 20 cents 2,700 puds walrus at 65 cents, materials for	 10,000 103
Mr. John Meek, *Crusader*, goods and supplies for	2,123	Bill of exchange on Main Office and in materials	2,000 123
1832			
Mr. Barker, ship *Smyrna*: goods for	14,657 41	Bill of exchange of 7 April (n.s.) on Main Office	14,657.41
Brig *Llama*, Captain MacNeil: goods for	4,090 15	Bill of exchange on Main Office for usual ten days	
Brig *Bolivar*, Captain Underwood	5,583 48½	Bill of exchange on Main Office for usual 20 days	
Brig *Crusader*, Mr. Dzhonid, supercargo Thompson: goods for	12,888 13	2,080 funts of whale bone for 20 days borne for usual 20 days for	12,672
Brig *Diana*, Mr. Orteaga Katran Little: goods for	14,000	For ¾ paid in other things and materials	

According to these figures, it is evident that from 1818 to 1826 a trade amounting to 205,652½ piasters took place with foreigners (considering the piaster at five rubles, this would amount to 1,028,262 1/5 rubles); this sum includes 109,479 seal furs, 2,900 river otters, 200 piasters and 500 chervonets. In addition to goods, we also purchased three ships from them: *Brutus*, *Arab* and *Lapwing*, which were renamed *Golovnin*, *Baikal* and *Okhotsk*. During this time, the price of seal furs remained constant, even when they were being sold in Canton at 1 ruble 35 kopeks. It was then agreed that it was necessary to pay higher prices for purchased goods than to sell goods at lower prices. As it is well known, a high price in Canton is 2(00) to 220 piasters. Mr. Thomas Meek obtained necessary goods from Boston and Canton at a 50 percent markup from the price of purchase. Goods we purchased from Mr. Blanchard had a 10 percent markup.

According to the chief manager, Fleet Captain P. E. Chistiakov, from 1826 to 1831 a trade amounting to 188,461 piasters took place with foreigners (considering the piaster at five rubles this amounted to 942,305 rubles). This sum includes 97,378 seal furs and various goods and materials valued at 11,000 piasters. In addition to goods, we purchased the brig *Tally-ho* (*Chichagov*) for 8,500 seal pelts.

The following charts [b. and c., pp. 103-107] will show what prices were paid for goods; the prices are in piasters.

2. Methods of Trade with California

The ship *Kutuzov*, commanded by Captain Hagemeister, stopped at Fort Ross in September 1817 on its way to Sitkha, and at Mr. Kuskov's advice Captain Hagemeister stopped in San Francisco in order to negotiate with the governor to release several Aleut hunting parties that had been captured by the Spanish and to request permission to trade there. Governor de Sola himself did not come to the port, but with respect to our wishes did send two Aleuts who told us that the rest had been sent far away; he gave us permission to trade.

The following year Captain Hagemeister left Sitkha for California where he had a private audience with the governor. From that time on every year our ships traded there; the following quantities of goods were received from California [see Tables a and b, pp. 108, 109].

[b. Table Showing When and for How Much Goods Were Purchased from Foreign Merchants in Novo-Arkhangel'sk, in Spanish piasters, 1818-1825]

Goods	Measure	1818 from Mr. Meek		1819 from Meek, Gyzelaar and Nye		1821 from Mr. Meek		1822 from Clark and John Meek		1822 from Thomas Meek		1823-24 from Newell and Meek		1825 from Blanchard	
		In piasters and cents													
		p.	c.	p.	c.	p.	c.	p.	c.	p.	c.	p.	c.	p.	c.
Tar and pik	barrel	5		6										18	
Vinegar	gallon		50		50										30
Pepper	funt		25												
Molasses	gallon		75	1		1		1		1				1	
Glass	box		15												
Paper	ream			5											
Tin	sheet				12										
Mustard	dozen cans			6											
Olive oil	dozen cans			7											
Gin	gallon			1	50	2		8	75 boxes	6	25 boxes	6	25 boxes		
Taro	100 [funts]			1	50										
Salt	picul			2											
Sushon tea	funt				40				75		75		75		50
Iron	ton			80											
Rum	gallon			1	20	2		1	75	1	50	1	75	1	65
Millet	100 [funts]			8		8			11½ piculs		9 cwt	8		7	
Peas	funt				40							3	50 barrel		
Large blankets	[piece]			3						3		3	25		
Frieze	yard			2						2	20	1	75	1	45

Table [b.] — continued

Goods	Measure	1818 from Mr. Meek		1819 from Meek, Gyzelaar and Nye		1821 from Mr. Meek		1822 from Clark and John Meek		1822 from Thomas Meek		1823-24 from Newell and Meek		1825 from Blanchard	
		In piasters and cents													
		p.	c.	p.	c.	p.	c.	p.	c.	p.	c.	p.	c.	p.	c.
Wool stockings	dozen			4											
White sugar, granulated	100 [funts]			15					20 cwt	15			14 piculs	10	
Eng. doublets	funt						35								
Virginia tobacco	100 [funts]					21				21	[100 funts]	21	[100 funts]	12	
Cognac	gallon					2	50								
Ship biscuit, white	100 [funts]					6		9				9		8	
Soap	picul							15							
Wheat flour	picul							7	10						
White sugar	picul							41	10						
Sugar	[picul]							34	28	21	[per funt]				
Bohea tea	[funt]										33				
Hyson tea	[funt]									1	12				
New Hyson tea	[funt]									1	20				
Short nankeen	[yard?]										81				
Blue nankeen	[yard?]									1	65				
Serge kerchiefs	packet									13	50				
Canton teaware	box									10					
Ground whiting	barrel									8		7	50		

Table [b.] — continued

Goods	Measure	1818 from Mr. Meek		1819 from Meek, Gyzelaar and Nye		1821 from Mr. Meek		1822 from Clark and John Meek		1822 from Thomas Meek		1823-24 from Newell and Meek		1825 from Blanchard	
		In piasters and cents													
		p.	c.	p.	c.	p.	c.	p.	c.	p.	c.	p.	c.	p.	c.
Drying oil	gallon									3	50				
Coffee	funt										30			2	40
Thread	English lb.											3	30		
Rifles	piece											5			
Steel	funt												11		
Madeira wine	gallon													3	
Flour	barrel													15	
Salt meat	barrel													13	

English and American goods are purchased at English weight and measure, but often with differences for rusks and wheat as sold by the hundredweight, consisting of 112 English pounds, and many are held at the same price per hundred pounds — 36 English pounds equal 40 Russian, 7 English yards are equal to 9 arshins, and 10 gallons of fluid equal three buckets.

From 10 to 15 percent is added to prices at which goods are purchased from foreigners, but it is not possible to make such a disposition of all goods; it would be necessary to add to other prices in order to agree with existing prices, and because one leaves always the predetermined profit for the benefit of the company.

[c.] *Table of Principal Goods Purchased from Americans at Novo-Arkhangel'sk during Tenure of Chief Manager P. E. Chistiakov, [1826-1830]*

Goods and Supplies	Measure	1826 from Hammet and T. Meek		1827 from Michael Cushing, Blanchard, and Meek		1828 from Allen, Carter, Meek		1829 from Hammet, Taylor, Stilia, Diubrot		1830 from Genchman	
		In piasters and cents									
		p.	c.	p.	c.	p.	c.	p.	c.	p.	c.
White sugar	funt		20		18 & 20		20		20 &		20
Yellow sugar	funt		12½-15		12		15		25		17
Sugar candy	funt				20		20		7		
Sushon tea	funt		75		75		60				55
Kongo tea	funt				75		55				55
Hyson tea	funt	1		1	25						
Molasses	gallon	1			90		75		60		40
Rum	gallon	2		1	80	1	50	1	40	1	40
				2	—					1	
Gin	gallon	2		1	80	8	per box	1	50	1	40
Vinegar	gallon		30	—	33		40			1	50
Groat flour	barrel	15		10 & 12		12				10	
Millet	funt		10		7 & 9		4½-7 & 8				
Virginia tobacco	funt		22 & 30		15 & 20				20		10
Plug (vatoi) tobacco	funt		40		40		30		22		
Soap	funt		18 & 20		15, 18 & 20		14				
Sicilian wine	gallon	2	75	2	50	1	75	1	75	1	40
		8		3		1	50				
Frieze	yard										

Table [c.] — continued

Goods and Supplies	Measure	1826 from Hammet and T. Meek		1827 from Michael Cushing, Blanchard, and Meek		1828 from Allen, Carter, Meek		1829 from Hammet, Taylor, Stilia, Diubrot		1830 from Genchman	
		In piasters and cents									
		p.	c.	p.	c.	p.	c.	p.	c.	p.	c.
Cloth	yard	4 to 8									
Grey Am. calico	yard	4			20 & 30		15				
Bengal calico	yard	7			20 & 30		15				
White E. India calico	yard				30 & 40						
Blue nankeen	piece	2		1	50	1	70				
				1	75						
Flesh color nankeen	piece										
Large blanket	piece	2									
Small blanket	piece	1	50								
Bleach [*belil*]	barrel	7 & 9		10		6		8		4	20
Tar and pik	barrel	16		8, 10 & 13		6					
Biscuit	quintal	10		8 & 10		8					
Coffee	funt		40		30						
Chintz	yard		15 & 20								
	piece				40 (wide)	12					
Drying oil	gallon	2 & 3									
Salt	100 [funts?]	1	75	1	75	1	75	1			
								1	50		

[Table a. Supplies Purchased in California by Vessels from Novo-Arkhangel'sk, 1817-1832]

Where and with which Vessels Provisions Were Obtained	Wheat in fanegas	Barley in fanegas	Peas and Beans in fanegas	Flour in arrobas	Tallow and Butter in arrobas	Dried Meat in arrobas
1817 To San Francisco on *Kutuzov*	358	256	109	180	203	
1818 To Monterey and Santa Cruz on *Kutuzov*	3,140	500	904	114	1,083	540
1820 To Monterey and Santa Cruz on brig *Buldakov*	3,376	250	163	242	390	260
1821 To San Francisco on brig *Golovnin*	737		24		263	
1821 To Monterey on ship *Kutuzov*, Capt. Dokhturov	1,160	300	306½		480	729
1821 To San Francisco on brig *Buldakov*	1,880			15	258	
1822 To Monterey on brig *Volga*	129	280	25			
1822 To Monterey on brig *Buldakov*	1,026	200	152	163	318	180
1822 To Santa Cruz on brig *Volga*	520		120		6	
1823 To Monterey and Santa Cruz on brig *Riurik*	742	115	86	101	188	170
1824 To Monterey on brig *Baikal*	1,317	400			510	
1824 To Monterey and Santa Cruz on brig *Kiakhta*	1,316		25		92½	181
1824 To San Pedro on brig *Buldakov*	1,885				140	
1825 To Monterey and San Francisco on brig *Kiakhta*	1,510		39		258	
1825 To San Pedro and San Francisco on brig *Baikal*	530½	6			22	

In addition to those aforesaid supplies, we received rawhide from California; when necessary we obtained soap, salt and always live cattle, both for food for the crew and to make corned beef on Sitkha Island. The amount of meat varied every year from 200 to 300 puds. beef on Sitkha Island. The amount of meat varied every year from 200 to 300 puds.

The prices of supplies varied in California. During the first years we were almost the only ones who could sell goods,

Table [b.] Trade in California [1826-1832]

	Where and with which Vessels Provisions Were Obtained	Wheat in fanegas	Barley [in fanegas]	Peas and Beans in fanegas	Marrow and Butter in arrobas	Tallow and Fat in arrobas	Salt Beef in puds	Salt [in puds]
1826	San Pedro, San Diego, Monterey and Santa Cruz on brig *Baikal*	1,469½	49	162½	150	264	323	
	San Francisco on brig *Okhotsk*	850	maize 42					
1827	Monterey and Santa Cruz on brig *Golovnin*	689	270	185		15 p. 28 f.	11 p. 10 f.	
	San Francisco on brig *Okhotsk*	290	maize 70			150 puds	188 p. 10 f.	
	San Pedro and San Diego on brig *Baikal*	591	104	30	80	212		
1828	San Francisco on brig *Kiakhta*	1,036½	maize 26 maize 28	peas 8	27	217	133 [puds]	
	Monterey and San Diego on brig *Okhotsk*	623½	maize 3	beans 5 peas 73½	56 puds	40 puds	50 puds	
	San Quentin on *Baikal*							9,700
1829	Because of draught and consequently no trade, the schooner *Baikal* sailed to Chile to purchase wheat							
1830	In Monterey and San Francisco on the sloop *Baikal*	2,210		peas 100		362 puds	340 [puds]	
1831	In Monterey and San Francisco on sloop *Urup*	2,087		maize 50 beans 60		365 [puds]		
1832	In San Francisco on sloop *Urup*	2,442		maize 5 peas 37				

but when the constitutional King of Spain opened all ports in America to foreign trade, from 1821 and every year thereafter English and American ships came with their goods to trade, while whalers came to get fresh supplies.

From that moment on we were obliged to sell our goods at cheaper prices and to buy our supplies at higher prices. Wheat from California was exported only to Peru, which was still under the king's authority, and to Chile, a rich agricultural region which had become a republic. Subsequently, both countries established mutual trade. The Americans and English buy steer hides, grease and tallow. The hides are taken to America and England, and send the grease and tallow along the coasts of Mexico and Peru. They sell the hides at a 200-percent profit, but they sell their grease and tallow at a loss. Here is a table [Table c, p. 111] of prices of supplies at various times.

The money used in California is called the *real*, eight of which make up a piaster. If something costs one piaster and one real or one piaster and four reales, they usually say that it costs nine or twelve reales and so forth to twenty-four reales. Even numbers are counted in piasters. A fanega is a weight measure, which depending on the quality of the grain, contains 3½ to 4 puds. According to Mr. Hagemeister, they usually measure in the following manner: a fanega of wheat equals 3 puds 30 funts; barley, 3 puds; peas and beans [frijoles], 4 puds. An arroba equals one-fourth of a quintal and contains 24 Spanish or 28⅛ Russian funts. Tallow and grease are bought in sacks which usually contain one-half an arroba, although many weigh much more.

Trade in California takes place in the following manner. When one arrives in port a manifest must be handed to the port commandant; the manifest must show the name of the ship, tonnage, its point of origin, to whom it belongs, the names of the captain and supercargo, and the number of crew members and of guns. One must also present the ship's passport and verification of the ship's tonnage. The captain must also declare the amount of goods on board the ship. Before, a list of prices had to be handed in, but this is no longer necessary.

In order to give an idea of where and at which prices the goods were sold, we present the charts following [on pp. 112-113].

[Table c. Trade in California, 1817-1825]

	Measure	1817		1818		1820		1821		1822		1823		1824		1825	
		Piasters and reales															
		p.	r.	p.	r.	p.	r.	p.	r.	p.	r.	p.	r.	p.	r.	p.	r.
						2	4	2									
Wheat	fanega	2	4	2	4	2	6	3	4	3		4		3		3	
						1	2			1	6	3					
Barley	fanega	1	6	1	6	1	4			1	2	2		2			
Peas	fanega	2	6	2	2	2	4	2	2	2	4	2	4	3		2	4
Beans	fanega	2	6	2	2	3		1	6	2	4	2	4				
Frijoles	fanega			3						3		3		3		3	
Millet	fanega					2		2				3				2	
Garbanzo	fanega			3												3	
Flour	arroba	1	6	1	6	1	6	2				1	4				
Tallow	arroba	2		1	6	1	6	1	5	2		2		2		2	
				1	6	2				2		1	6	2			
Dry meat	arroba					2				2	2						
Marrow	arroba			1	6	2	2			3		3		3		3	
Soap	arroba									4		4		4		4	
Salt	arroba									2			4		4		4
							4				4						
Hides, steer, dry	piece				6		6				6	1		1		1	
Large steers	one	5		6				6		8		8		8		8	
Medium steers	one							4		6		6				7	

[*Table d. Prices of Provisions Purchased in California, 1818-1825*]

Goods	Measure	1818 on *Kutuzov*		1820 on *Buldakov*		1821 on *Buldakov*		1822 on *Buldakov*		1823 on *Riurik*		1824 on *Kiakhta*		1825 on *Kiakhta*	
		[in piasters and reales]													
		p.	r.	p.	r.	p.	r.	p.	r.	p.	r.	p.	r.	p.	r.
Iron	quintal	16		13		16		12				12			
Cast iron kettles	quintal	18				18		18		16		16		16	
Stell	quintal	40		40		40		24							
Wax candles	quintal	120		120		100		100		100				120	
Lump sugar	quintal	22				30									
Sugar candy	quintal			40				40							
Granulated sugar	quintal			28		30		30				24		40	
White wax	quintal			80		75									
Virginia tobacco	quintal	80		80		16		60		56				banned	
Wheat	quintal			12		16		14		12				12	
Shot	quintal			30		24		24		20		24		30	
Ropes	quintal	28		17						16		16		18	
Lead	quintal														
Bohea tea	funt	2													
Sushon tea	funt														
Coffee	funt			1	2										
Copper teapot	funt	1		1		1				1		1		1	
Copper kettles	funt	1		1		1				1		1	2	1	
Pepper	funt						4						6		4
Sealing wax	funt					2	2								
Thread	funt					2						5			
Silk [thread]	funt							16				16		16	
Broadcloth	vara	1	50	1		1	2				6				

[Table d.] — continued

Goods	Measure	1818 on *Kutuzov*		1820 on *Buldakov*		1821 on *Buldakov*		1822 on *Buldakov*		1823 on *Riurik*		1824 on *Kiakhta*		1825 on *Kiakhta*	
		[in piasters and reales]													
		p.	r.	p.	r.	p.	r.	p.	r.	p.	r.	p.	r.	p.	r.
Good calico	vara	2		1	4	1	4					1		1	
Medium calico	vara					1	2	1		1			6		6
Bengal calico	piece	15		12		10				8		9			
Grey Flemish linen	piece	50		48		45		50		42		35		40	
Raven duck	piece	38		25		35				50		32			
White Kiakhta nankeen	piece	4				4		4				3	2	3	
Blue Canton nankeen	piece	3	4	4				3	4	3	4	2	4		
Flesh-colored nankeen	piece			2	4	2				2	4	3			
Broadcloth	vara					12		12						12	
Cloth, 6-golovk.	vara	6	4	8	4	7				6				6	
Baize	vara	1	4	2		2	4			1	6			1	6
Frieze	vara							3	2	2	6	3	4	2	4
Plush	vara	2	4	3	4	3				3	4	2	4	2	4
Ordinary flannel	vara	1												1	2
Double flannel	vara					2	4							1	6
Men's cotton stockings	dozen	30								24		18		1	6
Women's cotton stockings	dozen							15						1	2
Beaver hat	piece	6		6		6		6		6					
Axes	piece	2	4	1	4	2								2	4
Flat files	dozen	9		8		5	4								
Yellow plates	dozen	4				5				3	4	3	4		
Needles	thousand	3		4											
Spanish socks	piece			2		2		2		2		2		2	4
Ticking	vara						9		6						5

Here we have only indicated those goods which change little in quality. However, all kinds of trifling goods come to California, especially white calico, various kerchiefs, haberdashery goods, glass and crockery, carpenter's tools and much more.[38]

It was mentioned earlier that during the first years of our relations with this region we were the only foreigners who openly traded goods (the English and Americans smuggled all along the shores of the Spanish colonies in America); as a result of that trade we made a profit. In 1817 the *Kutuzov* traded 3,906 rubles' worth of goods (St. Petersburg prices) or 2,641½ piasters according to the Spanish prices; but considering the piaster at that time to be valued at 5 rubles 35 kopeks, it amounted to 14,132 rubles 37 kopeks. Consequently, the profit was 254 percent. In 1818 in Monterey the *Kutuzov* exchanged goods valued at 36,719 rubles 40 kopeks (according to Sitkha prices) or 17,221½ piasters considering the piasters to be valued at 5 rubles 35 kopeks. This amounted to 92,725 rubles 52 kopeks. Based on these calculations there was 150 percent profit. In 1820 in Monterey the *Buldakov* exchanged goods worth 21,444 rubles (Sitkha prices) or 8,995¼ piasters, considering the piaster to be valued at 5 rubles; an amount of 44,976 rubles 25 kopeks; this amounted to a 110 percent profit. In subsequent trading there was sometimes a 35 to 70 percent profit. It is a fact that rare goods are still sold at more than 100 percent profit, but other goods which are obtained from the Americans and the English are often sold at the original price of purchase. The reason for this is that the goods are bought for cash money, which is then used to procure the goods. In 1823 we were shown a declaration of prices paid in previous years; the governor told us that we could purchase wheat in exchange for goods at four piasters a fanega or at three piasters a fanega if we paid cash.

Goods can be sold either aboard the ship or ashore, for which purpose we were given a room in the Presidio. Sometimes inspectors appear ashore in order to record the goods brought down by merchants for us to buy; but most of the time they trusted us and we simply handed them over a declaration of goods sold and prices paid for them.

With the increase of trade so did taxes (duties) increase. In 1817 we paid no taxes for anything, but beginning in 1818 we were asked to pay 7½ percent on all goods sold and 12½ percent for goods purchased. In 1820 the duty for goods sold went up to

12½ percent, while the duty for goods purchased remained the same. In the following years, in accordance with the constitution of the Mexican republic, a 25 percent duty was imposed on goods sold and 2½ piasters for each ton. Before the constitution there had been a duty of 6 percent on goods purchased, but this was lowered later. The 25 percent duty on sold goods is figured in the following way: if the total value of sold goods is estimated to be 4,677 piasters, they deduct 12½ percent or 564.4 piasters as an import tax. That leaves a total of 4112.4 piasters. From this sum another 25 percent or 1,028⅛ piasters is deducted.

It costs 3 piasters for one fanega of wheat, or, a fanega being 3 puds 30 funts, 4 rubles for a pud. But after considering the cost and duties and other goods to be purchased, then 1 pud of wheat really comes out to be 3 rubles and 80 kopeks; peas and beans cost the same, and barley costs 4 rubles.

Although trade with California is not carried out for commercial gains but out of necessity to supply the colonies with grain and other supplies, it is, however, necessary to deduct expenses from the various transactions for the maintenance of the crews. For example, in 1825 the brig *Kiakhta* sold 29,060 rubles in goods to the Spanish; we purchased supplies at local prices, which when converted amounted to 29,803 rubles. In this exchange we made a 18,422-ruble profit on goods sold and a 4,931½-ruble profit from goods purchased; from other transactions we made a 1,776-ruble profit, so that there was a total profit of 25,030 rubles and 55 kopeks. If we deduct the loss of goods, duties at 2½ piasters per ton and duties for goods sold at 25 percent from the entire amount, the total equals 8,044 rubles, and the remaining profit is 16,986 rubles and 44 kopeks. The maintenance of the crew for five months, several presents for officials and other minor expenses amounted to 3,903 rubles 64 kopeks; subsequently, after subtracting this sum we are left with 13,082 rubles and 80 kopeks, which can pay the salary of the crew and pay for the ship's cargo.

This example, however, cannot be considered to be typical, because it all depends on the kind of transaction, the quantity of goods sold and at times the amount spent on the voyage.[39]

3. Methods of Trade with the Sandwich [Hawaiian] Islands

After Dr. Shaeffer was thrown out of the islands, the islanders were afraid the Russians would take revenge. In 1819 Mr. Schmidt was sent there on the brig *Brutus*, which had been bought from Mr. Nye. He went to buy provisions and a ship, and should the opportunity arise he should find out from the king of the Atuvai [Kauai] Island, King Tomari [Kaumualii] what his feelings were about the Russians. After accomplishing his business, Mr. Schmidt sailed to the Island of Atuvai and met with the king who told him that even though Dr. Shaeffer had given him several gifts, he was willing to pay for them. He admitted having 8 bolts of frieze, 4 bolts of blue wool, 80 axes, 10 flasks of powder, a schooner with arms and sails, two cast iron cannons and two bronze cannons. For these the king felt obliged to pay 200 piculs of the best sandalwood, on the condition that he be paid 15 barrels of English powder for maintaining our company personnel. After this our ships had no particular relations with the islands until we experienced shortages of goods and food. In 1823 Mr. Etolin was sent there on board the *Golovnin*, and after buying the brig *Arab* from Meek, along with its cargo, he returned to Sitkha with both ships, as mentioned earlier. Mr. Meek and his crew had to be taken back to the island, so the brig *Riurik* was sent to the Sandwich Islands where Mr. Meek arranged to have the brig loaded with salt. Such an agreement had been made with Mr. Blanchard in 1825, who after selling his brig the *Lapwing* was taken back to the Sandwich Islands. Here we present a table of goods bought through Mr. Meek and Mr. Blanchard.

[Table a. Goods Purchased by Russian-American Company Vessels in Sandwich Islands through Messrs. Meek and Blanchard, 1824-1825]

	Goods	piasters/	cents	Goods
	1824 received on brig Riurik:			
1,000	hundredweight of salt	1	75	2,000 fur seals
217	gallons of rum at:	1	50	300 Spanish piasters
133	gallons of cognac	2		
1,270	English lbs. hardtack	8*		
502	English lbs. of spermaceti candles		45	

[Table a] — continued

Goods		piasters/ cents		Goods
18	kegs of tar	8		
39	kegs of tutui nuts	3	40	
	Total	3,086†		

*One must suppose that an English lb. of hardtack cost not 8 piasters but 80 cents.
†Calculating the price of an English lb. of hardtack not at 8 piasters but at 80 cents, the total cost of the goods would be 3,860 piasters.

Goods		piasters/ cents		Goods	piasters/ cents	
1825 [Received] on brig Lapwing						
1,160	cwt salt at 1.75	2,030		1,323 fur seals at	1	75
378	English lbs. of sugar candy at 12 hundred [sic]	72		piasters	90	10
100	various small things for	128	36			

Goods which can be obtained from the Sandwich Islands are salt, tutui nuts, rum, taro root and jute rope, which is very useful for outfitting ships.

Many travellers, who have praised old Tomeamea (Kamehameha), King of the Sandwich Islands, have shamelessly claimed that he was an educated man and that he had sailed to Canton and along the shores of Northwest America. The fact is that when the Americans found out that the island abounded with sandalwood, which could be sold at a profit in Canton, they returned to the islands to buy it. Since the islanders did not know the value of sandalwood, they sold it for trifles, but when the merchants began competing with one another, the islanders raised the price to 8 piasters a picul. The sandalwood sold in Canton for 10 piasters. Whalers, on their way to hunt sperm whales [cachalots] along the Japanese shore, often set anchor at these islands for refreshment.

The Americans, English and the Spaniard Marini settled on the island and got the king's trust. They impressed the king with the value of money and made him understand how business really worked. On their advice, the king only took piasters for the sandalwood; when it could not be paid in coin, he then accepted trading goods such as cloth, calico, and other goods; he traded for 14 sailing vessels, one of which was a 200 ton brig. He only used these ships to travel among the Sandwich Islands. It is true that the Europeans surrounded him advised the king to send a ship of sandalwood to Canton under his own flag. In 1818 the American Adams sailed there aboard the *Forester*; but when he arrived there and sold his shipment, he was barely able to pay the duty imposed by that country. Meanwhile, because the ship was dilapidated, it needed repairs. In order to pay for these repairs and for maintaining the crew, the captain had to borrow money from his friends (Americans) on the king's account; and he returned in debt. This venture killed any inclination on the king's part to engage in trade. The king never sent any ships to Sitkha but he had contact with Mr. Baranov through American acquaintances, and they sent one another presents until everything was ended by Dr. Shaeffer's expedition.

When the old king died, there were 300,000 piasters left, which his son and successor spent on himself, taking the remaining 80,000 piasters he left for England where he spent the rest of his life.

This king was called Rio-rio [Liho-Liho] or Tomeamea [Kamehameha] II. His 12-year-old brother succeeded him; his name was Kaiki-ora [Kauikeaouli]. An elderly minister, Kari-maku [Kalanimoku] and the queen mother declared themselves regents. When Kari-maku became ill in 1825, each chief (elder) ruled the way he wanted. The English missionaries are also members of the council and have significant influence on island matters; the Spaniard Marini has managed to earn special trust and also participates in council affairs. Upon hearing the news of Rio-rio [Liho-Liho]'s death the islanders thought of rebelling; but those in charge took preventive measures; they took away all firearms and gunpowder; as a result those who had planned the rebellion failed and had to satisfy themselves by smashing a few drinking houses.

There was an uprising on the island of Atuvai which had begun in favor of the son of the late king Tomari, but as soon as the news reached Ovagi, the main rebels were captured, taken to Voagu [Oahu], and replaced by other people. Thus the rebellion was put down. Tomari's son lives freely on the island of Ovagi, but he is strictly watched.

In 1825 the late king Rio-rio still owed the Americans money for ships and goods which he had purchased in exchange for sandalwood. Kari-maku has promised to pay the debts off but has paid little back. Many of the creditors have left their agents on the island in order to regain what money they can. It is common knowledge that the Americans now make no profit from trade with the islanders. In 1824 they had many stores with goods; but by 1825 there was only one left. They had no permanent arrangement and sold their goods as best they could.

b. Supplementary information on the Sandwich Islands

I. Royal Income

Every year the king receives 20 to 25 thousand piasters. The sources of this income are the following:

1. Every year 100 to 200 vessels, mainly whalers, enter these islands. The whalers come from the coasts of Peru, enter the Sandwich Islands in April and from there proceed along the Japanese coasts. After hunting for the cachalot there for four to five months they return to these islands in order to resupply their ships. Each ship buys provisions worth 100 to 200 and sometimes 300 piasters.

The prices of supplies are the following: a large 150 pound pig costs 7½ piasters; a piglet of up to one and a half feet long — 1 piaster; a barrel of potatoes — 2 to 3 piasters. The Spaniard Marini owns up to 200 head of cattle and sometimes gets 35½ piasters for a large animal. When the ships arrive the islanders bring their goods to market; two of the king's commissioners are assigned to sell supplies; after coming to an agreement with the foreigners they sell them supplies; after they receive their money, they keep half of it for the king's use, and give the other half to the owners of the supplies. Earlier on Ovagi several head of cattle ran away into the mountains, and now they have become numerous; they have become wild and do not ever come down into the valley. Sometimes the king used to send his people to shoot the wild cattle; those who have seen the herd think that they number at least 10,000 head.

2. The king releases the islanders to work on English and American merchant vessels; the price paid per person is 10 piasters a month; the king receives part of this money for his own use.

In 1827 there were up to 300 Sandwich Islanders working on various vessels.

II. The Royal Vessels

The king allows foreigners to use his ships for half of the profit, taking upon himself half of the expenses and the maintenance of the crew. Many of the ships sail along the shores of California, Mexico, Peru and Chile, sometimes to hunt for whales and at other times to go on smuggling expeditions. In 1826 Captain Dany (Deni) of the schooner *Veveli* [*Waverley*?] killed up to 8,000 seals on the island of Guadalupe.

In 1827 the Frenchman Debrot, sailing to the islands of Galápagos and Galea, killed up to 15,000 seals on his five-month voyage at sea and gave half of the catch to the king.

The schooner *Washington* was sent there also and got 7,000 funts of tortoise shells, part of which was sent to Canton.

The price of tortoise shell in Canton was as follows: a large one — 11 piasters, a small one 5 to 7 piasters a funt. The first ship to come to Sitkha under the Sandwich flag was the brig *Tomari* under the command of Mr. Marini. In July 1828 the same ship under the command of Mr. Meek delivered 700 barrels of salt to Sitkha and loaded his ship with construction timber. The crew consisted of two Americans and islanders.

III. Sandalwood

Sandalwood trees cut down in 1827 yielded 15,000 piculs; in 1828 it was no more than 5,000 piculs. Several *kanakas* are sent into the hills by the king in order to cut the trees down; up to 5,000 men and women and boys and girl and men and women are then sent out to drag the trees from the hills. The distance from the harbor to the area where the trees have been cut down is 12 to 18 miles. They usually bring the trees down on their shoulders. Those who gather the trees are given half by the king either in trees or money at 4 piasters for 1 picul.[40]

The islands of Voagu [Oahu], Atuvai [Kauai] and Movi [Maui] have the best type of sandalwood; the largest quantity is located on Oahu, but even the poorest kind is of good quality. The

Americans buy this tree at 8 piasters a picul in goods; and sell the sandalwood in Canton at 9, 10 and 11 piasters a picul.

NB. Besides getting the sandalwood from the Sandwich Islands and the Marquesas Islands, Canton gets it from Bombay and Timor, but no more than 100 piculs of the best quality and it is sold at 25 to 30 piasters a picul.

IV. The Number of Inhabitants

There are no more than 60,000 inhabitants of both sexes on the Sandwich Islands, the most populated of which is the island of Ovagi [Oahu].

V. The Crustacean Bêche-de-Mer

Bêche-de-mer can be found on the Caroline Islands and other islands in the Pacific Ocean. The Americans gather them, dry them and ship them to Canton. They ship 25 to 50 piculs, sometimes 100 to Canton and sell them at 60 piasters a picul. The Chinese use them in soups.

Bêche-de-mer looks like a crustacean. In Sitkha we call it a baidarka, but it is without a shell, although it has a thick protective membrane; it is one-half foot long, and green in coloration; the best are those with red stripes on them.

About Whale Hunting

Whalers get 80 to 90 barrels of oil from a large whale; 35 to 40 from a small whale. A barrel contains 200 English pounds. A whaler can load 1,500 to 2,000 barrels into its cargo hold.

VI. The Expedition to the [New] Hebrides Islands

In 1830 three vessels were sent out from the Sandwich Islands — one English and two belonging to the king (one was the *Tomeamea*) with 600 men — in order to cut down trees on the island of Arromango [Erromango; Soniano].

On the way they stopped at the island of Ratoma [Rotuma] where they let off 400 men out of 1,000. The brig *Tomeamea* had a lot of gunpowder on board and it is thought that it exploded. The brig blew up and all 500 people on board, including the governor, Boki Kosoviatu, an Englishman, and his family perished. The two vessels stopped at Arromango, where many of those on board were killed and eaten by the islanders, while others died of disease. After killing the Sandwich islanders, the people of Arromango cut them up and ate the human flesh raw. Only seven men returned alive to the Sandwich Islands.

4. Methods of Trade with the Kolosh

After Mr. Baranov was replaced, trade with the Kolosh continued in the same manner. But for their pelts they were now paid one-half or two-thirds they had agreed on in the general contract. At that time the Americans paid them five to six large blankets, in addition to several containers of molasses, dried rusks and groats. We could not pay that much because the price would have been double its cost, and because there were times when we did not have sufficient goods to trade. So that our trade was limited all the time. Finally, the chief manager, Matvei Ivanovich Murav'ev, considering the resolution of the Main Office, stated in dispatch No. 388 to the Novo-Arkhangel'sk office on October 14, 1825:

1) Trade with the Kolosh must be carried out based on the quantity and quality of goods stored in our magazines (warehouses).

2) This trade should not be carried out on the sole basis of making a profit for the company, but it should also be conducted in order to make friends with the Kolosh and to establish goodwill between them and the Russians and the company.

3) The company can order the payment in goods worth 100 to 150 rubles for sea otters and sometimes more, depending, of course, on the quality of the pelts.

The office may pay more for other pelts, compared to sea otter pelts, but I would not pay more for land animals than is paid at the present time. However, if this will improve the company's benefits, then the chief manager can increase the payment a little. Trade was begun in 1826 on that principle (regulation), but much has changed since then as attested by the following table [p. 123].

[Table a. *Number of Furs Obtained from the Kolosh by the Novo-Arkhangel'sk Office, 1818-1831*]

Names of Fur Animals	1818	1819	1820	1821	1822	1823	1824	1825	Total	1826	1827	1828	1829	1830	1831
Sea otters and yearlings	54	54	27	21	20	24	16	22	236	95	79	79	75	59	40
Sea otter pups	27	33	17	2	3	1	11		94	27	3	11	19	4	6
Sea otter tails	95	62	42	16	13	15	38	1	282	48	55	81	64	58	37
Yearling tails	21	31	7	9	1	5	1	2	83						
River beaver, various	265	147	115	41	39	177	198	74	1,058	347	299	524	449	255	451
River beaver, various	262	242	137	75	48	120	187	63	1,134	122	175	246	244	175	269
Foxes:															
silver	17	17	8	4		8	6	11	71	14	127	69	62	35	51
cross	20	29	12	3	2	5	3	7	81	109	178	88	102	60	91
red	6	8	3		1		1	4	25	46	71	43	92	49	61
Mink, various	1,807	1,302	842	272	137	433	602	165	5,569	503	692	900	564	186	668
Sables of various colors	62	73	166	1	85	76	133	27	633	20	13	4	2	2	9
Bears:															
black	40	36	30	20	20	26	24	34	230	49	97	79	26	4	158
brown	3	1		3		2			9						4
Wolverine, various	1	2	1		2	6			12	1	10				6
Lynx, various	1	24					6		31		6	3			13
Muskrats, various		2	11	2			5		20	12	3				86
Sea *kechki*[?], various	2	3	1				2	2	10						
Wolves, various				2					2				2		
Squirrels, various		17	12						29						
Seal skins		95	86	7					188						
Beaver castors*					3	5¾		1½	10¼	16½	22	13	13	58	129
Sables															82

In all, at such prices in the course of eight years were traded from the Kolosh goods worth 29,987 r. 36 k. For amount paid for these goods, see special list.

*In funts.

[Table b.] Extract, Payment for Furs Bartered from the Kolosh, [1821-1825]

				r.	k.
1821	March	1 sea otter	1 copper armór	25	
			40 sea lion whiskers	1	20
		1 sea otter	2 blankets, large, for	24	
	April	1 sea otter	2½ arshins of frieze	22	
		1 sea otter	1 razor set	39	
		1 sea otter tail	1 one-funt caldron	2	
		1 otter	10 ermine	6	
		1 otter	3½ arshins Flemish linen	6	
		1 otter, medium	1 ax	3	
		3 otter, medium	10 arshins of calico	12	50
1822	January	2 river beaver	6½ arshins Flemish linen	11	20
		1 river beaver	10 ermine	6	
		10 mink	1 mirror	1	65
	March	2 black bear	1 25-funt caldron	6	25
		3 cross fox	3 large blankets	36	
	November*	1 sea otter	1 sheet copper	21	
		1 sea otter	3 armor, native 15 [slats] 3 arshins of frieze 26, 40	41	40
	June	1 yearling	1 blanket	12	
	August	1 cross fox	1 blanket	12	
		2 river beaver	2 axes	6	
		1 river beaver	10 ermine	6	
		2 otter	10 arshins of calico	12	50
		1 black bear			
		1 bear, medium	5 arshins Flemish linen	8	50
1825	August	1 river beaver	10 ermine	6	—
		2 large black bear	2 large blankets	[. . .]	
		4 medium black bear	20 arshins unbleached linen	[. . .]	
		8 mink	1 funt Virginia tobacco	[. . .]	

*[Sic.]

In addition to these furs, the Kolosh trade *tsukli*, or lime shells of worms, found on the [Queen] Charlotte Islands, which the natives of North America love so much. The Kolosh are paid 30 rubles a 100 in goods for them.

The reasons why we were not able to strengthen our trade with the Kolosh up to now were the following:

1) Without the permission of the chief manager, we could not pay a price comparable to that paid by the Americans in order to attract them to our side. Now we are paying seven medium blankets worth 15 rubles and sometimes more depending on the situation.

2) American trade in the straits is now declining. They have acknowledged that three to four ships come here and pick up 500 sea otter pelts per ship. They pay six large blankets in addition to various goods equal to two blankets.[41] According to Mr. Hammet, these payments and the high cost of maintaining a crew are the reasons for this decline. Americans pay 10 to 30 percent for the insurance on the ship and cargo, depending on the time of the sea voyage. The captain and supercargo receive from 2 percent to 5 percent of the transaction. A sailor earns a monthly wage of 12 piasters, and one and a half funts of rusks, one funt of meat and a cup of rum a day. In the morning and evening he also receives tea and coffee. Each sailor gets 200 piasters in wages a year.

Because of these circumstances we can hope that their trading along this coast will soon come to an end and that in the next ten years they will no longer visit here.

3) Sometimes when we had shortages, the company would trade with the Kolosh for halibut, whale oil and seal oil; and in the spring for tree bark to cover our barns, kazhims and other buildings which could not possibly be covered with boards because we have no sawmill. In exchange for these goods the Kolosh receive tobacco, cast iron pots, axes, beads, paints, Flemish linen, calico and other items. The supply of fish would ease the question of foodstuffs for the company if the promyshlenniks and Creoles and their wives and daughters who live at company expense (many of whom are Kolosh women) would observe this rule: to pay moderate prices for fish; but they often pay without thinking about the prices they are paying. In addition to these necessary items, the Kolosh bring in in the spring the following: sea gull eggs, and eggs from other birds: ducks, geese, grouse, roots and herbs; in the summer they bring berries; in the winter — mountain sheep, crab, shellfish and other crustaceans; they also bring many handmade artifacts such as hats, blankets, masks, pipes and other trifles which they sell to the promyshlenniks, Creoles, Aleuts and their wives for goods and foodstuffs which are sold in our stores, including great quantities of potatoes and even flour and provi-

sions of grain. This practice is a major evil and the welfare of the company demands that it be eliminated as soon as possible. It often happens that a promyshlennik will give a scarf worth two rubles for a bowl of berries and then go into debt to the company. The Kolosh exchange everything with the Americans and even buy guns which are sometimes of high quality.

In addition to these business dealings, the Kolosh have found another way of making profit necessary in their every-day life. Many bring their slaves and women and invite the Russians to make use of them; whatever the girl receives for her services is taken away by the owner; this new business activity also causes the promyshlenniks to give away whatever they own for the girl's sustenance. Many of the company employees and visitors from European ships have become involved in these relationships. It is clear that many of the promyshlenniks have come to financial ruin by dressing their vile lovers. Others have tried to run to them and have greatly spread diseases. This is also an evil, but a necessary one if we are to avoid unnatural acts against nature which we have observed due to the shortage of women.

It is impossible to estimate the harm which comes from such exchanges. Without this, on the other hand, we would have a greater quantity of goods and other things, which our employees and the Aleuts buy as necessities and give away as mere trifles; on the other hand, there would be an increase in the purchase of furs. The Kolosh say that when they are given the same thing for a fish as they would for a fox, he would rather give the first instead of having to wander through the forest hunting for fox.

At the beginning of 1831, the chief manager, Baron Ferdinand Petrovich Wrangell, established a tax on all goods bought from the Kolosh; he designated a special area for a daily market, except for holidays, and assigned a person to oversee the trading. This overseer was to turn in a list of the items bought every day.

[Table c.] Payment to Kolosh for Furs, 1830

[Name of Animal]	[Quantity, Measure and Type of Goods]	Price: r.	k.
1 sea otter	9 blankets	10	
	2/8 [bucket] of rum	5	
	1 funt cinnabar	10	

[Table c.] — continued

[Name of Animal]	[Quantity, Measure and Type of Goods]	Price: r.	k.
	1 funt cinnabar	1	50
	4 funts of tobacco	4	
1 sea otter	5 arshins of calico, depending on quality, with diminution: 2nd, and sometimes one blanket, depending on quality of the animal; or with it still furs, even happens that a quintal [of furs] and nine blankets	[...]	
1 sea otter yearling	4 blankets, sometimes	5 & 16	
	1½ rum	5	
	72 [funts] cinnabar	10	
	2 funts tobacco	1	50
1 newborn sea otter pup	7½ arshins of calico	1	
1 genuine sea otter pup	2½ arshins of calico	1	
1 tail of sea otter and sometimes	7½ arshins of calico	1	
4 tails of sea otters	2 blankets	16	
1 yearling tail	2½ arshins of calico	1	
	1 funt tobacco	1	50
2 large river otter	2 blankets	16	
1 medium river otter and sometimes small	1 funt tobacco and sometimes 2 funts	[. . .]	
1 large otter No. 1	1 blanket	16	
2 otter, medium	2 blankets	16	
1 otter, small	1 or 2 funts tobacco	1	50
4 sea otter, small black	2 blankets	16	
1 sea otter pup, large	10 arshins calico	1	
1 sea otter pup, medium	7½ arshins calico	1	
1 sea otter pup, small	5 arshins calico	1	
1 sable cloak (27 sables)	3, sometimes 4, blankets	16	
3 mink	1 funt tobacco	1	50
1 cross fox	1 blanket, depending on quality, added to tobacco		
2 silver fox	1 blanket		
1 red fox	7½ arshins of calico		
1 prime sable	7½ arshins of calico		
1 sable cloak	3 blankets		
	2 sazhens of calico		

[Table c.] — continued

[Name of Animal]	[Quantity, Measure and Type of Goods]	Price: r.	k.
1 pair otter castors	1 small bunch of tobacco		
1 muskrat	1 small bunch of tobacco		
1 fur seal	5 arshins of calico		

The Koloshi measure by arm sazhens, calculating a sazhen as 2½ arshins.

[Table d.] Analysis of the Kolosh Trade, 1831

What Went to [the Kolosh] in the Barter of Furs			Price: r.	k.	Total: r.	k.
736	[pieces]	blankets	16		11,776	
170	[pieces]	blankets	22		3,740	
1,261	arshins	calico	1	10	1,387	10
1,221¼	arshins	calico		80	977	
435	papers	cinnabar	1		435	
2	[pieces]	horn combs			1	
1¼	funt	tobacco			2	
1½	arshins	English cloth	10		24*	
½	arshins	English cloth			10	
55½	arshins	blue cloth	6		333	
64¾	arshins	blue cloth	5		323	75
9 puds 17¾ funts		Virginia tobacco	60		566	63
2	funts	Circassian tobacco			3	
6⅛	buckets	rum	40		245	
14¼	arshins	flag bunting	1		14	25
9 puds 22 funts		cast iron vessels	10		95	50
2¾	funts	copper vessels			8	25
4	funts	powder			6	
7	[pieces]	andirons copper	15		105	
18	[pieces]	axes	2		36	
4	clusters	string beads			2	
					20,090*	48
For purchase of bark [tree bark for roofing]:						
749	arshins	calico		80	599	20
11	[pieces]	mirrors			2	75
8 puds 24 funts		cast iron vessels			86	
4	clusters	beads			10	

[Table d.] — continued

What Went to [the Kolosh] in the Barter of Furs		Price: r. k.	Total: r.	k.
96 [pieces]	axes		192	
			889	95
		Transport:	20,980	43
	For purchase of clay:			
3 puds 1 funt	cast iron vessels		30	25
11 funts	Virginia tobacco		16	50
7 [pieces]	axes		14	
6¼ arshins	calico		5	
			65	75
	For purchase of fat:			
47½ arshins	calico	80	38	
3 funts	tobacco		4	50
1 [piece]	ax		3	75
6 arshins	calico		6	60
			52	85
	For purchase of foodstuffs per detailed inventories:			
1,477½ arshins	calico		1,274	
891½ arshins	ticking and cloth		469	
78 puds 20¾ funts	tobacco, various		4,763	86
19 puds 27½ funts	cast iron vessels		196	87
	for various small items		1,296	27
			8,000	
		Total	29,100*	

Total of main goods received:

306 [pieces]	blankets
4,768 arshins	calico
88 puds, 15 funts	Virginia tobacco
40 puds, 34 funts	cast iron vessels
122½ arshins	cloth
891 arshins	cloth and ticking
122 [pieces]	axes
435 [pieces]	papers red [cinnabar]

*[Sic.]

[Table e.] Price Schedule for Foodstuffs [in 1831]

	r.	k.		r.	k.
Sheep:			Goose or swan	1	25
large	12		River duck		75
medium	10		2 Small ducks		75
small	8		1 Bucket red bilberries	2	
Sheep:					
very small	5		1 Basket of mussels		75
legs	3-1¾				
Halibut:					
2½ puds	3				
pud	1	50			
Cod, each		75			

[Table f. Record of Foodstuffs Purchased from the Kolosh, January to 1 June 1831, According to General Schedule]

Bartered			Paid		
[Amount]	[Goods]	[r. k.]*	[Amount]	[Goods]	[r. k.]
33	goats		49 puds, 8½ funts	Virginia tobacco per 60 [r.]	2,952.75
111	goat legs			twist tobacco	
1,376 puds	halibut		7 funts	per 2 [r.]	14.00
232	geese and swans		309½ arshins	calico	309.10
315	river ducks		657½ arshins	ticking	334.00
198	grouse and partridge		114 arshins	cloth	68.40
2	heron		51 arshins	striped linen	25.50
2,503	cod		19 puds 7½ funts	cast iron	191.87
512	perch, flounder		1 [each]	handkerchief	4.00
25,060	herring and smelt			pigment worth	3.25
145 baskets	raspberries		1 [each]	axe	1.50
[. . .]	baidara hooks				
50	crabs				
6 puds, 26 funts	sheep fat				
62 vedros	fat				
3¼ vedros	red bilberries				
96 bundles	various greens				
8 baskets	iukola				
9 puds, 10 funts	whale meat				
					3,934.37†

*The prices are not entered. †Error in original; should be 3,904 r. 37 k.

[Table g. Record of Foodstuffs Purchased from the Kolosh, June through September 1831]

Bartered				Paid			
Amount	Goods	[r.	k.]	Amount	Goods	[r.	k.]
10	sheep	44		37¼ arshins	calico [at] 80 [r.]	297	
4	sheep legs	3		20 arshins	striped linen	10	
155 puds	halibut	121		3 puds 4½ funts	tobacco [at] 60 [r.]	185	25
59	cod	12		2 puds 2½ funts	molasses	33	
2	ducks		75				
20	perch	3	75				
103	king salmon	167	75				
½ vedro	fat	2	50				
3	geese	4	50				
1	grouse		75				
2	cuttlefish	2	25				
2,960	gull eggs	148					
	greens and raspberries	15					
		525	25			525	25
1	sheep	4		3 arshins	calico	3	60
6	sheep legs	5	50	61¼ arshins	calico	47	
1,000	eggs	42	60	5 arshins	ticking	6	
2½	buckets of fat	5		15 arshins	ticking for trousers	7	50
2 puds 15 funts	whale	13	25	5 arshins	cloth	3	
5	live geese	5	75	3 puds 19¾ funts	Virginia tobacco	209	62
1	tufted puffin		37	22½ [funts?]	twist tobacco	45	
13 puds	halibut	12					
	berries	233	25				
	[Total]	321	72		[Total]	321	72

[Table g.] — continued

Bartered				Paid			
Amount	Goods	[r.	k.]	Amount	Goods	[r.	k.]
			For August [1831]				
5	sheep legs	6		103¼ arshins	calico	83	
7	sheep	28		2¼ arshins	calico	3	
18 puds 30 funts	funt halibut	20	25	5 arshins	calico	3	
107 puds	pink salmon	25		2 puds 10½ funts	tobacco	135	75
32 [puds]	chum salmon	9		1 pud 9¾ funts	Virginia tobacco	99	50
43 [puds?]	silver salmon	10	50	1 pud	soap	1	30
6	geese	7	50				
1,000	eggs	55					
	berries for	164	30				
	[Total]	325	55		[Total]	325	55
			For September [1831]				
125 puds	halibut	158	75	53¼ arshins	calico	43	
34 [puds?]	silver salmon	10	50	5 arshins	ticking	6	
	berries for	109	85	5 puds 10 funts	Virginia tobacco	315	25
63	river ducks	26	25	27¾ funts	twist tobacco	55	50
15	geese	18	75	2	red cloth [cinnabar]	1	60
236 fish	chum salmon	53					
2	sheep	13					
26	sheep legs	24					
11	woodcock	6	50				
2 funts	tallow		75				
	[Total]	421	35		[Total]	421	35

[Table h.] *Estimated Annual Purchases in the Kolosh Market, 1831*

	r.	k.
January to June	3,934	35
June	525	35
July	321	72
August	325	55
September	421	35
October	639	02
November	627	62
December, approx.	600	
	7,394	98*
Besides the market, approx.	615	02
Total for the year for foodstuffs	8,000†	

*Error in original; should be 7,394 r. 96 k. †[Sic]

[i.] *Notes on Ozerskii Redoubt*

1831 Ordered to preserve fish and salt-beef in salt:

red salmon—	30 [thousand fish]
pink salmon —	10 [thousand fish]
silver salmon —	10 [thousand fish]
Total:	50 [thousand fish]

Estimated Salt:

for small sort —	18 [puds]
for large sort —	22 [puds]

In all, 20 puds* per thousand fish, and therefore, 1,000 puds of salt per 50,000 fish.

*Should be 40 puds.

[j. *Purchase Record for Foodstuffs from the Koloshi, October-November 1832]*

Bartered				Paid			
[Amount]	Goods	[r.	k.]	[Amount]	Goods	[r.	k.]
For October 1832							
25	sheep	171	25	300 arshins	calico	240	
185	ducks	109	30	8 arshins	ticking	9	60

Table [j.] — continued

Bartered				Paid			
[Amount]	Goods	[r.	k.]	[Amount]	Goods	[r.	k.]
16	geese	26	62	10 arshins	ticking	5	
117 puds	halibut	111	25				
33 fish	chum salmon	10	25	6 puds, 7¾ funts	tobacco	371	62
211 fish	silver salmon	71	25	1 funt	twist tobacco	2	
1 vedro	fat	3	60	4 funts	cast iron	5	
13 baskets	raspberries	9	75	2 funts	red cloth [cinnabar]	5	
12 baskets	turnips	9					
1	crab (cuttlefish)			1 funt	red cloth		80
6	sheep legs	8					
5 vedro	red bilberries	8	50				
1 pud, 20 funts	whale meat	4	50				
	iukola for	1	50				
	berries for	44	25				
12	cod	4	50				
	[Total]	639	02*		Total	634	02†
For November [1832]							
78 puds, 20 funts	halibut	109	50	267½ arshins	calico of various sorts	249	
18	silver salmon	6		6 puds, 11¾ funts	tobacco	377	62
21	sheep	176	50				
686	cod	196	50	1	red cloth	1	
5	geese	6	50				
67	ducks	41	87				
40	sheep legs	42	50				
3	grouse	2	25				
3½ vedros	red bilberries	6					
30 baskets	mollusks	21	75				
4 baskets	mussels	3					
3 baskets	turnips	2	25				
3 funts	tallow	1	50				
½ vedro	fat	2	25				
15	iukola	3	75				
	iukola for	5	25				
	[Total]	627	62‡		[Total]	627	62

*[Sic.] †Error in original; should be 639 r. 02 k. ‡[Sic.]

5. Domestic Trade Methods

Under this heading one should understand everything that deals with the supply of all necessities to all the inhabitants of the colonies. Stores were built in Novo-Arkhangel'sk: one was built for the storage of furs gathered from the various areas; these are then shipped to Russia and elsewhere; the second store is used to stock Russian and foreign goods — imports from Russia or bought from foreigners. The goods are stored, shipped to the various offices and departments and sold in the various stores; the third store is a building supply store [*material'nyi magazin*], which receives, stores and distributes building materials for houses, ships and projects in port; the fourth is a general store [*obshchii ili naskhodnyi magazin*] which is in charge of issuing rations; it stores and distributes all household goods such as lavtaks, kamlei, etc. This store also exchanges goods with the Kolosh and pays the Aleuts for the furs they gather; the fifth is a trading store which receives goods on a monthly basis wholesale from the warehouse and sells them at retail prices for cash to officials, employees and Aleuts. A price list, signed by the chief manager, is issued to each office, and this is posted on the wall of each store so that every customer knows the prices of the goods and the shopkeeper [*prikazchik*] cannot by any means charge an extra kopek for any of the goods. We affix a list of such prices:

[a.] Extract from Price Schedule [for Foodstuffs] and Goods for 1825

		r.	k.
Sugar, loaf	funt	1	50
Sugar, best granulated white	funt	1	20
Sugar, yellow	funt		60
Sugar, hard	funt	1	25
Sugar, molasses	funt	40	
Rice	funt	40	
Tea, baikhov	funt	8	
Tea, sushon	funt	4	
Tea, bohee	funt	3	
Rum, cognac and gin	os'mina	5	
Vinegar, sharp	os'mina	3	
Vinegar, rhine	os'mina	1	50
Flour, large-grained Bostonian	pud	15	
Flour, wheat	pud	5	
Peas	pud	4	80
Meal barley	pud	6	
Salt beef, English	pud	13	

		r.	k.
Salt beef, California and Kad'iak	pud	6	
Butter, Iakut	pud	36	
Butter, Kad'iak and Russian	pud	20	
Kazan soap	pud	30	
Tobacco, Circassian	funt	1	50
Tobacco, Virginia	funt	1	25
Thread	funt	6	
Leather, iufta	funt	2	
Leather, dubbed	funt	1	60
Nuts, cedar	funt	1	60
Hops	funt	1	50
Pepper, bitter	funt	1	50
Mustard, California	funt	50	
Coffee	funt	2	
Shot	funt	50	
Powder	funt	1	50
Copper ware	funt	3	50
Nankeen, large Kiakhta	piece	9	
Nankeen, large Canton	piece	10	
Blankets, large American	piece	17	
Blankets, small American	piece	11	
Blankets, large English	piece	18	
Blankets, medium English	piece	14	
Frieze, best	arshin	8	
Frieze, medium	arshin	6	
Frieze, kamluk	arshin	6	
Calico, best English	arshin	3	
Calico, medium English	arshin	2	
Calico, Russian	arshin	2	25
Cloth, best English	arshin	36	
Cloth, Holland	arshin	25	
Cloth, ordinary	arshin	10	
Cloth, calico	arshin	8	60
Cloth, soldier	arshin	5	
Cloth, Lenskoe	arshin	1	50
Calico	each	40	
Kerchiefs, pocket Bengal	each	2	50
Stockings, cloth men's	pair	5	
Stockings, women's cotton	pair	3	
Stockings, cotton thread	pair	2	25
Stockings, wool	pair	2	
Cloth, Romanovskii	arshin	60	
Ticking, striped linen	arshin	1	20
Ticking, blue	arshin	50	
Ticking, blue	arshin	56	
Flemish cloth	each	75	
Ravenduck	each	50	

In order to show the quantity of goods sold in the store in Novo-Arkhangel'sk, we affix two extracts of monthly sales:

[b.] Extracts from the Record of Monthly Profit from Sale of Foodstuffs and Goods in the Novo-Arkhangel'sk Store for 1824 and 1825

1824	[r.	k.]	1825	[r.	k.]
January	10,587	39	January	19,729	65
February	11,745	08	February	13,164	44
March	17,984	66	March	15,999	20
April	14,377	20	April	16,102	61
May	19,881	80	May	24,349	30
June	11,328	07	June	11,457	35
July	6,356	18	July	947	08
August	11,974	35	August	14,537	43
September	12,024	51	September	18,728	80
October	13,261	66	October	20,212	78
November	12,360	24	November	13,481	96
December	13,361	77	December	13,062	58
	155,239	91*		190,243	18†

*Error in original; should be 155,242 r. 91 k. †[Sic.]

At the beginning of each year all promyshlenniks receive 50 rubles at the same time in order to equip themselves, and after that they receive 15 to 20 rubles a month. When ships sail out of the port they are also supplied for a three- to four-month voyage; as a result of this there is a great sale of goods at that particular time. In 1825 there were more than sufficient goods and as a result, the amount of money spent was greater. It is necessary to note that at that particular time the military sloop *Predpriiatie* was in port from February to September; then the ship *Elena* was here from August to November. Their officials and crews also bought their goods from our shop.

H. THE SETTLEMENT'S FACILITIES

The Siberian promyshlenniks call a rocky headland which juts out into the sea and is separated from the shore by an isthmus a *kekur*. The Novo-Arkhangel'sk fortress, consisting at the present time of three towers and a battery of 30 cannons of 3- to 6-funt caliber and a two-storied building with a mezzanine which is used by the chief manager, is located on such a kekur. This formation consists of native rock, rising 77 feet above water, topped by a flat area 60 sazhens in diameter. Below the manager's housing there are the barracks which accommodate 40 workers. Below this on the rocky slope there are warehouses, barracks and other quarters, which will be mentioned later. These form the middle fortress.

1. Buildings

When Mr. Baranov was replaced all the buildings were dilapidated. The house of the chief manager, the barracks and others were maintained by constant repair until new buildings could be built in the following order:

1818. During Mr. Hagemeister's management

Tower No. 1, with two stories, octagonal, with eight cannons.

1819. During Mr. S. I. Ianovskii's management

1. Tower No. 2, two-storied, octagonal, with eight cannons.
2. Pier near the shore.
3. Windmill.

1820

1. Chief manager's house in the upper fortress, eight sazhens in length, with barracks and kitchen below; the manager's room on the first floor and a billiard room above the gates; two rooms upstairs in the mezzanine.
2. Tower No. 3 in the upper fortress, the same size as the others; with six cannons.
3. A battery on the seaside; with eight cannons.
4. Lower barracks, divided into three parts by hallways (with a mezzanine on both sides); these rooms can house 80 men; they are nine sazhens in length; there are three rooms for officials upstairs.
5. An apartment house, two-storied, nine sazhens in length; they house the priest, the doctor, two officials, the office, pharmacy and hospital.
6. House of the office manager.
7. Bathhouse for officials.

8. Bathhouse for the garrison.
9. Spinning (weaving) shop.
10. Bakery.
11. A new harbor on pilings to replace the old one, eaten by worms.
12. Three stairways to the upper fortress and a reviewing stand.
13. A two-storied arsenal for small arms.
14. Gates and a wall for the middle fortress from the barracks to the priest's house, with a battery of two cannons.

From 1826 to 1828 Under the Management of Petr Egorovich Chistiakov

1. A three-storied store 18 sazhens in length; the lower floor contains a section for storage in general; there are two rooms for storing materials, and two for storing goods and supplies; the central floor is for materials and furs and supplies; the floor under the roof is used for storing various types of goods.
2. A two-storied house for apartments of officials; downstairs there is a barracks, a school; three separate apartments for officials; upstairs — six separate rooms and two kitchens. Both buildings are covered with metal roofs.

After receiving orders from the Board of Directors to move the main offices from Sitkha to Kad'iak, no new buildings were built except for those which were needed: that is, storerooms, granaries, and kitchens for the doctor, priest and the hospital, with a wall which was part of the central fortress.

1830. July and August

Two new pilings have been put in place for the building of the harbor area.

A large warehouse, 18 sazhens long, is now being built; in it there will be various sections to house various workshops, and storage areas for goods and supplies.

Some of the old buildings can still stay up awhile; others are falling apart; these include:

In the central fortress: general store, trading store (both were torn down because of their disrepair).

Inside the fort: workshops, blacksmith's shops, quarters for the shop workers and a metalwork shop, the general kitchen, the stable, three kazhims for the Aleuts, the carpentry shop and saw shed.

Outside the fort: the church, a clay-walled cottage, where the school and teacher's quarters used to be.

Due to the shortage of company housing the company has bought small private homes from the prikazchik Sungurov and from the employee Stepanov.

In addition to the company buildings, there are 20 small private homes outside the fortress along the shore.

2. Specialized Trades

In surveying the population of Novo-Arkhangel'sk, we listed all the craftsmen found here. Now we would like to list their occupations.

1. Blacksmiths work at three forges. One and sometimes two mainly repair sailing ships, which is always needed. These repairs mainly take place in the spring when the ships prepare to sail; one forge is used for the making of axes and repairing old ones; this is its main function. If time allows it, the smithies also make plough shares, which are traded in California; these ploughs are made in a style designed to be used there. These tools can be sold at a 200 percent profit.

2. Metalworkers in two shops. One worker is responsible for cleaning and repairing firearms from the arsenal; the other for repairing instruments in port and performing work on ships; for building, repairing locks, etc. Due to the large amount of work, it is seldom impossible to perform any new work.

3. The coppersmiths have three shops. In two of them they make new copper and tin cauldrons, cups, teapots, coffee pots, siphons, funnels and other types of vessels, part of which is used for trade in California and with the savages of North America and to supply the other colonies because other kitchen utensils are not ordered from Russia; one shop is especially responsible for making small ship fittings; sometimes they cast pins and hinges for the ships' rudders and bells not more than five puds in weight; small bells are used on ships and large ones are traded or sold in California.

Creole apprentices work in these blacksmith and metalwork shops, but not a single one has yet become a master smith. On the other hand, all copper and bronze masters are now all Creoles. They learned from masters here and know their work well.

4. Coopers have the permanent occupation of repairing barrels for the ships and making new barrels, and tanks and other ship equipment. Barrels are used extensively to ship grain to the colonies. Therefore the main task of the coopers is to repair old ones which become damaged in shipping. New barrels are rarely made.

5. Woodworkers are constantly busy working on ships, making pulleys, blocks and capstans, repairing old ones and making other necessary items; sometimes when necessary they make new pumps for the ships, etc.

6. Boat-wrights build rowboats for the port and for sailing ships. They build excellent launches, whaleboats, gigs and skiffs of various sizes.[42]

7. Rope makers make small ropes, line-ropes, out of twine and other matter. They make log lines, lot lines, marlins and other things out of white flax. They are also kept busy.

8. Candle makers make tallow candles out of California tallow; because of its wide usage to light the houses of officials and ships, 120 puds are used each year. Two to four puds are issued per vessel depending on the time spent at sea. From September to May 30 puds a month are issued to officials; and from May to September — 15 candles a month;[43] when necessary, soap has been made from California tallow.

9. The painter and his assistants constantly make paint and oil out of coconut or hemp. Sailing vessels have to be painted almost every year, not so much for appearance sake as to prevent them from rotting because of the incessant damp weather. Every two or three years they paint the metal roof of the chief manager's quarters and the barracks. All houses are covered with a compound of chalk or yellow ocher to prevent the wood from rotting.

One of the workshops is devoted to distilling oil from turpentine; the oil is used in great quantities in making oil paints.

One man is assigned to make flags because six to ten flags are used for vessels and by the colonies and ships per year.

10. Bricklayers are kept busy building and repairing house stoves. Bricks are brought from Kad'iak and sometimes from Ross. There is little clay here, and that is of poor quality, brought with difficulty from various places around the settlement.

3. Occupations

Occupations in the fortress and port consist of the following:

1. Carpentry for ship and house construction. After Mr. Baranov was replaced, only one cutter was built in Sitkha. It was named the *Baranov*. Ten to twenty of the best carpenters and joiners are used yearly for the purpose of re-timbering and making masts and spars. Sometimes more men are needed. Ten to twelve men are also used for building new homes and repairing old ones.

2. Cutting, hauling and floating logs for building ships and houses is also a major occupation. Nearby trees have been cut down; they are now at 50 sazhens, sometimes 200 sazhens from the shore, which makes the work difficult. In the fall a detachment of 20 men is sent out for a month, sometimes two, for the purpose of cutting trees for lumber. Two men can cut up to five trees, which make logs of six to twelve sazhens long and six to ten vershoks thick. Three-hundred to four-hundred logs are prepared for construction; when the trees are cut down, 40 to 50 men are sent out to haul them to shore. The shore areas are generally uneven, hilly and blocked by fallen trees, all of which creates a special hardship. On some days they cannot even manage to haul ten such logs to the shore, but normally they haul out ten to fifteen logs. Bad weather increases the difficulty. By 11 May the logs are brought into port. Ten to sixteen logs are towed in by rowboats; sometimes they can tow 30 to 40 logs which are pulled in by two or three vessels. Sometimes when there are not enough Russians, Aleuts help in this task.

In addition to spruce, they use thorn apple trees for building purposes; this straight lumber is used to deck row-boats; the curved pieces are used for framing. Spruce roots are used for gussets and other purposes in shipbuilding.

In addition to the lumber prepared for local use, lumber is prepared for Unalashka and the Pribylov Islands yearly; now lumber is also shipped to the Andreianovskie Islands. Keels and framing for the baidarkas are also shipped to these areas; traps for catching fox; barrel staves and special clubs to kill seals and sea lions.

3. There is also the constant and arduous task of cutting wood and making charcoal. The wood is gathered into piles in an area of 10 to 16 sazhens. Then it is covered with dirt and burned. The burning lasts up to 15 days. Seventy to 150 baskets of charcoal is produced in this process, depending on the size of the pile. The charcoal is used by blacksmiths, metal workers and coppersmiths at a rate of five to eight baskets a day. A large amount of charcoal is also used to smoke out rats before ships sail out to sea. No sooner has a pile disappeared than more wood is cut for another pile. One important visitor to the colonies wisely noted that he saw only labor there, that they made axes for cutting timber, which were used for making charcoal, which in turn was used to make axes.

4. The thorn apple is used for firewood because it is softer and more thorny, but the wood crackles noisily when burning. The best firewood and more appropriate to burn in houses are spruce twigs, which, even though they are resinous, give off a more even and warmer heat. In the winter two or three large launches bring firewood into port every week for heating the barracks and houses; for baking and drying bread into rusks. Enough wood is prepared for each ship ready to sail. If time allows, it is, however, necessary to peel off the bark from the trees and not load them wet because, as experience has taught us, wet wood soon becomes mouldy and rots; the mould then affects goods which are being transported aboard ships.

5. In the spring the Aleuts are paid one ruble a day by the company to work in the gardens; more than 20 barrels of potatoes are planted and 150 barrels are harvested; in addition

to potatoes, they plant turnips, lettuce, cabbage and cucumbers; the latter only ripen in greenhouses.[44]

6. Getting hay ready during the summer is hard work. It begins in the middle of July and if the summer is rainy, the work continues till October. It often happens that the mowed grass gets wet because of the rain and rots. They seldom have enough time to gather enough hay for ten head of cattle. The hay remains in place till autumn or winter and is transported dry on boats. It often happens that the shallow bays, where the hay is located, freeze. Because of this, there is the problem of transporting the hay until the ice melts.

4. Vessels and Communications

Sailing vessels in use in 1825:

Best:	*Baikal*, American-built	230 tons
	Golovnin	140 tons
	Okhotsk	180 tons
	Rurik [*Riurik*], Finnish-built	180 tons
Fair:	*Volga*, California-built	140 tons
	Kiakhta, California-built	180 tons
	Fortuna, Mexican-built	60 tons
	Baranov, Sitkha-built	30 tons
Poor:	*Buldakov*, California-built	200 tons
	Konstantin, Okhotsk-built	80 tons
	Total:	10 [vessels]
Useless:	*Otkrytie*	
	Chirikov	
	Rumiantsev	
	Platov	

In navigation of that year, the following voyages were made:

	May:	Brig *Volga* to Okhotsk	1
		Riurik and *Fortuna* with [hunting] party	2
		To Nushagak, *Konstantin*	1
First period	June:	To Sandwich Islands, *Okhotsk*	1
		In the colonies, *Baikal*	1
	July:	To Nuchek, *Baranov*	1
		To Unalashka with wood, *Buldakov*	1
			8

		To California for wheat	
Second period	September:	*Kiakhta* and *Baikal*	2
		To Kad'iak with Aleuts, *Riurik*	1
			3

Attempts at building ships in the colonies were made, but it seems that it is more advantageous to buy ready-made ships from the Americans for the following reasons:

1. Quality. All the ships bought from them are of a superb quality and are suitable for many purposes; they sail well, handle easily and drift very little. Of the ships built at Ross the *Rumiantsev* and the *Volga* were of good quality but they lacked other conveniences.

2. Durability. The brig *Golovnin*, purchased from the Americans in 1819, had already been used, and was constantly in use until 1825. Only after six years was it necessary to re-timber it. All ships bought from them were made of solid American oak and the frame (hull) reinforced with copper. Of the ships built in Ross, the *Rumiantsev*, which entered service in 1819, could hardly last until 1822; after a short voyage to Yakutat it was found to be completely useless and beyond repair. The brig *Buldakov*, built in 1820, was used until 1825 and was also found to be defective. Of the ships built in Sitkha, the *Chirikov* was used from 1809 to 1824. It was timbered repeatedly. It is certain that the lumber in Sitkha is more suitable for building, but even though the wood is cut in nearby forests, it has to be hauled a long distance with great difficulty; this task takes up a lot of time and workers who are busy with other necessary tasks in the settlement itself. It is impossible not to give praise to the simple carpenter, who built the two ships in Sitkha and after that the four ships at Ross. But one must also realize that any person sailing on these ships in tempestuous seas cannot have complete faith in a man who has no knowledge of the art of shipbuilding.[45]

3. Price. The following was paid for the ships purchased from the Americans: 5,000 otter pelts for the *Brutus*; 11,000 for the *Arab*; 8,000 for the *Lapwing*; considering a pelt to be worth 8 rubles 75 kopeks, the first ship cost 43,750 rubles; the second, 96,250 rubles and the third, 70,000 rubles. The *Brutus* was already eight years old, and had less space; its sails and tackle had

to be replaced in two to three years. The *Arab* had the best qualities, had lots of space, was four years old and was well armed. Excluding 11,250 rubles paid for its rowboats, artillery shells and other things, it cost 85,000 rubles with full armaments; the brig *Lapwing* was two years old and had new guns; excluding 10,000 rubles for the cost of rowboats and artillery shells, the ship cost 60,000 rubles.

Thirty to forty thousand rubles' worth of materials were used to build ships in Ross; this does not include the price of labor; but if we take the average, even then the price exceeds the price of the ships purchased from the Americans. Take for example:

Materials worth	35,000 r.
30 craftsmen for 1½ years, figuring salary and ration at 400 r. [per year] apiece	18,000 r.
Bonuses to craftsmen up to	5,000 r.
	[Total] 58,000 r.

The only reason why shipbuilding was attempted was to keep the people in that area occupied. When it was discovered that the California oak rots quickly and is unsuitable for shipbuilding, it was necessary to stop this activity; the people were put to work at agriculture.

[a.] Addendum Regarding Shipbuilding in Sitkha [1826-1832] During Petr Egorovich Chistiakov's Management

Soon after taking office, the chief manager found it necessary to tell the various offices to begin shipbuilding. Subsequently the following ships were built:

1826

In November 1825 the building of the boat *Unalashka* was begun; it had a 35½-foot deck, a 45-foot keel. It was built by Master Grudinin. It was launched on 6 July and sailed to Unalashka on 3 August. The Creole Fedor Stepanov was assigned as its captain. Considering the materials used for its construction, the ship cost 13,000 rubles in capital; comparing it to other vessels, it was appraised at 28,000 rubles, of which 15,036 rubles were paid out for labor. With supplies, materials, instruments and artillery shells, it cost 29,464 rubles and 72 kopeks. This ship was assigned to the Unalashka office.

1828

In November 1827 two boats (*Bobr* and *Sivuch*) were begun; 35½-foot in keel, 45-foot deck. Both were built simultaneously by Master Ioganson.

On 21 April, the boat *Sivuch* was launched and on 21 May it sailed to Atkha under the command of navigator Ingstrom.

The materials along with full armament for this ship cost 18,000 rubles; 9,218 rubles 82 kopeks for labor; with supplies (such as anchor and other parts) it cost a total of 28,101 rubles 55 kopeks. This ship was assigned to the Atkha Office. On 28 July the boat *Bobr* was launched. It was equipped and used after that to be in contact with Kad'iak. For building this ship, 16,924 rubles and 34 kopeks were spent on materials; 8,075 rubles 66 kopeks on labor; with armament the total cost came to 25,000 rubles. All three boats were trimmed with copper.

1829

On 2 December 1829 the ship *Urup* was begun by Master Ioganson. It has an 85-foot keel and a 97-foot deck. On 30 November 1829 it was launched from its berth. With copper reinforcement, trimming and full armament, the ship cost 70,664 rubles; 17,665 rubles were tagged on; by 1 September 1830 the ship cost 100,727 rubles for all materials, labor and instruments.

1830

On 16 March the boat *Aleut* was begun by Master Ioganson. It had a 37-foot keel.

Under Chief Manager Baron Ferdinand Petrovich Wrangell

1830	Laid foundation of church seven sazhens long, [. . .] width . . . Altar.
3 March 1831	Boat *Aleut* was launched, at cost of 16,575 r. 26 k. for materials and full armament, and 25,000 r. in capital.
On 1 May	Surrounded (with pickets from *Amethyst* to hill and from there to the suburbs behind Mr. Benseman's house. On

	the hill a watchtower was built, in which nine cannon were placed, and facing the Kolosh, a battery was built consisting of 21 cannons and falconets.
September	The church was completed and dedicated on the 27th.
September	Foundation for workshops were laid, one sazhen long and one sazhen wide. In the middle, a smithy; on both sides, two other shops in which must be constructed locksmith shop, carpenter shop, block shed, copper smithy and an apartment for two shipmasters.
12 October	Master Netsvetov began work on cutter *Morekhod* with a keel 52 feet long.
November	Workshops begun [. . .] sazhens long.
May 1832	Workshops finished with smithy in center; on right side a carpentry shop and two apartments; on left a copper smithy, lock smithy and lathe shop.
1 June	Galiot *Morekhod* launched, which cost, for materials with full armament, in capital.
During summer	Built barn for cattle.
until 1 September	In lower fort on both sides built wall with embrasures for guns.

5. The Ozerskii Redoubt

A settlement known as the Ozerskii Redoubt was built twelve miles from the fort near the source of a river which flows into a lake. Fishing was the main reason for establishing this settlement; because the waterfall is dammed at its outlet fish traps have been built there and fish are caught there. The redoubt has the following buildings at the present time:

1. The house of the redoubt commander, and barracks for the people who work there; this area is surrounded by a stockade for defense purposes; it also has a tower with eight guns; this tower is situated outside the stockade.

2. A special barracks with six rooms built for the promyshlenniks, outside the stockade.

3. A mill, which was built originally for grinding flour. It has an oak crusher.

4. The mill was built in 1825 with two grindstones. Storage bins have been built inside; they have the capacity to hold 1,500 fanegas of wheat.

5. A tannery to make leather uppers and soles. Yearly they can tan from 100 to 150 hides from California steer.

6. A fish factory, where there is a dam and a small fish pond where the fish come in.

There are always 25 to 30 men at the redoubt.

The men cut granite for grindstone in the mountains beyond the lake which is near the redoubt.[46] The lake is surrounded by hills (mountains) which are covered by thick forests. There they cut trees for lumber and float them down to the settlement which is located amidst snow-covered peaks at the edge of a narrow bay. Entrance from the sea and from Novo-Arkhangel'sk is impeded by rocks and a sailing vessel can sail through there but with great difficulty. One cannot anchor there in the bay; the water is deep everywhere, and the bottom is rocky.

Five to six miles from the redoubt there are mineral springs [hot springs] where two small cabins have been built; the water flows into a basin where visitors can lie in the water.

J. CAPITAL TURN-OVER IN NOVO-ARKHANGEL'SK

As the seat of colonial rule Novo-Arkhangel'sk has at its disposition greater capital than the other offices in the colonies.

As an example we present the use of capital for the year 1825, when Chief Manager Matvei Ivanovich Murav'ev was replaced. As of 1 January 1825 the capital in cash and goods was the following:

	r.	k.
During the year, goods were delivered from Russia on the ship *Elena* and on the Okhotsk transport and transfers made for	873,242	
Transferred to the Novo-Arkhangel'sk office from colonial offices and districts	193,928	51

	r.	k.
Profit from trade with foreigners, from adding markups on Russian goods, and from hunts of furbearing animals	470,493	43
Owed by the office to officials and employees to January 1826	107,481	26
	3,810,066	30*
From this capital, the office owed officials and employees at the beginning of 1825	133,985	99
Transferred for furs to the Main Office and to the Okhotsk office	330,484	03
Transferred to the colonial offices for goods and transfers of capital	427,875	22
Trade expenditures in the course of the year	403,368	80
Remaining capital as of January 1826	2,514,351	56
	3,810,066	30*

One must note that during this year [1825] a capital sum of 172,869 rubles was transferred from the Okhotsk Office to Novo-Arkhangel'sk; this sum was considered to belong to the detachment in Atkha, but since this area came under colonial rule, the capital available increased.

In previous years the capital of the office, gains and expenditures were the following:

Year	Capital Turnover		Taxes on Production		Expenses for Production	
	r.	k.	r.	k.	r.	k.
1818	2,833,555	59	184,420	59	152,851	19
1819	2,009,769	13	113,275	73	204,935	98
1820	3,257,212	52	487,274	52	358,433	98
1821	3,479,107	49	188,889	28	321,447	49
1822	3,305,411	51	256,938	74	355,496	96
1823	2,865,946	76	79,287	81	366,668	02
1824	3,037,446	21	571,001	96	396,682	18
1825	3,810,066	30	470,493	43	403,368	80
1826	3,463,609	08	306,624	56	464,300	76
1827	3,776,025	68	574,072	89	454,222	12
1828	3,414,044	68	244,373	19	425,597	50
1829	3,514,317	75	132,381	13	404,951	34
1830	3,070,096	61	211,973	77	471,812	87
1831	2,905,165	96	137,518	61	426,891	15

Here, it may seem that there is more than a double return on expenditures, but it is necessary to note: (1) that during the first two years there were fewer officials receiving significant wages, and there were fewer promyshlenniks, while the Creoles received little pay; (2) that sailing ships were assessed at the purchase price while the capital spent for repairs increased; as a result, depreciation and ships no longer considered seaworthy were not included; (3) the construction of houses (buildings) were assessed at the purchase price; after a house fell apart, it was entered as a loss; (4) during the first year the promyshlenniks were paid 300 rubles (in later years 50 rubles were added to their salaries) and there were no bonuses.

It must be noted that there was a profit, and significant at that, when we traded with foreigners and when Russian goods were shipped in from St. Petersburg, because of the 30 percent markup. But there is no way that profit from hunting can go beyond 100,000 rubles in the colonies.

Capital at the beginning and end of 1825 was the following:

To January 1825	r.	k.
Cash on hand in Spanish piasters at going rate and colonial coins at	53,456	89
Furs, Russian and foreign goods	1,118,245	48
In arsenal, weapons and shells worth	129,547	90
Sea-going, sailing and rowing boats	489,828	69
Debts owed by officials, promyshlenniks and Aleuts	165,653	32
Church possessions	14,315	04
All buildings, including furniture, library, pharmacy, etc.	116,671	55
At Ozerskii Redoubt	25,160	42
Commissions owed by agents	52,041	81
Total	2,164,921	10
To January 1826		
Cash on hand	22,704	11
Furs, Russian and foreign goods, foodstuffs and materials	1,224,577	75
In arsenal, weapons and shells	140,637	27
Sea-going, sailing and rowing boats	623,337	68
Debts owed by officials, promyshlenniks, etc.	180,487	96
Church possessions	18,133	05
All buildings, furniture, library, pharmacy, etc.	122,626	41
In Ozerskii Redoubt	29,484	74
Commissions owed by agents	152,362	60
Total	2,514,351	56*

*[Sic.]

1. A Note on Paper Money

In order to facilitate payments in the colonies, the Main Office supplies paper currency in denominations of 10, 5, and 1 rubles and 50 and 25 kopeks. In 1817 it issued a sum of 12,000 rubles. Later, when it was discovered that this paper money had become worn out with time, 30,000 rubles were issued in 1822.[47] The earlier notes were exchanged and sent back, and the new currency was sent to all the colonies and is now used by the Russians and Aleuts.

The colonial authorities always kept a certain sum of Spanish piasters at their disposal in case they were unable to exchange goods for wheat in California. Thus, by January 1825 they had accumulated a sum of 7,591 piasters. These piasters were sometimes obtained by trading goods with military ships; sometimes they were taken from the officers and given to the Main Office, but these sums were small. Mr. Klochkov, from the *Riurik*, left the office 3,647 piasters.

When ships are sent out annually to California, they are issued 1,000 to 2,000 piasters, and they are instructed to try to save them, unless it becomes necessary to pay for wheat or duties.

2. Quantity of Main Goods and Their Consumption

By January 1826 there was a considerable quantity of Russian and foreign goods in our stores. These goods had been obtained in 1825 from the *Elena* which had come from St. Petersburg and from England. A complete cargo was also bought from the American Blanchard. The following goods were sent to the colonies that year:

154	arshins of English cloth at 36 r.	199	puds of wheat
316	arshins of English cloth at 20 to 26 r.	104	puds butter
1,533	arshins of English cloth at 10 to 20 r.	288	funts Circassian tobacco
2,018	arshins of English cloth at 6 to 10 r.	911	buckets rum, cognac, arrack and gin
1,260	arshins of English cloth from 5 r.		
2,095	arshins of Lena cloth	35¼	buckets vinegar
5,900	arshins Kalmuk	344	puds sheet copper
3,183	arshins of various frieze	1,200	puds lead
3,965	large blankets from 14 r.	200	puds shot
1,532	small blankets	940	puds iron nails
1,329	pieces of nankeen	170	puds copper nails
3,358	arshins of various calicos	2,900	puds new anchors
284	pierces of calicos	2,973	puds wheat, unmilled
1,907	arshins of various coarse calico	552	puds barley

2,837	pieces of kerchiefs of various sorts
1,286	pairs of various stockings
23½	puds of various thread
55,800	arshins of various canvases
42,160	arshins of ticking and striped linen
240	puds of yarn
67	puds of various tea
35	puds of wax candles
92	puds of loaf sugar
1,358	puds of granulated sugar
206	puds of molasses
3,525	puds cable and tackle
320	puds twisted cable
7,780	puds iron
96	puds tin
442	puds chalk
167	puds pik
50	shtof turpentine
30	puds tutui nut oil
27	puds of drying oil
1,100	sheets of tin plate
265	puds sheet iron

And a considerable number of tools for the many workshops.

It must be noted that a shore and port tax of 10 to 20 percent and 15 percent are added to the price of goods which are purchased by the Main Office; in addition to that another 30 percent is added for shipping costs. As a result, 40 to 45 percent is added to the goods brought in from Russia. Moreover, these goods are distributed on the basis of need, quality and quantity. These goods are distributed or divided into three categories: (1) goods to be used by the company for sailing, agriculture and local distribution; (2) those which are to be used to supply officials and employees of the company; (3) goods to be used for trading with the Spanish, Americans and savages. With this understanding, the following interests should be taken into consideration:

1. Goods, which can never be used in any manner (sold) but which remain part of the overall capital, must remain at a fixed price. (Such as firearms.) Because of the climate and time, these firearms become damaged so that they can no longer be of any use. They bring only a loss.

2. Twenty-five to thirty percent should be added to goods which cannot be sold or exchanged immediately. [These are luxury or expensive items.]

3. A markup of 40 to 45 percent should be imposed on materials and tools used for house and shipbuilding.

4. Goods for the promyshlenniks and Aleuts, such as tobacco, canvas, ropes, skins (leather), soap, thick linen, socks, and other such items should also be taxed at the same amount.

5. Goods, which are not considered extremely necessary, but are available for sale, such as glass, and chinaware, mirrors, cloth, calico and other similar items, should be taxed at a different percentage rate. Depending on quality, quantity and use should be marked up 50, 60, and 70 percent.

Goods used for trading in California, from which we can hope to make a profit or exchange them for ready cash, should be spared and not sent to the various colonies except in cases of extreme necessity. These main goods are the following:

Glass wares of middling sort
Straw-colored and porcelain dishes of middling sort
Printed and coarse calico
Flemish linen cloth, not wide
White and other threads
Blue and ruby red cloth
Pig iron vessels

Each year the colonial offices send in their requisitions to the Main Office in Novo-Arkhangel'sk. The chief manager then distributes the supplies depending on the quantity of goods in the warehouses. The various requests are studied by the chief manager, and the goods are issued after he has approved each requisition. Communications with Unalashka, the Ross office, Atkha, the Aleksandrovskii fort and the Northern Islands district were maintained once a year. Therefore, they receive enough goods to last them a year; Kad'iak receives goods two to three times a year. Therefore the amount of goods they receive is never the same.

Sometimes when requests are not made, then goods and materials are sent out in accordance to requests based on previous years.

3. Sailing Vessels

In order No. 22 of the Novo-Arkhangel'sk office, made 20 March 1821, Chief Manager Matvei I. Murav'ev suggested a discount of 10 to 15 percent for materials used to repair ships, depending on the age and quality of the ship.

It is understandable that ships age and lose their value and become useless. When this is so, they should be excluded from capital, except for materials and instruments which can be used again.

In an order to Mr. Baranov, Nikolai Petrovich Rezanov stated that sailing vessels made of dry lumber usually last twelve years; one made of wet lumber eight years; when their time has come these ships should be revalued; should a ship be wrecked, then, after excluding any reusable materials, it should be written off as a loss. He ordered that all old vessels in bad condition be sent to Unalashka where there are no forests, so that the lumber from these ships could be used in some way so that it might be counted as capital.[48]

The Novo-Arkhangel'sk office keeps annual accounts of the vessels; it adds to the capital value of all ships materials which have been used to repair them. At the end of each year, information dealing with such matters are sent by each captain to the office. On this basis the value of the ship is set. (Materials which have been used on other purposes are excluded, while those used to repair the ships are added to the value.)

We present the following assessed values of ships in 1825:

		r.	k.
From the brig *Golovnin*, at present prices	10%	6,672	10
From the brig *Buldakov*, for uselessness	30%	14,702	70
From the brig *Volga*	10%	4,140	62
From the schooner *Chirikov*, to be broken up	50%	10,219	38
From the schooner *Fortuna*	10%	2,913	93
From the sloop *Konstantin*	15%	2,556	50
From the cutter *Baranov*	10%	1,563	84
From the brig *Riurik*	10%	8,651	52
From the brig *Kiakhta*	10%	4,772	52
From the brig *Baikal*	5%	4,794	68
From [the ship] *Otkrytie*, for dilapidation	25%	7,254	05
From [the galiot] *Rumiantsev*, for breaking up		1,916	24
From various row boats		1,619	98
	Total	71,777	54*

*[Sic.]

Excluding the estimate, sailing vessels remained in capital as follows:

	[r.	k.]
Golovnin:		
Brig with armament, reserve materials and rowboats	71,911	13
Mathematical instruments	821	13
Firearms and artillery shells	2,356	78
Total	75,088	91*

		[r.	k.]
Brig *Buldakov*		41,426	20
Brig *Volga*		49,328	81
Brig *Riurik*		77,863	69
Brig *Kiakhta*		52,268	05
Brig *Baikal*		101,771	40
Brig *Okhotsk*		93,431	23
Schooner *Chirikov*		14,206	19
Schooner *Fortuna*		31,417	56
Sloop *Konstantin*		18,846	29
Cutter *Baranov*		22,758	95
Ship *Otkrytie*		31,970	95
Crew of the *Amethyst*		1,046	16
Row boats in port		10,666	86
Mathematical instruments		1,236	43
	Total	623,337	68[†]

[†][Sic.]

4. Notes on Debts

Promyshlenniks who come from Russia usually owe debts between 400 and 700 rubles. Many of them accumulate this debt during their seven-year stay here. Through negligence, few of them ever thought of repaying their debts and instead become even more indebted. As a result, their pay is small. As proof of this, there is the fact of 400 men on salary, whose debts amounted to 150,585 rubles and 4 kopeks in January 1826. The Aleuts owed 11,723 rubles and 46 kopeks, while the debts in California amounted to 18,178 rubles and 95 kopeks. The debts owed by the Aleuts date back to Mr. Baranov's time, and it appears that it may be impossible to get money from them because of the now insignificant hunt.

Many promyshlenniks and officials have received money from the company; this has amounted to 70,528 rubles. Some officials who have credit (capital) from the company transfer it to savings banks. The Main Office receives requests from these officials to deposit their money, and they receive receipts [shares in the Russian-American Company] for the capital they have sent in.

There are people who look at everything cynically and see nothing else but harm inflicted against society by the Russian-American Company. These people contend that the colonies are starving the people and the company brings no advantages to the Russian government. In order to convince them otherwise, we can offer a most detailed and true information on the number of people who came to the colonies from Russia and of those who returned to Russia. Here, it can be seen how much the company paid out in wages: this statement will prove that many earned a living from the company, not to mention the amount paid yearly for services rendered and pensions to relatives. The death rate in the colonies, thank God, is in the order determined by nature!

[Table a. Arrivals and Departures in Colonies, Indebtedness and Payments, 1819-1831]

Arrivals			Departures		
	No. of Men	*Debt* r. k.		No. of Men	*Credit* r. k.
			1818. To Okhotsk on		
			schooner *Chirikov*:		
			officials	2	
			crown seamen	7	
			promyshlenniks	23	2,400.27
			1818. On *Suvorov*:		
			promyshlenniks	3	1,486.30
			1818. On *Kutuzov*:		
			officials	2	
			promyshlenniks	4	
			Creoles	9	6,132.45
1819. On *Chirikov*:			1819. To Okhotsk on		
officials	3		*Rumiantsev*:		
promyshlenniks	35	30,164.32	promyshlenniks	19	9,029.74
1820. From Okhotsk			1820. On *Konstantin*		
on *Rumiantsev*:			and *Finliandiia*:		
officials	4		officials and		
promyshlenniks	62	45,729.91	promyshlenniks	25	6,357.54
1820. On ship *Borodino*:					
officials	6				
promyshlenniks	19	8,865.50			
1821. From Okhotsk:			1821. To Okhotsk on		
on *Konstantin*	21	16,682.35	*Rumiantsev*:		
on *Rumiantsev*	20	14,996.57	officials	2	
			promyshlenniks	25	13,040.40
From St. Petersburg					
on *Kutuzov*:			1821. On *Borodino*:		
officials and			officials	2	
promyshlenniks	28	27,829.36	promyshlenniks	14	4,147.93

[Table a.] — continued

Arrivals			Departures		
	No. of Men	*Debt* r. k.		No. of Men	*Credit* r. k.
1822. From Okhotsk on *Chirikov*: promyshlenniks	 50	 2,843.80	1822. On *Chirikov*: officials and promyshlenniks On *Konstantin*: officials and promyshlenniks	 3 15	} 71,542.87
			from Kad'iak	16	11,381.06
On *Rurik* [*Riurik*] officials crown seamen	 7 30	 10,900.00	1822. On *Kutuzov*: officials promyshlenniks and Creoles	 4 3	 2,886.96
1823. From Okhotsk on *Chirikov* and *Konstantin*: clergy and officials promyshlenniks	 3 33	 3,680.23	1823. To Okhotsk on *Chirikov*: officials promyshlenniks	 4 14	 10,469.25
1824. From Okhotsk on *Volga*: clergy promyshlenniks	 1 11	 8,438.21	1824. To Okhotsk on *Volga*: promyshlenniks	 17	 8,563.46
			1824. On *Kreiser*: officials	 1	 499.59
1825. From ship *Elena*: officials seamen	 2 3	 2,959.94	1825. To Okhotsk on *Volga*: clergy promyshlenniks	 1 15	 6,984.82
1825. From Okhotsk on *Volga*: officials promyshlenniks	 5 44	 47,391.49	1825. On *Elena*: officials and employees crown seamen	 10 7	 9,602.81
			1825. On *Predpriiatie* crown seamen	 20	 8,399.92
			1826. On brig *Okhotsk*: officials and promyshlenniks	 23	 9,114.91
Total	387	243,484.68*	Total	291*	182,040.18
1826. From Okhotsk on brig *Okhotsk*: officials promyshlenniks	 1 27	 5,636.50 15,196.52	1826. On brig *Okhotsk* to Okhotsk: officials prikazchiks	 3 4	} 4,300.00
			promyshlenniks	16	4,814.91
			from Atkha	1	1,127.62

[Table a.] — continued

Arrivals			Departures		
	No. of Men	*Debt* r. k.		No. of Men	*Credit* r. k.
On brig *Finliandiia*:					
officials	1	6,350.70			
promyshlenniks	9	2,950.71			
From St. Petersburg on sloop *Krotkii*:					
officials	1	2,500.00			
1827. From Okhotsk on *Chichagov*:			1827. On *Chichagov* to Okhotsk:		
officials	44	21,592.29	officials	15	7,416.31
On brig *Okhotsk*:			On *Okhotsk*:		
prikazchik			officials	1	583.70
Kostromitinov	1	1,350.00	promyshlenniks	19	8,294.44
promyshlenniks	36	18,551.29	from Bering Island	3	5,204.38
1828. From Okhotsk on *Okhotsk*:			1828. On *Okhotsk* to Okhotsk:		
clergy	1	8,064.45	officials	2	
officials	2	4,372.81	prikazchik	1	2,000.00
promyshlenniks	34	13,223.19	promyshlenniks	24	16,749.83
			On *Baikal*:		
			official Benevskii	1	144.88
1829. From Petersburg on *Elena*:					
officials	1	5,121.88	1829. On *Okhotsk* to Okhotsk:		
prikazchik	1	2,000.00			
arms master	1	836.03	seafarer Klimovskii	1	
promyshlenniks	1	282.92	promyshlenniks	18	7,392.60
From Okhotsk on *Okhotsk*:			To St. Petersburg on *Elena*:		
prikazchik	1	2,285.00			
promyshlenniks	21	11,694.69	promyshlenniks	4	1,235.68
			1830. To Okhotsk on *Urup*:		
On brig *Chichagov*:					
promyshlenniks	6	2,156.07	promyshlenniks	7	6,726.62
Total	189	124,165.05	Total	120	65,990.97
1830. From Okhotsk on *Urup*:			1830. To Okhotsk on *Urup*:		
officials and employees	4	41,748.80	from Kuril district, [promyshlenniks]	3	2,704.97
Fr. Okhotsk on *Okhotsk*:					
employees	2	10,114.84	1831. To Okhotsk on *Urup*:		
promyshlenniks	14	6,868.83			
Creoles	2	3,661.91	officials	5	27,821.90
Creoles	3	353.04	promyshlenniks	7	5,402.62

[Table a.] — continued

Arrivals			Departures		
	No. of Men	*Debt* r. k.		No. of Men	*Credit* r. k.
1831. From Okhotsk on *Urup*:					
officials	4	16,664.74			
promyshlenniks	8	3,762.37			
From Okhotsk on *Polifem*:					
officials	4	31,841.68			
promyshlenniks	16	7,710.23			
Total	261*	124,165.05*	Total	135	101,920.46

*[Sic.]

[b.] Extract on the Amount of Capital Paid and Encumbered for Payment to Employees of Various Ranks in the Colonies from 1818 to 1831

	[r.	k.]
By the first table for 1826		
Transfer of debts in the colonies	243,484	68
Transfer of credits	182,040	18
	425,524	86
By second table for 1831 (excluding the last third)		
Transfer of debts	124,165	05
Transfer of credits	65,990	97
	190,156	02
Transferred to banks for deposit:		
1820. Chief Manager S. I. Ianovskii	22,500	
1826. Chief Manager M. I. Murav'ev	55,000	
1830. Chief Manager P. E. Chistiakov	26,000	
1830. On 1 May	16,000	
1822. Doctor Bervi	6,000	
1828. Doctor Benevskii	9,000	
1830. Physician Ermolaev	5,500	
1830. Midshipman Etolin	8,000	
1830. Prikazchik Molvistov	6,000	
1830. Seafarer Tumanin	2,000	
1830. Manager Nikiforov	8,000	
1830. Manager Sizov	5,000	
	169,000	
1831. To Rodion Petrovskii	2,500	
1831. To Priest Veniaminov	5,000	
1831. To Mr. Ingestrom	3,000	

1831. To Obriadin	4,000
1831. To Ermolaev	2,500
1831. To Mr. Etolin from 1827 4,000 annually	16,000
	[33,000]

It must be noted that the payment above excludes the transfer of money from various officials to the Main Office to be deposited in banks, a situation mentioned above. Many of the old promyshlenniks who worked here as prikazchiks had debts which were sent to the Main Office; they were unable to settle their accounts and their debts amount to over 30,000 rubles. According to the chief manager the Main Office did not attempt to collect a debt amounting to 25,000 rubles, due to the fact that these employees had worked for the company a long time and because of the impoverished state of others. It must be said in all fairness that not every business organization can cancel debts which could be of interest to the company.

[c.] Above we have offered two lists of the population; one for all the colonies in 1818, the other especially for Novo-Arkhangel'sk in 1825. For clarification I append a detailed table for all the colonies in 1830.

	Russians		Creoles		Aleuts		Total		Total of both Sexes
	M	F	M	F	M	F	M	F	
In Novo-Arkhangel'sk	271	18	128	106	52	47	451	171	622
At Kad'iak itself	104	8	177	187	37	17	318	212	530
Kad'iak Island:									
Dwellings					1,230	1,271	1,230	1,271	2,501
Tribes on mainland					1,972	2,023	1,972	2,023	3,995
Unalashka District	23	7	51	52	562	701	643*	760	1,403†
Pribylov Islands District	8		17	24	98	92	123	116	239
Fort Ross	35	2	21	32	61	51	117	85	202
Atkha District	43	1	55	65	298	332	396	398	794
Kuril District	11		1		59	9	71	9	80
Total	495	36	450	466	4,376	4,543	5,321[a]	5,045	10,366[b]

*Error in original; should be 636. †Should be 1,396. ‡Should be 4,369. [a]Should be 5,314. [b]Should be 10,359.

By 1 January 1830, 975 people out of those mentioned above remained on the company payroll, including 100 women workers; due to the variety in framework I offer this general table:

[Table d.] Salaries of Officials and Non-official Employees, including Promyshlenniks, Creoles and Aleut Males and Females, to 1 January 1830

	Number	Salary [r.]	Total [r.]
Chief manager	1	30,000	30,000
Office manager at Novo-Arkhangel'sk	1	12,000	12,000
Naval officers	1	7,000	7,000
Naval officers	5	5,000	25,000
Naval officers	1	4,500	4,500
Employees, officials and non-officials	4	4,000	16,000
Employees, officials and non-officials	3	3,500	10,500
Employees, officials and non-officials	2	3,000	6,000
Employees, officials and non-officials	7	2,500	17,500
Employees, officials and non-officials	1	2,250	2,250
Employees, officials and non-officials	2	2,000	4,000
Employees, officials and non-officials	1	1,800	1,800
Employees, officials and non-officials	8	1,200	9,600
Employees, officials and non-officials	3	1,000	3,000
Employees, officials and non-officials	1	900	900
Employees, officials and non-officials	2	800	1,600
Employees, officials and non-officials	2	750	1,500
Employees, officials and non-officials	5	700	3,500
Employees, promyshlenniks and creoles	27	600	16,200
Employees, promyshlenniks and creoles	14	500	7,000
Employees, promyshlenniks and creoles	18	450	8,100
Promyshlenniks and creoles	29	400	11,600
Promyshlenniks and creoles	379	350	132,650
Creoles	36	300	10,800
Creoles	31	250	7,750
Creoles	9	240	2,160
Creoles	1	225	225
Creoles	9	200	200*
Creoles	19	180	5,420*
Creoles	4	175	700
Creoles	2	170	340
Creoles and Aleut workers	11	150	1,650
Creoles and Aleut workers	1	140	140
Creoles and Aleut workers	4	130	520

[Table d.] — continued

	Number	Salary [r.]	Total [r.]
Creoles and Aleut workers	6	125	750
Creoles and Aleut workers	59	120	7,080
Creoles and Aleut workers	51	100	5,100
Creoles and Aleut workers	17	90	1,530
Creoles and Aleut workers	86	80	6,880
Creoles and Aleut workers	18	70	1,260
Creoles and Aleut workers	32	60	1,920
Creoles and Aleut workers	14	50	700
Female workers	48	25	1,200
	975		388,125†

*[Sic.] †Error in original.

The table above applies particularly to Novo-Arkhangel'sk.

[Table e. Salaries of All Other Employees of All Ranks in the Colonies including Promyshlenniks, Creoles, Aleut Males and Females in Novo-Arkhangel'sk on 1 January 1830]

	Number [of people]	Salary r.	Total r.
Chief manager [P. E. Chistiakov]	1		30,000
Office manager [K. T. Khlebnikov]	1		12,000
Naval officer Mr. Etolin	1		7,000
Messrs. Lipinskii, Teben'kov, Zarembo, Til', and Benzeman	5	5,000	25,000
Mr. Ermolaev and wife	1		4,500
Messrs. Prokof'ev and [I. Ia.] Vasil'ev	2	4,000	8,000
Prikazchik Ivanov	1		3,500
Mr. Solodovnikov and bookkeeper Kondakov	2	3,000	6,000
Messrs. Chernov, Obriadin, prikazchik Petr[ovskii], Rikhter, Kashevar[ov]	5	2,500	12,500
Prikazchik Terent'ev, carpenter Ioganson	2	2,000	4,000
Prikazchik Popov	1		1,800
Priest Sokolov, Iv. Ul'ianov, Ia. Geints, Klimov[skii?] and Cherno[v?]	5	1,200	6,000
Teacher Koshevarov [Kashevarov]	1		1,000
Malakhov	1		800
Sub-officers Bykov, Sim[on] Matson	2	700	400*
Various employees	12	600	7,200
Various promyshlenniks	9	500	4,500

[Table e] — continued

	Number [of people]	Salary r.	Total r.
Various promyshlenniks and creoles	10	450	4,500
Various promyshlenniks and creoles	10	400	4,000
Promyshlenniks and creoles	223	350	78,050
Creoles and Aleuts	19	300	5,700
Creoles and Aleuts	9	250	2,250
Creoles and Aleuts	6	200	2,160*
Creoles and Aleuts	14	120	960*
Creoles and Aleuts	8	120	960
Total	360*		236,540†

*[Sic.] †Error in original.

[Table f.] Salaries in Colonies at All Levels for 1831

[No.]		Annual Payment [r.]	Total [r.]
	In Novo-Arkhangel'sk		
1	Chief manager	30,000	30,000
1	Office manager	12,000	12,000
1	Messrs. officials	7,000	7,000
1	Messrs. officials	5,500	5,000*
7	Messrs. officials	5,000	35,000
1	Messrs. officials		4,500
1	Messrs. officials		6,000
5	Messrs. officials	4,000	20,000
3	[Officials] and employees	3,500	10,500
2	[Officials] and employees	3,000	6,000
5	[Officials] and employees	2,500	12,000*
6	[Officials] and employees	1,200	7,200
3	[Officials] and employees	1,000	3,000
2	[Officials] and employees	800	1,600
1	[Officials] and employees		1,500
2	[Officials] and employees	900	1,800
1	Employee		750
2	Employees	700	1,400
9	Employees	600	5,400
7	Promyshlenniks and creoles	500	3,500
11	Promyshlenniks and creoles	450	4,950
16	Promyshlenniks and creoles	400	6,400
2	Promyshlenniks and creoles	360	720
249	Promyshlenniks and creoles	350	87,150
13	Creoles	300	3,900
4	Creoles	250	1,000

[Table f.] — continued

[No.]		Annual Payment [r.]	Total [r.]
8	Creoles	240	1,920
7	Creoles	200	1,400
1	Creole		230
15	Creoles	180	2,700
7	Creoles	120	840
1	Creole		150
395	persons	rubles:	286,510*
	In Kad'iak		
1	Office manager		4,000
1	Official		2,400
1	Employee		1,200
1	Employee		1,100
1	Employee		800
2	Employees	700	1,400
2	Employees	600	1,200
4	Employees	500	2,000
7	Employees	450	3,150
13	Promyshlenniks and creoles	400	5,200
56	Promyshlenniks and creoles	350	19,600
7	Promyshlenniks and creoles	300	2,100
6	Promyshlenniks and pensioners	250	1,500
13	Promyshlenniks and creoles	200	2,600
25	Promyshlenniks and creoles	180	4,500
1	Promyshlenniks and creoles		170
3	Pensioners and workers	150	450
5	Creoles	120	600
10	Creoles	100	1,000
14	Creoles	90	1,260
68	Creoles	80	5,440
6	Creoles	70	420
20	Creoles	60	1,200
4	Creoles	50	200
271	persons	rubles:	63,490
	At Ross		
1	Office manager		4,000
1	Employee		2,500
3	Employees	600	1,800
4	Promyshlenniks	450	1,800
32	Creoles	350	11,200
3	Creoles	300	900
2	Creoles	400	800
1	Creole		240
5	Creoles	180	900
1	Creole		175
53	persons	rubles:	24,315

[Table f.] — continued

[No.]		Annual Payment [r.]	Total [r.]
	In Unalashka Office		
1	Office manager		3,000
1	Employee		2,250
1	Employee		1,200
1	Employee		1,000
1	Employee		600
8	Promyshlenniks	400	3,200
13	Promyshlenniks and creoles	350	4,550
5	Creoles	300	1,500
6	Creoles	250	1,500
2	Creoles	225	450
2	Creoles	200	400
3	Creoles	150	450
1	Creoles	—	140
2	Creoles and Aleuts	130	260
5	Creoles and Aleuts	125	625
29	Creoles and Aleuts	120	3,480
10	Workers, male and female	100	1,000
1	Worker		70
3	Workers, male and female	60	180
1	Worker	50	50
96	persons	rubles:	25,905
	In Pribylov Islands Office		
1	Promyshlenniks		675
2	Promyshlenniks	500	1,000
1	Promyshlenniks	400	400
4	Promyshlenniks	350	1,400
1	Creole		300
3	Creoles	250	750
1	Creole		200
25	Workers	25	625
17	Workers	60	1,020
55	persons	rubles:	6,370
	In Atkha Office		
2	Office manager and official	4,000	8,000
1	Employee	—	1,200
1	Employee	—	750
4	Employees	600	2,400
3	Employees	500	1,500
3	Employees	500	1,500
1	Employee	500	450
37	Promyshlenniks and Creoles	450	12,950
2	Creoles	350	600
3	Creoles	300	660

[Table f.] — continued

[No.]		Annual Payment [r.]	Total [r.]
14	Creoles and Aleuts	180	2,520
8	Creoles and Aleuts	120	960
9	Creoles and Aleuts	100	500*
7	Workers	60	420
1	Worker		70
2	Employees	700	1,400
4	Promyshlenniks	400	1,600
1	Creole		150
6	Creoles	40	240
102*	persons	rubles:	36,370*
	In Kuril District		
1	Promyshlenniks		1,000
1	Promyshlenniks		450
8	Promyshlenniks	350	2,800
10	persons	rubles:	4,250
	Total		
395	In Novo-Arkhangel'sk		286,510
271	In Kad'iak district		63,490
53	At Ross		24,315
96	In Unalashka district		25,905
55	[On] Pribylov Islands		6,370
102*	In Atkha district		36,370
10	In Kuril district		4,250
982*	persons	Per year [in rubles]:	446,210*

*[Sic.]

5. A Note on Household Property

In his discourse concerning buildings in the colonies, Nikolai Petrovich Rezanov directed Mr. Baranov to assess all company buildings and to again make accounts based on the price of lumber used, labor cost and materials used. A wooden structure was set at twelve years; during the first three years the house was considered at the original price; the next three years the price depreciated by one-twentieth (20 percent); the next three years less than 40 percent; the next three years less than 60 percent. As for those buildings which last longer than twelve years, when they are torn down, all salvaged materials should be saved and the rest counted as a loss.

It was mentioned above that the buildings inherited from Mr. Baranov were dilapidated and worthless, but in order to have records, everything was appraised and counted as part of the capital and was then written off when new buildings were built. The new buildings were appraised at a price which included building materials and labor. In building these new structures special care was made to build them solidly out of milled beams instead of rough logs. Every year they are covered with a compound which prevents the wood from rotting. Chalk or ocher are added to the compound for the sake of color.

The mark-down is made gradually on the new ones from 10 to 15 percent, and the old ones from 15 to 50 percent.

In 1826 the capital consisted of the following:

		[r.	k.]
New:	House of the chief manager and things with it	24,259	38
	Bath	1,130	25
	House of office manager	2,508	55
	Wing for office, hospital and apartment	10,000	
	Barracks with apartments on mezzanine	9,977	43
	Arsenal	1,500	
	Three watchtowers	4,606	45
	Rope walk	641	50
	Mill	3,481	
	Stockade	991	80
	Pier and quay	3,323	28
	Bath for crews	1,464	28
	Three houses purchased for apartments	4,262	
	Old structures and various chapels, for exclusion, constitute	17,788	26
	Total	90,187	25

*Error in original; should be 85,934 r. 18 k.

According to the list above 10,385 rubles 19 kopeks was the amount for the depreciation of buildings for the year 1825.

If we were to take a more exact account of all labor, for example, cutting, hauling and delivering of lumber; the making of axes, and burning of charcoal; in a word all labor performed by the people, and count it towards the price of the buildings, we would have to raise the price by at least 100 percent. In such a

6. A Note on the Library and Instruments

The library in Sitkha consists of more than 1,200 volumes, which are valued at 7,500 rubles. In all there are 600 books in Russian, close to 300 in French, 130 in German, 35 in English, 30 in Latin and the rest in Swedish, Dutch, Spanish and Italian. The basis of this collection was laid in St. Petersburg, when they organized the first expedition around the world. Chancellor Nikolai Petrovich Rezanov set out on it as an agent of the company. He intended to bring civilization to this far-away land with all means at his disposal. He proposed his ideas to wealthy individuals who were concerned about the general well-being of the country. They responded by sending him volumes in various languages. Mr. Rezanov sent these to the Main Office, which bound them in rich bindings and shipped them to the colonies for the library. The following generous individuals made their contributions: Metropolitan Amvrosii, Count Nikolai Petrovich Rumiantsev, Count Pavel Aleksandrovich Stroganov, Admiral Pavel Vasil'evich Chichagov, Minister of Justice Ivan Ivanovich Dmitriev, Nikolai Nikolaevich Novosil'tsev, Aleksei Nikolaevich Olenin, Egor Borisovich Fuks, Senator Ivan Semenovich Zakharov and others.

The first [Russian round-the-world] expedition left with high hopes; at that time the Russians compared themselves to Columbus, Gama and Cook, and the names of these great men were associated with our travellers. In letters addressed to Nikolai P. Rezanov it is pleasant to read with what enthusiasm these generous people greeted this expedition. We cannot refrain from mentioning several excerpts from their personal comments, which deserve respect because of their high and incomparable feelings.

(*Letter from Ivan Dmitriev from Moscow 3 April 1803*). "I have had the pleasure to perform part of the task you asked of me. Mr. M. M. Kherasov has already sent two volumes of Epics — Cadmus, Harmonius and Polydor. Tomorrow I shall send them to you by post. Karamzin also wanted to send some books. When I read my name in your letter, I blushed and thought, what can I send along with the others? What could my insignificant contribution mean to this Russian venture? Finally, because of self-pride but more out of an obligation to you, I decided to send you my fables and stories. Let your Americans learn grammar from them until they come to a point when they can discuss rhetoric and so forth."

(*Egor Borisovich Fuks*). "Well, my beloved friend, we shall soon see you sail away from the granite shores of the clear Neva, with your brave voyagers across vast oceans. And you shall vanish from sight; soon pride but more out of an obligation to you, I decided to send you my fables and stories. Let your Americans learn grammar from them until they come to a point when they can discuss rhetoric and so forth."

(*Egor Borisovich Fuks*). "Well, my beloved friend, we shall soon see you sail away from the granite shores of the clear Neva, with your brave voyagers across vast oceans. And you shall vanish from sight; soon you shall hear for the last time the most sincere 'good-bye' from your countrymen and you will already be in foreign waters. Allow me now, my dearest friend, to marvel at your bravery, and if I may be bold enough to say 'to marvel' at your daring enterprise; allow me to express my ecstatic rapture which I feel because of your expedition.

By daring, Columbus
Discovered half the world

and Russia has its own Columbuses, Cooks and La Pérouses. From the first rowboat of Peter the First I address myself to a ship sailing to America! I have long been a witness of how we Russians have defeated our enemies on Caesar's and Hannibal's fields under Suvorov, scorning all dangers, and chose to die for the fatherland as a great honor, and now again they are seeking a new type of danger during the reign of our Tsar, a humble, philanthropic man, a man of peace.

"What autocracy, in its flight towards enlightenment, can compare itself to ours? Only at the beginning of the last century did our people awaken to their political existence through the creative inspiration of Peter the Great; our people has grown from its youthful crib; it has become greater, daring and already view with other enlightened nations and already surpasses the. And all of this has happened in this century. Now at the beginning of this monarchy, a charitable, and brightly lit Aurora is burning across our vast empire from the throne and marking the golden age of Astrei. Hasten, O worthy son of our fatherland to fulfill the will of our Lord, to glorify his name and power so that the savage peoples shall know the name of Ross. Tell them stories about our immortal ancestors in our fatherland, about their contributions to our general welfare, about their great and remarkable associates; show them the pictures of our heroic Suvorov. This is all I have to request.

"Not knowing science or art, the savage has a soul; he senses the wholesomeness of the sun and therefore he must be capable of honoring the valor of great men.

"Finally, when you return to your beloved fatherland, you shall bring back treasures from India, new knowledge to science, art and trade. Then you shall be granted our sovereign's recognition, the amazement of our compatriots and the pure satisfaction in your own heart. And history immortalizes those who benefit their nations above all dangers and sacrifices."

(*Pavel Aleksandrovich Stroganov*). "I am including a book, which I promised you, Sir, for your library to be established in our American colonies; it is with particular pleasure that I use this opportunity to disclose my enthusiasm for your useful intention."

(*Nikolai Nikolaevich Novosil'tsov*). "Upon sailing around the world at the request of our Almighty Emperor, your honor shall have the opportunity not only to look at distant lands but also to make various observations concerning the political relations of governments, nature and human knowledge. The Imperial Academy of Sciences will take a most active part in such an important undertaking. In this case we wish to participate as much as possible as a benefactor of the government, in particular in your philanthropic aims to spread the seeds of science among peoples alienated from Europe and consequently from enlightenment. We felt obliged to choose several classical books and maps of the world, which are being sent along with the attached inventory to you as requested. The Imperial Academy of Art has provided you with various art objects. Your devotion to the general welfare convinces the Academy that these objects will further your enterprise in teaching peoples who do not have the opportunity to rise above their own ignorance; they shall then sense the worth of your gifts, and your brief stay there among them will remain unforgotten in their minds because of your generous gifts."

(*Count Nikolai Petrovich Rumiantsev*). "I petitioned the Throne concerning the establishment and expansion of our trade in America, and have also felt that Orthodoxy and education would be the first gifts which an enlightened man should share at the edge of the New World.

"As a start I am sending with you to Kad'iak holy vessels to be placed on the altar to commemorate Our Savior Himself, hoping that the holy churches of that region will serve as an example of our church, of God, and of the Tsar.

"I am sending you the works of the Free Economic Society, hoping that these observations can make agriculture and farming easier for the peoples of that land, which will attract our trade to them.

"I am also sending textbooks on Russian grammar as proof that Russia not only does not endanger but wants to bring enlightenment to America.

"Likewise, I would like you to leave the books which I previously gave you. Unfortunately, not all of them are in our language due to the lack of translations, but I judged it best to supply the New World with everything necessary for its education, regardless of language.

"These are sincere feelings, which I leave you, Sir, to make sure that my small gifts reach the other side so that i might glorify our fatherland. It is not without pride, however, that I imagine that approaching hour, when the educated youth in the New World shall know that we thought of enlightening America during Alexander's reign. Enraptured with this feeling, I willingly admit before you that there is no pride greater than wishing to participate in this enterprise.

(*From a response to his honor from Nikolai Petrovich Rezanov*). "I would like to tell you here how opportune our trade is because of the loyal solicitations of the Throne, but I do not wish to dwell upon this idea. This freedom belongs to our heirs. On my part I have found no better sustenance in my soul than to let your honor know, that once I reach Kad'iak with God's will, I shall place the gifts which you have so generously entrusted in me, as well as your wonderful letter and this inadequate response concerning my strong convictions. Let those in time to come look at your charge in that far-away land; and let my pride be crowned, so that they can render tribute to my devotion.

Count Aleksandr Stroganov obtained various portraits, drawings and paintings from the Academy of Art for the colonies; the Minister of the Navy Pavel Vasil'evich Chichagov sent plans of various vessels; while the Reverend Metropolitan Amvrosii got books for church services. Many of the boys educated here used and still use the fruits of their knowledge. One cannot help but note that many of them have an inclination to draw, and that two, without education or training, using only pictures, have been successful in drawing portraits with great verisimilitude.

In the museum there are many mathematical, physical and other instruments of fine English work. In addition to that, all ships are equipped with sextants, octants and telescopes, chronometers and semi-chronometers; we also have for use ashore a theodolite, and a circular instrument made by Trouton. There are also an astrolabe and a very precise Jurgenson pendulum, telescopes, a large microscope, an electricity machine, natural and artificial magnets, barometers, thermometers, charts, maps, atlases and similar items. These instruments, which are a part of the museum, are worth 12,500 rubles, excluding those which are used in expeditions.

7. Note on the Pharmacy and Hospital

From the time that the Main Office sent a medical officer to the colonies in 1820, it has taken the responsibility of getting medications and sending them to the colonies every year. Medical officers are replaced every year. In 1825 three good rooms were assigned for the pharmacy and its medical personnel. Medications are kept in cupboards in an orderly fashion, and of course, there are as good in quantity and quality found in any pharmacy in any Russian city. Surgical and anatomical instruments are of superior quality. The present physician has four Creole boys studying medicine, anatomy and surgery.

There is a special room connected to the pharmacy which serves as a hospital. In it there are eight beds for those with serious illnesses; others, who live in their own quarters, come to the hospital in the morning to get their medicine. In general, the hospital is maintained with money set aside for the poor; that is capital which comes from the deduction of half a percent from profits made. In accordance with a decree from the company on 29 March 1802; this capital is transferred from the Main Office to Novo-Arkhangel'sk. In addition some of the capital comes from various sources which do not enter into the capital of the colonies. Now, in accordance with the orders of the chief manager, it has been ordered that five percent should be deducted from the profits of auctions held when officials leave the colonies; it has also been ordered that any furs which officials and promyshlenniks have been holding secretly above the legal number, should be confiscated and their value transferred to capital for the hospital's use.

The sick in the hospital receive fresh food in accordance with the physician's orders, including tea, and sugar at company expense; the sick are not charged for medicine either.[49]

We hope that several of the boys will succeed in learning how to heal and shall become physicians in other departments of the colonies where they can do good work towards their fellowman.

8. Note on the Arsenal

On 1 January 1826 the capital worth of the arsenal was considered to be 140,600 rubles. However, this did not include the artillery bombs with which our ships and outposts are equipped. Each department has its own account. The arsenal inventory includes guns in the fortress and in storage; these are kept in good shape and cleaned, in a specially built two-storied tower, which are under the supervision of a special man and an assistant.

The main articles of this capital are the following:

49	cast iron cannons and carronades	16,300	r.
15	falconets	925	
28	copper [brass?] cannons of various calibers	16,221	
43	various muskets	1,315	
1,368	various military rifles	40,963	
34	hunting rifles	1,166	
53	carbines	1,895	
291	pistols	3,837	
205	rifles	7,381	r.
95	carbines	3,730	
	sabers, cutlass, shot, canisters and various artillery shells	35,235	
	powder	10,064	
4	fire-pump and other fire-fighting equipment	1,585	
	Total	140,600*	r.

*Error in original; should be 140,617 r.

The cast iron carronades are twelve to fourteen funts in caliber; the cannons three to six funts; brass cannons on field carriages are of various calibers. Rare weapons provided by the Main Office include: two Persian carbines, one of which is worth 450 rubles; one saber inlaid with precious stones worth 560 rubles; two Persian *yatagans* made of silver, 210 rubles; one Dalmatian saber, 112 rubles; one set of Persian pistols made of silver, 300 rubles, and one rifle with gold inlay, 150 rubles. Most of the soldiers' weapons are of French or English make of high quality; [signal] rockets and flares are made here every year and are quite good. They are mainly used for signals on ships sailing at night. Every year they also make powder and ammunition for guns; 35 to 40 puds of gun powder are used every year for signals and salutes.

9. Note on the Ozerskii Redoubt

Above we mentioned the building of the Ozerskii Redoubt, which took a considerable amount of money. The buildings there consist of the following:

Two barracks and fort	7,000	r.
Old mill and stamp-mill	2,000	
Tannery	500	
Fishing structure and pier	3,108	
New mill	6,267	
Total structures	19,875*	
Instruments for establishments	2,187	
Artillery shells at	6,067	
	28,128†	r.

*Error in original; should be 18,875 r. †Should be 27,129 r.

The people at the redoubt include masters, that is, smiths, carpenters, stone masons, sawyers, a stonecutter and others. The preparing of lumber and other work is done in turns by the detachment; during the winter ten to fifteen men from the port are assigned to the redoubt.

10. Note on Trading Expenses

Capital, excluding trade expenditures, consist mainly of debts from which the salaries of officials and promyshlenniks are excluded in accordance with general agreement. Almost all expenditures are designated, except for some insignificant ones,

Mark-down

In the fort from old structures	10,385	19
In the port from vessels with expenditures	73,007	07
In Ozerskii Redoubt from buildings	1,500	07
	84,892	26[‡]
Expenditures in port from workshops and in fort from arsenal and in housing	9,800	43
Usual expenditures of goods for stores	2,644	64
	12,454	07[a]
Total	403,428	80[b]

[*] Error in original; should be 65,404 r. 50 k. [†] Should be 240,688 r. 7 k. [‡] Should be 84,892 r. 33 k. [a] Should be 12,445 r. 07 k. [b] Should be 403,429 r. 97 k.

K. ADVANTAGES OF SITKHA'S LOCATION

"There are no advantages without disadvantages," the proverb goes. This is certainly the case of Sitkha. It is hard to argue with this contradiction until the moment when the natives have been pacified. The local advantages, compared to the other colonies are as follows:

1. Landmarks at the Entrance to [Sitkha Bay] from the Sea and in the Roads

Mt. Edgecumbe, which rises out of the sea as a cape, serves as a good and precise landmark for all sea travellers who have not been here before. Approaching these shores during storms, it is of great help to navigators to have a reliable landmark. After he has spotted Mt. Edgecumbe and sailed through the bay with the aid of Lazarev Island and Biorka as bearings, he will find the lighthouse by taking a north compass bearing. During bad weather all the rocks are on this side of the course. We should mention that although there are many rocks in the bay, they stick out of the water and have been identified by the navigator I. F. Vasil'ev, and by the officers of the sloop *Predpriiatie*. Underwater rocks are also marked on the maps. It is true that those who are used to the best European ports do not like the entrance into Sitkha Bay. But it is the best of all entries in the colonies and subsequently the most useful. There are three ways to enter the bay: two from the east, one from the western side of the port. The roadstead is safe and convenient; it is possible to have 20 sailing ships in the bay near the fort. The depth in shallow water is

1. Landmarks at the Entrance to [Sitkha Bay] from the Sea and in the Roads

Mt. Edgecumbe, which rises out of the sea as a cape, serves as a good and precise landmark for all sea travellers who have not been here before. Approaching these shores during storms, it is of great help to navigators to have a reliable landmark. After he has spotted Mt. Edgecumbe and sailed through the bay with the aid of Lazarev Island and Biorka as bearings, he will find the lighthouse by taking a north compass bearing. During bad weather all the rocks are on this side of the course. We should mention that although there are many rocks in the bay, they stick out of the water and have been identified by the navigator I. F. Vasil'ev, and by the officers of the sloop *Predpriiatie*. Underwater rocks are also marked on the maps. It is true that those who are used to the best European ports do not like the entrance into Sitkha Bay. But it is the best of all entries in the colonies and subsequently the most useful. There are three ways to enter the bay: two from the east, one from the western side of the port. The roadstead is safe and convenient; it is possible to have 20 sailing ships in the bay near the fort. The depth in shallow water is five to nine sazhens; the sea bottom is silty in places; in others it is made up of small stones and sea shells. In the eastern roadstead the bottom is silty and the depth six to twelve sazhens. The roads are protected by islands. Strong southeast and northeast winds can cause the water to become quite turbulent. But very seldom do the ships drift. Ships are able to sail in the winter to southern latitudes and sometimes to Kad'iak. The roads are never covered with ice.

2. Tides

Tidewaters during a new or full moon are usually 14 feet; accompanied by winds the water rises 16 to 17 feet. According to observations by officers on the sloop *Predriiatie* the duration of the tide is 30 minutes.

The advantages of high tide allow easy access to the ships so that they can be examined and repaired without difficulty and danger. The ship, after it is unloaded, is brought close to shore, where it dries and is examined. If it is necessary to repair any ship or to re-timber it, then the ship is placed on blocks; a hole is made, and it is repaired. Minor repairs are accomplished in two tides [during the first and second omrubov] and then the ship is returned to its anchor site.

3. Construction Timber

One of the great advantages here is the abundance of excellent building material. Besides using this local lumber to build ships and houses, it could be important as a trade item in the form of beams and boards with the Sandwich Islands and the shores of California and even Mexico. This branch of trade has not yet entered into our economy, and for that reason no attention has been paid to it. If we were to build a sawmill near the Ozerskii Redoubt, we could, hopefully, open a new source of income. The trees near the fort have all been used for construction; those buildings built during Mr. Baranov's time have rotted or become dilapidated and must be torn down; therefore we need another period of building. Three hundred to five hundred trees are cut down every year for building materials; if we consider 400 trees to be an average, then since the settlement began in 1804, we have cut down around 8,000 trees for company use; and if we take into account the use of firewood, the preparation of charcoal, lumber for shipbuilding and housing for individuals, then it would not be an exaggeration to say that in 20 years 20,000 trees were cut down. Although the shores are as thickly covered with trees as wild animals are covered with thick furs, the nearest trees have been cut down, and getting lumber now has grown more difficult a task. In spite of all this we can use these forests for another century without the supply becoming exhausted.

4. Good Potato Harvest

Of all the areas in the colonies Sitkha is the best for growing potatoes. Some of the seeds are gotten from Siberia, others from California. The potato is rather tasty and large in size. The earth is rocky and is usually fertilized with seaweed or as they call it here, sea cabbage. In better places the harvest is twelve to fourteen fold; in the worst it is six to eight fold. The quantity of potatoes harvested reaches a thousand barrels or over 4,000 puds. No amount of soil remains unturned around the fort to make gardens. Taking into account the nutritious qualities of this product, we can say that it is taking the place of bread and that it is healthy when eaten with salted fish. When the harvest is good the price is 10, usually 15 rubles for a small barrel [keg?]. American seamen and government ships sometimes bought 100 barrels from the inhabitants. All of this together represents a local advantage.

5. FISH CATCH, TAKING MOUNTAIN SHEEP, RAISING PIGS AND CHICKENS

A well-constructed fish pond near the settlement supplies enough ocean fish each year. The year round fishing for herring is also an advantage, which does not exist everywhere. During the winter the Aleuts go out in their baidarkas to catch halibut, perch and other fish, which they sell to the Russians when they have enough for themselves. Cod at 50 kopeks; and halibut up to 3 rubles apiece, depending on the size. We can say without exaggerating that they get around 1,000 rubles for fish in the winter.

It is worth noting that the Aleuts hunt mountain sheep. They begin in November and end in May. It is impossible to say how many they catch, but it can be said for certain that in a very good year they have caught up to 200 head. This hunt supplies the officials' tables with good meat, and the Aleuts are paid 10 to 15 rubles per [mountain] sheep. With this catch it is sometimes possible to have fresh, cheap meat at the table. When they are fat, the sheep weigh nearly two puds.

We must note here that they raise a large number of pigs and chickens here; but the pigs, which are fed on fish and shellfish have a repulsive taste, while those fed on potatoes and grain are very tasty. The price of a piglet is 5 to 7 rubles; large pigs weighing 5 to 6 puds are sold for 60 to 80 rubles. The price of chickens is 4 to 5 rubles; 10 eggs are 3½ rubles, sometimes 5 rubles. Chickens and pigs can be bought from the inhabitants any time of the year.

6. TRADE WITH FOREIGNERS

When I wrote about the occupations of Sitkha, I said that trade with foreigners could not be an essential part of advantages because they would end up selling all their own goods everywhere. But this only refers to ships which have cargoes. There are ships which come into Sitkha from the straits on their way home with little cargo left because of their trading with the savages, and there would be little gain for them to go any further to sell those remaining goods. Ships have come from the Sandwich Islands and even Boston with goods which were not bought from them because they were either too expensive or unnecessary. But this example does not frighten others. And we expect that every year we shall see ships come from Boston, Canton or the Sandwich Islands. From here they go on to California on down to the coast of Chile, selling their goods. The business activities of the Americans are remarkable. They sail from Boston straight to Sitkha, after stopping to take on supplies and fresh water in the Sandwich Islands which lasts three to five days; their trip takes 140 to 160 days.

L. DISADVANTAGES IN NOVO-ARKHANGEL'SK

By their virtue, disadvantages are divided into real (which always exist) and relative ones, which can occur later. The latter are taken up in the following two paragraphs:

1. Dangers from Civilized Enemies

In a war against European powers, the fort would not be able to endure a blockade. Perhaps they think that England and the United States have no need to send military ships along the Northwest Coast of America to attack the insignificant fort in Norfolk Sound? or that such an effort would case damage to the ships used in such an expedition? But these powers would not send their squadrons from Europe or North America; they will come from the many ships which now cruise the shores of Peru, Chile, Mexico and even from the fleet of the East India Company. There would be many privateers who would encourage and help them. They are convinced that the fur trade of our company is the only source of income by which the colony exists. They are certain that they will find an abundance of furs, goods and materials, which they will be able to turn into money. In such an event, we shall have to surrender to the enemy since we are already surrounded by one enemy on the other shore and we would thus be under fire on both sides. All enemies use treason to their advantage and will not pass up the opportunity to join up with the Kolosh. With no hope of repulsing the enemy from the sea, there is only one thing that can possibly be done — to surrender the fort to the enlightened enemy [European powers], with the hope of getting satisfactory terms, rather than to allow the fort to be destroyed and have our garrison given over the barbarian peoples.

2. Disadvantages in Case of Grain Shortages

If for any reason we do not obtain grain from California, starvation will threaten our colonies; it is clear that in the winter the only product which can take the place of bread is the potato, which is not available in great quantities. It is also impossible to get enough fish or iukola. Salted fish, even if there were a surplus, cannot be enough without bread. And the people (as it happened during Mr. Baranov's management when shortages occurred) will have to purchase goods with their monthly wages and trade them with the Kolosh for fish. If the main colony were located on Kad'iak, then if such a shortage would occur, we would be able to use cod, iukola, sarana and berries.

3. Danger from Indigenous Peoples and Measures against It Now in Effect

The native inhabitants, the Kolosh, have remained our perpetual enemies since we defeated them and took this area a second time. The present colonial administration has used friendly and pacifying measures to prevent these people from becoming openly hostile; but their hearts are still filled with vengeance and they cannot wait for an open confrontation. Up to now their leaders, who have enjoyed our favors, have affirmed us that they have no intention of causing us any harm, but no sooner do they become dissatisfied or begin to fight with our promyshlenniks or Aleuts than they grab their guns and knives and with a rage, found only in savages, they wait for the moment that we will initiate the fighting. They are so shrewd that they never begin anything openly; although there have been several incidents when at the smallest provocation, they armed themselves, hid behind trees and bushes and waited for the consequences. Peaceful talks with their chiefs usually calmed their rage. Of course, it is easy to tame them at the fort with our guns. But the fact that we killed several hundreds of them must have left the seed of vengeance in several thousands of them; they can at any time seize isolated groups of our men while they are either hunting or crossing the wilderness to get lumber or to go fishing.

The most vicious of them make plans every year to attack our fortress; and the bravest to prove their daring sneaked inside the fort on dark, rainy nights and went behind the shallow waters where the *Amethyst* is anchored and stole some items from the admiralty and carried them as trophies to their tribesmen.

They claim that we have occupied these lands where their ancestors used to live, that we have deprived them of hunting animals, and that we use the best places to catch fish. On the contrary, we affirm that we gave them the opportunity to sell their goods at a profit; we supply them with necessary items; and we showed them how to raise and use potatoes and other items.

But all of these arguments are strengthened by a need for vengeance, which is an inherent disposition of all ignorant people. It has been noted by observers that savages do not abandon their way of life willingly and will not change their way of life for anything in the world; this has been supported by numerous examples: the Kolosh are agile, strong, have great stamina and are therefore capable of all kinds of physical skills. They would make great sailors, but it is not possible to get them to change their natural ways. There have been examples of their young people working for our company. They received a good job and room and board, but they became bored and left.

Only one thing will change this situation with time: and that is that the Russian ties with the Kolosh women may serve to strengthen an alliance between future generations. Perhaps our customs will influence them in such a way that they will accept them. The lack of American trade will also bring the Kolosh closer to us. But most of all, we hope that one day they will be enlightened by the Holy Word. God's grace has greater influence on the individual than any human thought. An intelligent priest knowing their language would be of great help. Many of the Kolosh, curious about God, agree about His existence; they believe in the immortality of the soul, reward for good deeds done in this lifetime and the punishment of evil deeds. They also agree that God is all-knowing and everywhere. This truth alone is already sufficient to reinforce the truths of our holy beliefs. We should begin these teachings which correspond to their understanding.

Careful watch is observed at the fort as a precautionary measure: each ship has two sentinels; and the main ships have three, who are relieved regularly. All six posts have two men per post. Two responsible men supervise and make rounds each day.[60] One extra man, a cook, is added at night to give them assistance. In the spring and summer they begin their rounds at four and at nine in the evening. The night watchmen send six flares up every hour; those who make their rounds of all posts also go aboard the various ships.

The cannons in the fort and ships are always loaded, and they are inspected every week. Those sent out for lumber to the Ozerskii Redoubt usually ride out with loaded guns. The number of Kolosh increases in the spring during the herring run, when they come down from various areas to collect roe. At that time nearly 1,000 of them set up camp near the fort, and sometimes there are the same number on the nearby islands. There are less of them in the summer, but it is not rare to see 500 to 600 people of both sexes near the fort. Mr. Baranov did not allow them to settle near the fort or even on the nearby islands. Any trading to be done took place during the day. At night the Kolosh would be sent back. Sometimes, but only rarely, a few were given permission to put up their huts near the fort but only for a short time. Mr. Baranov's first successors also continued this tradition. But the Kolosh guns were taken away and they themselves were under constant watch.

Chief Manager Matvei I. Murav'ev allowed them to settle near the fort. He thought that if their property, women and children were located under the cannon this would guarantee the security of the fort itself. And being there they could not very well carry out their secret intentions.

Usually persons are assigned to various posts in the fort with the necessary weapons. These posts are equipped with good artillery pieces. To give an example I would like to present the list of men and their post for the summer of 1826 during the absence of the chief manager:

	men		men
In upper fort with rifles	29	At cannon on *Amethyst*	4
In upper fort with cannon	27	On fire-fighting equipment	12
On barkazes armed with six cannon	21	On parade ground at mobile cannon	23
In upper fort at watchtower No. 1	12	At guns on brig *Kiakhta*	10
In upper fort at watchtower No. 2	11	With guns on brig *Buldakov*	8
In upper fort at watchtower No. 3	11	At guns on cutter *Baranov*	6
At palisade at watchtower No. 4	3	At guns on ship *Otkrytie*	16
At palisade at watchtower No. 5	3	At distribution of guns	2
At northern gates with carronade	3		

	men		men
At carronade at south gate	3	With sick	4
		Total	209*

*Error in original; should be 208 men.

It must be noted that this number includes boys, sick and weak men and those who can barely use heavy artillery pieces.

In regard to other safety measures, the acting chief manager, Mr. Ianovskii, published an order, which has been reissued several times, especially during the absence of the chief manager. The order consisted of the following:

> Should a fire occur outside the fort at night, only those assigned to fire equipment should go out to extinguish it; others with no special orders should not stray from the fort.
>
> Should the fort be attacked during the day the alarm should be sounded with drums, bells and rattlers, and the watchman should raise the red flag with a scythe and everyone, no matter where he might be, should hurry to the fort as fast as possible. At night the alarm should be wounded with drums, bells and rattlers.
>
> In case of fire, sound only the bell. Do not raise the flag.
>
> Every commander should inspect his guns as often as possible; they should be clean; the powder should be dry and flints and all supplies should be in readiness; it should be impressed upon those who are assigned to the various poses that they should have their guns in good working order and know their posts.
>
> During an alarm watchmen should be on time at their posts, except for those outside the fort; those men should run back to the fort as quickly as possible.
>
> Should the situation arise that someone cannot get to the fort, he should try to come across in a boat to the south gate; should anyone not be able to get to a boat, then he should defend himself in his own house, making sure his doors are closed.
>
> An inspector making his rounds outside the fort from sunset to sunrise should listen to strange sounds and movements in the forest and behind bushes. Should he see anyone

lying there he should report this to the guard who shall sound the alarm.

During the alarm the inspector with the keys should post himself at the north gate, identify his men and let them through.

Inspectors must check the guards often to see that they are not asleep, whether they are alert, whether their guns are in good working order, particularly in the watch towers; if a gun has been loaded for a whole week, it should be unloaded, cleaned and reloaded with new powder and shot; all guards should be aware that if anyone of them should fall asleep or not be alert or be missing from his post, he shall be punished severely. The inspectors have an even greater responsibility to perform what is assigned to them; everyone knows that we have enemies who watch us all the time, to see if they can catch us off guard. Should this happen, then we shall perish.

The fort is strongly guarded. Everyone depends on our guards. Inspectors and guards alike should be on the alert all the time.

The inspectors should check out any noise or disturbance. Anyone causing such a disturbance should be put under arrest and this should immediately be reported to the office manager as well as any other happening during his watch.

4. Status of the Aleuts Located in Sitkha

In the month of March the Aleuts begin to prepare their baidarkas. The company issues them enough laftaks, whalebone and whale sinews. In May they go out hunting on sailing vessels and return at the beginning of August. The Aleuts are used for hunting only for three months. In August and September they store fish for winter consumption; then for the next five months they spend their time in utter idleness, except for some who hunt mountain sheep.

According to the population count in Novo-Arkhangel'sk there are 145 free Aleut males who live here of their own free will. Sometimes they go to Kad'iak to visit their relatives.

In Sitkha there are many people and officials: military and foreign ships often come here. Aleuts sometimes get vodka and luxury items in exchange for fish, game and sheep. Since they are addicted to hard liquor, they try to get it through deceitful means, which indicates how immoral they are. In addition to this, they have developed a taste for tea and Russian food. Many of them have wives and in accordance with their traditions the wives have two to three husbands. But when the Aleuts go off on their hunt for several months, their wives are free to do as they want and these are not idle since there are four women for every man. Because of their immorality, the women usually become infected and subsequently become infertile, thus contributing to the colony's small birth rate.

The children who are born here not only get the mothers' milk but also pick up the bad habits from their mothers and fathers. As these children grow up they do not witness their ancestors' natural ways but the sailors' shouts, the hammering in the workshops, and the pranks of a noisy crowd, all of this strongly influences them.

In the other colonies the Aleuts wear bird skin parkas, which are warm, comfortable and attractive, but in Sitkha they do not want to wear clothing made from regular soldier cloth but from good quality frieze or fine wool. Many of them have frock coats and dress coats. In earlier times their wives were happy to have parkas made from beaver skins and cotton kamlei, but here they all want calico dresses, shawls, etc. All of this luxury is not only detrimental to them but also to the colony.

If the Aleuts did not live in Sitkha, but were instead taken to Kad'iak, then they would spend the fall hunting fox and otter; then they would be more useful to themselves and the company. There is no difference in taking the Aleuts from Sitkha or Kad'iak aboard ships to hunt sea otters in designated areas. At the present time there are not enough Aleuts living in Sitkha to make up such hunting parties; therefore some are brought from Kad'iak every year and then taken back on 20 to 30 baidarkas.

There are 250 Aleut men, women and children in Sitkha. Their present way of life here demands three times what they normally need in their own villages. Besides, the Aleuts and their wives get a lot of money from the Russians through various means: thus they want things such as tea, sugar, molasses, wheat and other things. They were taught to desire these items, and it would be unfair to deny them these things now. If they were taken back to their own settlements, then in time they would abandon their present whims and would be satisfied with local products.

5. Lack of Space for Gunpowder Storage

One of the main disadvantages in Sitkha is the lack of space to safeguard gunpowder. The fortress is situated on soft rock with its base subject to erosion. During Mr. Baranov's management the gunpowder was stored in various buildings, stores and towers, but because of the danger to neighboring houses these storage areas could no longer be used. The gunpowder had to be transferred to the ship *Otkrytie*, which is harbored in the roads. This ship, being in the front line of defense, is equipped with cannons and has a double number of guards. But is this storage area safe in case we are attacked by European powers? There is no other space in the entire fort.

6. The Impossibility of Introduction of Cattle-Raising

It is impossible for the Chief Manager not to have a few head of cattle to supply those travelling round-the-world and to provide milk for the officials and for the sick. That is the reason why eight head of cattle are maintained. If we are to take into account the preparation of hay, the labor, time, materials and other items used to maintain each head the cost is 100 rubles per head of cattle. Consequently, it costs the same during normal times to maintain a head of cattle as it does to maintain a human being; when hay is in short supply, it is necessary to feed the cattle grain; the cost then doubles. The main reason for the lack of cattle is the preparation of hay; dark and damp weather prevents the grass from drying; the mowed grass often rots after incessant rains, but people and time were necessary to prepare it. The area itself does not allow for more than ten to twelve head of cattle because there are only three to four places in the various bays which have valleys where you can cut [enough hay for] three to four stacks, but most of these valleys become covered with water during high tide; only during low tide can the grass be cut and raked to higher ground so that the tide does not carry it off.

7. The Damp Climate, Harmful to Ships and Buildings

This particular climate causes a lot of damage to ships and buildings, but if we were to compare this colony to the others there would be no great difference. Because of the constant bad weather in Kad'iak, the buildings also rot very fast; this disadvantage is the same all along the Northwest Coast of America. The ships, however, are well preserved because they are carefully painted every year. The tackle and sails become damaged quickly.

8. Expenses Not Commensurate with State of Colonial Industry

Precautionary measures against neighboring enemies force the colony to maintain a large garrison in Sitkha; this means that we have more people than we need; this situation causes us to assume losses. It can be said that we have an excess of 100 persons. The supplies for a 100 men is important because they could be used to supply 100 men at another time.

I do not speak here about moving the colonies, although I shall discuss this matter later on. I shall just remark that without the hostility of the Kolosh, we would not be experiencing this loss, and we would not have the expenditures from the Russians which I mentioned in my article about trading with the Kolosh. In the following articles comparing Sitkha and Kad'iak we shall set forth the losses that arise from being in Sitkha.

SUPPLEMENT

Estimate of quantities of goods, [various] items, provisions and materials requisitioned annually in [districts] of the colonies in shipbuilding and economic matters, for payment of officials and employees found in company service, for supply of hospitals and charitable institutions in various places, for payment for furs to Aleuts and other peoples within the company's jurisdiction and for trade with the Koloshi, North American natives, Chukchi and in California.

Presented to Mr. Chief Manager [F. P. Wrangell] in March 1832.

Goods and Supplies	Measure	At Novo-Arkhangel'sk office	In other offices and districts								See Notes pp. 197-202
			Kad'iak	Unalashka	Atkha	Ross	Kuril District	Nushagak	Pribylov Islands	Total	
Supplies											
Tea of various sorts	pud	120	20	15	15	15	3	3	5	196	No. 1
Sugar of various sorts	pud	600	75	50	50	50	14	10	5	810*	No. 1
Rum	bucket	500	50	40	40	40	10	8	12	700	No. 1
Gin	bucket	100	10	6	6	6				128	No. 1
Molasses	pud	300	60	40	40	40			20	500	No. 2
White wine	gallon	500	20	20	20	20				580	
Flour	pud	200	30	20	20					270	
Wheat	pud	300	80	50	50	50	10	5	10	655*	No. 3
Cow butter	pud	150	from own	20	20		5	5	8	208	No. 4
Marrow	pud	150	cattle	25	25					200	No. 4
Barley groats	pud	100	25	25	25	20				195	
Peas and beans	pud	300	100	100	100		50	50	100	800	No. 5
Wheat and rye flour	pud	7,300	2,000	1,000	1,000		200	200	300	12,000	No. 6
Corn	pud	300	25	25	50					400	No. 7
Salt meat	pud	500		40	40			10	10	600	No. 8
Salt	pud	1,500	500	250	400		50	50	250	3,000	No. 9
Honey for pharmacies and officials	pud	25	Of this quantity some are spared for the districts							25	
Pepper, pea	pud	6								6	
Vinegar	bucket	50								50	No. 10, 11
Textiles											
⅓ calico and half calico ⅔	arshin	2,000	500	400	400	200	150	150	200	4,000	No. 12
Printed linen	arshin	1,000	300	300	300	200	50	150	150	2,500*	No. 12

Goods and Supplies	Measure	At Novo-Arkhangel'sk office	In other offices and districts								See Notes pp. 202-203
			Kad'iak	Unalashka	Atkha	Ross	Kuril District	Nushagak	Pribylov Islands	Total	
Various nankeen	piece	500	300	200	300	100	50	50	100	1,600	No. 13
Blue plush for California	arshin	250	black 50	50	50					460*	No. 14
Thin white calico	arshin	500	100	100	100	200				1,000	No. 14
Grey American calico	arshin	7,000				1,000				8,000	
Cloth	arshin	1,000	300	200	200	200			100	2,000	
Poorer quality kerchiefs	piece	1,000	Of this quantity some is spared for the districts							1,000	
Medium kerchiefs	piece	700								700	
Large kerchiefs	piece	500								500	
Cotton stockings	dozen	10								10	
Cotton wicks	pud	3								3	
White & colored calico	piece	50	5	5	5	5				70	
Linen Goods											
Medium linen	arshin	10,000	2,500	2,000	2,000	2,000		1,000	500	20,000	No. 15
Romanovskii linen	arshin	10,000	2,000	2,000	2,000	1,000	1,000	1,000	500	20,000*	No. 15
Lords' linen from 80 [k.] to 1 r. 50 k.	arshin	600	200	100	100	100	50	50	100	1,300	
Napkin, various	arshin	1,000	Of this quantity some is spared for the districts							1,000	
Napkin linen, various	arshin	6,000	2,000	2,000	2,000	1,000	500	500	1,000	15,000	No. 16
Ticking and *deburetov* (?)	arshin	9,500	1,200	1,000	1,000	1,000	300	500	500	15,000	No. 16
Sewing thread of various sorts	pud	15	Of this quantity some is spared for the districts							15	
Sail thread	pud	15								15	

Goods and Supplies	Measure	At Novo-Arkhangel'sk office	In other offices and districts								See Notes pp. 203-204
			Kad'iak	Unalashka	Atkha	Ross	Kuril District	Nushagak	Pribylov Islands	Total	
Thin stocking thread	pair	400	100	75	75	50				700	
Thin half-stocking thread	pair	200	50	50	50	50				400	
Coarse cloth for bags	arshin	7,000	1,000			2,000				10,000	No. 17
Fishing cord	pud	30	40	30	20	10	10	10	20	170	
Sea otter cord	pud			10	30		10			50	
Grey Flemish cloth	piece	50	20	10	15	10	5	5	5	120	No. 18
Various white Flemish cloth	piece	20	10	10	10	10				60	
Woolens											
Soldiers' and coarse grey cloth	[piece]	1,000	500	500	500	300	200	200	200	3,400	No. 19
Cloth from 3 to 6 r.	[piece]	1,000	300	200	200	100	50	100	50	2,000	No. 19
Cloth from 6 to 8 r.	[piece]	500	100	100	100	50	50	100	50	1,000[a]	No. 19
Cloth from 8 to 12 r.	[piece]	500	Of this quantity some is spared for the districts							500	No. 19
Cloth from 12 to 18 r.	[piece]	200								200	No. 19
Frieze	arshin	800								800	No. 20
Baize, various	arshin	1,000								1,000	No. 20
Flannel	arshin	800								800	No. 20
Coarse woolens	piece	dark green 2		crimson 1	crimson 1				crimson 1	5	No. 21
Camelot for greatcoats	piece	15	Of this quantity some is spared for the districts							15	
Wool stockings	pair	1,000								1,000	
Half stockings	pair	500								500	
Wool	pair	500								500	
Blankets, various	piece	1,700	150	100	100	100	50	50	50	2,300	No. 22

Goods and Supplies	Measure	At Novo-Arkhangel'sk office	In other offices and districts								See Notes pp. 205-206
			Kad'iak	Unalashka	Atkha	Ross	Kuril District	Nushagak	Pribylov Islands	Total	
Bunting: white, 250 blue and red, 200	arshin	450								450	
Cloth, camel hair [*armiak*]	arshin	200								200	
Leather Goods											
Sole leather	pud	50	10	6	6		2	2	2	78	No. 23
English sole leather	pud	8								8	
Fine calf leather, Yufta	pud	25	6	5	5		2	2	2	47	
Dressed calf leather	pud	10	3	3	3					19	
Calf leather	pud	150								150	
Dressed calf shoe hooks	pair	250								250	
Calf hooks	pair	150								150	
Moroccan leather	piece	50								50	
Lacquered hide	piece	25								25	
Visors	piece	100								100	
Sheepskin mittens	pair	500								500	
Gloves, officers' uniform	pair	100								100	
Goat skins, Kazan	piece	200								200	
Miscellaneous Goods											
Virginia tobacco	pud	250				25				225*	No. 24
Circassian tobacco	pud	100	100	60	60	20	20	30	20	410	No. 25
Beads, white, light blue, red, black	pud	6	5			1		2		14	No. 26
Beads [*korol'ki*], small and large	pud	1	1					1		3	No. 26
Soap, ordinary	pud	120	30	20	20		5	5	5	205	No. 27

*[Sic.]

	[Measure]	In All Places	
Tobacco, smoking	box	10	
Tobacco, Turkish pipe	piece	500	
Pipe stems, ordinary	piece	100	
Candles, wax table	pud	50	
Candles, wax church, for California	pud	30	No. 28
Candles, local wax	pud	10	
Candles, wax, for colonies	pud	25	
Wax, white and yellow	pud	25	No. 28
Chalk, white	pud	50	
Chalk, red	funt[?]	10	
Glue, sturgeon	pud	20	
Glue, animal tissue	pud	18	
Ammonia	[. . .]	5	
Borax	funt	20	
Candles, tallow	pud	150	No. 29
Tallow	pud	150	
Whetstones, various sizes	piece	25	
Whetstones	piece	200	
Gun flints	piece	7,000	
Gunpowder (small ¼)	pud	100	
Combs, bone	piece	250	
Combs, cow horn	piece	1,000	
Snuff boxes, ordinary	piece	300	
Saltpeter	pud	3	
Earrings, ordinary	pair	1,000	
Copper rings	piece	1,000	
Crosses, copper	piece	1,000	
Crosses, silver	piece	100	
Glasses, semi-white	box	20	
Vegetable garden seeds	box	2	
Shipped on Demand			
Wall paper	lumps	500	
Paper edging	lumps	250	
Mercury	funt	20	
Steelyards for ships	piece	4	
Scales for artels	piece	16	
Icons, small, on wood	piece	200	
Icons, paper	piece	1,000	
Diamonds, glass cutting	piece	5	
Thermometers, plain	piece	4	
Spoons, maplewood	piece	1,000	
Sulfur, burning	pud	2	
Bristles	funt	20	
Pumice stone	funt	10	
Pharmacies, household	box	2	
Silk Goods			
Taffeta, various, especially black	piece	5	
Shawls, various sized, colored	piece	300	
Neckerchiefs, black	piece	200	
Silk [thread], various colored	funt	20	
Waistcoat material	arshin	50	
Silk cord	batch	20	

	[Measure]	In All Places
Ribbons, various	piece	50
Papers and Apparatus		
Thin paper	ream	5
Common writing paper	ream	50
Quill pens	piece	2,000
Pencils	dozen	20
Sealing wax	funt	10
Ink stands and sand boxes	piece	30
Wafers	funt	1
Gum and elastic [India rubber]	funt	1
Slate boards	piece	40
Slate pencils	piece	200
Pen knives	piece	5
Office books	piece	40
Alexandrian paper	quire	25
Ink set	pud	1
Vessels, Various		
Tea cups	dozen	75
Teapots, various	piece	100
Slop bowls	piece	300
Soup tureens	piece	100
Dishes, various	piece	200
Platters	dozen	75
Table pails	piece	5
Mugs, various	piece	500
Bowls, sugar	piece	100
Pitchers, milk	piece	100
Decanter, ordinary	piece	100
Glasses	piece	600
Wine glasses	dozen	35
Salt cellars	dozen	5
Bottle corks	piece	1,000
Metal Objects		
Kettle, copper	pud	7 } No. 30
Sheathing, copper	pud	150 } No. 30
Copper, bolt	pud	100 } No. 30
Copper, sheets	pud	3 } No. 30
Copper, bar, for bayonets	pud	40 } No. 30
Iron, sheet	pud	200
Iron, hoop	pud	50
Iron, thick hoop	pud	40
Iron, thin hoop	pud	30
Iron, soft bolt	pud	150
Iron, wide strip	pud	150
Iron, (*gunrepnogo*)	pud	30
Nails, hook	pud	25
Nails, (*pompennykh*)	pud	10
Nails, copper	pud	20

	[Measure]	In All Places	
Nails, roofing	pud	25	
Nails, ship, 4- to 8-inch	pud	100	
Nails, copper sheathing	pud	15	
Wire, various copper	pud	2	
Wire, iron	pud	10	
Steel, German	pud	40	No. 31
Steel, Russian or coarse	pud	20	No. 31
Steel, natural	pud	1	
Steel, spring	pud	1	
Sickles	piece	150	No. 32
Sickles, mowing	piece	80	No. 32
Various cast iron cauldrons	pud	150	No. 33
Large axes	piece	1,250	No. 34
Padlocks	piece	100	
Door locks	piece	30	
Knives, seaman's	piece	400	
Knives, table	dozen	25	
Spoons, iron	piece	800	
Candlesticks, various	pair	60	
Candle snuffers	piece	60	
Scissors, various	dozen	20	
Fishhooks, various	piece	500	
Needles, various	piece	20,000	
Needles, sail	piece	400	
Shovels, iron	piece	150	
Frying pans	piece	200	
Samovars, copper	piece	20	
Razors, good	dozen	4	
Buttons, formal	dozen	24	
Birdshot	pud	40	
Fired tin (pewter?)	half cases	2	
Pewter, burned (*ologo*)	funt	4	
Zincum metallium	pud	10	No. 35
Sheet lead in rolls	pud	100	No. 36
Flat iron [*glukhoi*]	piece	10	
Spigots, various sizes	piece	10	
Shipped on Demand: Bells, ship's	piece	3	
Shipped on Demand: Bells, church	piece	2	
Shipped on Demand: Hinges, iron, with screws	pair	100	
Shipped on Demand: Hinges, copper	pair	60	
Shipped on Demand: Hinges, cast iron	pair	100	
Shipped on Demand: Candle molds	piece	50	
Shipped on Demand: Awls, various	piece	500	
Shipped on Demand: Corkscrews	dozen	1	
Shipped on Demand: Kettles for melting metal	[funt]	100	
Shipped on Demand: Weights, large cast iron	pud	50	
Shipped on Demand: Weights, small cast iron	pud	5	
Pigments and Equipment			
Verdigris	pud	4	
Prussian blue	funt	20	
Red ocher	pud	60	

	[Measure]	In All Places
White lead	pud	25
Lamp black, Dutch	pud	3
Red lead	pud	2
Turpentine	pud	10
Auri [*gilt*] pigment	pud	1
Drying oil	pud	50
Varnish, polish	funt	5
Varnish, alcohol	funt	20
Varnish	funt	20
Spirits for varnish	pud[?]	1
Litharge	funt	10
Paint brushes	piece	30
Cinnabar, ground, for the Kolosh	pud	3
Paints for sketching	box	2
India inks	funt	2
Carpenters', Locksmiths' and other Tools		
Files, triangular, flat, and semi-flat, 5- to 8-inch	dozen	10
Various planes	dozen	5
Chisels	dozen	5
Augers	dozen	2
Gimlets	dozen	4
Carpenter saws	piece	10
Hammers, various sized	dozen	3
Blacksmith bellows	piece	2
Adzes, various	dozen	2
Anvil, large	piece	1
Drafter instrument, case	piece	1
Pincers [vice?], large	piece	1
Pliers, pointed and flat	dozen	1
Pal'movykh brace and bit [fine chisel like a pipestem]	piece	2
English foot ruler	piece	5
Caulker and *dorozhanov*	piece	100
Ship Equipment		
Sailcloth	piece	50
Semi-sailcloth	piece	50
Ravenduck, good quality	piece	80
Ravenduck, heavy-duty	piece	30
White hemp [for rope]	pud	5
Piku [for paint?]	pud	80
Liquid tar	pud	100
Harpius [white resin?]	pud	30
Deck glass	piece	10
Bokautu [?]	pud	25
Turpentine	pud	40
Kaluga ropes	pud	150
Marlines, *gotlinia*, *lorlinia*	bundles	300
Lines	bundles	100

		[Measure]	In All Places
	Loglines	bundles	50
	Sounding lines	rings	10
	Blocks, two-pulley, various	piece	500
Shipped on Demand	Glass, half-hour	piece	20
Shipped on Demand	Glass, small	piece	30
Shipped on Demand	Valves, sailcloth	piece	20
Shipped on Demand	Stream anchor for baidara, 2- to 3-pud	piece	8
Shipped on Demand	Tar paper	pud	60
Shipped on Demand	Stove, ship, heating	[piece]	8
Shipped on Demand	Stove, ship, galley	[piece]	1
Shipped on Demand	Compasses, fine quality	piece	10
	Cable, 3-year supply, 11-inch		2
	Cable, 3-year supply, 10-inch		3
	Cable, 3-year supply, 9-inch		4
	Cable, 2-year supply, 8-inch		4
	Cable, 2-year supply, 7-inch		6
	Cable, 2-year supply, 6-inch		6
	Hawsers, 2-year supply, 5-inch		6
	Hawsers, 2-year supply, 4-inch		6
	Hawsers, 2-year supply, 3½-inch		8
	Shroud lines, 2-year supply, 6-inch		2
	Shroud lines, 2-year supply, 5-inch		2
	Shroud lines, 2-year supply, 4-inch		4
	Lines, 2-year supply, 4-inch		6
	Lines, 2-year supply, 3½-inch		16
	Lines, 2-year supply, 3-inch		20
	Lines, 2-year supply, 2½-inch		24
	Lines, 2-year supply, 2-inch		24
	Lines, 2-year supply, 1¾-inch		16
	Lines, 2-year supply, 1½-inch		12
	Lines, 2-year supply, 1-inch		70
	Lines, 2-year supply, ¾-inch		20

[1. Notes]

[Table a. Supplies Used at Novo-Arkhangel'sk for a Year]

	Rum		Sugar		Tea		
	Month	Year	Month	Year	Month	Year	
	bucket	bucket	pud*	pud	funt	pud	funt
By position							
To chief manager	1	12	2½	30	3		36
To office manager, officers	7/8	10½	20	6	2		24
and officials — 16 men	6/8	144	20	96	2	9	24

[Table 1] — continued

	Rum		Sugar		Tea		
	Month	Year	Month	Year	Month	Year	
	bucket	bucket	pud*	pud	funt	pud	funt
Prikazchiks — 10 men	3/8	45	15	45	1½	4	20
Various duties — 10 men	2/8	30	10	30	1½	3	24†
For celebration — 300 workmen	1st bottle	19					
To each per year sold for holidays	3/8	112½	30	270	1	90	
Expenditures on Company Account							
Portion on ships		120		10			12
Ten times on holiday charka of rum for 350 Aleuts	35						
For entertaining Kolosh 2½ buckets a month [per man]	30						
For towing vessels at unusual time	6						
For Aleuts working gardens, making trips on baidarkas and other work	9						
To the pharmacy	10	90					
For unforseen cases		17					
To the hospital				10		2	20
Supplement for family of worker, 1 funt sugar per person				33			
For unforseen needs				80		8	
Total		600		600‡		120	

*[Sic; should be funts.] †[Sic.] ‡Error in original; should be 610 puds.

2. Besides sugar, one bottle of molasses per man a month was produced:

For 300 men [a year]	225	puds
For beer at hospitals	25	
For crew on vessel with tea	30	
For officials with tea	20	
	300	puds

3. If it becomes impossible to obtain wheat, then finely ground barley and buckwheat should take its place. Millet has been used since the founding of the settlement in Sitkha. It is still used because people have grown used to it.

Workers per man per month	from 3 to 5 funts
Officials per man per month	from 10 to 20 funts

4. *Concerning butter.* Out of the nearly 200 puds used every year, it is necessary to order 100 puds from Okhotsk, 80 puds from Fort Ross and to purchase up to 150 puds of good marrow [*monteka*] from California with cash. Kad'iak produces up to 30 puds of butter from the local cattle. The product is used by the people of that area.

5. *Concerning peas and frijoles [beans].* In accordance with regulations peas are issued to ships at the rate of eight funts per month per person, and is sold by the store at a ration of five to ten pounds a month; the same applies to frijoles; the Aleuts of Unalashka and the Pribylov Islands have become quite fond of the latter; every year they send in their requests for them.

6. *Concerning flour.*

Expenditure on company account:

In Novo-Arkhangel'sk Port in 1831	[puds]
They gave shares per position to everyone	3,270
At Ozerskii Redoubt	230
	3,500
Each vessel requires 600 puds of ship biscuit per year, flour for which, at 28 funts of biscuit per pud, comes to	860
Flour issued to workers for cooking per year	100
Annual issue for cattle	40
For the priest per year, by agreement:	50
For Sale	
Above ration for all workers at 20 funts per month, per year	1,750
To officials per 14 men at approximately 5 puds per month	700*
For 10 men at 30 puds per year	300
	2,750
	7,300

In Kad'iak

For 119 shares by agreement, that is, by puds per month	1,421
Additional purchases above ration and for officials	863
Expenditures	70
	2,354
Subtracted from additional purchases	-354
	2,000

In Unalashka

At 40 rations per 1 pud	480
Additional, at 20 funts	240
Employees and officials	190
Priest	52
For Aleuts and in expenditure	38
	1,000
	1,000

In Atkha

For 61 rations of 12 puds	696
Purchases	up to 350
For officials and for bot	150
	1,200[†]
Subtracted from additional purchases	-200
	1,000

[*]Error in original; should be 70 puds. [†][Sic.]

7. *Concerning corn [kokoruza].* Corn is sold in Sitkha and other areas in order to feed cattle, chickens, ducks and other domestic animals.

A fanega of corn (4 puds) can be purchased in California at the cost of 2 piasters and sold at 3 rubles 20 kopeks. If corn is unavailable then wheat is used.

8. *Concerning salt meat.* Out of the 600 puds needed, 300 are prepared at Ross and 300 in the port of San Francisco. July is the fixed date for salting beef in the port of San Francisco. At this time barrels are brought into the port from Ross on baidarkas. The first time meat was salted there was a surplus of salt which had been bought in Monterey. In addition to corned beef, it is necessary to salt sea lion and seal meat on the Pribylov Islands; seal meat is the hunter's favorite meat.

9. *Concerning salt.* The Ozerskii Redoubt has the task of preparing fish for use in Novo-Arkhangel'sk: red salmon (30,000), pink or humpback (10,000), and silver (10,000) — in all 50,000 fish.

According to previous experience, 28 puds of salt is used for the small fish, 22 puds per thousand for large fish, or 1,000 puds for 50,000 fish.

In the port itself, they sometimes salt up to 20,000 fish, including herring. Up to 500 puds are used according to the above-mentioned example. In addition to the Pribylov Islands, the other departments use salt to prepare fish to be used in Novo-Arkhangel'sk (from 30 to 50 barrels of sea lion and seal meat). There are two ways of getting salt to the colonies: one is to buy it from the Sandwich Islands through the Americans or to procure it ourselves in California at port San Quentin.

In addition to these places, salt can be found in large quantities on Carmel Island, near Loretto in Southern [Baja] California and on the islands of Tres Marys near San Blas.

10. *About the Ross Office.* This office is not assigned its quota of butter, salt or corned beef because they obtain their goods in their own area, and it is from there that goods are shipped to Novo-Arkhangel'sk.

The Russians and Aleuts who come to Ross exchange goods for salt, peas, corn and monteka in the neighboring port of San Francisco. When meat is salted for use in Sitkha, salt can sometimes be bought in California, but the salt must be ordered ahead of time. Should the salt not have been ordered ahead of time, it must then be sent from Sitkha. (NB. Salt in California is sold at two to three piasters a fanega, which weighs more than five puds).

11. *Purchasing supplies from California.* Since the company took on the obligation of provisioning its promyshlenniks and employees 14 years ago, wheat for flour and other grain were mainly purchased in California, where the harvests were sometimes quite good, sometimes poor, but always sufficient to supply the colonies with goods. This, in many ways, amounted to a loss, in addition to wasting a month.

In 1829 there was no harvest in California, and the wheat had to be bought in Chile. Hoping that trade with California will continue, we can count on getting the following supplies from them every year:

Wheat	2,000 fanegas	to 8,000 puds
Dry meat	300 arrobas	to 200 puds

Peas and beans	100 fanegas	to 800 puds
Maize	100 fanegas	to 400 puds
Tallow	300 arrobas	to 200 puds
Monteka	200 arrobas	to 140 puds
Salt meat	40 steers	to 350 puds

At average prices these supplies will cost up to 8½ piasters. It is proposed to pay for them three-quarters in goods and one-quarter in cash. The main types of goods needed there for that sum will be as follows:

		Each	*Total*
Wax candles	quintal	10	1,100
Ticking	piece	100	1,200
Strip iron	quintal	25	300
Large shot	quintal	5	120
Sail cloth for sacks	piece	25	500
Yarn for sail thread	funt	100	50
Sewing thread	funt	100	200
Cast iron utensils	quintal	20	800
White, black and red beads	funt	200	400
Blue velveteen	var	200	300
Medium sort cloth	var	200	1,000
Iron nails, 2-to 3-inch	quintal	10	250
Copper kettles and teapots	funt	200	250
Table and glass vessels	[box]	[...]	130
			6,500*

*[Sic.]

12. *Concerning calico, etc.* Calico, semi-calico and printed linens are generally used in the colonies. Even the Aleuts have grown fond of using this cloth, and therefore it has become one of the necessary demands for women's clothes. Calico is used by the families of officials and clerks; the semi-calico is used by the promyshlenniks and Aleuts.

13. *Nankeen.* The colonies prefer getting Cantonese nankeen because it is larger in size, and one piece of it is sufficient to make someone a coat or dress, and the price is almost the same as that of calico. When there is no means of getting Cantonese calico, we can get Kiakhta nankeen, which is cherry-colored, glossy and non-glossy, and has great breadth. The Russian nankeen brought here on the ship *Elena* was of good quality, but it faded quickly, and could only be sold when needed. If the color of the cloth becomes more durable and does not fade, it may replace

the Cantonese and Kiakhta nankeen. This would be more advantageous because it is cheaper.

14. *Concerning coarse calico.* Thin calicos are designated for the officials, while the grey American calico is used mainly in Sitkha for trade with the Kolosh, who are paid in calico for small fur pelts; to a certain extent, by established custom, this material has now become a barter good. The Kolosh who sell bear skins of various sizes, price them as 2, 3 and 4 sazhens of calico or at 5, 7½ and 10 arshins. With the calico we buy sheep and other goods from them.

At Ross, calico is used to pay the Indians for working the soil and harvesting grain. The Indians use the calico to wrap themselves in instead of using blankets.

15. *Concerning linen.* Linen (canvas-like) cloth is used mainly in hospitals and schools, for sheets, pillow cases, shirts and towels.

In Sitkha this linen is exchanged for fish and other goods from the Kolosh. After supplying the hospitals and schools, the various offices sell this linen to the promyshlenniks and Aleuts so that they might make shirts out of it.

At Nushagak they make shirts for the neighboring peoples; at Ross they make them for the Indians as payment for their chores.

The unpacked linen is generally used to make shirts for the workers and Aleuts.

16. *Concerning ticking.* The promyshlenniks and Koloshes in general use ticking to make their shirts. The type they need are made of inexpensive linen. They rarely use half-cotton or full cotton cloth because of their cost.

Ticks and deburets are used to make hospital robes, sheets and light work clothes. The Aleuts especially like these materials. They are also used by the Kenais and Aglegmiuts, who make women's kamleiki out of them; these are exchanged for river otters. In California this material is in general use by the Indians because of its durability and is readily bought at the mission and by the Indians.

17. *Concerning sacking.* Sacks are extremely necessary in Sitkha in order to transport grain to the different offices, but because of the lack of them we have to ship the grain in piles and in barrels. In the first case the grain is wasted and becomes damaged because of the dampness from being enclosed inside damp boards; in the second case, when shipped in barrels, it takes up

more room on the ship and it makes it hard to unload; and worst of all, it is harder in places where the grain has to be unloaded at sea.

In order to buy wheat in California, it is always necessary to have up to 300 sacks to facilitate the loading of the ship.

In Kad'iak sacks are needed to transport grain to the various offices; in Ross they are needed to transport the ground grain from the fields, to the stores and granaries.

It would be more advantageous to send ready-made sacks from St. Petersburg; the sacks should be three-quarters of an arshin in width and one and a half arshins long in order to contain one fanega of wheat.

18. *Flemish linen.* In Sitkha it is used to make tents for workers who work in the forests; it is used as a trade item with the Kolosh and to make light summer sailor's clothing; part of it is sold in California.

This linen is used by the various offices to mainly make sails for baidaras, tents, clothing for the workers and Aleuts.

19. *Concerning broadcloth.* During Mr. Baranov's management of the colonies, frieze was generally used to make clothing; soon after it was replaced by linen; good soldier's linen and the ordinary type of linen are comfortable for worker's clothing.

Russian and Aleut promyshlenniks buy them willingly; but there is a competition among them because they want to have the best clothing for the holidays; that is why it is necessary to have linens of average prices; let us say 6 to 10 rubles per sazhen. Colors most used are blue and grey. The grey, dark-green, black and blue linens must also be of a high quality; part of them are needed in California.

20. *About friezes, flannelettes and flannels.* Part of the frieze cloth is designated for trade with the Kolosh; the rest, along with the flannelette and flannel, is used for winter clothing for the families of officials and workers. In the winter the temperature often reaches 10 to 15° celsius; since there are no pelts, except ground squirrel ones to make winter clothing, the men and women need flannels and flannelettes to make their clothes.

21. *Concerning woolen cloth.* The dark-green is designated for use by the officials; the red by the Aleuts who use the threads to embellish their kamleika, parkas and baidarkas, etc.

22. *About blankets.* Large, medium and small blankets of very good quality are needed by officials, workers and hospitals

throughout the colonies. The blankets are used mainly as trade items for the sea otters with the Koloshes. This type of blanket must be medium, of average quality and cost 14 to 16 rubles.

European goods: friezes and linens have become familiar to the Kolosh since the Northwest Coast became settled by the English and Americans; these goods were brought yearly in large quantities. At first, as it is well known, all these goods were bought up readily by the natives; but time and experience have shown the Kolosh that blankets alone can be used as a comfortable piece of clothing and bedding, and blankets are more becoming to their natural clothing (coats made of wool, and cloaks made from animal pelts); therefore after giving up their taste for frieze and linen, they mainly demand blankets; the blankets are used as a price measure for other European goods and fur goods. The exchange of blankets for friezes occurs only conditionally; instead of giving a certain number of blankets; they are given a definite measure of frieze or linen; but this happens when there is a surplus of otters or when there are no blankets.

23. *About tanned hides.* Half of the tanned hides can be gotten from Ross every year where the raw hides are processed. Every year we obtain up to 78 puds of hides (each hide weighing 30 funts). The hides are gotten from the cattle at Ross or from trade in California; the holds of the ships are always lined with hides before the wheat is loaded; then it is covered with canvas-sail to protect it from dampness; these hides are then sent to Ross to be processed. The quality of the Ross hides is rather good, and few are inferior to the Russian hides.

24. *Virginia tobacco.* A lot is spent to buy tobacco which is used by officials and workers, but it is mainly used as a trade item with the Kolosh. With this tobacco we buy inexpensive fur items from them; and the tobacco pays for food supplies in the market place as well as for the seaweed which is used for fertilizing gardens, for tilling the gardens, for wood and other things. Because of its necessity, five to ten funts of tobacco is sold monthly to officials and one funt to the promyshlenniks. In Ross it is needed to pay the Indians for their work and at times to pay the Californians.

25. *Circassian tobacco.* In designating 100 puds of tobacco to Sitkha, trade with the Chukchis and others throughout North America has been taken into account. The workers are given one funt per month according to previous regulations. The Kolosh do not like this brand of tobacco.

In addition to it being used by the Aleuts, the tobacco is sent from the Kad'iak office for trade with the Kenaitsy, the Chugach, the people along the Copper River; and from Nushagak to the Kuskokwimtsy and the Aglegmiuts.

26. *About seed beads.* Out of the six puds of beads assigned to Sitkha, five puds are supposed to go to California. The following colors are sent there: red, white and black; the rest of the beads, blue and white, are used for trading with the Chukchis and with the Americans in North America.

The Kad'iak office needs blue, white, red and black beads for the Aleuts, and for trade with the Kenais, Chugach and other natives.

Transparent coral beads, especially blue ones, of various sizes are needed. But other colors are needed besides these.

27. *Concerning soap.* A certain amount of requisitioned soap is used to wash clothes. Five funts are issued to the officials for this purpose; the Aleuts and workers receive one funt per month.

In case of shortage, it can be bought in California, where it is sold at 16 to 18 piasters a quintal; it can also be bought from the missions at 12 piasters a quintal; its quality is fair but it does not come up to the quality of Kazan soap.

28-29. *Concerning candles.* Wax table candles are designated for the use of the Chief Manager and officials, but they are issued according to regulations: in the summer (from March to September) and for winter use (from September to March).

[Consumers]	Units per Month			
	Wax		Tallow	
	In summer months	In winter months	In summer months	In winter months
To the chief manager and officials	10	20	10	20
Officials of middle ranks	5	10	15	30
Lower ranks		15		30

Church candles are needed for churches in Sitkha, Kad'iak and Unalashka, Atkha and small candles are also needed for the men on watch duty in the various offices. California needs a special type of candle, which is used in Catholic churches. These candles are of an average height and width; no taller than three feet and one and a half inches around.

Tallow candles can be obtained in the following quantities: half can be gotten from Okhotsk (that is, 75 puds); the rest can easily be made from California tallow; at least 200 puds is gotten there.

30. *About copper.* One hundred fifty puds of copper plating (sheets) is usually needed. Each sheet weighs 7 funts; that means getting 587 sheets; 500 sheets are needed to plate a 150 ton ship; 700 sheets for a 200 ton ship; and a few extras to repair previously made mistakes. Copper utensils such as teapots, pots, etc., are never imported to the colonies but over 100 of them are required annually; these are made in the workshops in Sitkha and other districts; 100 sheets are used yearly for this purpose.

31. *Steel.* The large amount of axes used in the forest demands constant repair; but the Russian shops have gotten so used to the Russian way of fixing axes that they cannot adapt themselves to working with English steel, which we have in large quantities and is considered useless. Therefore it is necessary that the steel and materials needed to fix axes is of Russian make.

32. *About sickles and scythes.* Sickles are needed by the Ross office in order to grow grain, but if more of these were to be shipped they could be sold in California at a profit. In order to prepare hay, the scythe is needed, especially the *gorbusha* [the humped one] a type of scythe which is used in Russia proper and in parts of Siberia. At the beginning a great quantity of straight scythes were shipped to Sitkha, but because they were not used, they rusted and became useless.

33. *About cast iron cauldrons.* Small and medium sized cast iron cauldrons from four to ten to twelve funts are used everywhere among the Aleuts. They are used as barter with the Kolosh and are easily sold in California. In addition the usual cauldrons, several large ones (3 to 20 buckets) are needed in order to prepare food in the artels; to render fat, etc.

34. *About axes.* A wide standard size axe is used throughout Sitkha for work in the forest and for carpentry. In Russia this axe is generally known as a carpenter's axe. It is of good quality, well tempered, with strong butts and thick sides. All the other types of axe are narrow and otherwise worthless in the colonies.

35. *About zincum metallium.* This metal alloy is used in the smelting of copper to make hooks, and hoops for ships, bells, etc.

36. *About sheet lead.* The common English lead sheets are used locally for various needs about ship; part of these sheets are used to sheath the stern of ships; part of which must be thicker than normal.

[B.] Estimate of Needs

	[r.	k.]
Supplies	228,446	
Textiles	52,900	
Linens	73,155	
Woolens	92,010	
Leather goods	14,953	
Various goods	82,631	50
Silk goods	3,790	
Cloth and desk sets	1,508	
Dishes	4,335	
Metallic things	51,081	50
Paints and apparatus	5,822	
Carpenter and other tools	1,578	
Ship stores	55,380	
	617,590	00*

*[Sic.]

[C. Estimate of Company Expenditures]

From the full sum of goods, etc., must be expended on account of the company:

For ship building and household furniture:

	[r.	k.]
Ship stores	55,380	
Carpentry and other tools	1,578	
Paint and apparatus	5,822	
Metallic things	51,081	50
Paper and fittings	1,508	
	115,369	50

Foodstuffs:

6,000 puds of flour in rations 860 puds of flour for sea biscuits	} 7,460 puds	37,300
210 buckets of rum estimated as		8,400
Salt, estimated as		12,000
		57,700

For ship provisions per previous expenditure, 1831:

	[r.	k.]	[r.	k.]
200 puds salt beef at	6		1,200	
50 puds monteka at	20		1,000	
50 puds butter at	27		1,350	
130 puds groats at	10		1,300	
130 puds peas at	4	50	585	
20 funts tea at		04*	80	
20 puds molasses at	16		320	
3 puds granulated sugar	36		108	
In the hospital:				
10 puds granulated sugar			360	
2½ puds tea	1	60	400	
Candles for apartments of officials				
20 puds of wax at	100		2,000	
80 puds tallow 40 puds tallow *na suda*	26		3,120	
			11,823	
Yarn for fishing nets			3,400	
To Kolosh for work:				
15 puds tobacco at	60		900	
500 arshins calico at			550	
			4,850	
Total needed for company expenditures			189,742	50
Estimate for other accounts			427,847	50
			617,590	

[D.] General Estimate of Needs [1831]

	[r.	k.]
Per tables for 1831 of all employees	446,210	
Assuming that from all sums, one-quarter remains in the economy with officials in general and on the average among promyshlenniks in payment of debts	111,522*	
	334,658*	
For this sum goods and supplies are needed for maintenance of officials and employees		
For Trade		
In California, by estimate, approximately	17,500	
For purchase from the Kolosh, for goods, etc., to company at	21,000	
For trade with Chukchi and Americans in North, approximately	2,000	

For trade at Kenai and Chugach forts and Nushagak	10,000	
For Aleuts in payment for furs, birds, whales, ground squirrels, etc., in all districts	60,000	
Total	495,158*	
Goods after expenditures on company needs	427,847	50
Balance	17,310	50
	445,158	

*[Sic.]

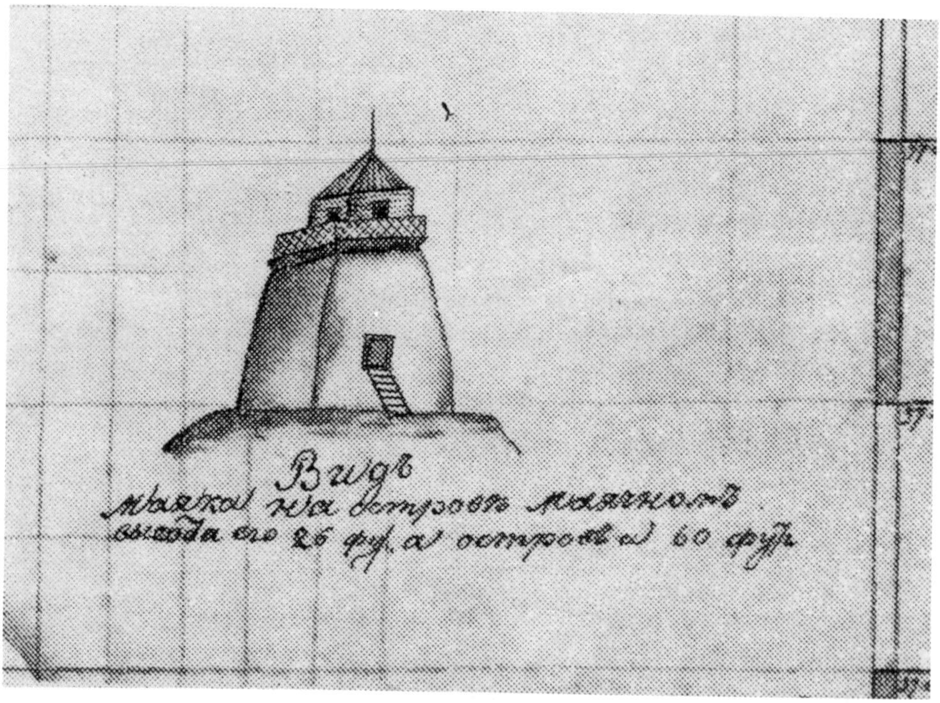

Miachnoi Ostrov [Signal I.], Sitka. Detail from a map of Novo-Arkhangel'sk by I. F. Vasil'ev, 1809.

ADMINISTRATIVE DISTRICTS OF THE RUSSIAN COLONIES IN AMERICA, 1821-1825

The Colonies of the Russian-American Company, which are under the immediate supervision of the chief manager, are in the course of affairs divided into five areas, run by separate offices and bailiffs. They consist of the following: (1) the Novo-Arkhangel'sk office, (2) the Kad'iak office, (3) the Unalashka office, (4) the Ross office, and (5) the Northern Islands district.

Dealing with the local districts, each of the offices has specific tasks in various fields: that of hunting sea and land animals; of preparing fish; of building ships, of growing gardens; cultivating a certain amount of grain; of raising cattle and performing other chores.

A description of the areas mentioned above and their relationships to trade, farming, etc., follows.

I. THE NOVO-ARKHANGEL'SK OFFICE ON BARANOV ISLAND

The company was established here in 1799, and it is common knowledge that a small fortress was built (a little more westward than the now existing fortress) with the agreement of the natives (a considerable amount of goods was given to the natives for ceding this area); in 1802 the Kolosh attacked and took the fort, killing the Russians and Aleuts who were in it.

In 1804 immediately after this incident occurred, the area was taken from the Kolosh with the help of the ship *Neva* which was under the command of Captain Lisianskii. The fort has been in existence since then.

The apartments of the chief manager are located here, and the office under his direct supervision. He is responsible for all company buildings, goods, ships, Russian promyshlenniks and Aleuts; the office receives furs from various areas in the colonies and according to the orders of the chief manager they are sent to Russia either around the world or through Okhotsk. From Novo-Arkhangel'sk, all Russian and foreign goods, supplies, materials and other things needed by the settlement, are sent to the other offices and districts.

In Novo-Arkhangel'sk to 1 January 1821 the population stood at:

Russian officials serving from civil callings and promyshlenniks	235
Their wives and children	92
Creoles educated by the company, taught various trades and as	76
Their wives and children	22
School pupils	30
Aleuts for sea otter hunting	155
Their wives and children	89
Total	639*

*Error in original.

All Company capital is concentrated in this office. It verifies reports of other offices and sends them to the chief manager and to the Main Office [in St. Petersburg].

	r.	k.
In 1820, turnover of capital in this office came to	3,257,212	52
Personal and material capital of the office on 1 January 1821 amounted to	2,572,569	16
Which included the following items:		
Cash in foreign money and assignats	11,270	58
Furs and other goods per tariff	281,198	50
Russian and foreign goods, materials, foodstuffs, etc.	1,395,477	62
In the fort and arsenal firearms and other arms and artillery shells	90,628	25
Seafaring sail and rowing boats with arms	359,226	89
Debts of officials and employees, promyshlenniks and Aleuts	229,880	83
In the church of the Archangel Mikhail various utensils supplied by company, except for applied things	11,789	73
Household furniture in structures and with them in various needs, furniture, library, etc.	86,481	53
Various capital at Ozerskii Redoubt managed by the office	6,046	66
Entrusted to the agent for trade in California and other expenditures	100,568	93
Total:	2,572,569	16*

*Error in original.

There are eight sea-faring vessels on active duty and two which remain in port because of disuse.

The ships are sufficiently equipped with rigging and sea provisions in accordance to a special and permanent regulation, which has been in effect for some time.[51] These ships are sent out to sea for three- to five-month voyages (the same amount of time they spend at sea is still in effect). As soon as fall arrives all ships gather in port.

The Novo-Arkhangel'sk office supervises the Aleuts' hunting of sea otters, which takes place under the escort of one or two well-armed vessels and three to four rowboats. Up to 80 baidarkas were used in hunting in 1818, 1819 and 1820, but now (in 1821) there are up to 100.[52] In the last three years we have obtained 250 to 400 otter pelts of various types. It is unclear whether this type of industry can continue.

Trading of furs between the Kolosh for Russian goods takes place in the fort (Russian goods are exchanged for furs and other items by the Kolosh); they bring in up to 50 sea otter pelts a year; 100 river otters and other pelts. This amount of furs is, however, insignificant; the value of the furs do not compare to the cost of items used to maintain our ties with the Kolosh.

Officials, employees and promyshlenniks receive a salary in accordance with their positions. This is set by the offices and the Main Office; they are paid in monies or bonds; each trading store buys necessary goods and provisions based on prices set by the company.[53]

Creoles and other wards occupy many of the positions within the company and receive a standard salary; all Creoles who have learned a trade and the sailors receive 60 to 150 rubles a year, a pud of flour a month, a pair of socks and coat; now we have to raise their salaries.

In order to hunt sea otters, the Aleuts are issued laftaks for their baidarkas and also get kamleiki, all at company expense. The company pays one-fifth of the price of the fur according to a tax established when the colonies were established.[54]

When hunting furs or whenever there is a shortage of food in port, they get food from their relatives or subsist on fish, sea lion, and sometimes berries and roots; and if these are in short supply, they bake bread from peas, groats or beans. For the work they perform, the Aleuts are paid 50 to 70 kopeks a day in port by the company; this happened more than once last winter (1820/21). When work begins at noon, they are paid 25 kopeks a day, depending on the hardship of the labor. With the money the Aleuts earn, they have the right to buy goods and supplies from the stores, when there are no significant shortages.

All promyshlenniks receive a pud of flour a month from the company, but also have the right to buy a predetermined amount of flour, groats, peas from the stores. The amount issued depends on his family status: a single person — 26 pounds; married — 48 pounds; married with families (depending on the number of members in the family); the same applies for the Aleuts and creoles and salaried employees.

In the school, located near the fort, they teach grammar (reading and writing) and basic arithmetic. On 1 January 1825 there were up to 30 students; they are issued winter and summer clothing by the company, clean undergarments, a provision of flour and other products and supplies, as approved by the chief manager of the colonies (1820-1825), Fleet Captain-Lieutenant and Cavalier Matvei Ivanovich Murav'ev.

The hospital, which is near the port, has enough coats, undergarments and various dishes; the care of the sick is now under the direction of the chief manager and the colonial physician.

Because the buildings have fallen into disrepair, it is impossible to have quiet, clean sleeping quarters such as barracks; the chief manager has already taken strong measures to remedy the situation.

The following buildings stand near the port: a windmill to grind grain; when there is a shortage of soap, it is made out of available fat; there is a spinning shop to make nets; there are shops such as a smithies, a copper foundry, a metal shop, cast iron and bronze smithies; there are sail makers, caulkers, glaziers, roofers, sawyers, carpenters, tailors, boot makers, turners, furriers, painters, and a watchmaker.

The Ozerskii Redoubt [This District Belongs to the Novo-Arkhangel'sk Office]

The Ozerskii Redoubt is under the supervision of a baidarshchik who is in charge of thirteen Russians and four salaried Aleuts. The fish are caught in traps; it is then salted and smoked and sent to the port of Novo-Arkhangel'sk; near the redoubt there is a water mill to grind grain; there is a fair tannery used to process hides and other furs; they crush millstones nearby; near this area there is a sulphur spring which the Russians and Aleuts from the fort use all year round.

The Ozerskii Redoubt has a fort, barracks, stores and granaries, barns, etc. There are two small buildings near the hot springs.

II. THE KAD'IAK OFFICE ON KAD'IAK ISLAND

The eminent citizen Grigorii Ivanovich Shelikhov established a colony here in 1784; and after his death [in 1795] it came under the supervision of the Russian-American Company. At the present time it supervises areas and trade relations under its jurisdiction.

In Pavlovskaia Harbor there are the following buildings: a church, the house of the Kad'iak office manager, barracks, stores, trading post, shops and various private homes (which according to recent information are becoming dilapidated).

The 1821 census reported the following people:

Russians, employees and laborers	83
Creoles and Aleuts on salary	23
Aleut kaiurs of both sexes	32

Aleuts on the entire island of Kad'iak by the new census:

Males	1,176
Females	1,429
Total	2,605

Kaiurs of both sexes in all settlements on Kad'iak Island: 183.

	r.	k.
During the year 1820, company capital amounted to	625,925	
At the present [1825], cash and household furniture, various goods, furs, cattle and debts amounted to	405,386	58

Under the supervision of the Kad'iak office the Aleuts hunt sea otters; they hunt fox, otter, beaver, sable, bear, wolf and other animals on Kad'iak Island and on the American mainland. These furs are then collected in the Kad'iak office and then sent to Novo-Arkhangel'sk.

A small sailing vessel is used to transport furs and processed food from the various artels.

At Pavlovskaia harbor there are privately owned horses, cattle, swine and barnyard fowl.

The promyshlenniks and Aleuts catch Arctic fox. In the summer a party of 100 baidarkas is sent out to hunt otter. The party sometimes separates in two — half sails south of the island, the other goes along the Kenai and Chugach bays.

The fishing is fine at the proper time of the year.

The Kad'iak office gathers furs from various areas and sends them jointly to the Novo-Arkhangel'sk office in the following quantities:

	[No. of skins]		[No. skins]
Sea otter	from 150 to 200	Lynx	200
River beaver	from 150 to 400	Wolverine	60
River otter	from 150 to 500	Black bear	from 100 to 200
Sables	from 600 to 1,200	Muskrats	to 500
Various foxes	from 600 to 1,200	Whale bone [baleen]	100 puds
Beaver castors	from 1 to 2 puds		

Under the Kad'iak office in various places:

Horned cattle	up to 300
Horses	5
Iaman [goats?]	5
Swine	100

In order to facilitate food processing, several Russians work with the Aleuts during the winter, catching fish and hunting fox.

The following districts come under the supervision of the Kad'iak office:

OCCUPATIONS OF THE RUSSIANS ON KAD'IAK ISLAND

1. *Chiniatskaia artel.* Two Russians live here. The company buildings consist of barracks, stores and granaries. Up to 40 head of cattle graze here. They hunt fox here.

2. *Igakskaia artel.* It consists of four Russians. They live in barracks and store food in granaries. The Aleuts prepare iukola and hunt whales. In the spring they hunt fox. There are up to 100 head of cattle and up to 60 pigs.

3. *Three Saints artel.* Has two Russians, who have barracks, granaries and stores. There are few head of cattle here; they process fish; in the winter they hunt fox and in the summer whales.

4. *Alitokskaia artel.* There is one Russian. Here they process food and hunt fox in the winter.

5. *Karlukskaia artel.* Consists of three Russians. The buildings are: barracks, barns, granaries and others. There are up to 50 head of cattle. In the summer they catch fish in traps, and they hunt fox in the winter.

ON THE ISLANDS NEAR KAD'IAK

6. *Afognakskaia artel.* There are five Russians on Afognak Island. They have a house, barracks, granaries, bathhouse and other buildings. They hunt whales, process fish and hunt fox. There are a few cattle.

7, 8 and 9. On the nearby islands of Dolgii, Lesnoi and Elovyi — there are several buildings where the Russians stay: on the first island they hunt sea otter, on the latter island lives Father Herman, a monk who has withdrawn from the world.

10. *Ukamokskaia artel* on Ukamok Island. It has one Russian, quarters and storage areas. They hunt ground squirrels here.

11. *Katmaiskaia artel* on the Aliaska Peninsula. There are two Russians here and rather good buildings: a house, a barracks,

a store, a shop, granaries, etc. They have more than 20 head of cattle. Some process fish. They hunt sea otter and purchase beaver, fox, reindeer and bears. According to the 1818 census there are many Aleuts in this artel on the Aliaska Peninsula:

Males	386
Females	451
Total	837

12. *Nikolaevskaia Fort* in Kenai Bay [in Cook Inlet] It has good buildings. There are thirteen Russians and four salaried Aleuts. At the fort they keep up to 25 head of cattle. The commander of the Nikolaevskaia Fort listed the following in the 1818 census:

Kenaitsy males	636	
Kenaitsy females	1,054	
Chugach males	23	
Chugach females	40	
Of both sexes	1,753	persons

The Commander of the Nikolaevskaia fort trades Russian goods for land animals with the Kenaitsy; the majority of them consist of: river beavers and otters, sable, bear, lynx, fox and beaver castors. Hunting parties are sent from here to hunt sea otters.

13. *Fort Konstantinovskaia* in Chugach Bay on Nuchek Island in Prince William Sound. The buildings here are in good shape: the fort has four cannons, a house, barracks, granaries and others.

As in Fort Nikolaevskaia, the commander here trades with the Chugach for amphibious animals. Parties are sent out from the fort to hunt sea otters.

Russians	15	
Aleut employees	4	
Kaiurs	15	persons

Under Fort Konstantinovskaia, the 1820 census shows:

Chugach males	153
Chugach females	164
Male inhabitants on Copper River	328
Female inhabitants on Copper River	340
Kolchan of both sexes	128

Ugalentsy of both sexes		105
	Total	1,218

At Fort Konstantinovskaia, like Fort Nikolaevskaia, various products of amphibious animals are traded. Parties are sent from that fort to hunt sea otters.

14. *Voskresenskaia artel* in Chugach Bay, located on the mainland on the Kenai Peninsula. There is one Russian here and a small building. There are some cattle.

The following people are under the jurisdiction of this department:

Male and female Kenaitsy	133	
Chugach	162	
Total	295	persons

15. *Fort Aleksandrovskii* in Bristol Bay on the Nushagak River was founded in 1820. There are twelve Russians. Goods are exchanged for river otters from the surrounding peoples known as Aglegmiuts.

This settlement is to be transferred to Hagemeister Island, which is near Cape Newenham.

III. UNALASHKA OFFICE ON UNALASHKA ISLAND IN KAPITANSKAIA HARBOR

There are a few small buildings. The settlement known as Selenie Soglasiia [Accord Settlement] has no forests and it is difficult to improve it in a short time.

According to the 1818 census the following inhabitants have been listed in the various islands under the Unalashka Office:

Males	463	
Females	559	
Total	1,012	persons

There are ten Russians at the settlement of Selenie Soglasiia and several kaiurs who perform various chores.

Business of the Unalashka office in 1820; the capital turnover consisted of 146,900 rubles and 83 kopeks.

On 1 January 1821 it had in its possession 73,005 rubles 79 kopeks.

The Unalashka office sends parties out to hunt sea otters along the islands and buys the pelts of land animals from the Aleuts; most of the furs are fox of various types.

The pelts collected by the Unalashka office are then sent to the Novo-Arkhangel'sk office in the following amounts:

Sea otters of various sorts	up to 150 [skins]
Foxes of various sorts	from 1,500 to 2,000 [skins]
Walrus tusks	up to 100 puds
Whalebone	up to 40 puds

On the various islands there are buildings where Russians live when they hunt animals. These districts are as follows:

DISTRICTS BELONGING TO THE UNALASHKA OFFICE ON THE ISLAND OF UNALASHKA

1 and 2. Makushinskaia and Koshiginskaia artels have one Russian each who hunt fox.

3. At Sannakhskaia artel on Sannakh Island there is a company building under the supervision of one Russian; here they hunt fox and sea otter.

4. The Unganskaia artel in Unga Island is under the supervision of one Russian; here they hunt mainly walrus and reindeer.

5. In the Umnakskaia artel on Umnak Island there is one Russian; they fish for halibut and hunt sea otter.

6 and 7. A Russian is assigned to each of the Akun and Unimak artels (on Akun and Unimak Islands) to hunt for pelts.

IV. THE ROSS OFFICE ON THE SHORES OF NEW ALBION

With permission from the Russian government a settlement was founded at Little Bodega Bay in 1812. It consists of a small fort, the commander's house, barracks, offices, shops and barns to store wood and a windmill for grinding flour.

Vegetable gardens are well cultivated; fruit trees have been planted; experiments with growing grain have not met with success; but there was a harvest in 1819:

	puds	funts
Wheat	92	—
Barley	64	22
In 1820:		
Wheat	173	20
Barley	11	20

Besides company gardens, the various promyshlenniks also have their own little plots and gardens.

They build sailing ships near the settlement.

Up to this time trading and the settlement itself have been under Mr. Ivan Aleksandrovich Kuskov. The settlement has around 25 Russians and 100 or so Aleuts and Kad'iak [Eskimos].

This particular office has up to 340,000 rubles in capital at its disposal.

On 1 January 1821 it had 215,369 rubles and 3 kopeks in cash.

The Aleuts were brought here to hunt sea otters, since the latter soon moved away from the coasts, the hunt does not take place nearby.

Sometimes parties are sent out to the northern parts of the coast, but few otters have been found there.

Various types of livestock animals are raised in the Ross settlement. On 1 January 1821 there were:

Various horned cattle	134
Sheep	670
Swine	150
Horses	20

[1.] *District belonging to the Ross settlement [Farallon Islands].* One Russian and several Aleuts are assigned from the Ross office to the Farallon Islands, which are located near Cape Drake. Those assigned to this area hunt sea lion and fur seals of various types and gather up to 1,000 furs a year.

V. THE DISTRICT OF THE NORTHERN ISLANDS: THE ISLANDS OF ST. PAUL AND ST. GEORGE

These islands are run by a special person under the jurisdiction of the Novo-Arkhangel'sk office.

Along with the person in charge there are six Russians on St. Paul and three on St. George.

The Aleuts brought in from Fox islands numbered:

Males on St. Paul Island	105
Females on St. Paul Island	110
Males on St. George Island	77
Females on St. George Island	88
Total	341*

*Error in original; should be 380.

On both islands they hunt sea animals in the following number:

	On St. Paul		On St. George	
Fur seals	40,000		12,000	
Foxes:				
blue	100		700	
white	100		200	
Walrus tusks	80	puds	30	puds
Whalebone	100	puds	15	puds

On St. George they hunt up to 2,000 sea lions and all hides are sent to the Novo-Arkhangel'sk office.

The Aleuts hunt fur seals and receive 20 kopeks for each of them; for cleaning the hides they et around 100 kopeks apiece.

The Russians process seal meat with salt; the Aleuts catch cod and kill sea lions; they gather large quantities of bird eggs, kill various birds and dry meat. All of these products together consist of food for the islanders. In addition to these products they get grain, goods and other supplies from the Novo-Arkhangel'sk office every year.

In addition to these settlements, which come under the supervision of the chief manager, there are also other areas under the management of the Okhotsk office. These are the following:

1. Komandorskii or Bering Island

This artel consists of ten Russians and some Aleuts from the island of Atkha. Here they hunt fur seals, river otters, foxes, which are then sent to the Atkha office to the manager there.

2. Andreianovskie Islands

The manager of this detachment is situated on the island of Atkha along with 30 Russians.

The settlement is near Korovinskii Bay.

According to local information the population of the Andreianovskie Islands consists of 330 people of both sexes.

Here they hunt sea otter, fur seals, fox of various types along the shores. The pelts are then sent to the Okhotsk office. One ship is used for this purpose.

A rather large number of cattle and fowl is raised on the island of Atkha.

APPENDIX

[Questionnaire for collection of information about the Koloshi, compiled by V. P. Romanov.]

I respectfully ask that the following information be gathered as far as possible.

ABOUT THE KALOSH

1. The conception of the Kalosh about a supreme being, life after death, creation of the world and mankind, and about evil spirits?
2. Have they a concept of the soul and what happens to it after destruction of the body?
3. About the intellect of the Kaloshi and their enterprise?
4. Their morals?
5. Marriage, fidelity of husbands and wives, and the number of wives?
6. Marriage customs?
7. The form of their domestic life?
8. Do they even marry their mothers, sisters or daughters?
9. Love for children, rearing them, and their devotion to their parents?
10. Customs regarding birth?
11. Other funeral customs, include the killing of their slaves?
12. Do they have sorcerers?
13. At what time of the year do they prepare food and of what does it consist, does it last all year, and if there is none, what do they use for food?
14. Is it known whether in recent times they have used human flesh for food?
15. Are the Kalosh superstitious and of what do their superstitions consist?
16. Do they use the women for work, and do they take part in councils and important matters?
17. Are there traces of [earlier] faiths?

18. What games do they have?
19. For what do the savages here make was, and what form of war?
20. What are the main illnesses and the causes among the Kalosh and means for their cure?
21. Of what does their wealth consist?
22. The authority of the taëns?
23. Do they have power over the lives of their kalga [slaves]?
24. About the occupations in New Albion, the place for the settlement of Ross, why was this occupation made?

Are there any anecdotes about the late Baranov or about the Aleuts and promyshlenniks which would show unusual esteem or honesty or unusual love toward the parents or toward others, etc.?

Cathedral of St. Michael the Archangel, Novo-Arkhangel'sk. Artist unknown, 1830s.

The Song Composed by Baranov on the Northwest Coast of America [1799]

Russian wit plunged in adventure,
Has scattered free men across the seas,
To seek new lands, for trade and profits,
For the good of the fatherland, for the honor of the Tsar. (Repeat)

God the Almighty is helping us here,
Supporting Russian courage everywhere,
As soon as we discovered the land, we quickly settled it,
A very important strip of the mainland.

Forming society and companies,
We don't need the muse of the Greeks,
We need but learn the simple rules of nature,
And to follow its laws.

To erect buildings in parts of the New World;
The Russian is moving, Nootka is his goal,
Savage peoples, of barbarous natures,
Have now become our friends.

Peter the Great! If you could only awake,
You would see, that you made no mistake,
Suspecting land nearby, knowing great advantage,
Your offspring found it, and settled there.

The Argonauts were drawn by glitter,
The Golden Fleece they tried to find;
It have been to their fatherland's advantage,
Had they only known about this land.

Here exists no Golden Fleece,
But precious gold is flowing to us.
Were it not for intruders — our European friends —
We should be richly rewarded for our risks.

APPENDIX

The Tower of Sukharev beautifies Moscow,
The Bell and Tsar's Cannon astonish all;
There are wonders aplenty, as the bell tower of Ivan the Great,
But they could be no use to us.

Honor and glory brought us here,
Brotherly friendship unites us,
Let us build and expand,
This so useful for Russia American land.

Here though there is the wildest nature,
Bloodthirsty customs of the natives,
But the advantages important, and needed by the country —
Make labor and loneliness bearable.

In the New World, in the lands of midnight,
We stand among mighty people.
The tribes make peace, respecting bravery,
Take hear, friends — we are Russians.

Neither rank nor riches are important to us,
All we need is harmonious friendship,
All that we have created, all of our efforts,
Will be valued by patriots in times to come.

Aleut, Kad'iak Islander, and Kolosh (Tlingit) noble in ceremonial dress. On right, Kolosh commoners or slaves. Artist unknown (*Zhivopisnaia russkaia biblioteka*, 1859).

ABBREVIATIONS

AVPR	Arkhiv vneshnei politiki Rossii [Archive of Russian foreign policy], Moscow
AGO	Arkhiv Geograficheskogo obshchestva SSSR (Leningrad)
GAPO	Gosudarstvennyi arkhiv Permskoi oblasti (Perm')
GIM	Gosudarstvennyi istoricheskii muzei [State Historical Museum] (Moscow)
LOANN	Leningradskoe otdelenie Arkhiva Akademii nauk SSSR [Leningrad Division of the Archives of the USSR Academy of Sciences]
LOII	Arkhiv Leningradskogo otdelenie Institut istorii AN SSSR [Archive of the Leningrad Division of the Institute of History of the USSR Academy of Sciences]
MAE	Muzei antropologii i etnografii im. Petra I AN SSSR [Peter I Museum of Anthropology and Ethnography of the USSR Academy of Sciences] (Leningrad)
OR GPB	Otdel rukopisiei Gosudarstvennoi publichnoi bibilioteki im. M. E. Saltykov-Shchedrina [Manuscript Division of the M. E. Saltykov-Schedrin State Public Library]
Otdel IZO	Otdel izobrazitel'nykh materialov Gosudarstvennogo istoricheskogo muzeia (Moscow)
RAK	Rossiisko-Amerikanskaia kompania [Russian-American Company]
TsGA VMF	Tsentral'nyi gosudarstvennyi arkhiv Voenno-Morskogo Flota SSSR [Central State Archive of the USSR Navy] (Leningrad)
TsGIA	Tsentral'nyi gosudarstvennyi istoricheskii arkhiv SSSR [Central State Historical Archive of the USSR]
TsGIA ESSR	Tsentral'nyi gosudarstvennyi arkhiv Estonskoi SSR, g. Tartu [Central Historical Archive of the Estonian SSR, Tartu]
Roll	The Russian-American Company, 1802-1867. National Archives Film microcopy No. 11 (92 vols., 77 Rolls), 1942, Washington, D.C.

NOTES

CHAPTER 1

1. Nearly 500 baidarkas were used on this expedition, and between 100 and 200 baidarkas were usually sent along other parts of the Kad'iak and Aliaska coasts; as many as 700 baidarkas could be gathered from Kad'iak and from the Kenai and Chugach peoples, and sometimes even more.

2. During the first winter after the fort was built a food shortage caused the death from scurvy of seven settlers and thirteen promyshlenniks, not counting women and children. Two prikazchiks who had been assigned to various regions constantly fought with one another.

3. In South America the highest mountains in the Andes are: (1) Chimborazo, (2) Cayambe Urcu, (3) Antisana, and (4) Cotopaxi, which has a height of 18,891 feet. The others are lower than 18 thousand feet. See *Spanish America*, London, 1818, Vol. 2. [This footnote was written in by K. T. Khlebnikov in AGO-111, *l.* 3 *ob.*).

4. The height of one mountain does not refute the idea of the gradual decrease of heights of most of the earth [in relation to sea level) from the equator to the poles. [In the margins of LOII-447, *l.* 5, written in by F. P. Wrangell.]

5. The day after the hunting parties left Sitkha they stopped in Khutsnov Strait; the Aleuts ate their fill of black mussels and then suddenly felt nausea and cramps, and in two hours more than 100 of them died. In place of an emetic the leaders of the party administered tobacco mixed with gunpowder and managed to stop the epidemic. But another 15 men died. This place is called Perish Bay because of this incident, and it still bears that name. [The last sentence in this footnote was written in by K. T. Khlebnikov in AGO-111, *l.* 4.] (It is now called Peril Strait — R.A.P.)

CHAPTER 2

6. The hunt was supposed to last 10 to 14 months, and the catch was to be divided into two equal parts; the leader of the party enjoyed the rank of captain. The Aleuts were given food by the company; in case of shortages in supplies the captain was obliged to feed them. The captain paid the Aleuts 2½ piasters for a prime sea otter, 1½ piasters for a yearling and 1 piaster for a pup. If an Aleut was taken prisoner by the Spanish or killed by the savages, the captain was obliged to pay his family 250 talers.

7. A tael equals 10 mes; 1 mes equals 10 kondorins; 1 kondorin equals 10 kems; 100 catties equal 1 picul, which equals 133 English pounds or 148 Russian funts. [This footnote was written in by K. T. Khlebnikov in AGO-111, *l.* 15 *ob.*]

CHAPTER 3

8. Mr. Baranov himself acknowledged this several times and wrote to certain people concerning the unfortunate end of the O'Cain expedition to Canton and to Dr. Shaeffer's in the Sandwich Islands. [This footnote was written in by K. T. Khlebnikov in AGO-111, *l.* 17 *ob.*]

9. According to a previous agreement, Mr. Baranov received ten shares and three more because he was the manager of Sitkha, of which he gave one and a half to his assistant Mr. Kuskov, who received five shares according to the contract.

10. Included in these goods there were also cargoes delivered from St. Petersburg on the ships *Suvorov* and *Kutuzov*. The first [. . .] and the second had a cargo worth 190,000 rubles. [This footnote was written in by K. T. Khlebnikov in AGO-111, *l.* 19.]

CHAPTER 4

11. Subsequently, in 1826 the administration of the Atkha department was combined with the newly established Kuril Islands department. As insignia for seals, the Atkha [office] was given # and the Kuril [office] =. [This footnote was written in by K. T. Khlebnikov in AGO-111, *l.* 24.]

CHAPTER 5

12. The declination of the compass is 27°30′00″ (easterly); the inclination of the magnetic needle is 78°24′; these observations were made by the officers of the sloop *Predpriiatie*. [In AGO-111, *l.* 24 *ob.*, this footnote was written in by K. T. Khlebnikov.]

13. The Spanish navigator [Bodega y] Quadra was the first to reach this area in 1775, then Cook in 1778, the Spanish Captain Martínez on the corvette *Princesa* in 1779, La Pérouse in 1787, Malaspina in 1791, Dixon in 1786; [Bodega y] Quadra named this [cape] Hyacinth. Sitkha Bay he called *Justo* (Horror). [This footnote is found only in AGO-111, *l.* 25, written in the margin by K. T. Khlebnikov.]

14. All the mountains have sharp crests, and many have very conical shapes. Being an extinct volcano, Edgecumbe has a caved-in crest. [This footnote was written in AGO-111, *l.* 25 by K. T. Khlebnikov.] According to the measurements made by navigator Malaspina, Mount Fairweather was 5,068 California vars or 15,060 English feet from sea level. It is situated at a 59°42′ latitude, 131°33′15″ longitude from Kad'iak.

15. The following observations were made to give a sampling of the weather:

August 1819: five clear days; thirteen days with rain during which the sun showed; dark days with rain — thirteen; the highest barometer reading was 30 inches 20 lines; the lowest was 29 inches 3 lines. It was observed that various efficient barometers, which showed changes in weather quite well, tended to show a reading of 29 inches 50 lines and 29 inches 70 lines in bad weather. And even higher readings.

September: six clear days; eleven rainy days during which the sun showed; dark days with rain — thirteen.

October: seven clear days; three rainy days with sun showing; nineteen dark rainy days; two snowy days.

December: eight clear days; four dark days, eight rainy ones; eleven with snow. The average temperature at the best time of year is 18° in the shade. Scientists believe that the snow-covered mountains draw away half of the heat which in the summer should be in the atmosphere at such a latitude.

16. On 9 January 1832, with a northwest wind and dark sky present, there was a rather strong earthquake which lasted more than a minute. This was the first time this happened.

[This footnote is only available in AGO-111, *l.* 25 *ob.*, and is written in by K. T. Khlebnikov.]

17. While it rains and the sun is shining there is always a rainbow to be seen; in the spring and summer there is no thunder or lightning; there is thunder and lightning in the fall and winter but not much. On 21 November 1826 there was an unusually strong west wind accompanied by loud thunder and uninterrupted lightning, which burned down the windmill in Sitkha, but this was the only time it happened.

18. The sound *g* is pronounced like the Latin *h*.

19. Orphans and children who have no relatives and who are unable to earn a living because of illness are looked after by those who have means and who really want to bring them up. [This footnote is written in AGO-111, *l.* 29, by K. T. Khlebnikov.]

20. When the Kolosh get up early in the morning they do not wash themselves but begin to eat immediately; the same for noon and evening; usually they eat when they feel like eating. [This footnote is written in AGO-111, *l.* 31, by K. T. Khlebnikov.]

21. Each large boat is named, for example: Sun, Moon, Stars, Earth, Island, Shaman, Eagle, Raven, Man, etc. The representation of that name is carved into the nose of the boat with various figures. [This footnote is lacking in *Materials for History . . . vyp.* 3, *s.* 43.]

22. In the lake near the redoubt there is the tasty loach, better than the ocean type. The lake never freezes; it did freeze during the severe winters of 1830 and 1832. The ice then was half an arshin thick.

There was a lot of snow in the winter of 1830; on a hill 300 feet high there was a snow avalanche which rolled down into the sea razing a path of spruce 80 sazhens wide. Some trees were cut above the roots; others were taken from the surface of the ground; others taken with their roots. [This footnote is only available in AGO-111, *l.* 31 *ob.*, and written in by K. T. Khlebnikov.]

23. In June 1828 the thermometer showed the following air warmth:

Near the pool	50°	Reaumur

In the pool	35°	Reaumur
The air above the pool	20°	
The air on the seashore	16°	
In a pool of cold water on the shore	10°	

[This footnote is in AGO-111, *l.* 32, written in by K. T. Khlebnikov. This is missing from *Materials for History . . .*, *vyp.* 3, *s.* 43.]

24. The captain of the French ship *Bordelais*, Mr. Roquefeuille, writes that the following number of sea otter pelts were brought to Canton:

1804-1808	59,346
1808-1813	46,692
1813-1815	6,200
1815-1818	12,627
In 1818	4,800
Total	130,425*

*Error in original; should be 129,665 sea otters.

Considering each pelt to go for 31 piasters the sum comes to 4,043,485 piasters. The usual price in Canton was 35 to 45 piasters. But the best otter pelts from the Northwest Coast of America went for 60 piasters. The California otter 24 to 30 piasters. [This footnote is in AGO-111, *l.* 32 *ob.* and 33, written in by K. T. Khlebnikov.]

25. It is not unusual that after long storms, the sea will throw fish of various types upon the shores. Crabs crawl out of the sea and cluster in large piles and die out of the water. The water along the shore looks red. This was observed in Sitkha in 1816 and in Kad'iak in October 1825. During that time they could get no fish until spring.

26. The odor comes from a small membrane on the spine, but the spines themselves are also made of a limestone-like material. The spines of large sea urchins can be used like an engraving tool on slate. [This footnote is in AGO-111, *l.* 34 *ob.*, written in by K. T. Khlebnikov.]

27. Chief Kuakan reassured us that they winter in tree trunks and that they are alive. And that they found their nests there, but the Kolosh do not know how they feed them-

selves in the winter. [This footnote is in AGO-111, *l.* 35, written in by K. T. Khlebnikov. This is missing from *Materials for History . . .* , *vyp.* 3, *s.* 49.]

28. It is not known where they grow, but the Kolosh gather this moss which grows on mountain cliffs and hills; they use it to dye the wool from mountain sheep, out of which they make blankets which only the chiefs or respected elders are allowed to wear. [This footnote is in AGO-111, *l.* 35 *ob.*, written in by K. T. Khlebnikov.]

29. In Kad'iak Bay there are mountains which are made of slate; the upper strata are made of clayey layers of various types. [This footnote is only available in AGO-111, *l.* 36, written in by K. T. Khlebnikov.]

CHAPTER 6

30. According to regulations established by Baron Ferdinand P. Wrangell on 23 December 1825 6/8 [of a bucket] of rum was to be issued to each officer per month; the prikazchiks and officials were to be issued 3/8 of a bucket per month; the workers 2/8. [This footnote is in AGO-111, *l.* 38 written in by K. T. Khlebnikov.]

31. According to regulations made by the chief manager, Mr. Matvei I. Murav'ev, salaries were raised as follows: master craftsmen such as smiths and coppersmiths, master carpenters, shipbuilders and others from 400 to 450 rubles; boatswains first class, 450 rubles; boatswains second class, 400 rubles.

32. The chief manager has the right to award bonuses; the sum of these awards can go up to five thousand rubles a year; these awards are given to the promyshlenniks engaged in trade; those who work as sailors and perform in other capacities; these people receive from 25 to 100 rubles a year.

Subsequently the Main Office of the company allowed the chief manager 10,000 rubles for such awards yearly. At the end of the year these bonuses are given out based on the recommendations of the chief manager and office managers.

33. When sufficient flour came from California in 1824, the chief manager decided to sell twenty funts of flour to each man and three funts of groats and peas. [This footnote is in AGO-111, *l.* 40, written in by K. T. Khlebnikov.]

34. It must be agreed that in a wet, unhealthy climate the moderate use of hard liquor is one of the best means to stay healthy. Experience has proven that scurvy, which was at one time widespread here, is almost unknown now; perhaps rum, tea and potatoes are responsible for this. Every employee gets four to five cups of rum a month during the rainy season; they drink tea twice a day and potatoes are always available; sometimes these are issued by the company; sometimes they buy it from the artel. [This footnote is in AGO-111, *l.* 44-44 *ob.*, written in by K. T. Khlebnikov. See table on p. 82 for the amount of potatoes harvested from personal and company gardens in 1833.]

35. Up to now, this article has not been submitted to the government for its approval. [This editorial note is only available in the book *Materials for History of Russian Colonization of the Eastern Shores*, *vyp.* 3, St. Petersburg, 1861, *s.* 67.]

36. It must be noted that: (1) millet was a necessary item for travel if peas and groats were lacking in warehouses, but now it is sold as an item for money; (2) the *Kiakhta* was sent to Kad'iak with a full cargo of wheat, which should last four to five years; (3) above these expenditures, the ship *Elena* when it sailed had 228¼ puds of flour, 201 puds and 16 funts of rusks; and (4) in the list of expenditures, the loss in the warehouses has not been listed; this loss amounted to 100 puds.

37. If there is a shortage of barrels, then fish is salted in chests or bins which are lined with cloth. Such a bin is 15 6/12 feet long, 5 10/12 wide, 6 8/12 high and has a volume of 891,800 cubic inches; figure 231 cubic inches to the gallon, this would be equal to 3,860 gallons or 1,158 buckets by Russian measurements. [This footnote is in AGO-111, *l.* 49, and written in by K. T. Khlebnikov.]

38. Note: Weight is measured in quintals: 1 quintal has 4 arrobas; an arroba has 25 Spanish pounds; 89 Spanish pounds equal 100 Russian funts.

Length is measured in vars: 84 vars equal 100 Russian arshins.

39. The trade amounted to the following in the last few years:

	r.	k.
1828 to the beginning of 1829		
Goods sold and money exchanged into Russian currency	39,450	
With a profit of 31 percent	12,247	
1830 Goods sold	59,443	
Profit at 43 percent	25,546	
1831 Goods sold	17,781	
Profit at 94 percent	8,386	61

[This footnote is in AGO-111, *l.* 58 *ob.* written in by K. T. Khlebnikov.]

40. According to the latest information in 1832: the sandalwood tree is of no use in Canton and has no value; the reason for this is unknown, but there are no advantages with it. [This footnote is in AGO-111, *l.* 111 *ob.* written in by K. T. Khlebnikov.]

41. According to information received from the Americans in 1829 the three ships owned by the company Bryant and Sturgis of Boston received in trade with the Kolosh the following pelts in 1828: 600 sea otters of various types and 6,000 river otters. Captain Thompson said that in 1830 he was paying the Kolosh ten blankets and a gun, axe, knife, scissors, gunpowder, pellets, ten bullets, ten flints, a little wheat and tobacco for one otter pelt worth up to 25 piasters; this price was established by the owners in Boston.

In 1831 the Americans were unable to obtain 100 sea otter pelts. [This footnote is in AGO-111, *l.* 62 written in by K. T. Khlebnikov. The last sentence is only available in AGO-111, *l.* 62 in the margins.]

42. At the end of each month all masters give the harbor master, or the office manager (in the harbor master's absence), a detailed account of all work performed. This is entered in a special book and presented to the chief manager monthly. [This footnote is in AGO-111, *l.* 60 *ob.*, written in by K. T. Khlebnikov.]

43. In 1825, 31 puds of tallow were used aboard ships; 84½ puds were used by the fortress, barracks, and in the quarters of the officials; the chief manager used four puds of spermaceti and seven puds of wax. The prices for candles were the following: those made in Sitkha, 25 rubles; made in St. Petersburg, 30 rubles; made in Okhotsk, 40 rubles; spermaceti, 88 rubles; wax, 120

rubles a pud. This totals 4,300 rubles. [This footnote is in AGO-111, *l.* 67, written in by K. T. Khlebnikov.]

44. In 1824, 493 rubles 60 kopeks were paid out to till the gardens and 222 rubles 60 kopeks for harvesting potatoes, a total of 716 rubles 20 kopeks; 150 barrels of potatoes were harvested; each barrel was thus worth 4 rubles 20 kopeks. The inhabitants sell them at 12 to 15 rubles a barrel. In 1826, 331 rubles were paid out to till the gardens, in addition to a cup of rum per man which was issued daily. [This footnote is in AGO-111, *l.* 68, written in by K. T. Khlebnikov.]

45. Each time ships are sent out, they smoke out the rats with charcoal. This is a necessary precaution. It has happened that the smoking was badly done and that the rats returned on ship and multiplied on board. In such a case many goods were lost. [This footnote is in AGO-111, *l.* 69, written in by K. T. Khlebnikov.]

46. The main mountains consist of clear granite; the boulders come in various shapes: rhombus, cube, cylinders and others. In one cliff hanging above the sea, there is a boulder ten vershok in diameter and three-quarters of an arshin long. The Kolosh who used to live near the lake left a myth that a crab of terrible size lives deep in lake. One day this crab came up to the top and with his foot pushed down a boat and its people to the bottom; those who witnessed this scene drew a picture of the crab's foot, which is harmless now. [This footnote is in AGO-111, *l.* 70, 70 *ob.*, written in by K. T. Khlebnikov.]

47. Out of which 6,000 were sent to Kad'iak, and 3,000 rubles to Unalashka and Fort Ross.

48. Chief Manager Petr Egorovich Chistiakov sent old, useless ships to the various departments:

		Commander
1826	In May the *Konstantin* to Unalashka	Mr. [I. Ia.] Vasil'ev
1828	In June the *Finliandiia* to Unalashka	Mr. Pometilov
1828	In July the *Volga* to Atkha	Mr. Benzeman

[This footnote is in AGO-111, *l.* 74 *ob.*, written in by K. T. Khlebnikov.]

49. Article No. 93, issued by the chief manager in Novo-Arkhangel'sk on 4 December 1820, states what items are needed and to be issued to the hospital:

List of Things Needed for the Hospital

	[Each]		[Total]	
	[r.	k.	[r.	k.]
Clothing				
30 linen shirts	4		120	
10 robes of ticking with lining of crash	16		160	
20 pair of wool socks	2	25	45	
10 canvas mattresses	11	50	115	
20 linen sheets	6	75	135	
20 pillow cases		90	18	
10 cash pillows with wool	1	20	12	
10 flannelette blankets	10		100	
10 wool nightcaps	1	50	15	
			720	
Copper Vessels				
1 ewer, 2 basins, 2 teapots } 11 funts	3		33	
Straw-colored [Ceramic] Vessels				
4 teapots			4	50
4 chamberpots			8	
10 slop basins			4	50
1 dozen plates			3	90
Glass Vessels				
10 mugs	1	80	18	
Iron vessels				
2 cast iron pots of 7 funts			1	50
			73	40

50. The watch, making their rounds, report those who are sick in the fort in the morning and the number of Kolosh who spent the night in the fort, listing the men, women and chiefs. In the evening the watch gives an oral report to the chief manager about the number of Kolosh in the fort; the chief

manager gives those making the rounds the password. [This note is in AGO-111, *l.* 88, written in by K. T. Khlebnikov.]

ADMINISTRATIVE DISTRICTS OF THE RUSSIAN COLONIES IN AMERICA, 1821-1825

51. Each seaman was assigned the following for each 24 hours at sea:

Hardtack	1¼ funts	Marrow [per 24 hours]	5 funts
Corned beef or California dried meat per month	½ pud	Rum [per 24 hours]	5 shots
Groats [per 24 hours]	8 funts	Vinegar	as needed
Peas	8 funts	Salt	as needed

52. Formerly, hunting parties of up to 300 baidarkas were sent from Kad'iak, but because of fragmentation and decline in the number of Aleuts, it is now impossible to assemble [such a force].

53. By firm rules of the Main Office, [markups] of 30 percent are proposed for goods delivered around the world from St. Petersburg and 10 percent for goods purchased en route, which sum sometimes equals the expenses of delivering the goods.

54. Prices are fixed as follows:

	r.	k.		r.	k.
Sea otter	50		Fox:		
Yearling	20		mainland red	3	50
Pups	4		mainland silver	5	
Large river beaver	6		mainland cross	15	
Large river otter	8		Fur seals	2	
Large black bear	10		By quality and size, walrus ivory	12	

COMMENTARIES

CHAPTER 1

Page 1: *"It is common knowledge that during several years after occupation of Kad'iak Island by Mr. Shelikhov's company (1783) . . . "* — This event occurred a year later. On 16 August 1783 G. I. Shelikhov's vessels, the *Tri Sviatitelia*, the *Sv. Simeon Bogopriimets i Anna Prorochitsa* and the *Sv. Mikhail*, set out from Okhotsk for the coast of America. On 13-22 July 1784 the first two took on supplies at a Russian settlement at Captain's Harbor on Unalashka Island; and only on 3 August 1784 did those vessels (and later the *Sv. Mikhail*) reach the southern tip of Kad'iak Island and stand at anchor in the harbor which Shelikhov named "Gavan' Trekh Sviatitelei" (G. I. Shelikhov, *Rossiiskogo kuptsa Grigoriia Shelikhova stranstvovaniia iz Okhotska po Vostochnomu okeanu k Amerikanskim beregam*, edited by B. P. Polevoi, Khabarovsk, 1971, pp. 35-43).

Page 1: *"In an order of 11 May 1794 addressed to Mr. Shelikhov, the Governor-General of Siberia, Mr. Pil', directed him to accomplish the following: 'In accordance with an Imperial Decree, you have been assigned twenty families in order to build shipyards at Cape St. Elias and ten families to settle and cultivate the land there . . . '"* — According to "an order of the Governor-General of Irkutsk I. A. Pil' to G. Shelikhov of 11 May 1794," Catherine II by an ukaz of 11 December 1793 had "deigned to order: that at your request [the company of G. I. Shelikhov and I. I. and M. S. Golikov], in order to build with your own funds at Cape St. Elias a wharf and to establish agriculture at suitable places along the mainland of America and on the Kuril Islands, were to be given as artisans for the first up to twenty peasant exiles, and for the second up to ten families (which, by my order, has already been done) . . . " (*Russkie otkrytiia v Tikhom okeane i Severnoi amerike v XVIII v.*, edited by A. I. Andreev, Moscow, 1948, p. 323, No. 43). The number of "settlers" is defined more precisely in Shelikhov's report to I. A. Pil' of 18 November 1794: in August 1794, 45 settlers of both sexes were sent from Okhotsk to the Russian settlements in America on the vessels *Tri Ierarkha* and *Sv. Ekaterina*. Moreover, besides the group of men and women, it was proposed to send six "settlers" from Okhotsk to the 18th Kuril Island, Urup (*ibid.*, pp. 354-355, No. 45).

According to "A list of people wishing to leave the colonies next year [of 1 May 1819]" sent to the Main Office by the chief manager of the colonies S. I. Ianovskii, out of 37 persons were named "four settlers: Shchukin, Krylatskii, Podomarev and Sokolov, who by the personal ukaz were given to Shelikhov for crafts and agriculture and are not to be freed except by authority of the management." The reply of the Main Office of 16 January 1820 was brief: "No one is to be allowed to leave until he has paid his taxes" (AVPR, *f.* RAK, *op.* 888, *d.* 964, Roll 2, *f.* 10 [*Records of the Russian-American Company, Correspondence of the Governors General, Communications Received*: Main Office to Chief Manager Murav'ev, 16 January 1820, Vol. 2, f. 10, National Archives, Washington, D. C. Hereafter cited *RAC, CR*].).

Thus, of all the Russian colonists in Russian America, the "settlers" appear to have been in the category most deprived of rights. In 1809 two of them, Ivan Popov and Vasilii Naplavkov, led an uprising of the promyshlenniks, caused by dissatisfaction with the company's economic demands and protest against oppression by the chief manager of the colonies A. A. Baranov: both were sent from the colonies to Russia. The directors of the Main Office of the Russian-American Company wrote to A. A. Baranov on 22 March 1817: "The case of the culprits Naplavkov, Popov and their comrades is now in the Governing Senate for decision, which, hopefully will be soon, and in the opinion of the Criminal Court, the Civil Governor here who sentenced them, they will be given the punishment they deserve. It is to be hoped that, upon learning of this, other promyshlenniks will take the fate of these criminals as a lesson and shun similar activities." To the document is appended a letter of 1815 without a signature: "the case brought to me from the St. Petersburg Tribunal for Criminal Law has been presented to the Governing Senate [Supreme Court] with an abstract and a short covering memorandum about the former promyshlenniks of the Russian-American Company: namely, the settler's son, registered peasant of Yakutsk okrug, Amginsk volost, Vasilii Naplavkov; the retired copyist Prokhor

Verigin; and the Tiumen townsman [*meschanin*] Ivan Chernyshev. They were charged with conspiracy to engage in seditious acts and kill the manager of the Russian-American provinces Collegiate Councillor Baranov and other company employees. The Tribunal, finding [the two accused] Popov and Naplavkov guilty, has sentenced them to deportation in Siberia instead of to labor, exempting them from corporal punishment, by authority of the [Imperial] manifesto of 30 August 1814, but Verigin and Chernyshev, because they did not confess to participation with Popov and Naplavkov, nor was it proved, were freed by the section of the court and sent to Siberia for settlement under supervision, without right to engage in the fur trade" (AVPR, *f.* RAK, *op.* 888, *d.* 963, Roll 1, *f.* 58-59 [*RAC, CR:* Main Office to Chief Manager Baranov, 22 March 1817, Vol. 1, No. 192, f. 58-59]).

The fate of Ivan Shchukin, Semen Krylatskii, Fedor Valakin, Aleksandr Golovin and their families is traced in an article by the American historian W. L. Sarafian ("Alaska's First Russian Settlers," *Alaska Journal* 7(3):174-177, 1977).

Page 4: *"On 20 April 1800, [Mr. Baranov] left for Kad'iak on a galley, leaving Medvednikov in charge with 20 Russians. In 1802, because of the garrison's carelessness, the Kolosh attacked and destroyed the settlement."* — The events in the Russian settlement of Novo-Arkhangel'sk on Sitkha [Baranof] Island in 1802 and their causes are most fully described in "Reports of I. A. Kuskov to A. A. Baranov on Kad'iak regarding an armed encounter between the party of promyshlenniks and the local tribes and the destruction of Novo-Arkhangel'sk by the Indians. Yakutat, 1802, July 1" [*K istorii Rossiisko-Amerikanskoi kompanii, Sb. dok. materialov*, Krasnoiarsk, 1957, pp. 106-123, No. 9). An extract of this document was published earlier by P. A. Tikhmenev (*Istoricheskoe obozrenie obrazovaniia Rossiisko-Amerikanskoi kompanii, ch. 2*, St. Petersburg, 1863, Appendix 2, pp. 180-182). Khlebnikov used this source and others in writing his work published under the title *"Pervonachal'noe poselenie russkikh v Amerike"* (*Raduga*, Revel', 1833, *Kn.* II, III, and V). The work was again reprinted in *Materialy dlia istorii russkikh zaselenii po beregam Vostochnogo okeana* (St. Petersburg, 1861, No. 4, pp. 40-56). Preserved also is the scribe copy of this article with the signed dedicatory letter of K. T. Khlebnikov (Novo-Arkhangel'sk, 21 June 1831) to Baroness Elizaveta Vasil'evna Wrangell, the wife of the chief manager of the Russian possessions in America, F. P. Wrangell (TsGIA ESSR, *f.* 2057, *op.* 1, *d.* 354, *l.* 1-25 *ob.*).

CHAPTER 2

Page 6: *"The first contact with Americans took place on Kad'iak in May 1801 because there had been a shortage of supplies due to the unfortunate accident suffered by the ship Phoenix."* — The Russian three-masted vessel *Phoenix*, built in Voskresenskaia Harbor, was wrecked en route from Okhotsk to the Russian possessions in America in 1799. Eighty-eight people perished and a considerable cargo was lost. "For a long time it was hoped that the *Phoenix* had found shelter somewhere from the storms which were then raging, but the subsequent casting ashore at Sitkha, Kad'iak, and Otter Bay of many items belonging to the ship finally forced acceptance of the sad truth" (Tikhmenev, *op. cit.*, *ch.* 1, p. 79).

Page 6. *"In 1802 the Englishman Barber and the American Ebbets ransomed several prisoners from the Kolosh and brought them to Kad'iak."* — "Depositions, made in the Kad'iak office of the American Company by the promyshlennik Abrosim Plotnikov, by Ekaterina, wife of Zakhar Lebedev, and others who were witnesses to the massacre at the Novo-Arkhangel'sk fort [sic] and who escaped from the Kolosh . . . " (Tikhmenev, *op. cit.*, *ch. 2*, Appendix 2, pp. 174-180).

Page 8: *"In May of that year [1810] another party was sent out into the straits . . . After reaching Dundas Island, near the Queen Charlotte Islands, they began their hunt under constant danger of Kolosh attack."* — In order to ingratiate themselves with the Kolosh, the Russians entered into wedlock with the native inhabitants. "Many of our Russian promyshlenniks are married to the daughters of these Americans, and vice versa, Kolosh whom we held as hostages, married Aleut women. The inhabitants of these parts of America held in particular esteem the late manager Baranov, who often invited them as guests. Baranov, who had in Kargopol in Russia a legal wife Matrena and a daughter Afanas'ia, took to wife in Russian America the daughter of a native leader, baptized Anna Grigor'evna, and had by her three children: Irina, Antipatr and Ekaterina. Commercial Councillor Kuskov, the former assistant manager, was married to a native American from a place lying about latitude 52° [the latitude of the Queen Charlotte Islands, inhabited by the Haida and Tsimshian

Kolosh]. He himself recounted frequently that he did that for political reasons, for he voyaged from Novo-Arkhangel'sk to California annually for ten years. During his passage, all the inhabitants down to Nootka came to him with esteem, bearing various provisions and each time gave his wife, their countrywoman, valuable presents" ("On the rights of Russians to possession of the Northwest Coast of America from latitude 52° N to Icy Cape or to the supposed Polar Sea, 1825," in the book *Arkhiv grafov Mordvinovykh*, St. Petersburg, 1902, v. 6, p. 688, Document No. 1245).

This document was found in the archive of the Russian state figure Count N. S. Mordvinov (1754-1845), who was a shareholder of the Russian-American Company from 1805 and from 1818 possessed 20 shares of this company, which give him the right to active participation in making decisions on the most important affairs of the company. The document not only expands our knowledge of the colonial practice of the Russian-American Company, but carries existing corrections in the biography of Ivan Aleksandrovich Kuskov himself. As is known, the English term *Indian* has two meanings when translated into Russian: *Indiets* and *Indeets*. This was probably the reason for the error in the article by the first biographer of I. A. Kuskov, the Vologda historian and regional specialist E. V. Kichin, who wrote that the wife of I. A. Kuskov, Ekaterina Prokhorovna, "was the daughter of an Ustiug burgher, living in India. On the death of her father and mother, she was left an orphan and somehow met up with Kuskov, who married her . . . Here [in Ross settlement], as in our other settlements in America, Mr. Kuskov treated the heathen mildly and gently, but nevertheless they more than once intended to kill him. For his salvation from such malefactors he was obligated to his wife, acquainted with the language of the wild Americans" (E. V. Kichin, "Ivan Aleksandrovich Kuskov: A Biography," *Vologda gub. vedomosti*, 1848, 21 February, No. 8, *chast' neofitsial'naia*, p. 84). One must suppose that E. V. Kichin was misled by the translation of the English word *Indian*, so near in sound but so different in essence.

Nevertheless, on glancing at the portrait of E. P. Kuskova, done on thick cardboard in oil and kept in the Tot'ma regional studies museum (Vologda oblast), the question arises: if this is a Kolosh woman before us (the oval face, slant eyes and other signs permit this supposition), why does she not have a labret in her lower lip? To wear the labret was the privilege of women of the upper classes (wives of chiefs wore a large labret) and free Kolosh women; slaves did not wear labrets at all. However, it is difficult to suppose that I. A. Kuskov would have married a Kolosh woman not of a better class, for only blood ties with one of the Indian chiefs could promise the Russians necessary diplomatic advantages. However, in I. A. Kuskov's account are mentioned only "valuable gifts, which for ten years he received annually with esteem" from the Kolosh of the Queen Charlotte Islands for his wife, "their countrywoman" and "various provisions," but nothing is said about the social origins of E. P. Kuskova. One can suppose that among the well-to-do, important Kolosh Haida and Tsimshian women in the 1810s were already some whose lower lip was not pierced with the labret inserted. A decline in the custom of wearing the labret was noted by the Spanish seafarer Jacinto Camaño, coming up from San Blas to the north coast of the Queen Charlotte Islands on the corvette *Aransasu* in March 1792: "All the actions of these people clearly indicated that in five years of contact with Europeans they had learned superficial patterns of behavior. The chief's daughter was judged a good-looking girl, perhaps partly because she did not wear the labret" (E. Gunther, *Indian Life on the Northwest Coast of North America as Seen by Early Explorers and Fur Traders during the Last Decades of the Eighteenth Century*, Chicago and London: University of Chicago Press, 1972, p. 134).

Three and a half decades later, in 1827, F. P. Litke noted among the Sitkha Kolosh the same tendency to retreat from traditional customs: "The women are much less handsome than the men, but would not be quite so repulsive if they did not disfigure themselves . . . with pieces of wood pierced into their lips — the most absurd custom that despotic fashion has ever imposed on man. However, even this custom is not as widespread as it used to be, and now, without these three inch long pieces of wood implanted in her lips, a young Kaloche woman still has some hope of pleasing and thus of finding a good catch" (F. P. Litke, *Puteshestvie vokrug sveta na voennom shliupe "Seniavin," 1826-1829*, Moscow, 1948, p. 77).

With this commentary the author wants to correct her own research about the Kuskovs (see S. G. Fedorova, "Russkaia Amerika i Tot'ma v sud'be Ivana Kuskova," in the book *Problemy istorii i etnografii Ameriki*, Moscow, 1979, pp. 229-254).

Page 9: *"Shvetsov and Tarakanov were assigned to the expedition along with 20 baidarkas."* — In 1803 Afanasii Shvetsov and Timofei Tarakanov were the first Russians from Kad'iak to reach the shores of California, where they hunted sea animals under protection of the American vessel *Eclipse*, Captain O'Cain. [An error. The vessel was the *O'Cain*, commanded by O'Cain on her 1803-1804 voyage. — R. A. P.]

Page 9: *"In California Winship and Slobodchikov quarreled. While on the island of Seros, Slobodchikov bought the schooner* Nikolai *in exchange for 100 sea otter pelts and 50 yearlings. He persuaded an American to sail the schooner to the Sandwich Islands, and from there returned to Sitkha on 22 August 1807."* — The Captain of the American vessel *O'Cain*, Jonathan Winship, in May 1806 concluded in Kad'iak with A. A. Baranov an agreement for a joint hunt of sea otters from the mouth of the Columbia River to the coast of California with the aid of Aleut and Russian hunters on baidarkas. At the end of the agreed period Slobodchikov managed to buy on the California coast a small American vessel with all armament, named the *Sv. Nikolai*, load in it furs acquired as the company's share and persuade the former skipper of this vessel to conduct him and the baidarkas to the Sandwich Islands, whence Jonathan Winship also set out on his vessel. "King Kamehameha received the Russians very kindly and sent to Baranov, of whom he had heard much from the American captains, a colorful feather helmet and cloak, as a sign of his special respect" (Tikhmenev, *op. cit.*, *ch. 2*, p. 169).

Pages 10-11: *"The unfortunate wreck of the* Nikolai *and the immediate imprisonment of the crew were described by Mr. Tarakanov . . . "* — The author had in view "the wreck of the Russian-American Company vessel *Sviatoi Nikolai*, under the command of navigator [*shturman*] Bulygin, on the Northwest Coast of America at a latitude of about 47½°, at the island Vancouver called Destruction Island, 1 November 1808." The "Wreck . . . of the vessel *Sviatoi Nikolai*" is based on the account of the voyage, 1808-1809, of the prikazhchik of the Russian-American Company Timofei Tarakanov obtained by V. M. Golovnin in Russian America in 1810 from Chief Manager A. A. Baranov and also notes on Golovnin's personal conversations with Tarakanov and his fellow voyagers.

Published in 1822 was *Opisanie primechatel'nykh korablekrushenii, v raznye vremena sluchivshchikhsia. Sochineniia*

Archibal'da Dunkena. Chetyre chasti. Perevod s angliiskogo, popolnennyi primechaniiaimi i poiasneniiami V. M. Golovnina (St. Petersburg, 1822). The "Supplements and Remarks" constitute a fourth part, in which V. M. Golovnin included "the wreck . . . of the vessel *Sviatoi Nikolai*" (also appearing later in the book *Sochineniia i perevody V. M. Golovnina*, Vol. 4, St. Petersburg, 1864, pp. 406-428). The schooner *Sv. Nikolai* (the same that Sysoi Slobodchikov obtained from the American captain in 1806 on the California coast) under command of navigator N. I. Bulygin, set out from Novo-Arkhangel'sk to the California coast on 29 September 1808 but was wrecked on 1 November 1808 on the north mouth of the Columbia River, near what Vancouver named Destruction Island (47°33′, according to T. Tarakanov; 47°38′, according to V. M. Golovnin). Going ashore, the crew began to head south toward Grays Harbor, where I. A. Kuskov, who had left Novo-Arkhangel'sk after the *Sv. Nikolai* and was the head of this expedition, was to arrive on the vessel *Mirt-Kad'iak*. Pursued by the Kolosh Indians, Tarakanov and his comrades at the end of 1809 had to surrender to the Indians; those remaining alive were held prisoners until 10 May 1810 when the American Captain Brown, arriving on the brig *Lydia*, purchased them from the Kolosh and on 9 June 1810 took them to Novo-Arkhangel'sk. An analogous version of the wreck of the schooner *Sv. Nikolai* and the presence of its crew as prisoners among the Indians was written in the 1850s in Novo-Arkhangel'sk from the words of the then 70-year-old Timofei Osipovich Tarakanov to a "visitor" (N. M. Bogomolov, *V plenu u Indeitsev: Istinnoe proisshestvie (1808) iz vospominanii moriaka*, St. Petersburg, 1885, pp. 1-29). [Bogomolov's account is only a piece of hack-work plagiarized from Golovnin and is without scholarly merit. — R. A. P.]

Page 12: *"In 1815 Mr. Baranov sent out the brig* Il'mena *with a party of Aleuts under the command of Tarakanov with trading goods with prikazchik Nikiforov. . . . Eliot . . . was eventually caught by the Spanish who also took a few Russians and many Aleuts."* — The date this voyage began varies in different sources: Khlebnikov himself in his *Zhizneopisanie Aleksandra Andreevicha Baranova* (St. Petersburg, 1835, p. 155) noted that this expedition was sent in December 1813. The American historian R. Pierce states that A. A. Baranov acquired the brig *Il'men'* (the former *Lydia*) from the Americans at the end of 1813 and sent her on a voyage from Novo-Arkhangel'sk to the shores of California in January 1814

(R. A. Pierce, *Russia's Hawaiian Adventure, 1815-1817*, Berkeley and Los Angeles, 1965, p. 9). A. Ogden states: "In 1814 the *Il'men* arrived at Fort Ross with supplies and with 59 Aleuts under Tarakanov" (A. Ogden, "Russian Sea-otter and Seal Hunting on the California Coast, 1803-1841," *Quarterly of the California Historical Society*, Vol. XII, No. 3, September 1933, p. 231). The Bancroft Library of the University of California at Berkeley, California, has an undated manuscript headed "Statement of Vassili Petrovitch Tarakanoff, a hunter in the employ of the Russian American Company" (Manuscript Division of the Bancroft Library, Russian America, PK P-K 2:2, 42 pp.) written in the hand of Ivan Petrov (a Russian co-worker of H. H. Bancroft from 1875) and published as "Statement of My Captivity among the Californians" by Vassili Petrovitch Tarakanov (written down by Ivan Shishkin and translated from the Russian by Ivan Petroff, with notes by Arthur Woodward, *Early California Travels*, Series No. XVI, Los Angeles: Glen Dawson, 1953, p. 47).

Tarakanov's account contains such interesting and instructive details about the ways and customs of the California Spaniards and Indians that it continues to attract the attention of historians and ethnographers. However, it must be noted that, although the Russian original text is stated to have been published in *Morskoi Sbornik* in November 1852, that number does not contain any such item by Tarakanov. This bibliographic inaccuracy in turn led to an error by the publishers of a guide to the manuscript collections of the Bancroft Library (Dale L. Morgan and George P. Hammond, eds., *A Guide to the Manuscript Collections of the Bancroft Library*, Berkeley and Los Angeles: University of California Press, 1963, p. 178), which lists the Tarakanov memoir and the list "Russian round-the-world expeditions (1849-1852)" in *Morskoi Sbornik* for November 1852 (pp. 415, 415a, 416). Lack of the Russian original of Tarakanov's notes or their publication; the impossibility of finding any information about an Unalashka priest Ivan Shishkin, supposed sometime to have written down Tarakanov's account; and the incorrect rendering of Tarakanov's given name and patronymic give reason to suppose that the notes on life as a prisoner of the Spanish in California (in 1814 or 1815) ascribed to Tarakanov were actually an artful forgery by Ivan Petrov. See Prof. R. A. Pierce, "New Light on Ivan Petroff" (*Pacific Northwest Quarterly*, Vol. 59, No. 1, January 1968, pp. 1-10) and *Russian America: A Biographical Dictionary* (Preliminary Survey, 1983, for the Alaska Historical Commission, Anchorage).

Eliot de Castro and three Russians (among whom T. Tarakanov is not mentioned) were freed from Spanish captivity by Lieutenant O. E. Kotzebue in San Francisco on the ship *Riurik* in October 1816, en route to the Hawaiian Islands (O. E. Kotzebue, *Puteshestviia vokrug sveta, 1815-1818*, Moscow, 1948, pp. 113, 117). Bancroft in his *History of California*, in the writing of which I. Petrov took part, noted that several of the Russians and Aleuts remaining in custody of the Spaniards were delivered by Lieutenant Ia. A. Podushkin, arriving in San Francisco and Monterey on the schooner *Chirikov* at the end of March 1817, and then returning to Novo-Arkhangel'sk in June 1817: "One of the liberated prisoners was Tarakanov, or Tarasov, as the Spaniards called him" (H. H. Bancroft, *History of California, 1801-1824*, Vol. XIX (Vol. 2), San Francisco, 1886, p. 313). However, this version appears doubtful. According to N. N. Bolkhovitinov, T. Tarakanov already arrived at Oahu Island (the Hawaiian Islands) from the California coast in May 1816 on the *Il'men'*, Captain W. Wadsworth, where he met Mr. Shaeffer and took an active part in the realization of his plans (N. N. Bolkhovitinov, *Russko-amerikanskie otnosheniia, 1815-1832*, Moscow, 1975, pp. 97-98).

Page 13: *"Two shipwrights began building it in September, and in June 1806 it was launched and named the* Avos'*."* — The two craftsmen were "Koriukin, who had come around the world on the *Neva*, and Popov, who had come via Okhotsk" (K. T. Khlebnikov, *Zhizneopisanie Aleksandra Andreevicha Baranova: glavnogo pravitelia Rossiiskikh kolonii v Amerike*, St. Petersburg, 1835, p. 98).

Page 13: *"Since [A. A. Baranov] lacked vessels, he bought some from the Americans, but he thought it would also be more advantageous to build some himself."* — F. P. Wrangell wrote: "The company has for a long time built ships in the colonies. The first and most active period took place in Okhotsk using larch wood of excellent quality. From 1799 to 1819, 14 vessels were built there, mostly brigs of 150 to 200 tons. On Kad'iak four vessels were built; in Resurrection Bay [between Chugach Bay and Port Chatham] one, and at Yakutat two, also from larch. Four brigs of 160 to 200 tons were built at Ross settlement from 1816 to 1824, but, being of a poor quality of wood, these rotted very quickly. Finally, in Sitkha the tender *Avos'* was launched in 1806 and in 1810 one brig of about 160, one ship of about 320 and one schooner of about 120 tons were built. By purchase from foreigners and construction at Okhotsk and Ross, the company was fully provided with vessels; in the same year [1810] work in Novo-Arkhangel'sk was stopped, and except for one small boat launched in 1819, the wharf there did not put out a single vessel until 1826. Work then started again and in 1834 four tenders of 55 tons were launched, three schooners of 65 to 100, and one ship of 230 tons. Meanwhile, at Okhotsk one schooner of 70, one brig of 190 and one ship of 320 tons were built in 1829, 1830 and 1832. Now all the other wharfs have been abandoned and sea vessels are built only in Novo-Arkhangel'sk. The dockyard is in excellent order, supplied with good craftsmen, and shipbuilding is carried out under a roof by the Creole Netsvetov, born on the island of St. Paul, educated in his craft in St. Petersburg. In Novo-Arkhangel'sk the ribs are made of a type of cypress called here 'fragrant wood,' which being dense, dry, and of astonishing lightness, is superb for shipbuilding, particularly for rowboats, built here both for colonial needs and for sale to foreigners. For sheathing vessels, they use larch and on deck, spruce; however, this wood does not last long because of the wet ground and climate.

"Thus, from 1799 to 1834, in the course of 35 years, the company management has by its own means built 41 vessels, including three three-masters. Besides the vessels bought from Americans of the United States visiting Sitkha for trade, eight vessels (of 150 to 230 tons) were acquired; two vessels arriving from Russia were left in colonial service, so that in 35 years 51 vessels were regarded as belonging to the company. Currently, they have present and in good condition (besides three blockships used as magazines) 12 vessels displacing about 1,565 tons, including three tenders, three brigs, three three-masters — a number entirely sufficient for undertaking maritime colonial service" (F. P. Wrangell, "Kratkie statisticheskie zamechaniia o Rossiiskikh koloniiakh v Amerike," *Teleskop*, 1835, *ch. XXVIII, otd. Nauka*, pp. 119-121).

A list of vessels built in the colonies compiled by F. P. Wrangell indicates the following: (1) At Kad'iak: the small vessels *Ol'ga* and *Del'fin* at Wood Island, the *Zlatoust* at [Pavlovskaia] Harbor, and the *Karluk* at Afognak Island. (2) At Voskresenskaia gavan': the *Phoenix*, a three-masted vessel. (3)

At Yakutat: the small vessels *Ermak* and *Rostislav*. (4) At Sitkha: the old artel built a vessel which the Kolosh burned on the ways [in 1802]. At Novo-Arkhangel'sk port: the tender *Avos'*, the schooner *Sitkha*, the three-masted vessel *Otkrytie*, the schooner *Chirikov*, the tender *Iaroslav*, the bots *Unalashka*, *Sivuch*, *Bobr*, and *Urup* — launched 30 May 1829. (5) At Ross from 1816 to 1824: the galiot *Rumiantsev*, the brig *Buldakov*, and the brigs *Volga* and *Kiakhta* (TsGIA ESSR, *f.* 2057, *op.* 1, *d.* 338, 1829-1836, *l.* 12).

Page 21: *"But when O'Cain died in a shipwreck at the same island . . . "* — Joseph O'Cain, captain of the American vessel *Eclipse*, was shipwrecked on Sannakh Island in September 1808. After a year building a brig from the remains of his former vessel with the aid of local Aleuts, he tried to reach Unalashka in February 1809; however, off Umnak Island he again suffered shipwreck and perished (see "Popolnenie izvestiia o razbitii [sudna] O'Keina [v 1808] na Sannakhe," in *Russkaia Amerika v neopublikovannykh zapiskakh K. T. Khlebnikova*, Leningrad, Nauka, 1979, p. 143).

Page 21: *"Mr. Ebbets, an agent of the rich and powerful merchant Mr. Astor . . . "* — According to Astor's instructions, which Captain Ebbets showed V. M. Golovnin by error at Novo-Arkhangel'sk in early July 1810, Ebbets was instructed: "To penetrate in detail the course of company affairs in America; learn their strength there, means of defense and defensive condition of forts; get trustworthy information on how much trust the company enjoys in Russia and from the government; what ties Baranov has in Petersburg; whether he has any support in the court; how great his power in this region; what are his abilities in the position he occupies, etc., etc." (V. M. Golovnin, *Puteshestvie na shliupe Diana iz Kronshtadta v Kamchatku sovershennoe pod nachal'stvom flota leitenanta Golovnina v 1807-1811 gg*, Moscow, 1961, p. 326).

CHAPTER 3

Page 26: *"' . . . [T]he advanced age of the chief manager . . . and his 25-year stay there . . . '"* — A. A. Baranov concluded a contract with G. I. Shelikhov in 1790 and on 19 August 1790 set out from Okhotsk on the vessel *Tri Sviatitelia* under command of D. I. Bocharov. Wintering in Koshigin Bay on Unalashka Island after shipwreck, he reached Kad'iak only on

27 June 1791. From the moment he took over the duty of manager (1791) until compilation of the cited document (1816), 25 years passed. Baranov's entire presence in Russian America may be stated as 28 years (19 August 1790 to 27 November 1818).

Page 26: *"'After deliberating on the matter, the Russian-American Company asked Mr. Hagemeister to write to Mr. Baranov, so that the latter would relinquish his power, capital and business affairs.'"* — We give here the text of the letter of the Main Administration of the Russian-American Company to A. A. Baranov of 6 April 1817 sent after Hagemeister's departure from Kronshtadt 8 September 1816 on the ship *Kutuzov* by L. A. Hagemeister:

> Dear Sir, Aleksandr Andreevich!
>
> Do not think that we have not esteemed your advanced years and attacks of illness, nor especially, your many years there in such a remote region and all the labors you have undertaken. All the more if, contrary to our wish, you should not be there, and for want of someone able to govern it, even for only a short time, would it not then be in jeopardy?
>
> Also, do not think that we, not deaf to all that was said above, were so remiss that we did not seek a successor for you. Two were sent, but did not reach you. Frankly, we cannot find a trustworthy person, although we try every day. That is why we have been so long sending you a successor.
>
> We hope, however, if only conditions will permit, to have one soon. We cannot agree to appoint the person you recommended [German Nikolaevich] Molvo as your successor because of his youth and lack of experience in dealing with savage peoples of the region where you are living. You make the observation that there is danger from old age and infirmity not to make a false step. This trait is your wisdom. But what person does not make mistakes? If you will be guided by our wishes and councils, adapting them to your local conditions, that, it seems, will not be a great mistake.
>
> And so, wishing you all the best from God, and spiritual and bodily strength, we remain, as before, with un-hypocritical sincerity and esteem. [The registration number and date of receiving the letter are written in:] No. 220, 6 April 1817.

> PS. You would do well if jointly with Leontii Andreianovich [Hagemeister] you would recommend your best people for rewards of ranks and medals, such as: your son [Antipatr Aleksandrovich], but not calling him son, clerk Creole Terent'ev and others, who are there with you, describing their deeds and conduct. We will try to do as you wish [AVPR, *f.* RAK, *op.* 888, *d.* 963, Roll 1, *l.* 83-84, scribe copy, no signature (*RAC, CR:* Main Office to Chief Manager Baranov, 6 April 1817, Vol. 1, No. 220, f. 12)].

Page 27: The Atkha district included the Komandorskie Islands (Bering and Mednyi islands), beginning with Attu Island (the most westerly island of the Aleutian chain) and to the east all the islands as far as Iunaska Island (that is, the Blizhnie, Krys'i and Andreianovskie islands). The Atkha district was under the Okhotsk office. The date the Atkha district was placed under the Novo-Arkhangel'sk office varies: According to Khlebnikov, this transfer took place in 1825 (see p. 150); according to F. P. Wrangell, only in 1826 (F. P. Wrangell, "Kratkie statisticheskie zamechaniia," pp. 105-106). The office of the district manager was on Atkha Island.

CHAPTER 4

Page 35: *"The truth is incontestable. It is a fact that under the terms of previous companies and regulations the promyshlenniks were able to exist only on shares, on the basis of which they received animal skins in kind, selling them at free prices, thus obtaining some profit. When a set price was substituted, the profits disappeared completely."* — From April 1803 A. A. Baranov, and then in 1806 N. P. Rezanov, experimented with a complex economic reform aimed at basic changes in compensation for labor: the promyshlenniks were to forego "partaking" in the company income and a salary substituted with additional assignment of a certain quantity of provisions [rations]. A consequence of this worsening material position of the promyshlenniks was the plot of a group of promyshlenniks and employees in July 1809, led by Vasilii Naplavkov. Baranov discovered the plot and put it down. The reform proposed by L. A. Hagemeister in 1818 had not only adherents but also opponents in St. Petersburg: for example, the chief bookkeeper of the Russian-American Company, Platon Bokovikov, wrote in wrath: "What did Hagemeister ever do in America for the company? He dismissed Baranov and nothing more . . . His dispositions regarding the internal administration in America are so petty and insignificant they are not worth talking about. For example, he liquidated the shares and put the promyshlenniks on salary. This change is detrimental both for the company and for the promyshlenniks. It was bad for the company, because the promyshlenniks, counting on a certain set salary, have stopped caring about improvement of the industry and for that reason the take in recent years has noticeably decreased; the accounts and business correspondence prove this" (AVPR, *f.* RAK, *op.* 888, *d.* 232, *l.* 3 [*RAC, CR:* Main Office to Chief Manager Baranov, 6 April 1817, Vol. 1, No. 220, f. 12]; cited in A. I. Alekseev, *Sud'ba Russkoi Ameriki*, Magadan, 1975, p. 177). Having firmed up the monopoly on the entire fur take and similarly getting rid of competitors from their own employees who used to sell their "half-shares" at much lower prices, the company strengthened its position in the fur market.

Page 36: *"From this time [20 February 1818] paper tokens came into general use and the practice of using notes for goods issued from the store on credit was stopped; instead, even salaried employees received tokens from the cashiers office every month and used them to buy the items needed."* — Until April 1803, as long as labor compensation in the Russian colonies in America was made in half-shares (that is, in furs), the Main Office of the Russian-American Company had no need to worry about delivery of "hard currency" [coins] to the colonies from Russia or to invent its own monetary system. With the abolition of "half-shares" and introduction of wages (in April 1803) at a time when the company did not have its own monetary symbols, the currency consisted of "notes" issued by the chief manager and locally by the local office manager against which the company stores issued goods. Large-scale mercantile deals between colonists most often were formulated by notes (which later on were honored in the company offices in Okhotsk or St. Petersburg), or at a later time, by means of credit notes, which were honored by the company commissioners on return of the holder to Russia from the wages due the creditor upon return of the creditor to Russia. However, there can be no doubt that the Russian "hard currency," along with paper money [*assignatsii*] was brought by the colonists to Russian America. This is supported by G. I. Davydov's notes about his voyages in 1802-1803 in the Kuril Islands: A small baidarka came to the vessel with five Kuril islanders. "They all spoke Russian, and the one who came aboard gave us a fox fur and asked us to sell him powder and that we told him that we could not sell him anything, but we would give him some powder, even without the fox fur. Then we gave him three pounds of powder, two pounds of tobacco, several biscuits, and each of them a glass of vodka. Then the Kuril islander asked if we would give him all these things for ten rubles, and he showed us a note for that amount. We asked him how he had come by our currency, and told us that each year Russians would come to his island from Kamchatka to collect iasak and to barter for animal pelts . . . The islanders who came out to us lived on Paramushir" (*Materialy dlia istorii russkikh zaselenii po beregam Vostochnogo okeana*, St. Petersburg, 1861, *vyp.* 4, p. 62). While at Fort Ross in June 1824, K. T. Khlebnikov gave the assistant manager of the office, P. I. Shelikhov, the following written notification: "As ordered by Mr. Chief Manager [M. I. Murav'ev], I request that you turn over to me all sums subscribed for construction of a chapel [at Fort Ross], with an extract from the book as to how much has been subscribed and by whom. This sum went directly to Mr. Chief Manager and the Ross office will eventually receive information about where by his order it is to go. In response to this memorandum the Ross office has presented me with a list of contributors of the following sum:

	r.	k.
42 Dutch 10-ruble coins	420	
122.6½ Spanish piasters	614	06
Russian silver	2	80
copper coins	11	14
Russian-American Company tokens	1,573	
Total	2,621	

(AGO, R-99, *op.* 1, *d.* 28; K. T. Khlebnikov, "Zapiski putevye, v Kalifornii i kreposti Ross na brigakh Baikale i Kiakhte vedennye v prodolzhenie 1824 g.," *l.* 26).

Recent archaeological finds at Fort Ross confirm that Russian "hard currency" circulated in the Russian colonies in America along with the Russian-American Company tokens. In 1979 the author of these lines acquired in the souvenir shop of the Fort Ross museum a reproduction of such a find — a copper five-kopek "Siberian coin" with the monogram of Catherine II (on the obverse side) and a Siberian crest (on the reverse). The copy (probably cast) is in appearance very old, as if it went through many hands, with dents and scratches. However, in order to inform the owner of the coin that his possession is a new creation, the inscription "Fort Ross" appears in relief under the Siberian crest on the reverse side of the coin. The text on the accompanying label makes it evident that not long ago in those same places still another was discovered, this time a silver 10-kopek "Siberian coin." From 1763 to 1781 the Kolyvan mint (at Nizhne Suzunsk) minted a special series of "Siberian coins" worth from a quarter kopek [*polushka*] to 10 kopeks, made from ore, which contained only a small amount of silver (and sometimes gold), but this amount was so insignificant that it was decided to mint "Siberian coins" of all denominations from silvery copper. From 1781 to 1847 they minted just ordinary copper coins (I. G. Spasskii, *Russkaia monetnaia sistema: Istoriko-numizmaticheskii ocherk*, Leningrad, 1962, pp. 177-179).

Page 36, Note No. 11: *"Subsequently, in 1826 the administration of the Atkha department was combined with the newly established Kuril Islands department."* — In 1795 G. I. Shelikhov founded "the Atkha company," which was to carry on fur hunting on the Kuril, Komandorskie, Aleutian, Andreainov and Pribylov islands. The vessel *Dobroe Predpriiatie Sv. Aleksandry* brought to Atkha an artel of 41 promyshlenniks. In the same year the interpreter Zvezdochetov was sent to the 18th Kuril Island with a group of 35 Russian promyshlenniks and 3 women (including "*posel'shchiki*" [settlers] with families). The settlement on Urup Island existed until 1805, when the promyshlenniks rose against the oppression of the peredovshchik Zvezdochetov and "burying arms and ammunition in the settlement" left the island, heading for Kamchatka.

Various dates are given for the subsequent reestablishment of the Kuril district: according to F. P. Wrangell, the Kuril district was again established in 1828 (F. P. Wrangell, *"Kratkie statisticheskie zamechaniia . . . "*, p. 105); by other sources, in 1830 (AVPR, *f.* RAK, *op.* 888, *d.* 343). The manager of the Kuril district was located on Urup Island.

In a letter of 18 April 1828 the chief bookkeeper of the Main Office of the Russian-American Company, P. V. Bokovikov, wrote from St. Petersburg to K. T. Khlebnikov in Novo-Arkhangel'sk: "Mr. Etolin has noted that there are many sea otters in the Kuril Islands and that promises good successes for the detachment sent there. God grant that this will occur, but even there, if we hunt constantly, we will also soon hunt them out or drive them out, so therefore it would be best to hunt intermittently: now in the Kuril Islands, then on the American coast, one after the other, hunting in one place a year or two and then giving it a rest. It is therefore necessary for us to hold on to the American coast and settlement [Novo-Arkhangel'sk]" (GAPO, *f.* 445, *op.* 1, *d.* 151, *l.* 70 *ob.*).

CHAPTER 5

Page 47: *"We became acquainted with the Kolosh in 1783 . . . "* — It would have been more accurate to say in 1741, for the first immediate direct acquaintance with the Kolosh took place during the great geographic discovery, by Russians, of North America from the Pacific Ocean: on the night of 15 July 1741, one of the two ships of the Second Kamchatka Expedition, the *Sv. Pavel* under A. I. Chirikov, reached approximately 55°10′ north latitude and 133°55′ west longitude when suddenly a "high land" appeared. This was America. The *Sv. Pavel* went to Baker Island, lying in the broad Alexander Archipelago (the name was given later). Seeking a landing place in order to replenish nearly exhausted supplies of water and fuel, Chirikov sailed north-northwest. On 18 and 24 July he sent 15 Russians (seamen, a soldier, a master, and interpreters), headed by a fleet master (senior shturman) Avraam Dement'ev, ashore in one of the bays of Iakobii Island. Their further fate remained unknown, and the Russians sought them and their descendants until the middle of the nineteenth century. The Kolosh, coming out of the bay in two boats, where the Russians had been sent, dared approach so close to the ship that their faces could be distinguished. The word "*agai-agai*" was their sole communication when "invited" on board the *Sv. Pavel* (for more details see: Ia. M. Svet and S. G. Fedorova, "*Istoriia piatnadtsati*," in the book *Brigantine: Sb. rasskazov o puteshestviiakh, poiskakh, otkrytiiakh*, Moscow: Molodaia gvardiia, 1971, pp. 48-64).

However, Khlebnikov did not note 1783 by chance: in that year shturman Potap Zaikov on the fur-hunting vessel *Sv. Aleksandr Nevskii* undertook to explore the coast of Chugatsk Bay. Informed by one of the Chugach, Zaikov wrote: "The Shugachi fight, make war, or trade with five types of Americans: (1) the Kaniags, the inhabitants of the island of

Kad'iak; (2) the Kenai, who dwell between Kad'iak and Shugach Bay, in the bay the and on the mainland; (3) the Iulits, living by the great river described above; (4) the Lakhamiuts, living along the American mainland from Kaiak Island to the east along the coast of America; (5) the Koliushi, living farther east, who at various times of the year travel in groups in large baidaras" (Extract from "The journal of Potap Zaikov kept on the vessel *Sv. Aleksandr Nevskii* in 1783," in Tikhmenev, *op. cit.*, *ch.* 2, Appendix 2, p. 7). This seems to be the first mention in Russian sources of the ethnic term "Koliushi" later transcribed as "Koliuzhi" or "Koloshi."

Pages 47-48: *"After the occupation [by the Russians] of Yakutat in 1794 and Sitkha in 1799, Mr. Baranov of course gathered important data, but they have been lost."* — V. P. Romanov, who first published in 1825 extracts from Khlebnikov's *Zapiski*, concerning the ethnography of the Koliush, evidently possessed a manuscript work in which the ideas of the author were set forth more accurately: "Mr. Baranov, of course, collected necessary information, but [the manuscript] has now disappeared" (V. P. Romanov, "O Koliuzhakh i Koloshakh voobshche," *Severnyi Arkhiv*, 1825, No. XVII, Statistika, p. 5). "In the papers of the late Baranov many curious things about these [Kolosh] peoples and also about the entire region are found. They must be saved from oblivion" wrote F. P. Litke, who also highly valued the "industrious Khlebnikov," collecting and making public ethnographic information about the Kolosh (F. P. Litke, *op. cit.*, p. 71).

The Canadian historian Stuart Ramsay Tompkins, trying to explain the scarcity of Russian manuscript historical sources on the history of Alaska from 1801-1817, supposed that the archival materials were carried on the ship *Kutuzov*, on which A. A. Baranov left Novo-Arkhangel'sk in 1818, heading for St. Petersburg. " . . . Since he died and was buried at sea, there was no one to look after the documents when the ship arrived at St. Petersburg and they too disappeared" (S. R. Tompkins, "Another View of Russian America: A Comment," in *Frontier Alaska: A Study in Historical Interpretation and Opportunity*, Proceedings of the Conference on Alaskan History, AMU Press: Anchorage, 1968, p. 82). "I tell you, in confidence, that the company business is in great disorder," wrote S. I. Ianovskii from St. Petersburg (not later than October 1823) to Khlebnikov in Novo-Arkhangel'sk. "The company has finally released to me, after much difficulty, Aleksandr Andreevich's [Baranov's] estate. I have already received the money and shares, and I am in the process of accepting other things. Many items [Baranov's effects, delivered in Kronstadt 16 September 1821 after his death on the ship *Borodino*] were spoiled. Others do not agree with the inventory" (GAPO, *f.* 445, *op.* 1, *d.* 393, *l.* 21 *ob.*). According to N. N. Bolkovitinov, Baranov himself took documents from Novo-Arkhangel'sk covering the period of his tenure as manager of the colonies, hoping to use them to justify his actions before the directors of the company. These documents shared the fate of the rest of the Russian-American Company archives (N. N. Bolkovitinov, *Rossiia i S.Sh.A.: Arkhivnye dokumenty i istoricheskie issledovaniia. Analiticheskie obzor*, Moscow, 1984, p. 20).

Page 48: *"My data consist of the following."* — V. P. Romanov preceded this phrase with this information: "I now convey the latest information about the Kolosh, received by K. T. Khlebnikov from an old toen or taion Saigina-kha, elder brother of the Sitkha taion Kotlean, and of other taions."

Further in the article Romanov describes Kotlean: "He is of medium height, has a very pleasant face, and a small beard and mustaches. He is said to be a very good shot: he always has twenty good firearms. Kotlean is brave and very intelligent. Although the toions here govern with their subordinates, their power is very limited" (V. P. Romanov, "*O Koliuzhakh . . .* ," pp. 11-12).

Page 51: *"They think that the herring asked the evil spirits to give them Kabachkov, because he did not give them any peace in the past."* — Kabachkov, a company official, spent much of his time catching herring and finally drowned while doing this (*ibid.*, p. 18). One can assume that Khlebnikov was the author of this reference.

Page 53: *". . . [the women] are also burdened with such chores as preparing wood, bark, etc."* — "Bark was used to cover most baraboras, or huts, and for baskets" (*ibid.*, p. 23).

Page 53: *"The preparation of food among the Sitkha Kolosh begins in February with the coming of herring."* — "The herrings appear only in one inlet near Old Harbor, called therefore Herring Strait. In Sitkha great schools of them appear in March at the fort itself and stay about two weeks. Also near Sitkha are many cod, and they catch halibut in different places even throughout the winter" (*ibid.*, p. 24).

Page 61: *"After discovering Port Nootka, Cook . . . "* — Port Nootka on Vancouver Island was not discovered by Cook, but by the Spanish seafarer Juan Perez in 1774, four years before Cook's appearance in North Pacific waters.

Page 62: *"Formerly, the Kolosh used to shoot sea otters with bows and arrows, but now they own and use firearms to hunt them."* — It became clear that the sound of gunfire only frightened the sea otters soon enough. K. S. Zelenoi, who made the voyage on the corvette *Abrek* from Kronshtadt to the shores of Russian America (1861-1864), wrote as follows about the hunt for sea otters: "In order not to frighten them, they do not hunt the sea otters with firearms: if they kill a sea otter hauled out on the shore, on that rock where only a drop of its blood falls, there will never be sea otters again, and therefore the use of firearms is forbidden" (K. S. Zelenoi, "Iz zapisok o krugosvetnom plavanii (1861-1864)," *Morskoi Sbornik*, 1865, Vol. 80, No. 9, *ch.* III, p. 56).

Page 64: *"The esteemed Dr. B . . . "* — This probably refers to Doctor of Medicine V. F. Bervi, who served in the Russian colonies in America from 1817 to 1824 and later was professor at Kazan University. Bervi's letters from Kazan to Khlebnikov in Novo-Arkhangel'sk, dated 18 November 1835 and 3 September 1836, are kept in GAPO (*f.* 445, *op.* 1, *d.* 147, 6 *l.*).

Page 67: *"Minerals"* — Khlebnikov gathered a fine collection of minerals while in Russian America. Many company employees and ordinary Russian promyshlenniks helped him in this, as may be seen from letters he received in Novo-Arkhangel'sk from various corners of Russian America: "I beg you to accept, as a token of my heartfelt thanks, a box of some of the rarities here, namely various corals, as many as I could find," wrote Ivan Kriukov from the settlement of Good Accord [Dobrogo Soglasiia] on Unalashka 6 August 1820 (GAPO, *f.* 445, *op.* 1, *d.* 234, *l.* 3-4); "I got a small stone from interpreter Andrei Chistiakov. I gave it to Afanasii Klimovskii to test it on a whetstone, but when his brother [Nikolai] arrived, he gave it to him without my permission. Should Nikolai deliver it to you, please accept it. If you do not get it, I will create difficulties for him. In appearance, it looks like a small egg, the color is like clear water, yellow, and a little rubbed on one side," wrote manager of the Kad'iak office Stepan Nikiforov in April 1828 (GAPO, *f.* 445, *op.* 1, *d.* 227, *l.* 27 *ob.*).

Upon return to St. Petersburg, Khlebnikov began to analyze the mineral collection. "With this aim he [L. A. Perovskii] introduced me to the scholar, mineralogist Mr. Kameror, who volunteered to make a catalogue of all the minerals which I brought from our colonies, and to this catalogue I attach my 'Notes on the Colonies'" wrote Khlebnikov in Novo-Arkhangel'sk to F. P. Wrangell 20 December 1833 (TsGIA ESSR, *f.* 2057, *op.* 1, *d.* 489, *l.* 26 *ob.*). This catalogue has so far not been located.

Khlebnikov bequeathed the entire collection to F. P. Wrangell. As stated in a letter of the Main Office to F. P. Wrangell of 29 November 1838, while still alive Khlebnikov compiled a "will, written in his own hand and signed, in which he asked the Main Office of the company to transfer to Your Excellency from his estate the sum of five thousand rubles, also the ores, fossils and other things in raw and polished state and the entire collection of minerals. Thus fulfilling the will of the late Kirill Timofeevich [Khlebnikov], the Main Office of the company is transferring to Your Excellency five thousand rubles of Russian paper money with a humble request that you confirm its receipt and provide a receipt for the ores and minerals preserved in a special cabinet in the company headquarters. Directors: Ivan Prokof'ev, Andrei Severin, N. Kusov" (TsGIA ESSR, *f.* 2057, *op.* 1, *d.* 376, *l.* 23, 23 *ob.*). So far we have not attempted to trace the fate of this unique collection of minerals of Russian America further.

CHAPTER 6

Page 73: *"The company will get him a passport valid for seven years."* — Receiving passports for its employees and promyshlenniks, the Russian-American Company was obliged to pay the state a duty, which they then expected to recover from the owner of the passport. Thus, the orders from the Main Office to Chief Manager M. I. Murav'ev, dated 20 May 1820 (for No. 310), state: "Sixty-two promyshlenniks, now in the colonies, have sent to the Main Office a request that the company obtain new seven-year passports for them. The Irkutsk office transmitted this petition to the local government administration and received the desired passports, but it also received an instruction to make a payment for each of the petitions for the period in which they did not have the passports because of the expiration of the former and because the cost of some was 174 rubles and more, and for some more than 300 rubles. For the passports given out now, the cost was 86 rubles each. The company management, having consulted the laws and regulations, finds that by the Imperial Manifesto of 2 February 1810 the fees for burghers and peasants for one year was 3 rubles; for two years, 8 rubles; for three years, 15 rubles; for four years, 24 rubles; for five-year passports, 35 rubles. Another manifesto, 17 February 1812, ordered that the fee for passports given out by all districts be doubled. According to this legislation, the fee for a five-year passport, doubled, would come to 70 rubles; for two years, 16 rubles, and we get the sum which the Irkutsk government has demanded, namely 86 rubles. Consequently, the company management has no choice but to comply, even though it deplores the burden which has fallen on the promyshlenniks. Directors: Mikhail Buldakov, Venedikt Kramer, Andrei Severin" (AVPR, *f.* RAK, *op.* 888, *d.* 962, Roll 1, *l.* 92 [*RAC, CR:* Main Office to Chief Manager Murav'ev, 20 May 1820, Vol. 2, No. 310, f. 92-93]).

Page 74: *"Those who travel through Siberia . . . "* — Even F. P. Wrangell, setting out with his family from St. Petersburg to Novo-Arkhangel'sk to assume the post of chief manager of the colonies, had to overcome the difficulty of this route. They left Irkutsk on 27 May 1830, reached Yakutsk 16 June and arrived in Okhotsk on 4 August. They left on the sloop *Urup* 25 August and entered Sitkha Bay 29 September. Thus, under the most favorable conditions created by the company, the route from Irkutsk to Okhotsk took two months, and the sea voyage from Okhotsk to Novo-Arkhangel'sk took a little over a month (F. P. Wrangell, "Putevye zapiski admirala barona Vrangelia," *Istoricheskii vestnik*, October 1884, Vol. XVIII, pp. 162-180).

Page 75: *"The Payment of Taxes"* — State taxes were an unbearable burden for both the promyshlenniks and the Russian-American Company. Explaining why the debts of the promyshlenniks to the company rose constantly and trying to exempt their subordinates from paying state taxes at the place of origin, the Main Office of the Russian-American Company addressed the Ministry of the Interior 31 January 1818:

> When the promyshlenniks are hired, they agree by contract to the condition that the company will send to their administration [that is, to the peasant or burgher community of origin] a sum which they themselves determine sufficient to satisfy the taxes. Others [make the sum] considerably larger and include for their relatives the same amount needed for their subsistence. Every promyshlennik setting out for America is already in debt to the company either for settlement of his own debts, or to executors for supplying him for the voyage, or for other reasons. Some incur a debt of well over a thousand rubles even before they arrive at their destination, and what their take [of furs] would be remains uncertain. Such a burden upon the promyshlennik of such sums and in such a distant location depresses him and robs him of the spirit of zeal and effort. This in turn harms the company, which would derive much greater benefit if the promyshlenniks were not in debt to it, and could acquire their benefits and return able to get their own profits and land at an earlier age. Directors: Mikhail Buldakov, Venedikt Kramer, Andrei Severin" (AVPR, *f.* RAK, *op.* 888, *d.* 962, Roll 1, *l.* 197 *ob.* [*RAC, CR:* Main Office to Ministry of Interior, Department of Manufacturing and Domestic Commerce, 31 January 1818, Vol. 1, No. 71, f. 196-198]).

For more details about the position of promyshlenniks in the Russian-American Company colonies, see: S. B. Okun', *Rossiisko-Amerikanskaia kompaniia*, Moscow and Leningrad, 1939; W. L. Sarafian, *Russian-American Company Employee Policies and Practices, 1799-1857*, Ph. D. dissertation, University of California, Los Angeles, 1970.

Page 96: *"Mr. Baranov had intended to occupy several of the Sandwich Islands. His commissioner, Dr. Shaeffer, had begun this venture quite successfully, but it eventually ended in failure."* — At the end of January 1815, the Russian-American Company ship *Bering*, with a cargo valued at 100,000 rubles, was wrecked on the coast of Kauai Island. The cargo fell into the hands of the ruler of Kauai, King Tomari [Kaumualii], a vassal of King Kamehameha I, overlord of all the islands. In early October 1815 A. A. Baranov sent Doctor of Medicine Georg Shaeffer from Novo-Arkhangel'sk to King Kamehameha to try to retrieve the cargo. Shaeffer was to travel on board the American vessel *Isabella* (Captain Tyler) "as a traveler for research in natural history, and even on a foreign vessel, so as not to give the slightest suspicion of a conflict or hostility." He was to develop trade ties with the islands and if possible build a Russian factory there. Gaining the confidence first of Kamehameha and then of Tomari, and utilizing the hostility between them, Shaeffer succeeded in founding Russian factories and establishing plantations on Oahu, Kauai and Lanai islands. However, from the very beginning Shaeffer encountered the active opposition of the "Bostonians," who were afraid of losing their privileges and influence on the islands. In April 1817 "Kaumualii seized Shaeffer, wrecking all his scheme for the Sandwich Islands, and handed him over to an American ship, on which he was taken to Canton" (K. T. Khlebnikov, *Zhizneopisanie Aleksandra Andreevicha Baranova*, St. Petersburg, 1835, pp. 157-167). The positions of Baranov, Shaeffer, the Main Office of the Russian-American Company and the Russian government strongly differed from each other about the question of the Hawaiian Islands. On the basis of many sources and literature investigations, N. N. Bolkhovitinov concluded that the tsarist administration from the very beginning had no sort of relation to the adventure of Doctor Shaeffer, and as a result categorically rejected the very idea of annexing the Hawaiian Islands to Russia (N. N. Bolkhovitinov, *Russko-amerikanskie otnosheniia, 1815-1832*, Moscow: Nauka, 1975, pp. 86-141).

Page 120: *"The Royal Vessels"* — Kamehameha I had a passion for sea-going vessels. Abandoning worthless ones, in three years (1816-1818) he acquired six large ships of good maritime qualities, thereby significantly increasing the power of his fleet. In exchange for sandalwood, he received nails, drying oil, kettles, copper for sheathing, flour, rice, sugar, tea and medicines. Cannon, guns, powder and other military armament occupied a prominent place in the list of bartered goods (D. D. Tumarkin, *Gavaiskii narod i amerikanskie kolonizatory, 1820-1865*, Moscow, Nauka, 1971, p. 30.

Page 120: *"Sandalwood"* — Large American businesses, becoming convinced that Chinese merchants in Guanchzhou were eager to buy Hawaiian mountain sandalwood and that trade in this wood could with profit replace fur, from 1816 entered the "sandalwood trade" and the demand for sandalwood rose sharply. In 1816-1817 King Kamehameha sent large numbers of men to the mountains to cut and fell sandalwood trees. Thousands of Hawaiians were ordered to transport the prepared sandalwood to the shore jetties. As a result, many fields remained untilled and in the winter of 1817-18 a bad famine began. This occurrence somewhat sobered Kamehameha I, so he ordered the cutting of sandalwood limited and not long before his death (1819) forbade felling the young sandalwood trees, apparently wishing to prevent the destruction of the resource. Nevertheless, the felling continued. Mass preparations of sandalwood in the 1820s and 1830s helped cause the dying out of the original population of the Hawaiian archipelago. A number of seafarers pointed out that if the Hawaiian sandalwood had not been exterminated by the 1830s, continued exploitation of this resource would have caused extinction of the native population (*ibid.*, pp. 29-30, 48-49).

Pages 121-122: *"On the way . . . [t]he two vessels stopped at Arromango, where many of those on board were killed and eaten by the islanders, while others died of disease."* — One must assume that Khlebnikov refers here to the religious-magical form of cannibalism. This custom was based on the conviction that the strength and other qualities of the slain person transferred to the person partaking of the body. Religious-magical cannibalism was found throughout Oceania, particularly on the Marquesas and Solomon Islands and in New Zealand.

Page 122: *"Governor Boki . . . undertook this expedition and set out with his wife and children on the vessel* Tomeamea *and perished. It is supposed that the [vessel] was lost from an explosion of powder, loaded carelessly."* — Boki (Kamehameha II whom Khlebnikov erroneously calls an Englishman) tried to preserve many features of the original Hawaiian culture and channel relations with the foreigners into a stream most favorable for the islanders. Boki sent vessels under the Hawaiian flag to Petropavlovsk-on-Kamchatka, Manila, and Guanchzhou, and tried to establish trade relations with Tahiti. However, the situation on the Hawaiian Islands had changed substantially since the beginning of the nineteenth century. Boki was a plaything in the hands of the foreigners, who cleverly profited from his trade enterprises. He incurred a considerable debt, which he tried to recoup with sandalwood. In the fall of 1829 Boki learned from a sailor arriving from Sydney that there was sandalwood on the island Arromango (Vanuatu). He at once ordered two of the royal brigs (the *Kamehameha* and the

Keokoi) equipped, put 400 Hawaiians aboard them and set out for the distant island. The vessels were separated near the island of Ratuma and never met again; the brig *Kamehameha*, on which Boki sailed, disappeared without a trace. Only the second vessel finally reached the island of Arromango, but not getting any sandalwood because of quarrels with the local inhabitants, after five weeks the *Keokoi* returned to Hawaii, where the surviving crew members recounted Boki's disappearance. Some said that Boki had settled on the Samoan Islands, but this has been rejected by contemporary scholars (D. D. Tumarkin, *op. cit.*, pp. 43, 378).

Pg. 142: "*One man is assigned to make flags because six to ten flags are used for vessels and by the colonies and ships per year.*" — The Russian national commercial flag, which all merchant companies used, had a rectangular width with three horizontal stripes of equal width: red (the lower), blue and white. During its first years, the Russian-American Company also used this flag. On 28 September (10 October) 1806, Aleksandr I signed an ukaz introducing a special company flag. The project of introducing the flag was undertaken by Minister of Commerce N. P. Rumiantsev, who devoted much attention to company affairs. After Imperial confirmation the ukaz was heard in the Senate and on 19 October 1806 was sent for execution to the Main Office of the Russian-American Company, and also to the Admiralty and Commerce colleges. Distributed simultaneously with this institution were "copies made at the heraldry office" of a confirmed drawing of the flag and the following description: "The flag of the American company has three stripes: the lower — red, the middle — blue, and the upper broad one — white with the Russian state coat-of-arms on it, while underneath is drawn a ribbon hanging from the eagle's talons, with the inscription: 'Russian-American Company.'" The only original example of the flag is preserved in the State Hermitage in Leningrad (History of Russian Culture Section, No. 3n-Er-6024). It is made of thin silk cloth, with the state emblem and the inscriptions painted with oils. The general dimensions of the flag are 94 by 168 cm, the width of the lower red stripe — 18.5 cm, the blue — 19.5, the white — 56 cm (for a fuller account, see S. G. Fedorova, "*Flag Rossiisko-Amerikansoi kompanii,*" in the book *Ot Aliaski do Ognennoi zemli*, Moscow, 1967, 121-129; English translation: S. G. Fedorova, "The Flag of the Russian-American Company," translated by Paul Woolf and edited by Wayne Colwell, in *Pacific Historian*, Winter 1970, Vol. 14, No. 1, pp. 25-32).

Page 142. *"Bricklayers are kept busy building and repairing house stoves. Bricks are brought from Kad'iak and sometimes from Ross. There is little clay here, and that is of poor quality, brought with difficulty from various places around the settlement."* — When in August 1825 the general meeting of Russian-American Company shareholders approved the proposal to move the capital of the Russian possessions in America from Novo-Arkhangel'sk back to Kad'iak, the lack of clay at Sitkha and the impossibility of manufacturing the needed quantity of bricks played no small role in the decision. A "Memorandum of the Main Office about the need to move the capital to Kad'iak" noted:

> Clay is lacking on the island [of Sitkha]. Bricks for stoves must be brought from Kad'iak, therefore it is useless even to think about stone fortifications, which would once and for all secure a man's labor. Therefore, all construction has to be of wood. The constant rains permeate the trees at Sitkha with moisture and produce rot. Hardly a structure can be finished before it already requires significant repairs. Many laborers are used exclusively in repairing buildings. This labor is made even more difficult in that there is no construction timber near the fort. Men must be sent to distant bays for it. There, it takes ten men an entire day to fell and transport six suitable logs. The cost of tools and [the use] of a considerable number of skilled laborers, such as blacksmiths, locksmiths and charcoal burners, in repair work increases the cost of such unsuitable [wood] construction. This makes it necessary to retain at least 25 men in the [Novo-Arkhangel'sk] fort for these tasks. The abundance [on Kad'iak] of clay suitable for brick-making makes it possible eventually to build brick fortifications and main buildings. Besides, the better quality of the timber makes the wooden buildings there much more enduring. Near Kad'iak, on the mainland, are places rich in timber very suitable for shipbuilding (AVPR, *f.* RAK, *op.* 888, *d.* 966, Roll 4, *l.* 510-511 [*RAC, CR:* enclosure of Main Office to Chief Manager Murav'ev, 13 August 1825, Vol. 4, No. 640, f. 506-512]).

The Canadian historian James Gibson notes that whereas in 1800, 3,000 to 6,000 bricks were fired annually on Kad'iak, by 1831 this amount had increased to 10,000. The Russians also fired brick in many other places: at Fort Ross, at Novo-Aleksandrovsk fort (Nushagak), at St. Dionysius redoubt (Stikine), and Nikolaevskii redoubt (Kenai), where the best bricks in the colonies were made. From all these places bricks were transported on vessels to Novo-Arkhangel'sk, where by the beginning of the 1850s 12 to 15 thousand bricks were needed annually (J. R. Gibson, *Imperial Russia in Frontier America: The Changing Geography of Supply of Russian America, 1784-1867*, New York: Oxford University Press, 1976, p. 41.)

Bricks were also brought from Europe as ballast on round-the-world vessels. In August 1967, on Lincoln Street in Sitkha near an unused storehouse for plant equipment, a brick wall two feet high was found under a layer of ash on the site of an old Russian structure; the bricks bore the inscription "Stenswik" (letter from R. A. Miller, 6 September 1967). In the last decade interest has developed in archaeological investigation of old Russian settlements. In 1978-1982, the Department of Natural Resources (Anchorage) investigated sites at Yakutat Bay (the eighteenth-century Russian settlement of Slavorossiia) and at Middle Bay of Chiniak Bay on Kad'iak Island. On Kad'iak a small structure with arches was found made of two kinds of bricks: one, almost square, for the walls, and another, oblong, for the arches. This structure was under a thick layer of ash deposited after the eruption of Katmai volcano in June 1912. The building material merits more detailed study and more precise dating (T. L. Dilliplane, "The 1978 Archaeological Survey for New Russia," paper presented at the Conference on the Problems of Russian America sponsored by the Kennan Institute for Advanced Russian Studies at Sitka, Alaska, August 1979, 13 pp.; and T. L. Dilliplane, "Brickmaking in Russian America: Research Results through March 18, 1981," Department of Natural Resources, Anchorage, Alaska, 1981, 23 pp.).

Page 143: *"One important visitor to the colonies wisely noted that he saw only labor there, that they made axes for cutting timber, which were used for making charcoal, which in turn was used to make axes."* — Axes for felling timber and for carpentry which were manufactured in the Russian colonies in America ("of good quality, well tempered, with strong butts and thick sides"), as stated in No. 34, Supplements to Khlebnikov's "Notes," pp. 208-209, later on attracted the close attention of specialists in Russia.

In TsGIA SSSR (*f.* 410, *op.* 2, *d.* 514) there is a file "About axes invented in America for felling timber." This file contains correspondence for the period 13 September 1851 to 12 April 1856. A letter from the War Ministry in 1851 "sent with 25 axes," explains that:

> the vice-president of the Imperial Free Economic Society has ordered from America an ax of a special type, which was introduced there for felling the thickest possible timber. The main advantage of this ax lies in its being almost entirely cased in steel along the plane of the butt and the length of the head. It is convenient for making a wide swing and for felling trees at a considerable distance from the worker. Desiring the introduction and spread in Russia of useful economic tools, the Actual Privy Councilor Prince Dolgorukov has proposed to the War Ministry that a number of axes of the American type be distributed to peasants of the Tver landholder Major General Baron Reikhel'. [These peasant] earned an award for the axes they submitted to the local exhibition of farm tools. His Imperial Majesty, having listened to the presentation, has directed that 100 axes of the type presented by Prince Dolgorukov be ordered. He also directed that special attention be paid to the quality and durability of the wood used for ax handles. When these axes were ready, some were to be sent to the Caucasus for testing and the others distributed to the departments of the Navy and Engineering and the Military Settlements Office.
>
> By order of the Emperor, I have the honor to transmit to Your Excellency for testing one such ax fixed to a handle as a model and 24 without a handle (for convenience of shipping) with the appropriate number of ax handles of birch wood. I humbly beg that you inform me about the results of the testing of those axes. As for the wood used for the rough handles, Mr. Reikhel' replies that on his estate there is nothing better and that, when the peasants manufactured axes, they sent them for sale without handles. We ask that the money due for those axes, 1 ruble 50 kopeks silver apiece, be paid from the general funds of the War Ministry, including delivery in St. Petersburg.

On 16 July 1852, the Naval Ministry and the Department of Ship Timbers reported on the results of the tests:

> In accordance with instructions the axes delivered to us were sent to the regional administration and to the foreman of the work crew, which works [details of axes] out of Kurland oak to Captain Dmitriev for testing them on the spot and for reports about the quality and advantages of those axes by the people responsible for preparing timber.

The regional administration and Captain Dmitriev now report that in their present form the American axes are unsuitable for felling trees at the roots, because the handle cannot bear the weight of the ax itself and breaks with the first blows. Besides, the ax head also crumbles, and therefore when used in preparation of timber those axes require frequent and considerable repairs. This caused work stoppage. In working the felled timber, clearing the top and side branches, and in trimming the trunk, those axes do not offer the same convenience as do the Russian ones. The latter permits, during the trimming, the use of one's own judgement whether to take thick or thin cuts. The American axes are deflected from the timber during blows aimed a small angles toward the flat place of the tree trunk. When wedges have to be driven in, the butt end of the Russian ax can be used as a hammer. The head of the American ax more often splits the end of the wedge itself. The American ax cannot be used at all in the trimming of side branches and the crown when the crown is being turned or moved. It is also unsuitable for determining the quality of the timber to be felled by a blow of the butt end of the ax, the American ax having a narrow and very heavy butt. In a word, the Russian ax is suitable for use under all conditions encountered in preparation of timber; the American ax can be used only if the form of the blade and butt are modified. The American ax is convenient only for felling trees and for cutting roots and working tree stumps. The administration of the *nizhovyi* [lower] regions explains why the *lashman* [a type of state peasant engaged in woodcutting], who for over 150 years have been preparing ship timbers, used two types of axes for this work: one, with a wide head and wide butt, on a long handle, with a narrow blade, used specifically for felling trees; and the other just the ordinary Russian ax, used for trimming tree trunks.

Conclusion. In view of the information presented above, it is clear that axes manufactured in the manner of the America ones are unsuitable for preparation of ship timbers, and in accordance with tests conducted with felling timber in the guberniias of Olonets, Arkhangel'sk, Vologda, Kostroma, Viatka, Kazan, Simbirsk, Nizhegorod and Kurland, they cannot replace the Russian ax, which is suitable for all phases of the enterprise. Therefore, the Department of Ship Timbers proposes to return the furnished axes to be returned to the War Ministry with explanation of the unsuitability of their use in timbering operations conducted by the naval institution . . . "

(Signatures:) Director Matiushkin and
Department Supervisor Baron Wrangell

On the original is written: "Conclusion, 20 July 1852. Prince Menshikov."

Finally, in a letter from the War Ministry (St. Petersburg, 6 April 1856) to the office of the Naval Ministry, there is a request to submit [to it] one ax of the American type with handle . . . to be preserved in the archive of the Engineering Department."

Page 147: *"1830. Laid foundation of church seven sazhens long, [. . .] width . . . Altar."* — The church in Novo-Arkhangel'sk was built in 1806, then reconstructed in 1816 as a cathedral named for St. Michael the Archangel and was again reconstructed in 1831 (drawing on p. 158) while F. P. Wrangell was in charge of the colonies (I. E. Veniaminov, *Sostoianie pravoslavnoi tserkvi v Rossiiskoi Amerike* [The condition of the Orthodox church in Russian America], St. Petersburg, 1840, pt. II).

Page 148: *"On 1 May. Surrounded (with pickets) . . . On the hill a watchtower was built, in which nine cannon were placed, and facing the Kolosh, a battery was built consisting of 21 cannons and falconets."* — Within range of one of the shore batteries on the sea side to the west lies the Kolosh settlement, sometimes comprising more than 1,000 natives" (F. P. Wrangell, "Kratkie statisticheskie zamechaniia o Rossiiskikh koloniiakh v Amerike," *Teleskop*, 1835, ch. XXVIII, *otd., Nauka*, p. 110). For a detailed description of the artillery used in the Russian fleet for fortification of the fort at Novo-Arkhangel'sk, see F. P. Wrangell, *Ocherk puti iz Sitkhi v S.-Peterburg* (St. Petersburg, 1836).

Page 149, Note 46: *"The Kolosh who used to live near the lake left a myth that a crab of terrible size lives deep in lake."* — This tradition, involving the lake near the site of the Ozerskii redoubt, calls to mind the legendary denizen of Loch Ness in Scotland.

Page 150: *"One must note that during this year [1825] a capital sum of 172,869 rubles was transferred from the Okhotsk Office to Novo-Arkhangel'sk; this sum was considered to belong to the detachment in Atkha, but since this area came under colonial rule, the capital available increased."* — There is a small discrepancy in the dates here: according to F. P. Wrangell, "the Atkha district, which came under the colonial administration in 1826, includes the Komandorskie Islands, namely Bering and Mednyi, and, beginning with Attu (the western-most island of the Aleutian chain), all the islands to the east from Iunaska, including the Near, Rat and Andreianov groups. This district is managed from an office on Atkha Island" (F. P. Wrangell, "Kratkie statisticheskie zamechaniia, *op. cit.*, pp. 105-106).

Page 152: *"A Note on Paper Money"* — The monetary tokens [*marki*] of the Russian-American Company, circulating only in the Russian possessions in America, have long attracted the attention of historians (see, for example, P. A. Tikhmenev, *Istoricheskoe obozrenie . . . , ch.* 1; S. B. Okun', *Rossiisko-Amerikanskaia kompaniia*, Moscow-Leningrad, 1939; and articles on the monetary system of the Russian-American Company: A. Doll and R. A. Pierce, "Alaskan Treasure: The Russian Skin Money," *Alaska*, November 1969, p. 22; I. S. Shikanova, "Kozhanye den'gi Rossiisko-Amerikanskoi kompanii" [Leather money of the Russian-American Company], *Priroda*, 1979, No. 8:127-128; I. S. Shikanova, "Denezhnye znaki Rossiisko-Amerikanskoi kompanii pervoi poloviny XIX v" [Monetary tokens of the Russian-American Company in the first half of the nineteenth century], in *Pamiatniki russkogo denezhnogo obrasheniia XVIII-XIX vv. Numizmaticheskii sb.*, ch. 7, *Trudy Gos. Istoricheskogo muzeiia*, 1980, pp. 159-168, 189-194; I. Shikanova, "Russian America issues own private notes," *Coin World International*, July 30, 1980, p. 40; N. V. Ivochkina, "Marki Rossiisko-Amerikanskoi kompanii," *Trudy Gos. Ermitazha*, 1981, v. 21, pp. 193-202; also interesting is the catalog: M. M. Gould and B. Kenneth, *Alaska's coinage through the years: An illustrated catalog listing all the recorded issues of tokens used as money by the pioneer settlers of Alaska including all the souvenir gold issues and list of transportation tokens and medals covering the entire history of Alaska*, Racine, Wisconsin, 1960; and others.)

The largest collection of Russian-American Company tokens [*marki*], or, as they are sometimes called, "skin money" [*kozhanye dengi*], consists of 15 specimens of various denominations in the numismatic division of the State Historical Museum (Moscow). Four specimens exist in the collection of the State Hermitage (Leningrad), and there are separate specimens in private collections in the Soviet Union and abroad.

We will deal here only with several questions causing differences among numismatists. Researchers note that

Khlebnikov lists tokens of 10, 5, and 1 rubles, and 50 and 25 kopeks circulating in the Russian colonies in America in 1817 and 1822, without naming the denominations of 25 r. and 10 k., which are mentioned in 1861 by P. A. Tikhmenev (*op. cit.*, *ch.* 1, p. 225). One must suppose that the tokens of 25-r. denomination simply were not included in the first two issues of tokens in 1816 and 1826 (when Khlebnikov wrote his "Notes"), but this denomination appeared in the issue of 1834 and was also prepared in small numbers in the issue of 1852. This most rare 25-r. token exists only in the private collection of a Canadian numismatist (letter, Prof. R. A. Pierce). It is harder to explain the absence in this list of the first denomination of 10 kopeks, for one can suppose that such a denomination would be the most used and indeed this denomination is present in most collections. Without conjecturing further about Khlebnikov's forgetfulness, we can try to explain the number and dates of issue of the Russian-American Company tokens.

There are said to have been three issues of tokens — 1816, 1826 and 1834 (Shikanova, 1980). However, there is reason to believe that there were five issues — 1816, 1822, 1826, 1834 and 1852 (Ivochkina). Combining the data at our disposal, we have concluded that there were four issues (1816, 1826, 1834 and 1852). This makes it possible to date the tokens in a new way. Although numismatists did not have enough data to ascribe the tokens before us to definite issues, they have divided them into two significant groups by one distinct sign — the presence or absence on the reverse side of the tokens of the signature: "Dir[ector of the Russian-American Company] Andr. Severin."

Next arose the need to establish more accurately when this signature appeared. We will be so bold as to date the tokens which lack Severin's signature to three issues — 1826, 1834 and 1852 — for the issue of 1826 followed soon after the scandal which burst forth in the Main Office of Russian-American Company, where serious financial abuses were revealed.

> Mr. [I. V.] Prokof'ev discovered this and asked the shareholders to appoint a committee to conduct an audit, which was done. They found great carelessness, negligence and misuse of funds. From their number the shareholders elected as president Nikolai Semenovich Mordvinov. The shareholders, however, agreed to keep Severin in the company. Out of sympathy with his situation (he was bankrupt) and the fact that Kramer had done everything and that Severin was only

guilty of having heard of the affair [without reporting it] . . . [In place of Kramer] the shareholders elected the newly elected city mayor, Nikolai Ivanovich Kusov (letter of 30 June 1824 from S. I. Ianovskii, St. Petersburg, to K. T. Khlebnikov in Novo-Arkhangel'sk: GAPO, *f.* 445, *op.* 1, *d.*, 393, *l.* 27-28).

The future Decembrist V. I. Shteingel' wrote of this:

> Arriving in St. Petersburg the next year [1824], I stayed in the Russian-American Company headquarters in the apartment of Director Prokof'ev and found Ryleev managing company affairs. This drew us still closer together especially when it was necessary to deal with the affairs of directors Kramer and Severin, who almost drove the Company to bankruptcy (Notes of Baron V. I. Shteingel', in the book *Obshchestivennoe dvizhenie v Rossii v pervuiu polovinu XIX v.* [Social movement in Russia in the first half of the nineteenth century], St. Petersburg, 1905, p. 411.)

Thus, one can state with certainty that the tokens with the signature "Dir. Andr. Severin" relate to the issue of 1816. His signature cannot be on the tokens of the issue of 1834, inasmuch as A. Severin's name is not even in the "List of shareholders having the right to vote, invited in the General [Russian-American Company] meeting of 7 March 1835 (GAPO, *f.* 445, *op.* 1, *d.* 105, *l.* 1-2). And although later A. Severin was again given the right to sign financial documents of the company (as for example RAC shareholders' certificates, issued in 1845 — see the picture on pp. 212-213 [of the Russian edition]), his signature was not on the tokens of the issue for 1852 (it is known that A. Severin was still one of the directors of the Russian-American Company as late as 1847). As confirmation of this we have an eye-witness account of the tokens circulating in the colonies in 1867:

> A handful of Russians lived an Old Testament existence in Novo-Arkhangel'sk. Even the money was on leather made from local lavtak (skins from sea mammals) in St. Petersburg, where the [Russian-] American Company, giving the lavtak a certain color, shape and its seal, supplied their colonies with such money. Besides this Russian-American Company money, called colonial tokens [*marki*], there was no other. The 25-, 10-, 5- and 1-r. tokens, colored gray, red, blue and yellow, were of rectangular shape which diminished in size in accordance with value. On this rectangle was the seal of the Russian-American Company, and an indication of worth of the token. *Poltinniki* [50-k. notes], *chetvertaki* [25-k. notes] and *grivenniki* [10-k. notes] were also on skin, yellow in color, with

the seal and the proper inscription, but the *poltinniki* rectangles had their upper corners cut off, the *chetvertaki* had all four corners cut off, and the *grivenniki*, which were like the 1-r. tokens, only smaller, were rectangles with holes punched in them. There was no reason to fear counterfeiting; the small population made each person's lifestyle, social position, activity and means known to all. Therefore, if the skin *poltinniki*, *chetvertaki* and *grivenniki* became stretched or dirty and then found their way as rubles into the till of the Novo-Arkhangel'sk office or more often into the rum store in payment for vodka, this was not regarded as criminal in nature and the guilty were not even sought. In the Russian colonies on the Northwest Coast of America money did not have a significance which it has in the civilized world; it fully replaced credit and vodka; and what could one do with skin money, when sometimes it could not be used to obtain even the most necessary items in the company stores, not to mention items of comfort and luxury, and with that the salary due remained as credit or the tokens were even lost at cards, drunk up or spent on those needs which could be satisfied from the company storehouses (M. I. Vavilov, "Poslednie dni v Russkoi Amerike. Iz zapisok ochevidtsa 1867 g." [Last days in Russian America. From notes of an eyewitness, 1867], *Russkaia starina*, v. 51, September 1886, pp. 609-610).

In the colonies the tokens were always in short supply. Visiting Fort Ross in October 1822, K. T. Khlebnikov wrote: "Mr. [K. I.] Shmidt asked that because of lack of tokens, notes of 500 r. be issued to settle accounts. I advised him to issue the same from his [Ross] office under the signature of his bookkeeper and the seal. He keeps the treasury in proper order, has good accounts in the stores and the clerk keeps the books from his notes" (AGO, R-99, *op.* 1, *d.* 18: K. T. Khlebnikov, "Putevye zapiski vtorochno o pokhode na *Buldakove*, 1822 g.," *l.* 44).

Tokens of 50, 25, and 10 k., issued for the "mining expedition" (in Kenai Bay), signed by the mining engineer E. H. Furuhjelm exist in a private collection in Finland (R. A. Pierce, "The Russian Coal Mine on the Kenai," *The Alaska Journal: History and Arts*, Spring 1975, 5(2):104-198).

A delay in sending tokens from St. Petersburg in 1835 led to the appearance of counterfeit tokens in the colonies. "Because we did not receive new tokens from you," wrote Novo-Arkhangel'sk office manager P. I. Shelikhov from Novo-Arkhangel'sk on 25 April 1835 to K. T. Khlebnikov in St. Petersburg, "we had great difficulty here in issuing them: only four thousand rubles' worth of tokens were in circulation, but they too are so worn that it would be difficult to distinguish their worth, so clever promyshlenniks made use of this; first appeared false tokens made from lavtaks, but when this was noticed, [the promyshlenniks] began to color the ruble [tokens] with blue paint, in which guise up to 40 1-r. tokens were discovered which had long been in circulation as 5-r. [-k.?] ones. In order to put a stop to the counterfeiting and coloring of yellow tokens blue, it was necessary to take all tokens out of circulation on which the blue is obliterated, so that now there are in circulation [*marki*] worth two thousand, and for that reason 2 thousand in [credit] notes were issued (GAPO, *f.* 445, *op.* 1, *d.* 375, letter of P. I. Shelikhov to K. T. Khlebnikov, *l.* 36 *ob.*-37).

The committee formed in the 1860s to decide the fate of the colonies and of the Russian-American Company itself noted: "One must still remember the lack of all money in the colonies; all officials and workers were paid exclusively in skin tokens, of which 36 thousand rubles' worth are now in circulation, and since these have no significance either for foreigners nor even for independent natives, the inhabitants of Novo-Arkhangel'sk not only are deprived of the possibility of buying something brought on foreign vessels which happen to visit the port, but it still makes the hire of Kolosh workers difficult, who cannot be attracted otherwise as they ask to be paid in rum, contrary to local police regulations" (*Doklad komiteta ob ustroistve russkikh amerikanskikh kolonii* [Report of the committee on organization of the Russian American colonies], St. Petersburg, 1853, pp. 165-166). However, the statement that the Sitkha Kolosh were not paid for labor in tokens is not quite true. Although at first the company paid only officials, promyshlenniks, and Aleuts in tokens, they gradually began to use them in trade with the Kolosh. Here is a description of the Novo-Arkhangel'sk market in 1863 by an eye witness: "The Kolosh village is separated from the town by a wooden wall with a battery and a market. Entry into the settlement is via the market, which is nothing more than a hut without a roof. Here the Kolosh women bring their goods for exchange, such as fish, *iamany* (a type of wild goat), wild ducks, red and black bilberries, dewberries, and so forth. For all this they receive from the company prikazchik *laftaki*, that is, paper money, for which the company gives them blankets, flour, sugar and other supplies" (K. S. Zelenoi, "Iz zapisok o krugosvetnom plavanii [na korvete *Abrek*] (1861-1864)," *Morskoi sbornik*, 1856, v. 80, No. 9, ch. III, pp. 51-88). "It seems," remarked K. S. Zelenoi, "that the American company calculates everything in paper money [*assignatsii*]: look at the amount of salary — the figure is large, but if you change it to silver, it amounts to so little that what you are looking at is insignificant" (*ibid.*, p. 56).

Finally, let us again consider the absence of the 10-k. denomination in Khlebnikov's list of tokens. This denomination had different forms: it circulated as an ellipse, with the signature "Dir. Andr. Severin," as a rectangle with holes in the two upper corners, and as a rectangle without holes. Thus, if our view is correct that Severin's signature can be associated with the first issue (1816), it follows that the omission is due simply to a lapse of Khlebnikov's memory, for 10-k. tokens circulated in the colonies from the very beginning. Furthermore, since F. P. Litke used Khlebnikov's "Notes" in his voyage account and Litke also fails to mention the 10-k. token, he was simply repeating Khlebnikov's error (F. P. Litke, *Puteshestvie vokrug sveta na voennom shliupe Seniavin, 1826-1829* [Voyage around the world on the naval sloop *Seniavin*, 1826-1829], Moscow, 1948, pp. 56-57).

Page 154: *"Communications with Unalashka, the Ross office, Atkha, the Aleksandrovskii fort and the Northern Islands district were maintained once a year."* — "The Northern district, under the commandant of the Mikhailovskii redoubt, established in 1833 near Stuart Island, includes the area of the Kvikhpak River and the coast of Norton Sound. Geographically, the remainder of Northwest America, from Norton Sound to Bering Strait and farther, belongs to this coast. The islands of this strait [i.e., the Bering Sea], St. Lawrence and St. Matthew, lie outside the area of activity of this redoubt and are visited by vessels sent directly from Novo-Arkhangel'sk" (Wrangell, *Kratkie statisticheskie zamechaniia . . .* , p. 107).

Pages 169: *"The library in Sitkha consists of more than 1,200 volumes . . . The basis of this collection was laid in St. Petersburg, when they organized the first expedition around the world."* — "Mr. Rezanov supplied the colonies with a library, which later received various donations and now [in the 1830s] includes 1,700 volumes of Russian and foreign works. There are up to 400 volumes of Russian periodicals, excluding newspapers. This library, located in Novo-Arkhangel'sk and open to all wishing to use it, has a good collection of maritime charts, atlases, and mathematical and astronomical instruments. Every year the company sends here the best journals and magazines published in St. Petersburg and Moscow (*Ibid.*, pp. 117-118). The archive file "on the beginning of the first Russian round-the-world expedition" includes a "Register of books from the Imperial Academy of Sciences sent to America" (TsGIA, *f.* 15, *op.* 1, *d.* 1, 1804, *l.* 125 *ob.*-126 *ob.*). This lists 48 titles, amounting to 213 volumes. They include histories of Russia, Rome, and America; works on mineralogy, crafts, Euler's letters on physics, primers, Polenov's guide to home medicine, and a French lexicon. There are well-known books, such as M. V. Lomonosov's *A Russian Chronicle* and *A Russian Grammar*, S. P. Krashenninikov's *Description of Kamchatka*, and Daniel Defoe's *Life of Robinson Crusoe*. There are three maps of the Russian Empire and "four maps of the hemispheres." Unfortunately, data on the books is incomplete; in most cases the names of the authors and the years of publication are lacking, and some titles are inaccurate.

Another register (*ibid.*, *l.* 129 *ob.*-130) lists 28 titles of textbooks (348 volumes), and maps of Europe, Asia, Africa, America and "both halves of the globe" (in all 10 items), small atlases (12 items), school texts "figures belonging to natural history," 27; slate boards, 12; slate pencils, 185). Finally, third and last, there is "A register of books given by His Eminence the Member of the Synod Amvrosii, the Metropolitan of Novgorod and St. Petersburg, for use in the Russian American institutions" (*ibid.*, *l.* 125-125 *ob.*), including 44 titles of church books.

The library also contained a number of Khlebnikov's own works: In October 1835 he sent to Sitkha 20 copies of *Zhizneopisaniia A. A. Baranova* (St. Petersburg, 1835). He also sent copies to a number of fellow employees, including I. A. Kupreianov, A. K. Etolin, M. D. Teben'kov, N. Ia. Rozenberg, D. F. Zarembo, D. F. Chernov, Kh. M. Benzeman, A. G. Rotchev, A. K. Til', I. E. Veniaminov, Ia. E. Netsvetov, P. I. Shelikhov, V. I. Solodovnikov, V. I. Kashevarov, P. S. Kostromitinov, F. A. Kashevarov, P. M. Kondakov, and K. V. Shaiashnikov (GAPO, *f.* 445, *op.* 1, *d.* 45, *l.* 2 *ob.*).

As L. A. Zagoskin justly wrote in April 1840: "in normal, everyday life it is safe to say that Sitkha seems nearer to

St. Petersburg than the great majority of our provincial towns" (Zagoskin, *Puteshestviia. . .* , pp. 369-370).

In forming the world view of the Russian settlers in America, including formation of a definite "reading circle," the future Decembrists played a notable role. We have already noted in the introduction that in 1824 V. P. Romanov sent [the file of] *Poliarniaa zvezda* for 1823 from Kronshtadt to K. T. Khlebnikov in Sitkha. The archives contain a list, "Periodical publications of 1825 sent to the colonies via Okhotsk by the post, 27 March 1825:"

Syn Otechestva	Nos. 1 through 4
Severnyi arkhiv	Nos. 1 through 4
Vestnik Evropy	Nos. 1 through 4
Severnaia pchela	Nos. 1 through 7
Invalid	Nos. 1 through 6

and of books: *The Collection of Russian Laws on Military and Maritime Affairs*, Ryleev's *Thoughts*, and Colonel Vut'e's *Notes* (3 volumes). These books are to be sent with the first heavy post. [Signed by] Office manager [of the Main Office of the Russian-American Company] Ryleev" (AVPR, *f.* RAK, *op.* 888, *d.* 966, Roll 4, *l.* 413, 414 [*RAC, CR:* Main Office to Chief Manager Murav'ev, 27 March 1825, Vol. 4, No. 348, f. 413-414]).

"In accordance with Your wish, declared through Mr. Lieutenant Romanov," wrote a director of the Russian-American Company to Chief Manager M. I. Murav'ev in Sitkha 15 July 1824, "the collection of facades for private structures in Russian towns are sent for the colonial library. This description is hitherto unpublished. Include this book in the main catalog of the library. A. Severin, I. Prokof'ev, office manager K. Ryleev" (AVPR, *f.* RAK, *op.* 888, *d.* 966, Roll 4, *l.* 197 [*RAC, CR:* Main Office to Chief Manager Murav'ev, 15 July 1824, Vol. 4, No. 508, f. 177]).

After Khlebnikov arrived in St. Petersburg and entered the Main Office of the company, he continued to receive requests from Sitkha for books: "Perhaps you, Kirilo Timofeevich, could ease our monotony, by asking messrs. directors for a measly sum of 500 rubles for books to be sent to Sitkha — the ones which have been published recently, many new and all useful if one is to believe our good acquaintance, the *Telegraf,*" wrote N. Ia. Rozenberg on 30 April 1835 (GAPO, *f.* 445, *op.* 1, *d.* 318, *l.* 6 *ob.*).

Among Khlebnikov's papers has been preserved "A catalog of books sent by the Main Office of the Russian-American Company on the ship *Elena,* under command of M. D. Teben'kov" (GAPO, *f.* 445, *op.* 1, *d.* 112, 2 *l.*). I. S. Kostromitinov, departing for Novo-Arkhangel'sk as a passenger on this ship, wrote to Khlebnikov in St. Petersburg 16 September 1835: "If it were not for books, of which we have many, one could become very bored for idleness, but thanks to our books, and uplifting conversations in our wardroom we passed the time very pleasantly" (GAPO, *f.* 445, *op.* 1, *d.* 228). The ship *Elena* arrived in Novo-Arkhangel'sk 15 April 1836.

Thanks to Khlebnikov's active nature, the books of the Novo-Arkhangel'sk library traveled throughout Russian America and were read in its remotest corners. Here are several extracts from the letters of readers, addressed to K. T. Khlebnikov in Novo-Arkhangel'sk:

"It is very boring here. We have read and reread the books that are here. . . " (GAPO, *f.* 445, *op.* 1, *d.* 279, *l.* 2 *ob.*; letter of M. Nosov from L'tua Bay, 17 July 1823).

"I have the honor to return to you the following books: five volumes of *Christian Philosophy* and two volumes of *The Sufferings of Our Lord Jesus Christ,* for which I send heartfelt thanks. I wish I could have kept them until the next transport, so that I could reread them, but I did not want to hold them so long. Please lend me other such books, Kirill Timofeevich, to be received via Grigorii Terent'ev; they could be very useful to help me pass the time here" (GAPO, *f.* 445, *op.* 1, *d.* 273, letter from priest Iakov Netsvetov, from Atkha Island, 24 August 1829).

"I am returning your books via Korsakovskii, except for Boz[?], which I will be so bold as to keep until next year. I will read it again and someone else wants to read it and make some notes" (GAPO, *f.* 445, *op.* 1, *d.* 161, *l.* 29 *ob.*, letter of I. E. Veniaminov from Unalashka, 6 August, not earlier than 1831).

"And here [in Pavlovsk harbor on Kad'iak] there are also many books. Besides medicines, there are handbooks on rural medicine, how to cure with simple substances: for if one does not have those substances [medicaments] they remain like a book, idle, so that even the sick are without help" (GAPO, *f.* 445, *op.* 1, *d.* 277, *l.* 2 *ob.*, letter of the Kad'iak office manager, Stepan Nikiforov, 26 March 1827).

"Regarding the books: Krylov's *Fables*, as far as I can see, reveal human affairs objectively in the guise of animals (lions and tigers), famous people, etc. The work by Khemnitser is similar to that. As for Dmitriev's work about a young woman . . . I thought Pushkin's work seemed obscure." Then follow notes on works by P. S. Nakhimov and Iu. F. Lisianskii (GAPO, *f.* 445, *op.* 1, *d.* 277, *l.* 8 *ob.*, letter of Stepan Nikiforov, 9 October 1827).

And so, before us is literary Russian America! And therefore one need not be surprised to find in the hands of a Russian in Alaska a copy of Herzen's journal *Kolokol* (V. A. Chernykh, "*Kolokol* in Russian Alaska (A new document from the archive of A. I. Herzen)," in the book *Istochnikovedenie i arkheografiia Sibiri*, Novosibirsk, 1977).

And K. T. Khlebnikov's personal library, which he willed to his hometown of Kungur — was it with him in Novo-Arkhangel'sk? He probably had it all, although a considerable part of the new books had already appeared during the St. Petersburg period of his life. A list of literature (No. 93-385) has been preserved, including editions of 1774-1837 (GAPO, *f.* 445, *op.* 1, *d.* 34, 23 *l.*). Although the name of the owner of this book collection is nowhere stated, there can be no doubt that these books belonged to K. T. Khlebnikov, for under No. 264 is "*Zhizneopisanie Aleksandra Andreevicha Baranova, Glavnogo pravitelia Rossiiskikh kolonii v Amerike* [Life of Aleksandr Andreevich Baranov] by Kirill Timofeevich Khlebnikov, 1835 — 37 volumes of the same work, without portrait [of A. A. Baranov by M. T. Tikhanov]." Only the author himself could have supplied so many copies of his own book! The circle of interests of the owner of the library is unusually wide: history, geography, ethnography, economics, cartography, painting, and poetry in Russian and foreign editions. They include a work by A. S. Pushkin, *Istoriia Pugachevskogo bunta* [History of the Pugachev revolt] (1833). And the heart beats with concern when one reads item No. 303: "Report of the investigating commission to find out about bad thinking societies, 1826 . . . " (in a paper cover). The theme "the Decembrists in Russian America" still awaits further study.

However, let us turn to the first stage of the library, which was assembled in St. Petersburg, then was taken on the *Neva* to Kad'iak in 1804, and later moved to Novo-Arkhangel'sk. Several American historians and librarians have tried to ascertain the whereabouts of these books. Several years ago the Alaska Historical Library, at Juneau, received from the widow of the historian of Russian America A. F. Dolgopolov (Doll) his large collection of books, pictures, photographs, maps, postage stamps, and photocopies of coins and medals. The books include several volumes said to be from the Rezanov library. They include volumes 4, 16, and 18 of *Sokrashchennaia istoriia o stranstviiakh voobshche po vsem kraiam Zemnogo kruga* [A short history of travels in all parts of the globe), published by N. Novikov, Moscow, 1783-1785; Ivan Zmievskii, *Novye Ital'ianskie razgovory s rossiiskom perevodom* [New Italian conversations with Russian translation], Selivanovskii publishing house, Moscow, 1819, 252 pp.; Dr. Gil' (Hill), *O deistviiakh i sile shalfeia, sluzhashchikh k prodolzheniiv chelovecheskoi zhizni* [On the action and power of sage for prolonging human life], Moscow: V. Sokolov, 1792, 61 pp; Ivan Andreevskii, *Novyi polnyi metodicheskii lechebnik konskii, skotskii, i prochikh domashnikh zhivotnykh* [A new, complete methodical handbook for diseases of horses, cattle, and other domestic animals], Moscow: A. Risheshnikov, 1793, 531 pp. One can assume that these books are from those sent by N. P. Rezanov from St. Petersburg on the *Neva* (P. Wilson and L. Tobiska, *A Guide to the Dolgopolov Collection in the Alaska Historical Library*, Juneau, Alaska, 1982, Nos. 102, 724, 1805, 2183). Unfortunately, the above-mentioned "registers" of books are compiled in such a fashion that they do not permit definite confirmation of the presence of these books in the original collection of the library.

Page 172-173: *"Count Aleksandr Stroganov obtained various portraits, drawings and paintings from the Academy of Art for the colonies."*

30 June 1803

Dear Sir [the director of the Russian-American Company]:

His Excellency Count Aleksandr Sergeevich Stroganov, as curator for the dissemination of the arts, has asked me to dispatch to America a portrait of His Imperial Majesty [Alexander I] painted by the well-known Madame Lebruno, and enclosed with this a register of drawings and pictures which by my order to Mr. Academician Kurliandtsev have been packed in boxes and delivered by barge to the company prikazchik for dispatch on the ship *Neva*. Informing you of this, I humbly request that you send me in a box and packing, 75 rubles. With sincere esteem for you, my dear sir, your humble servant Nikolai Rezanov.

Register

Portrait of the Sovereign Emperor in a rich gold frame
Pictures:

Figures from picture by Natuara	12
Figures from picture by Grëza	3
Figures from picture by Losenkov	4
Various heads	36
Vases with picture by Bouchardon	3
	58

Paintings:

1. Rotchev's *Mercury and Paris*
2. L. Egorov's *Noah offers a sacrifice to God after the flood*
3. Repin's *Christ drives the moneylenders from the temple*
4. Novikov's *Portrait of a sculptor*
5. Anoriev's *Portrait of a teacher and pupils*
6. Geniev's *Portrait of girls*
7. Remezov's *Portrait of a secretary*
8. Razvodnoi's *Portrait of a secretary*
9. Utkin's *Portrait of a graphic artist*
10. Starkov's *Ruins of the temple of Jupiter*
11. *Girl holding a heart in her apron*
12. *Boy beating a drum*
13. *Boy with a letter*

(TsGIA, *f.* 15, *op.* 1, *d.* 1; on the assignment of the first Russian round-the-world expedition, *l.* 128, 128 *ob.*).

The location of these paintings is now unknown. In 1979 I saw in the official residence of the governor of Alaska in Juneau a monumental male portrait standing, in parade dress, done in oils on canvas. In Alaska there is a legend that this is a portrait of Peter I (and, indeed, there is a certain resemblance) originally displayed in "Baranov's Castle" in Novo-Arkhangel'sk. Without destroying the legend, we would like to draw the attention of American researchers to the abovementioned list of canvases, brought on the *Neva* to Russian America in 1804-1805. It is possible that some may have survived for a long time as exhibits at the Novo-Arkhangel'sk museum: "One must also visit the church-archaeological museum in the Sitkha cathedral. It contains much data on characteristics of the Alaska bishops, beginning with the unforgettable Innokentii of Alaska [Veniaminov]. Tourists in Alaska consider it their duty to visit this museum without fail. The museum and its contents are looked after with honor by the local arch-priest, Sergei Kostromitinov, an old inhabitant and authority on the Alaska past" (from "Otchet o sostoianii Aleutskoi i Severo-Amerikanskoi eparkhii-missii za 1913 g." [Report on the state of the Aleutian and North American eparchial mission for 1913, compiled by the Archbishop of the Aleutians and North America, Platon, New York, 1914], TsGIA, *f.* 796, *op.* 442, *d.* 2562, 1913, *l.* 26 *ob.*-27).

Page 173. *"...the Minister of the Navy Pavel Vasil'evich Chichagov sent plans of various vessels."* — Letter, P. V. Chichagov to N. P. Rezanov, St. Petersburg, 9 July 1803:

> With reference to our lively discussion, I have the honor to send herewith to Your Excellency three drawings: one of a transport vessel of large size, another the same, but smaller; the third a bot, and also a model of the first-mentioned vessel, for better guidance of a shipbuilder. It ought to be very easy to construct one in this manner. A vessel like this would be most suitable in the Kamchatka trade, and therefore it will of course be in line with those aims, which the Emperor has entrusted to you to carry out and expand (TsGIA, *f.* 15, *od.* 1, *d.* 1, *l.* 130 *ob.*).

The above-mentioned model vessel was of such dimensions that it had to be erected at Novo-Arkhangel'sk in the open in front of the school (see the plan of Novo-Arkhangel'sk in the 1830s on page 142 [of the Russian edition] and also the town plan offered as an appendix to E. Blashke's *Topographia Medica Portus Novi Archangelscensis* [A medical topography of the port of Novo-Arkhangel'sk], St. Petersburg, 1842).

Page 188: *"I do not speak here about moving the colonies. . . "* This refers to the project for moving the chief manager's residence and the factories from Novo-Arkhangel'sk back to Kad'iak. The project arose after Baranov's removal and was presented at the end of 1820 by Chief Manager S. Ia. Ianovskii. It had both proponents and opponents. Ianovskii cited the following reasons for making the move: (1) Ever since the occupation of Sitkha Island the fur catch in that region had hardly covered a fourth of the expenses which the company bore there;

(2) maintaining the Aleuts there was very expensive, since it is necessary to have at least two hundred at the settlement, each separated from his family; (3) the proximity of the Kolosh presented great dangers for the settlement, since they were better armed than the Russians, and the fort which they had erected was protected with ten cannon. Finally, there were more furs and more abundant means of obtaining them on Kad'iak. In case the board of directors should accept his proposal, Ianovskii considered it necessary to leave fifty men on Sitkha Island under the command of a trustworthy leader" (P. A. Tikhmenev, *op. cit.*, p. 272).

F. P. Litke, on the other hand, basing his views on his own impressions and Khlebnikov's "Notes," wrote: "One can hardly question Mr. Khlebnikov's testimony, based on many years of observations. He knows the country in the greatest detail. He refutes the superiority of Kad'iak over Sitkha as regards climate." Litke examined in detail all the advantages and disadvantages of the project (F. P. Litke, *Puteshestvie...*, p. 61).

The head bookkeeper of the Russian-American Company in St. Petersburg, P. V. Bokovikov, was another opponent of the project: "And why is there such a hurry to move?" he wrote to Khlebnikov in Novo-Arkhangel'sk on 18 April 1829. "Truly, this is not the first year that the company has maintained Sitkha. And how is it going to look politically if we leave Sitkha and together with it the entire American coast? There is nothing advantageous for the company in this. Would it not be better to transfer the main factory to Kad'iak and leave the Sitkha fort under the defense of a garrison? It would probably not require over 400 men for this; their support would not bankrupt the company, and along with that we would keep the whole American coast and the local fur trade. The latter would help us maintain the upkeep of the Sitkha fort. Also, by terms of the conventions the Americans soon will have no right to visit our coasts, and yet we ourselves want to leave this coast" (GAPO, *f.* 445, *op.* 1, *d.* 151, *l.* 70-70 *ob.*). In 1832 the idea of moving the colonial administration from Novo-Arkhangel'sk to Kad'iak was finally dropped.

APPENDICES

Page 211: "*Administrative Districts of the Russian Colonies in America*" (TsGAVMF, *f.* 213; Ekspeditsiia v Severnyi

Ledovityi okean kap.-leit. M. N. Vasil'eva, v 1819-1822 gg., *op.* 1, *d.* 144, *l.* 1-10. This document was used in the work of S. G. Fedorova, *Russkoe naselenie Aliaski i Kalifornii: Konets XVIII veka-1867 g.* [The Russian population of Alaska and California: End of the eighteenth century-1867], Moscow, Nauka, 1971, pp. 179-186. The document was translated into English and published by James R. Gibson, "Russian America in 1821. The colonies of the Russian-American Company by K. T. Khlebnikov," *Oregon Historical Quarterly*, 77(2):174-188).

Page 226: *"The Song of A. A. Baranov, 1799"* (TsGIA ESSR, *f.* 2057 (*f.* Vrangelei), *op.* 1, *d.* 354, *l.* 18-19). A. A. Baranov wrote the song in honor of the founding of the fort St. Archangel Michael (now old Sitka) on the Island of Sitkha in 1799. The text of this song was written down in Novo-Arkhangel'sk by L. A. Zagoskin at the beginning of the 1840s and published by him with commentaries in the magazine *Moskvitianin* (St. Petersburg, 1840, March, No. 5, book 1, *otd.* 6, pp. 1-4). It appears again, with commentaries by M. B. Chernenko in *Puteshestviia i issledovaniia leitenanta Lavrentiia Zagoskina...* [Travels and research by Lt. Lavrentii Zagoskin], pp. 379-381. There are at least three English translations of the song, one by the American traveler and scholar of Alaska and the Pribylov Islands Henry Elliot in 1915 (H. W. Elliot, *Bibliographical sketches of authors on Russian America and Alaska*, transcription and bibliography by J. W. Carnahan, Occasional Paper No. 2, Anchorage Historical and Fine Arts Museum, 1976, pp. 43-45). Thus, the text of the song of A. A. Baranov of 1799, evidently put in writing by K. T. Khlebnikov, Baranov's first biographer, in Novo-Arkhangel'sk between 1817 and 1832, is apparently the earliest version of this song.

Using a couplet from Baranov's song in one of his articles written in Novo-Arkhangel'sk in 1840, L. A. Zagoskin wrote: "This fragment from the spare-time literary works of A. A. Baranov, who deserves the gratitude of the Russian-American Company, is invaluable to posterity as it reveals still another facet of the many-sided gifts of the first governor of our colonies" (L. A. Zagoskin, *op. cit.*, p. 365).

One of the officers of the sloop *Kamchatka*, visiting Novo-Arkhangel'sk in July 1818, wrote the following:

> As soon as we dropped anchor in the roadstead of Novo-Arkhangel'sk [19 August 1818], lieutenants Ianovskii and Podushkin and Commissioner Khlebnikov came out to us. When we sat down to dinner, they announced Baranov's arriv-

> al. The extraordinary life and deeds of this extraordinary man had aroused my curiosity and I had a great desire to see him. Baranov was of slightly less than average height. His age and his labors had left few traces of the fire which had inspired him in former times. His face was covered with wrinkles, he was hairless, his gait was hesitating, but with all this it was impossible to think he was eighty years old [he was 72 — S. F.], particularly if one knew of his laborious and unsettled life. On the next day he invited us to dine. When the meal was completed, a chorus of singers appeared on the scene, who spared neither their own throats nor our ears to entertain their foremost chief. When they began singing a song of his own composition, "The Russian Mind Has Gone to Work," the eighty year old Baranov could not help following a custom which he had had for twenty years. He stood in a circle of his comrades and joined them in proclaiming their common exploits in the New World (Tikhmenev, *op. cit.*, 244-245).

"Homesickness is a disease that attacks Russians everywhere and at all times," wrote L. A. Zagoskin in 1840 in Novo-Arkhangel'sk (Zagoskin, *op. cit.*, p. 369). He pays particular attention in his notes to things that allay this pain and longing — music and song. "The Russians have brought their Russian ways and songs to the north [Alaska], along with their manners, customs, and faith. Several times I have heard a young native girl singing correctly "I was walking under the arbor," "In a dark wood," or "On Kad'iak Island in Eighteen Three," a song composed by the old-time promyshlenniks about Baranov's return to Kad'iak from Sitkha. Naturally, they do not understand everything they sing, but at least they show musical ability. Some of them even do the kazachka with great skill, but only privately, never in public" (*ibid.*, p. 100).

In Sitkha in August 1979, thanks to the aid of American colleagues, I was able to visit an elderly woman of Aleut ancestry, Margaret Osbakken, and to hear her sing an old Russian folk song handed down to her by her mother, born in Alaska in 1861. Pronouncing each word precisely, she sang melodiously:

I shall comb my hair,
And let it fall to my silken belt,
I shall braid it tightly,
I will see my father off.

Father came to see me,
He brought us gifts,
He brought us some tea,
And three pieces of sugar.

I shall order the stove to be lit,
And the kettle to be brought to boil,
We shall pour the tea,
And remember father.

Mother dear, do not be sad,
Soon father will come,
Soon father will come,
And he will bring gifts.

The song of Baranov of 1799 was not unique. Still another, "In eighteen hundred and eight," was published by A. Doll (A. F. Dolgopolov) and R. A. Pierce in Russian with an English translation in "Songs of Russian America," *Alaska Review*, Spring/Summer 1970, v. 4:1 (13), p. 24-32.

[Editor's note: Almost unknown, this song was evidently composed by promyshlenniks in honor of Baranov after the repulse of a threatened Indian attack. It was never published, but survived in the Aleutian Islands until modern times. Before World War II, Father Makarii Baranov (no relation to Aleksandr Baranov), collected part of it. An authority on Russian America, who served for nearly thirty years on St. Paul Islands in the Pribylovs, Father Makarii traveled constantly — his parish included the entire Aleutian chain — and met old Aleuts who remembered fragments of the song. In the end he had four versions, each incomplete. They were pieced together to make what is provided here. The talent of the Russian people for creating songs makes it certain that still others were composed in Alaska, but only two survive to express the spirit of that far-off time.

Song to Baranov
(1808)

In eighteen hundred and eight,
In Novo-Arkhangel'sk port,
Ai liuli, ai liuli,
In Novo-Arkhangel'sk port.

Under the rule of the Monarch,
The Tsar of all Russia
Ai liuli, ai luili
Alexander the First.

On Sitka island,
Stands a fortress on a hill,
Ai liuli, ai luili
Stands a fortress on a hill.

Stands a fortress on a hill,
In all its pristine beauty,
Ai liuli, ai luili
In all its pristine beauty.

In it the hunters stood,
In the dark night they scarcely slept,
Ai liuli, ai luili
In the dark night they scarcely slept.

In the dark night they scarcely slept,
Guarding their fortress,
Ai liuli, ai luili
Guarding their fortress.

We looked here and we looked there,
Their boats were all around,
  Ai liuli, ai luili
  Their boats were all around.

In the boats were people indescribable,
Looking like beasts,
  Ai liuli, ai luili
  Looking like beasts.

They were naked,
Without shoes,
  Ai liuli, ai luili
  Without shoes.

Faces painted,
With feathered bodies,
  Ai liuli, ai luili
  With feathered bodies.

They thought, the scoundrels,
To catch us napping (so they thought),
  Ai liuli, ai luili
  To catch us napping.

But, despite their bravery,
We were able to repel them
  Ai liuli, ai luili
  We were able to repel them.

Let us sing, let us sing,
Of how in America we dwelled,
  Ai liuli, ai luili
  Of how in America we dwelled.

We in America dwelled,
And were dealt a hundred willow rods,
  Ai liuli, ai luili
  And were dealt a hundred willow rods.

And were dealt a hundred willow rods,
Many sorrows we received,
  Ai liuli, ai luili
  Many sorrows we received.

The beautiful spring came,
The snows slid from the mountains,
  Ai liuli, ai luili
  The snows slid from the mountains.

Little birds began to sing,
Our chores increased,
  Ai liuli, ai luili
  Our chores increased.

Despite the fog upon the bay,
Baranov came to see us,
  Ai liuli, ai luili
  Baranov came to see us.

We launched small boats,
And went to meet Baranov,
  Ai liuli, ai luili
  And went to meet Baranov.

We met Baranov,
And greeted him,
  Ai liuli, ai luili
  And greeted him.

Hail, father,
We make a wreath for thee,
  Ai liuli, ai luili
  We make a wreath for thee.

We make a wreath for thee,
From the depths of our simple hearts,
  Ai liuli, ai luili
  From the depths of our simple hearts.

We will place it on your head,
We will sing a boisterous greeting,
  Ai liuli, ai luili
  We will sing a boisterous greeting.

Many sorrows we received,
And we tossed down half a goblet,
  Ai liuli, ai luili
  And we tossed down half a goblet.

We tossed down half a goblet,
All our sorrows we discarded,
  Ai liuli, ai luili
  All our sorrows we discarded.

Novo-Arkhangel'sk. By Postels(?) ca. 1827.

Novo-Arkhangel'sk. By Postels(?), ca. 1827.

Novo-Arkhangel'sk. By Postels, 1827.

Kalosh (Tlingit) settlement at Novo-Arkhangel'sk. By Kittlitz, 1827 (*Vokrug sveta*, 1862).

Novo-Arkhangel'sk. By Kittlitz, 1827.

INDEX

Abbreviations: RA: Russian America
RAC: Russian-American Company
I.: island
Is.: islands
Vessels are grouped under "Shipping"

-J-

-K-

SEA OF OKHOTSK
SIBERIA
Shumshu I.
Kurile Islands
Bolsheretsk
KAMCHATKA
Petropavlovsk
Bering I.
Mednyi I.
BERING
SEA
Attu I.
ALEUTIAN
Amchitka I.
Unalga I.
Adak I.
ISLANDS
Atka I.
Amlia I.
RUSSIA
RUSSIAN
AMERICA
Yakutsk
Okhotsk
Irkutsk
Sitka
CHINA
PACIFIC
OCEAN
JAPAN
Ft. Ross
San Francisco
Sandwich I.